Faulknerista

SOUTHERN LITERARY STUDIES

Scott Romine, Series Editor

Faulknerista

Catherine Gunther Kodat

LOUISIANA STATE UNIVERSITY PRESS
BATON ROUGE

Published by Louisiana State University Press
lsupress.org

Copyright © 2023 by Louisiana State University Press
All rights reserved. Except in the case of brief quotations used in articles or reviews, no part of this publication may be reproduced or transmitted in any format or by any means without written permission of Louisiana State University Press.

Designer: Michelle A. Neustrom
Typeface: Calluna

Cover illustration adapted from iStock.com/Komarova Anastasiia.

LIBRARY OF CONGRESS CATALOGING-IN-PUBLICATION DATA

Names: Kodat, Catherine Gunther, author.
Title: Faulknerista / Catherine Gunther Kodat.
Description: Baton Rouge : Louisiana State University Press, [2023] | Series: Southern literary studies | Includes bibliographical references and index.
Identifiers: LCCN 2022023549 (print) | LCCN 2022023550 (ebook) | ISBN 978-0-8071-7917-8 (cloth) | ISBN 978-0-8071-7849-2 (paperback) | ISBN 978-0-8071-7924-6 (pdf) | ISBN 978-0-8071-7923-9 (epub)
Subjects: LCSH: Faulkner, William, 1897–1962—Criticism and interpretation. | American fiction—20th century—History and criticism. | Women and literature—United States—History.
Classification: LCC PS3511.A86 Z8725 2023 (print) | LCC PS3511.A86 (ebook) | DDC 813/.52—dc23/eng/20220913
LC record available at https://lccn.loc.gov/2022023549
LC ebook record available at https://lccn.loc.gov/2022023550

For Gooby, Fishbird, and the Dude

And for my students

Contents

PREFACE & ACKNOWLEDGMENTS * ix

Introduction: Musings of a Faulknerista * 1

1. Putting It All on One Pinhead * 15

2. Pulp Fictions * 29

3. Writing *A Fable* for America * 46

4. A Postmodern *Absalom, Absalom!*, a Modern *Beloved*: The Dialectic of Form * 85

5. Posting Yoknapatawpha * 107

Interlude * 126

6. "C'est vraiment dégueulasse": Last Words in *A bout de souffle* and *If I Forget Thee, Jerusalem* * 131

7. Making Camp: *Go Down, Moses* * 156

8. Unhistoricizing Faulkner * 180

Postlude * 198

9. What Television Is For; or, From "The Brooch" to *The Wire* * 201

NOTES * 223
BIBLIOGRAPHY * 269
INDEX * 283

Preface and Acknowledgments

The following chapters are the fruit of more than twenty-five years of reading, teaching, and thinking about the work of William Faulkner. A sustained engagement, to be sure—but not one that ever aspired to the traditional Faulknerian form of the single author-focused monograph. The reasons for this are at once mundane and unique, rooted not only in my preferred approach to the work but also in the realities of a particular type of academic woman's life, where the demands of research, writing, teaching, mothering, partnering, and institutional service achieve whatever balance they may only over the long haul, through a kind of syncopation: in time and over time. To put it more directly, I never aimed to write a book about the novels of William Faulkner. Rather, I wrote about Faulkner in a way that suited both my life circumstances and my habits as a writer: through a series of what were initially conceived as independent essays that aimed to account for what I found most moving or puzzling about a particular work. Looking back, I now see how each essay emerged as a something like an installment-plan payment into a sustained effort to account for the powerful paradoxes that structure Faulkner's *oeuvre*—paradoxes that imbue it with an astonishing responsiveness and resilience even in its most off-putting moments. Looking back, I see now that I have produced a book despite myself.

The chapters that follow are not organized wholly in the order of their initial publication. Instead, I've arranged them as a series of gradually deepening encounters with a core theme: how Faulkner's adoption of the tools of international literary modernism both shaped and was shaped by his tortured engagements with a set of peculiarly American themes and concerns—

themes and concerns that included race and racism, sexuality, and the emergent, rapidly growing power of commercial media—as challenges at once unique and imbricated. Of the previously published work, the oldest essay, a comparative reading of *Absalom, Absalom!* and *Beloved,* was written in 1995; the most recent (a discussion Faulkner's use of a racist epithet to describe television) was drafted in 2011. Because understanding emerges in time and over time, I've decided to present these chapters largely in their original form, with brief, retrospective postscripts offered in lieu of revision. Written between 2004 and 2007, chapters 6, 7, and 8 took shape around a constellation of concerns, and an interpretive approach, that I've come to see as central to my concept of the Faulknerista. Accordingly, they are framed (with an introductory "interlude" and concluding "postlude") in a manner meant to heighten these shared aspects.

The introduction, written expressly for this volume, explores the history of women's efforts to contribute to critical conversations about Faulkner's work and posits a definition of the Faulknerista. The first chapter then offers a brief overview of Faulkner's biography on the way to introducing interpretive threads that will be developed in subsequent chapters: Faulkner's tendency to excess, both stylistically and in his subject matter; his disavowed yet symbiotic relationship to mass cultural forms; and his fraught, fundamentally flawed efforts to sincerely engage with a national history of racial terror. From this general point of entry each chapter takes up a tightly defined set of concerns, usually from a single text, that open onto larger questions of form, meaning, and cultural effects. Faulkner's artistic influence is deep and widespread, and for this reason many of the chapters take a comparative approach, placing the novels in conversation with later work: Quentin Tarantino's *Pulp Fiction* (chapter 2), Toni Morrison's *Beloved* (chapter 4), Jean-Luc Godard's *A bout de souffle* (chapter 6), and David Simon's *The Wire* (chapter 9).

That final chapter, which investigates Faulkner's use of the N-word when asked what he thought about television as an artistic medium, offers perhaps the most vivid example of the difference between the Faulknerian and the Faulknerista in my decision to follow up on Stephen Railton's observation (noted in the introduction) that "Faulkner's thoughts . . . on social issues gain new meanings when they are connected with the way he spoke them."[1] While there has never been any question about what Faulkner said about television (the incident was first relayed in the second volume of Joseph Blotner's massive biography, published more than forty-five years ago), efforts to explore how that remark might inform our understanding of Faulkner's work, and the culture in which it continues to find purchase, have been virtually nonexistent. Rather than excuse Faulkner's use of the epithet (in the manner of Blotner's and Frederick Gwynn's silent emendations of the record in *Faulkner in the University,* discussed in the introduction), or cordon it off from consideration of the work, I explore the complications that ensue when Faulkner's language is taken seriously, seeing its ugliness as no less important to our understanding of his craft than its beauty.

These chapters first appeared in a variety of collections and journals, and I want to thank the editors who in some cases solicited the work and in every case made it better: Ann J. Abadie, Gordon Hutner, Carol A. Kolmerten, Martin Kreiswirth, John T. Matthews, Richard Moreland, Julian Murphet, Stephen M. Ross, Morag Shiach, Stefan Solomon, Annette Trefzer, Joseph Urgo, and Judith Bryant Wittenberg. Thanks also to the anonymous readers who gave generously of their time and energy in response to requests from editors at *American Literary History,* Blackwell Publishing, Cambridge University Press, *PMLA,* and the University Press of Mississippi. I am especially grateful for the thoughtful, generous, and generative comments of the anonymous reader of this manuscript.

Bouquets, applause, and many, many curtain calls to the women who came before me and who stand beside me in the project of reading, teaching, and writing about Faulkner, my sister Faulkneristas. Aliyyah Abdur-Rahman, Michaela Bronstein, Deborah Clarke, Deborah Cohn, Anna Creadick, Joanne V. Creighton, Pardis Dabashi, Thadious Davis, Joanna Davis-McElligatt, Susan Donaldson, Florence Dore, Leigh Anne Duck, Jeanne Follansbee, Doreen Fowler, Kristin Fujie, Sarah E. Gardner, Sarah Gleeson-White, Farah Jasmine Griffin, Minrose Gwin, Jaime Harker, Lillian Hellman, Katherine Henninger, Lisa Hinrichsen, Myra Jehlen, Anne Goodwyn Jones, Barbara Ladd, Cheryl Lester, Valérie Loichot, Kathryn B. McKee, Sharon Monteith, Gail Mortimer, Julie Beth Napolin, Rebecca Nisetich, Carolyn Porter, Diane Roberts, Jenna Sciuto, Evelyn Scott, Judith Sensibar, Erin A. Smith, Hortense Spillers, Melanie B. Taylor, Theresa Towner, Olga Vickery, Linda Wagner-Martin, Candace Waid, Lorie Watkins, Judith Bryant Wittenberg, Yung-Hsing Wu, Patricia

Yeager. Whether or not your work is cited in the pages that follow, the simple fact of your presence in Yoknapatawphan precincts—your persistence in "trying to say"—has been in itself sustaining, and will ever be so. Thank you.

* * *

Chapter 1 first appeared, in somewhat different form, as "William Faulkner: An Impossibly Comprehensive Expressivity," in *The Cambridge Companion to the Modernist Novel,* ed. Morag Shiach (New York: Cambridge University Press, 2007). Copyright © Cambridge University Press 2007. Reprinted with permission.

"Pulp Fictions" copyright © 1997 Johns Hopkins University Press. This article first appeared in *The Faulkner Journal,* Volume 12, Issue 2, Spring 1997, pages 69–86. Published with permission by Johns Hopkins University Press.

Chapter 3, "Writing *A Fable* for America," first appeared in somewhat different form in *Faulkner in America: Faulkner and Yoknapatawpha 1996,* ed. Joseph R. Urgo and Ann J. Abadie, 82–97 (Jackson: University Press of Mississippi, 2001). Reprinted with permission of University Press of Mississippi. Material from chapter 3 also appeared in "Unsteady State: Faulkner and the Cold War," in *William Faulkner in Context,* ed. John T. Matthews, 156–65 (New York: Cambridge University Press, 2015). Copyright © John T. Matthews 2015. Reprinted with permission.

Chapter 4, "A Postmodern *Absalom, Absalom!,* a Modern *Beloved:* The Dialectic of Form," first appeared in somewhat different form in *Unflinching Gaze: Morrison and Faulkner Re-envisioned,* ed. Carol A. Kolmerten, Stephen M. Ross, and Judith Bryant Wittenberg, 181–98 (Jackson: University Press of Mississippi, 1997). Reprinted with permission of University Press of Mississippi.

"Posting Yoknapatawpha" copyright © 2004 Mississippi State University. This article first appeared in *Mississippi Quarterly,* Volume 57, Issue 4, Fall 2004, pages 593–618. Published with permission by Johns Hopkins University Press.

Chapter 6, "'C'est vraiment dégueulasse': Last Words in *A bout de souffle* and *If I Forget Thee, Jerusalem*," first appeared in somewhat different form in *A Companion to William Faulkner,* ed. Richard C. Moreland, 65–84 (Malden, MA: Blackwell 2006). Reprinted with permission of John Wiley and Sons.

Chapter 7, "Making Camp: *Go Down, Moses,*" first appeared in somewhat different form in *American Literary History* 19, no. 4 (Winter 2007): 997–1029. Reprinted with permission of Oxford University Press.

Chapter 8, "Unhistoricizing Faulkner," first appeared in somewhat different form in *Faulkner's Sexualities: Faulkner and Yoknapatawpha 2007,* ed. Ann Abadie and Annett Trefzer, 3–20 (Jackson: University Press of Mississippi 2010). Reprinted with permission of University Press of Mississippi.

Chapter 9 first appeared in somewhat different form as "What Is Television For? (or, from 'The Brooch' to *The Wire*)," in *William Faulkner in the Media Ecology,* ed. Julian Murphet and Stefan Solomon, 34–48 (Baton Rouge: Louisiana State University Press, 2015). Reprinted with permission of Louisiana State University Press.

Faulknerista

Auditors at a Faulkner reading in Rouss Hall at the University of Virginia.
William Faulkner Foundation Collection, 1918–1959, Accession #6074 to 6074-d, Special Collections, University of Virginia Library, Charlottesville, Va.

Introduction

Musings of a Faulknerista

> Mr. Faulkner, this is a question about writing in general. I think maybe you just answered it—but they say until Hawthorne came along there were two ways to construct a story: either start with the characters and then a plot, or start with a plot and make up your characters. And they say that Hawthorne started with the idea and invented both. And I, I wonder—I know there's no one formula to producing a story, but I just wonder where you start most often and what you feel is most important, what pattern you've worked out to use?
>
> —STEPHEN RAILTON & MICHAEL PLUNKETT, eds.,
> *Faulkner at Virginia: An Audio Archive,* February 15, 1957

> I was trying to say, and I caught her, trying to say . . . and I was trying to say and trying . . .
>
> —WILLIAM FAULKNER, *The Sound and the Fury: The Corrected Text*

Any professor fortunate enough to have hosted a classroom visit by a celebrated author knows the moment. The excitement has been mounting for weeks. Your students have been reading the author's work with care and enthusiasm, and preparatory class discussions have gone well, establishing sensible interpretive baselines that leave ample room for deeper exploration. During those discussions you've dropped some large hints—perhaps even given explicit instructions—about questions or topics likely to generate a lively exchange with your visitor. On the momentous day itself, you introduce your class to the author and vice versa (though the author, of course, really needs no introduction—a phrase that, to your mortification, you find yourself actually uttering), then get things going with one or two questions of your own. The author may be shy; the author may be voluble: no matter. Whatever your talents as an interlocutor, and however kindly the author, there's no avoiding those early, awkward, empty seconds in which the class struggles to return the ball that's landed in its court.

The opening minutes of William Faulkner's first class meeting at the University of Virginia unfolded completely according to this script. Faulkner would be in residence at the university for the entire spring 1957 semester, and Frederick L. Gwynn was taking no chances with his graduate seminar in American fiction, the course that would inaugurate the Nobel laureate's residency. More than fifty years later, Ann Thomas Moore, a member of that class who received her master's degree in English in 1958, vividly recollected Gwynn's meticulous preparations for Faulkner's visit. "Several class meetings in advance" of the day, she remembers, "he had each of us submit . . . a list of tentative questions that we might ask our guest. These sheets came back to us in the next class, the last before the visitation, with the handwritten note, 'Ask this one.' An arrow pointed to the acceptable question."[1]

In Moore's recollection, Gwynn's advance vetting of student questions amplified an already high level of anxiety: "It was humbling to realize that any of our questions might have been unworthy." On the day of Faulkner's visit, "we sat, thoroughly coached, in silent anticipation, our sheets of questions on our desks before us." Gwynn ushered Faulkner into the classroom, where he took a seat "in the professor's chair, center front," as Gwynn sat off to one side, near the students. "A lengthy silence followed" in which Faulkner waited, "utterly serene," until, Moore writes, "Doug Day, veteran of the U.S. Marine Corps who sat in the first row (and later became a member of the UVA English department), stormed the silence with the first question."[2]

It's an affecting reminiscence, nicely capturing the students' timidity and awe (Faulkner, Moore writes, was "both mystery and object of admiration to us all"), and ending with a neat, poetic flourish that sees the tense silence bravely "stormed" by an ex-military man who would go on to become one of the department's most distinguished graduates and respected professors.[3] It's the sort of fateful encounter one finds less in real life than in fiction. Which, it appears, this reminiscence may well be.

For while there's no reason to doubt Moore's recollection of the events leading up to Faulkner's visit (her characterization of the awkward silence that descended once the author took his seat is thoroughly believable), the audio record of the session reveals that it was Gwynn himself who opened the discussion with two questions about *The Sound and the Fury*.[4] The first question asked by a student—the question that stands as the epigraph to my introduction—was posed not by Day, but by an earnest young woman whose identity remains unknown to this day.

* * *

In 2010, the University of Virginia launched the *Faulkner at Virginia* website, a digital archive of materials documenting Faulkner's two spring semesters, in 1957 and 1958, as the university's inaugural Balch Writer-in-Residence. Central to this project was the conversion into digital audio files of more than twenty-eight hours of reel-to-reel tape recordings of what have come to be called Faulkner's "class conferences": the readings and question-and-answer sessions in which he discussed his work with literature and creative writing students, members of the wider campus community, and, on four occasions, the general public. The material isn't entirely new: in 1959 Frederick Gwynn and Joseph Blotner, the UVA English professors who managed Faulkner's schedule during the residencies, published *Faulkner in the University,* an edited transcript of what they deemed "the most typical and significant" (*FIU* xv) questions and answers from these encounters, and that volume remains in print. But the record presented by *Faulkner in the University* is selective, whereas *Faulkner at Virginia* offers the comprehensiveness only a digital archive can deliver, complemented by compelling visuals (a trove of previously unpublished photographs of Faulkner in the classroom), contextual information that includes brief essays by participating students and faculty (Moore's reflections appear here), and complete, searchable transcripts of the audio files themselves, conveniently organized by date and labeled by subject and occasion.

Naturally, comparisons have been made between the condensed text of *Faulkner in the University* and the more complete record of *Faulkner at Virginia*. In the judgment of Stephen Railton, the curator of the *Faulkner at Virginia* website and thus in many ways the person best positioned to make such a comparison, "the choices Gwynn and Blotner made about what to print hold up well; users familiar with their book probably won't find many revealing new ideas among the passages that are being published here for the first time—though Faulkner's thoughts on his works, on writing and other writers, or on social issues gain new meanings when they are reconnected with the way he spoke them."[5]

Even as he approves Gwynn and Blotner's editorial decisions, however, Railton acknowledges what he calls "major differences" between *Faulkner in the University* and *Faulkner at Virginia.* To be sure, not all of these differences are of the sort that gives pause. Some are archival accidents or the result of insurmountable technical challenges: an audio record doesn't exist for three of the conferences that appear in Gwynn and Blotner's book, for example. Other differences, however, invite interpretation, producing those "new meanings" Railton sees emerging once we are able to connect Faulkner's comments to the way he spoke them, a connection the editorial decisions made by Gwynn and Blotner tend to obstruct or elide.

Railton singles out for special attention one particular difference between the edited version of the class conferences and the evidence of the recordings: Faulkner's use of the N-word "on at least three occasions" when he was speaking not as a character in one of his works but in his own voice. "When Gwynn and Blotner published Faulkner's remarks for the larger national and international audience they knew their book would reach," Railton observes, "they silently replaced the word with 'Negro.'" For Railton, this silent substitution was both understandable and appropriate. Faulkner's use of the racist epithet, he asserts,

> is a part of the complex story these tapes tell about him and about this time and place. He and his all-white audiences talk a lot about African Americans, though of course they never use that term. Sometimes they use "colored," but the term they use most often is "Negro." . . . [In] the southern accents on these tapes, especially Faulkner's, the word can sometimes sound so much like "nigger" that "Negro" seems euphemistic. . . . Unless there's no doubt in my mind about the term Faulkner uses, I've chosen to compromise (or maybe engage in evasion myself) and represent the sound of the word as "Negro." Because this is an audio archive, you can listen for yourself, and make up your own mind.[6]

It's tempting to linger over a twenty-first-century scholar's decision (admirably transparent, if also apologetic) to perpetuate a mid-twentieth-century decision to protect Faulkner's public reputation as a white southern liberal from the taint of his racist speech. But since Faulkner's use of the N-word is the subject of my final chapter, I'll forego that temptation and focus instead on another set of editorial decisions made by Gwynn and Blotner. These decisions go unnoted by Railton, but they raise a similar set of questions about the underlying assumptions guiding their approach to representing these historic encounters between Faulkner and his readers. These decisions merit interrogation because Gwynn and Blotner's version of Faulkner's Virginia residency played a critical role for generations of readers and scholars, shaping not only our sense of Faulkner's views of his work but also our assumptions about who spoke in Faulkner's classroom: who, exactly, had the insight and intellectual wherewithal to come up those "typical and significant questions" whose answers have had such an impact on our understanding not only of Faulkner's work but of the man himself.

Comparing the text of *Faulkner in the University* with the record of *Faulkner at Virginia* reveals Gwynn and Blotner to be orchestrators as well as editors, frequently deciding in advance of a class conference what would pass muster as a "typical" or "significant" student question. In listening to the complete recordings and reviewing accompanying materials, Railton concludes that Moore's recollection of Gwynn's micromanagement of Faulkner's inaugural class visit describes a frequent practice: "Gwynn and Blotner were much more active in helping script the sessions than they ever let on: not just asking many of the questions themselves, but, as Ann's piece makes clear, vetting at least some of the questions that others asked."[7] In choosing for publication particular colloquies and excluding others, they further shaped these already somewhat scripted encounters so as to emphasize certain interpretive themes: the New Critical, Cold War humanist Faulkner, launched ten years earlier in Malcolm Cowley's *Portable Faulkner,* is in full sail in Gwynn and Blotner's representation of the Virginia class conferences.[8] Beyond cleaning up Faulkner's speech, two additional formal decisions combine to even more consequential interpretive effect: (1) Blotner and Gwynn chose to render the text in an uninflected Q&A format beneath bare-bones chapter headings (for example, "Session Eight / March 13, 1958 / Undergraduate Course in Contemporary Literature" [*FIU* 57]) that provide minimal contextualization—or, to put it another way, that invite readers to provide their own assumptions about context; and (2) they erased Faulkner's habitual acknowledgment of speakers with a polite, "yes, sir" or "yes'm." Taken together, these decisions served to scrub the text of nearly all evidence of the gender of Faulkner's interlocutors, with the clear, measurable effect of making women's voices, and women's questions, appear far more marginal to the class conferences than they actually were.

When Faulkner was Writer-in-Residence, the University of Virginia was still largely a male preserve: undergraduate women would not be admitted until 1970. Still, there were women on the Grounds during Faulkner's years at UVA. Students at the Nursing and Education Schools were mostly women, and there were women graduate students in the Schools of Law and Medicine and in several graduate programs in the College of Arts & Sciences, English among them. Though you would never know it from the "gender blind" record of *Faulkner in the University*, women were in the room—and speaking up—from the very first class conference, the February 15, 1957, meeting of Gwynn's graduate seminar in American fiction: not only because they were in Gwynn's class, but also because Faulkner's class conferences were open to auditors, and women throughout the university took advantage of the opportunity.[9] Knowing what we professors know from our own experience about the courage it often takes for a student to directly address a famous class visitor, and keeping in mind the status of women at UVA in 1957, it is significant that the first student who dared pose a question in that first class conference was a woman. And it is also significant that, for more than fifty years, this fact was hidden from literary history.

Our unknown female interlocutor was not alone. Extensive comparison of the record provided by *Faulkner at Virginia* with the text of *Faulkner in the University* reveals that Gwynn and Blotner had a habit of silencing women's voices. Their edited text contains a total of 646 questions; of those that match up with the audio record (recall that *Faulkner in the University* includes material from class sessions for which no recordings can be found), 92 are posed by women, a little more than 14 percent. By contrast, 1,318 questions appear in *Faulkner at Virginia,* and 253 of them come from women: a little over 19 percent. Comparing the editorial decisions made in transcribing individual encounters also reveals sometimes startling differences between the edited text and the tapes. In the April 15, 1957, open session with students from several Virginia colleges, for example, the audio record shows that women asked eleven of the forty-two questions posed. Twenty of those forty-two questions were included in Gwynn and Blotner's edited version, and of those twenty, just two are asked by women. In the original encounter, women asked more than 26 percent of the questions; in the edited text, the figure drops to 10 percent. In deciding which questions were "typical" or "significant," then, Gwynn and Blotner were far more likely to choose questions posed by men than by women.

The problem extends well beyond the lack of numerical equity in representation; qualitative aspects of Gwynn and Blotner's text work not only to minimize women's contributions to the residencies' larger interpretive project but also to disparage them. At a time when UVA was commonly understood to be a men's college, Gwynn and Blotner's decision to identify two sessions as *uniquely* comprised of female participants—the April 25, 1957, session with students from Mary Washington College, then the undergraduate women's coordinate college to UVA, and the May 16, 1957, session with "Law School Wives" (at a time when, in fact, there were women law *students* at the university)—encouraged a view of the class conferences as otherwise exclusively masculine endeavors. The Mary Washington College session enjoys the further distinction of being the only session in which Gwynn and Blotner include in the text what in reality was a common feature of many class conferences: an explicit encouragement to the audience to speak up. Gwynn and Blotner include not only the invitation for questions ("Do you want to ask Mr. Faulkner anything?"), but also Faulkner's follow-up encouragement: "Whether it seems frivolous or not to you, ask it." The impression thus created is that the women required prompting and encouragement that the men did not. And however benign Faulkner's intentions may have been, the notion that women's questions tend toward the "frivolous" hovers over the entire session.[10]

The question posed by the woman student in that inaugural class conference was far from frivolous. On the contrary, it set the conversation on the road toward Faulkner's celebrated description of the "anecdote," the "picture"—in a word, the inspiration—for *The Sound and the Fury,* and his confession of his reasons for denying Caddy a chapter of her own to counterbalance the voices of her brothers. Faulkner's initial response to her question is hesitant and noncommittal:

> Three methods you just stated, all will work, but, but none, neither or none are more important than the others, and no one can say just what method the story demands. Apparently there's something inside the man or woman that must be, be told, must be written. It could be an anecdote. It could be a character. It could be an idea, but I don't think you could say which system to, which pattern to assume in order to, to create a story or a book.

Persisting, the student follows up—"You have no favorite pattern? It just depends on the individual?"—and Faulkner warms to the exchange, providing an example:

> That's right, that's right. It could be an anecdote. *The Sound and the Fury* came out of an anecdote, a picture of a, a little girl, the muddy seat of her drawers when she climbed the tree to look in a parlor window, and that's, the book came from that.

A pause ensues, then a second student, male (who, contrary to Moore's recollection, is not Douglas Day),[11] poses the question that Gwynn and Blotner chose to present as the opening query of the first class conference:

> Mr. Faulkner [Faulkner: Sir.], in *The Sound and the Fury*, the first three sections of that book are narrated by one of the, of the four Compson children, and in view of the fact that Caddy figures so prominently, is there any particular reason why you didn't have a section with, giving her views or impressions of what went on?

"That's a good question," Faulkner replies, then picks up where he left off: "That—the explanation of that whole book is in that. It began with the picture of the, the little girl's muddy drawers, climbing that tree to look in the parlor window with her brothers that didn't have the courage to climb the tree, waiting to see what she saw." Faulkner then moves to his now-famous explanation for Caddy's silence: that she was "to me too beautiful and too moving to, to reduce her to telling what was going on, that it would be more, more passionate to see her through somebody else's eyes."[12] The irony is obvious, and painful: in opening their volume with Faulkner's explanation of his decision not to give the courageous Caddy a voice, Gwynn and Blotner likewise deny a voice to the courageous woman who, stepping into the wake of silence following her professor's questions, was the first student to speak in this inaugural, "historical," class conference.[13] In silencing a woman so as to begin the narrative with a question about a silenced women, *Faulkner in the University,* no less than *The Sound and the Fury,* embraces the view that women's voices must be muted so that "passionate" or "significant" speech can be heard.

At a time when coeducation at UVA was the exception rather than the rule—a time when students were taught that the third-person masculine pronoun stood for the universal human subject—*Faulkner in the University* (unsurprisingly, but still deplorably) offered a view of the 1957 and 1958 residencies strongly implying that few women attended Faulkner's class conferences at Virginia, and that those few who did contributed almost nothing to the discussion. It should go without saying (!) that this matters. Not simply because it's a factual error in need of correction but also because it helped reinforce for years an already dominant notion of the "typical and significant" Faulkner interlocutor—or, to put it in the register that interests me most here, the "typical and significant" Faulkner *scholar*—as a white man, ideally a southerner.[14] There is probably no more powerful testimony to the tremendous influence so long wielded by this view than the fact that Ann Thomas Moore came to believe, despite her own direct experience, that Douglas Day had asked the first student question of the first class conference.

The now-expanded record of Faulkner's class conferences makes vividly clear that the traditional gendered view of who is authorized to pose "significant" questions to Faulkner is both ethically problematic and historically inaccurate—but, of course, this would also be evident to anyone undertaking an honest appraisal of the scholarly and critical record. For women have been reading Faulkner's work—and writing about it, talking about it and talking back to it—from the very beginning of his career, and they have had "significant" things to say all along. The digital archive of the class conferences shows how true this was for the women Anna Creadick has termed the "everyday" readers, women who attended the sessions that were open to the public and who asked shrewd, often pointed questions of the author.[15] But it is also true for the many women scholars and writers whose work advanced our understanding of Faulkner's art from its earliest years. We could start with Lillian Hellman's *New York Herald Tribune* review of *Mosquitoes,* or—even better—Evelyn Scott's pamphlet blurbing *The Sound and the Fury,* which not only offered readers a road map through the challenging text but also characterized the novel as a "tragedy [with] . . . all the spacious proportions of Greek art," thus introducing the parallel between Faulkner's novels and ancient tragedy that would become a signal feature of the post-Nobel criticism.[16]

Furthermore, women's writing on Faulkner has frequently scaffolded the work of male scholars writing after them, in much the same way that our unknown female student, by inviting Faulkner to muse on the relationship between plot, idea, and character, set the stage for his description of *The Sound and the Fury*'s generative scene and his extraordinary explanation of Caddy's silence. Women will recognize in this class conference an all-too-familiar classroom and workplace dynamic, in which our contributions to a serious discussion are ignored, only to be appropriated and rearticulated by a male colleague who is then credited with the idea.[17] Gwynn and Blotner's text helped fortify the equally misinformed belief that it took second stage feminism to bring women to the Faulkner studies table, and it is in part because of this mistaken belief that our contributions to the scholarly record most likely to be acknowledged are those offering explicitly feminist readings of Faulkner. In truth, however, we have been writing and talking about everything in Faulkner, and through multiple methodologies: sex and gender and the novels' female characters, to be sure, but also Faulkner's handling of literary form, race, history, and political economy. Olga Vickery, Myra Jehlen, and Thadious Davis produced pace-setting work that continues to repay study just as solidly as the work of Cleanth Brooks, John Irwin, and Eric Sundquist.[18] The issue, then, is not simply whether or not a woman is allowed to speak about Faulkner, but also about the conditions under which she is finally heard: whether or not her contributions are allowed to register, and resonate.

And yet. As Ann Thomas Moore's startling misrecollection hints, it's worth considering the possibility that we ourselves have been unwilling to wholly embrace our role and legacy as Faulknerians. Not because we are reluctant to claim our authority to speak about the author and the work but rather, perhaps, because we hesitate to embrace Faulkner in the typical, heroically masculinist manner. Minrose Gwin's claim that "only a very few exceptional women have participated *consistently* in Faulkner scholarship" is not only an acknowledgment of the daunting challenge presented by the "unarticulated but nonetheless powerful assumption that men understand Faulkner better than women do."[19] It is also an admission that a *consistent* engagement with Faulkner of the sort traditionally practiced by our male peers may not, on reflection, be the best use of our time. This is not simply because, as Gwin writes, "the politics of Faulkner criticism is male politics; the discourse of Faulkner criticism is male discourse" (57). Writing at the turn of the decade between the 1980s and the 1990s, Gwin was speaking at a particular moment in literary history, when the hesitation she describes arose around the issue of appropriate object choice, the fraught question of selecting an author to champion. As Gwin put it, "In writing about a canonized male author, in making a writer like Faulkner palatable to a broader readership, are we inadvertently participating in an academic discourse which relegates 'great writers' (usually white male) to positions within the literary canon, to the detriment of women and ethnic writers who remain marginal, often obscured, devalued, or ignored?" (57). That hesitation remains, to be sure, but it has been supplemented in recent years by an even deeper, more thoroughgoing ambivalence: whether championing the work of a single author—male or female, white or Black, "canonized" or marginal—is, in itself, an appropriate use of a scholar's time and energy.

And so, as a counterweight and response to the hazards presented by the traditional model of the Faulknerian, I offer for your consideration the Faulknerista. In the land of Faulkner scholarship, the Faulknerista treads the rocky, winding path of ambivalent attachment and authorial disidentification, feeling at once both a part of and apart from the Faulknerian discourse that preceded her and, to a not insignificant degree, still swirls about her.[20] The days of single-author scholarship as primarily an exercise in hagiography have (mostly) passed, but today's Faulknerian still, in significant ways, reads like an American exceptionalist. Quite often, to read contemporary Faulkner scholarship is to be given to understand that there is nothing in the culture, high or low, that Faulkner did not draw upon as a source for his fiction; there is no liberationist strategy the novels cannot be seen to entertain, no oppressive structures they cannot be made to critically interrogate. Of course, making large, often extraliterary claims for Faulkner's novels—as antiracist, as anticolonialist, as gender system critiques, as denunciations of the savageries of capital—may bring fresh readers to the fold even as they open new avenues of understanding to those already long acquainted with his work. Such aims are sincere enough.

Even as she dips into this contemporary scholarly discourse, however, the Faulknerista remains wary of the values implicit in its approach, mindful of its tendency to perpetuate daunting, unsustainably heroic notions about art and authorship and its straitening effects on literary scholarship. But the Faulknerista is no reactionary debunker, either. Seeking neither to praise nor to bury, she strives to dispassionately observe, accurately describe, and better understand, examining each novel for the aesthetic, cultural work it does, or doesn't do: not only the work it enables but also the work it obscures or blocks. She reads not in the name of but, rather, in the wake of, fully aware that the power of identifying oneself as a Faulkner scholar—a Faulknerian—is the power of identification as such, in which there is security, to be sure, but also limitation. It is the need to read not only Faulkner but post-Faulkner—both what he has enabled and impeded, the good he's done and the damage he's inflicted—that leads her to decline the traditional Faulknerian pact. She takes the subversive impulses animating Faulkner's best writing as licensing her own subversive approach, granting the possibility that the continued salience of the fiction arises in no small part from the sometimes startling ways in which Faulkner's work undoes or embarrasses itself. Finally, the Faulknerista eschews calls either to "lean in" or "step out": rather, she simply stands her ground. She knows that laying claim to, and cultivating, her own interpretive soil, even if it's little more than postage-stamp sized, can be reward enough.

A few words on this locution, which I cannot claim (that credit goes to the brilliant and amiable William Germano, who pegged me as a Faulknerista when we first met many years ago). To be sure, there are multiple associations connected with the *-ista* suffix that readers might be tempted to import into their understanding of what it means to be a Faulknerista, depending on what first comes to mind: Sandinista, fashionista, barista—all offer possibilities. But as the dynamic range of those three terms indicates, there is in fact no shared attitude or characteristic that the *-ista* suffix signifies. Much like the English

-*ist,* the Spanish *-ista* simply indicates an association, not its nature—or gender. But to English-native ears (and no doubt thanks to the presence of *-ist*), *-ista* sounds feminine. In other words, it seems to articulate a difference. And so I choose it to signify a way of "doing Faulkner" that differs from the Faulknerian approach. The Faulknerista may or may not be speaking as a woman. But insofar as she speaks from a position always already outside the dominant, heroicizing discourse, her speech will be heard as gendered. And it is this difference that is her strength.

The scholarship of the Faulknerista, then, could be understood as a kind of guerrilla practice: a series of localized and unpredictable engagements that serve to challenge the assumptions of larger, more established interpretive forces. Strip away the militaristic associations, and you have in the Faulknerista one who forwards an interpretive project by means of small but intensely focused actions: patiently, gladly, maybe even conversationally. Accordingly, I have come to think of the difference between the Faulknerian and the Faulknerista as the difference between the urge to master a subject—to the desire to be *seen* as a master, even *the* master, one who delivers textual verdicts designed to close a discussion in awestruck silence—and the aim to be proficient: an adept, fleet, and flexible participant in an ongoing conversation. We see this difference plainly in Gwynn and Blotner's approach to editing the February 15, 1957, class conference, in their decision to present Faulkner's comment on *The Sound and the Fury* as responding to a single, pithy question posed by a single, deeply thoughtful (male) interlocutor. As the unedited record reveals, however, Faulkner's musings on his reasons for declining to write a "Caddy chapter" flowed naturally out of a collaborative exchange with multiple participants: it was the interactions of the contributions of Gwynn, the women student, and her male classmate that made the breakthrough possible.

One more observation: the Faulknerista does not shy away from the flawed, damaged, imperfect, failed, and vulgar aspects of Faulkner's work. For the Faulknerista, the purpose in examining these aspects of the work is not to defend, apologize, or denounce (though, depending on the passage, that may happen along the way), but rather to *read,* and to do so in a way that issues Faulkner's challenges back to him. Faulkner as failure is a well-worn narrative, not only metaphorically (courtesy of his famous description of *The Sound and the Fury* as a "most splendid failure") but also in reality: the repetitions, misplaced emphases, garrulity, and redundancies all have been acknowledged in the scholarship. Less often directly acknowledged or explored are how those embarrassments are fused to the glory, mutually constitutive with it, living in the same skin. The Faulknerista reads Faulkner to understand what lies behind that fusion and then explain it in a way that recognizes the pain no less than the beauty. As much as we may want to believe that a particular voice, attitude, or action is "too beautiful for words," the Faulknerista understands that words are often all we have. Hers deserve a hearing.

1

Putting It All on One Pinhead

I went to the dresser and took up the watch, with the face still down. I tapped the crystal on the corner of the dresser and caught the fragments of glass in my hand and put them into the ashtray and twisted the hands off and put them into the tray. The watch ticked on. . . . Father brought back a watch-charm from the Saint Louis fair to Jason: a tiny opera glass into which you squinted with one eye and saw a skyscraper, a ferris wheel all spidery, Niagara Falls on a pinhead.

—WILLIAM FAULKNER, *The Sound and the Fury*

As regards any specific book, I'm trying primarily to tell a story, in the most effective way I can think of, the most moving, the most exhaustive. But I think even that is incidental to what I'm trying to do, taking my output (the course of it) as a whole. I am telling the same story over and over, which is myself and the world. . . . I'm still trying to put it all, if possible, on one pinhead.

—WILLIAM FAULKNER

By 1944 the literary critic Malcolm Cowley had been reading the novels of William Faulkner for some time. "Gradually and with errors of judgment," he had begun to "perceive a pattern" in the novels that had largely escaped him on first reading.[1] Among the first to describe the emergence of literary modernism in America, Cowley was struck by the inverse relationship between his own growing certainty of the monumental nature of Faulkner's fiction and what he termed the author's "quoted value on the literary stock exchange" (as he noted, by "the later years of World War II . . . [Faulkner's] seventeen books were effectively out of print"), and so he decided "to write a long essay on Faulkner . . . to see whether it mightn't redress the balance between his worth and his reputation" (5–6). To that end, he wrote to the author asking for an interview; three months later Faulkner replied, indicating his willingness to assist Cowley as he could. A kind of collaboration between author and critic ensued, and the result was something much more than an essay: *The Portable Faulkner* (published in 1946), an anthology comprised of short stories and excerpts from the major novels, all selected by Cowley and framed by his exegesis of the creation and meaning of Faulkner's "mythical" Yoknapatawpha County. The rest, as they say, is history.

The revaluation of Faulkner's work that Cowley helped set in motion should be viewed as an instance of a literary historical constant, for Faulkner's reputation has been subject to frequent revaluation. Largely dismissed (even reviled) during the 1930s as a purveyor of macabre tales of "rape, mutilation, castration, incest, patricide, lynching, and necrophilia," author of "a series of horror stories that are essentially false . . . diffused through the brilliant technique that promises us everything and gives us nothing,"[2] Faulkner saw his reputation undergo a near-complete reversal in the years after World War II, thanks in part to Cowley, whose work on *The Portable Faulkner* realized his larger dream of single-handedly elevating the work of a neglected artist such that "other voices will be added to the critic's voice, in a swelling chorus" of praise (3). In 1950, on the occasion of receiving the Nobel Prize, Faulkner delivered a brief address that called for a literature based on "the old universal truths lacking which any story is ephemeral and doomed—love and honor and pity and pride and compassion and sacrifice,"[3] and in doing so he seemed to ratify the claims of those critics who followed Cowley in arguing that, far from being "a combination of Thomas Nelson Page, a fascist, and a psychopath gnawing his nails," Faulkner was a model of contemporary liberal humanism, an affirmative author whose novels were best read not as peculiarly regional effusions of the gothic but rather as universalist articulations "of issues which are common to our modern world."[4]

A generation later, Faulkner's reputation again underwent revision, as literary scholars who came of age during the civil rights and feminist movements turned a critical eye on those American cultural figures whose work seemed consonant with a political and economic establishment undergoing deservedly rigorous interrogation. Faulkner's novels certainly address the race and gender ideologies of the United States, but they can hardly be said to deliver judgments quickly to hand, and attempts to clarify matters by examining the author's extraordinary engagements with civil rights through the 1950s don't do the work any favors. For example: 1956 was an especially busy year for Faulkner in terms of his engagement with civil rights, and it was spent mostly in efforts to control the fallout from a late February interview with the London *Sunday Times* correspondent Russell Warren Howe. Addled with drink and anxiety over Autherine Lucy's efforts to become the first Black student to enroll at the University of Alabama, Faulkner told Howe, "If it came to fighting I'd fight for Mississippi against the United States even if it meant going out into the street and shooting Negroes."[5] In an essay published some months later in *Ebony,* a somewhat chastened Faulkner characterized his comment as "a statement which no sober man would make nor any sane man believe"; yet his plea, one paragraph later, for Black civil rights leaders to "go slow now" did little to reassure anyone and in fact drew widespread criticism (being singled out for particularly scornful treatment in Nina Simone's 1963 ballad "Mississippi Goddam").

As the civil rights movement spurred an increasingly critical examination of Faulkner on issues of race, so, too, the reemergence of feminism prompted heightened attention to his representations of women. Was the theme of *Sanctuary* truly that women have, as a character claimed in another Faulkner novel, an "affinity for evil"?[6] Thus by the middle of the 1980s a new critical consensus on Faulkner began to take shape: far from being an author articulating universal truths, he was a deeply flawed product of a no less deeply flawed time, a problem in need of explanation.[7] In this second reevaluation, the rise of Faulkner's reputation after World War II was seen as symptomatic of the blindness, the willed "innocence," at the heart of the United States' Cold War imperial project. Lawrence H. Schwartz's 1988 study *Creating Faulkner's Reputation* offers the strongest version of this claim: "Faulkner's work was championed and canonized because his often supremely individualistic themes and technically difficult prose served an ideological cause," he asserted. "Unintentionally, he produced a commodity of enormous value as a cultural weapon in the early years of the Cold War."[8]

While it may be too soon to predict the shape it will take, or the critical judgments it will produce, Faulkner's work—and so, his literary reputation—

is undergoing yet another reevaluation. The selection of three Faulkner novels—*The Sound and the Fury, As I Lay Dying,* and *Light in August*—as the summer 2005 reading selections for Oprah Winfrey's book club was an early indicator that something was afoot. Advertised as "A Summer of Faulkner," Oprah's promotion of the novels included a special packaged edition of the texts, a linked series of websites filled with historical information about Faulkner and the South, and the services of three distinguished American scholars (Thadious Davis, Robert W. Hamblin, and Arnold Weinstein), who provided brief online interpretive essays and answered emailed questions from readers. This was a cultural development that few would have predicted, given Oprah's status as a Black television celebrity and actress whose best-known involvement in the world of literature, up to that point, had been her devotion to the work of Toni Morrison, and it perhaps indicates that one strand of what could be called the "identity critique" of Faulkner has run its course. At the very least, it raises the possibility that the past half century's worth of stark rises and precipitous falls in Faulkner's "literary stock" offers little by way of absolute knowledge about the merits of the work itself. Rather, they illustrate an ongoing critical habit wherein particular aspects of that stock are selected for reevaluation by particular readers making judgments at particular historical moments.

For Faulkner's work brings complex expectations into play, expectations driven equally by the novels' formal properties—derived as they are from modernist literary techniques developed in Europe—and by their content, which we could say, and speaking generally, centers on the disjunction between the vaunted promises of American democracy and equality and the lived realities of the American experience, a disjunction demonstrated most profoundly in the country's ongoing racial *agon* in its especially virulent southern strain. Thus what is important about Faulkner's fiction—and what is alarming about it, also—is its uncanny ability to highlight the relationship between form and content such that each not only animates the other (in traditionally good, modernist formalist fashion) but each also reveals the inadequacies of a reading strategy that would prize one more than the other. This is to say, in other words, that in Faulkner's novels history and literature emerge as projects simultaneously opposed and conjoined, sometimes violently, terrifyingly so. If this is to emphasize that Faulkner is crucial to contemporary critical efforts to rethink literary modernism's relationship to history, it is also to demonstrate the importance of Faulkner's engagement with literary modernism to his effort to "tell about the South."⁹

Here, I outline an approach to Faulkner's major work (from *The Sound and the Fury* to *Absalom, Absalom!*) that emphasizes not only what the novels accomplish in their engagements with modernist literary technique and southern American history but also what they have made possible in the work of others. Thus I have divided the remainder of this chapter into two sections, one focusing on the life and the work, the other on the legacy. The two epigraphs standing at the head of this chapter point to a key constitutive aspect of Faulkner's fiction. The first, drawn from the Quentin Compson section of *The Sound and the Fury* ("June 2, 1910"), describes Quentin's effort to destroy his grandfather's watch, a family heirloom passed down to him by his father and described as "the mausoleum of all hope and desire," the "'reducto absurdum' [sic] of all human experience" (47). The second comes from a letter Faulkner sent to Cowley in November 1944, at the very beginning of the process that would produce *The Portable Faulkner*. There is much that could be (and has been) said about both of these passages, but what interests me here is the unusual figure they share: the image of a pinhead supporting an impossibly comprehensive expressivity.

In *The Sound and the Fury*, Quentin's recollection of his brother Jason's watch-charm emerges in classically modernist fashion out of the flow of associations catalyzed by his attempts to destroy his own paternal souvenir. The absurdity of an effort to contain (and so to measure) space—the ludicrousness of drawing "Niagara Falls on a pinhead"—suggests the impossibility of Quentin's "time" (in 1910) resembling in any way the times of father or grandfather. Still, the fact that these impossibilities exist (and, in the case of the grandfather's watch, seem impervious to destruction) signals, in *The Sound and the Fury*, the larger impossibility that the novel boldly takes as its central artistic challenge: to represent memory loosed from its moorings in time, space, and even flesh. In the second passage, this effort to capture "Niagara Falls on a pinhead"—an effort impossible in every dimension, involving the arrest of temporal flow as well as the compression of geographic space—becomes "the attempt to put it all ... on one pinhead," a figure for Faulkner's understanding of his own writing. Yet if the image of the pinhead in *The Sound and the Fury* connects Faulkner's work to a modernism influenced by Bergsonian notions of time, matter, and memory, the second connects it to the near-reportorial realism and fanatical excess of detail grounded in Honoré de Balzac. The connections between Faulkner's fiction and the novels of Balzac are well known and do not need to be rehearsed here; my point is simply to note that Faulkner expresses his ambition in terms that are historical as well as aesthetic.[10] In sum, the image of the overloaded pinhead stands as a kind of metonym for a literary practice aimed at puncturing the membrane separating the historical and the literary, event and representation, fact and fiction, and it invites recognition of how Faulkner's prose operates as a kind of verbal suture, a prosthetic aesthetic that serves to highlight the gaps it ostensibly works to close. The South is what Faulkner knows and so what he has to tell, and *has* here signifies both possession and compulsion. The challenge of reading Faulkner lies in grasping how his fiction refuses to reduce a bloody, criminal history to the status of bourgeois fairy story (to paraphrase the critique of modernism articulated by Georg Lukács), even as it rejects the notion that this history can be properly understood only in a single, "realistic" way. Faulkner's best novels, produced in an almost white-hot frenzy out of the depths of the Depression, virtually vibrate with the intensity of this dialectical tension. Perhaps it is, finally, this grim, determined refusal, this neither/nor, that accounts for the extraordinary lability of Faulkner's reputation, as readers continue to struggle with the challenge of squaring a horrific, historically insistent content with prose at once beautiful and obscure.

FAULKNER'S LIFE AND WORK

The oldest of four boys, Faulkner was born in 1897 in Mississippi, and except for a few sojourns of varying lengths (notably in New Orleans, Hollywood, and Charlottesville), he lived all of his life there, spending most of his adult years in a large antebellum house in the university town of Oxford that he bought in 1930 and christened Rowan Oak. The fictional Yoknapatawpha County has recognizable antecedents in the actual Lafayette County; the fictional county seat of Jefferson likewise bears a more than passing resemblance to Oxford. Like the Dublin of James Joyce's *Ulysses,* then, Faulkner's Jefferson has strong roots in the actual; but, as with Joyce, Faulkner's literary concerns could not be said to begin, or end (or even to linger at some middle point), in verisimilitude.

Still, abetting these links between fictional and actual biographies and geographies are the strong connections that can be drawn between Faulkner's family history and the lives of some of his characters. Attributes of the Sartoris family as reported in *Flags in the Dust* (first published in 1929 as *Sartoris*), and of Rev. Gail Hightower's grandfather in *Light in August*, resemble in some particulars the more storied aspects of the lives of Faulkner's paternal great-grandfather, William Clark Falkner (a lawyer, politician, railroad entrepreneur, and sometime author known as the "old colonel" for his Confederate army service during the Civil War), and grandfather, John Wesley Thompson Falkner (the militarily innocent "young colonel," also a lawyer and politician, and founder of the First National Bank of Oxford).[11] For years shaped largely by the assumption that Faulkner's fictional engagements with his family history derived from the way his ancestors appeared to embody the genteel "cavalier" of southern antebellum myth, scholarly understanding of this past took an important turn in 1993 with the publication of Joel Williamson's *William Faulkner and Southern History,* a study pointing out that the "old colonel" was in truth more Snopes than Sartoris (a shrewd businessman, he owned slaves but never operated a plantation), and raising the possibility that the miscegenation and incest plot central to *Go Down, Moses* may represent Faulkner's meditation on the rumored practices of that same forebear.[12]

Thus the usual caveats regarding the use of biography in the study of literature, confronted with the case of Faulkner, manage to seem simultaneously both excessively restraining and insufficiently cautious.[13] In terms of the novels themselves, the difficulty is compounded by the persistence with which particular details of Faulkner's own life and family narrative are refigured both as intensely personal expressions of a scandalous and violent regional history (involving slavery, white supremacy, vote rigging, environmental degradation, and patriarchal abuse) and as excruciatingly public manifestations of personal depravity (think, for instance of the ravings of Doc Hines in *Light in August* or of Jason Compson in *The Sound and the Fury*). Cowley's reach for "mythical" allegory is understandable in such a literary landscape; but allegory does not, finally, account for all that is afoot in the fiction.

As literary apprenticeships go, Faulkner's was a rather prolonged one: *The Sound and the Fury,* universally regarded as his first great achievement, was his fourth novel and his fifth published work (the first publication, in 1924, was a collection of verse in a Symbolist vein, *The Marble Faun*). In a preface to the novel written several years after its first appearance and published only after his death, Faulkner tellingly likens the experience of writing *The Sound and the Fury* to the shutting of a door "between me and all publishers' addresses and booklists and I said to myself, Now I can write. Now I can just write."[14] Whatever its relations to the actual creation of *The Sound and the Fury*—and the novel's obvious difference from the work that preceded it would indicate that something transformative did indeed occur—this image of the scene of *writing* as a kind of ecstatic immuring in the world of art, a world conceived as a region apart from all mundane economic concerns (those "publishers' addresses and booklists"), does capture one aspect of the experience of *reading* it, as we move from the hermetic recesses of Benjy's consciousness through the gradually expanding spaces of Quentin's and Jason's narratives to the seeming amplitude of the third-person vista and its overview of the collapse of the house of Compson. This is a collapse punctuated, with no small irony, by the return of a traditional reading practice of a traditionally ordered text, metaphorized in Benjy's relief at riding through the town square "as cornice and façade flowed smoothly once more from left to right, post and tree, window and doorway and signboard each in its ordered place" (*SF* 191). The novel seems, in this way, to be entirely a meditation on memory conducted outside of history, with the imposition of direct (i.e., linear) causality appearing as a kind of numbing betrayal of some higher "truth." Certainly, Jean-Paul Sartre's famous reading of the novel as an "absurdity which is so un-novelistic and so untrue," a vision of "suffocation and a world dying of old age" that flows from a faulty metaphysics, responds to this aspect of the work.[15] And Eric J. Sundquist's view that *The Sound and the Fury* is important "only . . . in the larger context of novels to which it gives rise"—that is, those novels like *Light in August* and *Absalom, Absalom!* that more clearly address the southern racial theme—echoes this sense that the central flaw of the work is its failure to confront history.[16]

What Sartre's critique misses, however, and what more recent approaches to the novel capture, is the persistent sense in *The Sound and the Fury* that there is more at stake in the narrative than an expansion into prose of the possibilities of poetic dramatic monologue. In granting that novels like *Light in August, Absalom, Absalom!,* and *Go Down, Moses,* all more directly engaged in issues of southern history and American racial injustice, do indeed arise from the thematic concerns and literary techniques first deployed in *The Sound and the Fury,* Sundquist points the way toward a view of the novel that would track its swervings and silences as indicators of something beyond the representation of consciousness and that would attempt, however obscured that something may be in a psychological twilight, to acknowledge its presence and take some measure of its contours.

Analyses by John T. Matthews and Richard L. Godden have served to make that presence more palpable. As Matthews notes, the very first sentence of *The Sound and the Fury* "prefigures the whole novel's close concentration on the inner workings of a single mind," but the Compson grounds are surrounded by a fence—not a wall—"through" which Benjy can glimpse a world beyond that which encloses him.[17] For Matthews, the fact that Benjy, Quentin, and Jason attend to what lies beyond their yard only with reluctance and at considerable risk (Benjy is castrated as a consequence of his attempt to step outside the family gate) points precisely to the fetishization of the loss of their sister Caddy as a means of refusing to acknowledge other larger, political, economic, and social losses: "*The Sound and the Fury* appears to offer a case study of the breakup of the Southern rural aristocracy, a late but accurate example of the replacement of the agrarian economy by mercantile capitalism," Matthew notes. And in its obsession with time past, the novel "reflects the way in which the emergence of the New South created a nostalgically fictional version of the Old South that could thus be both honored and replaced" (97).

That Faulkner returns to the character of Quentin Compson in his masterpiece *Absalom, Absalom!*—a sustained critical examination of southern ideology whose remorseless demands on the reader are unprecedented in American fiction—is perhaps one clear indication that readings of *The Sound and the Fury* casting it as a modernist evasion of history are fundamentally flawed. As Godden has demonstrated in three interrelated essays on the novel, the highly experimental technical methods of *Absalom, Absalom!* are intimately related to its historical project. It is a commonplace in readings of the novel to note the parallel between fiction-making and history (as efforts to tell the story of Thomas Sutpen pass from Mr. Compson to Rosa Coldfield to Quentin and his Harvard roommate Shreve McCannon), but it is wrong to assume that, in doing so, Faulkner's novel means to question the knowability of history. As Godden notes:

It would be a mistake to read the novel's difficulty as raising primarily epistemological questions: while readers must ask, "Who knows what, when, and how?" this should not . . . induce a crisis of knowledge culminating in some form of the unanswerable question "How can they (or we) know at all?" In *Absalom, Absalom!,* a novel designed to explore a repressive class "design," difficulty begs the altogether more answerable question: "How can those who know so much, repress so much of what they know?"[18]

The textual difficulty of *Absalom, Absalom!,* in other words, enacts not the difficulty of knowing as such but rather the difficulty of remembering when everything in one's social, political, and economic surroundings demand a strategic and deliberate forgetting. Godden illustrates this point in his reading of the novel's postulate that Sutpen earned his fortune by working as an overseer on a sugar plantation in Haiti in the first third of the nineteenth century—a clear historical impossibility, given the Haitian Revolution of 1791. In tracing the tale of Sutpen's Haitian adventures to its narrative source—a campfire conversation between Sutpen and Quentin's grandfather, like Sutpen a planter, slave owner, and Confederate army officer—Godden demonstrates how the novel simultaneously elaborates and interrogates a deathly desire to dismiss Black revolution so as to ensure white supremacy.

I have lingered over *The Sound and the Fury* and *Absalom, Absalom!* because, taken together, the novels give us not only some of Faulkner's finest writing but also his most sustained engagement with the full range of techniques of literary modernism. Other important novels from this period can usefully be seen as local investigations into particular aspects of the relationship between literature and history. *As I Lay Dying,* which Faulkner termed a "deliberate . . . *tour de force,*" pushes to the limit the investigation of individual consciousness begun in *The Sound and the Fury.*[19] In its exploration of communal voice and the logics of conformity, *Light in August* presses off on a different tack; the daring aspects of this novel lie less in its technical properties than in its direct treatment of southern racism—an issue almost literally embodied in the character of Joe Christmas, whose doom arises from his status as a racially indeterminate subject caught in a world that demands racial certainty. Between *As I Lay Dying* and *Light in August* came *Sanctuary,* a *succès de scandale* whose gruesome tale of a young woman raped with a corn cob brought Faulkner to the attention of Hollywood, where he worked as a scriptwriter, off and on, from 1932 into the 1940s. Although Faulkner called the book "a cheap idea ... deliberately conceived to make money," the novel remains startling in its diagnosis of the parallels between the *noir* sensibilities of the pulp bestsellers of the day and the postural rectitude of the southern patriarchal order.[20]

Between *Absalom, Absalom!* and the appearance of Cowley's *Portable*, Faulkner produced three more novels of significance: *The Wild Palms* (republished in 1990 under its original title, *If I Forget Thee, Jerusalem*), *The Hamlet*, and *Go Down, Moses*. They can be viewed as discrete chapters of a continuing exploration of the dialectic between form and content in its engagement with the relationship between fiction and history, with each novel addressing a different social front: *The Wild Palms* develops technical modes and thematic territory first touched upon in *Light in August* (the double plot) and *Sanctuary* (the commercialization of sexuality in popular culture); *The Hamlet* revisits issues of class, gender, and rhetoric earlier engaged in *As I Lay Dying;* and *Go Down, Moses*—like *Absalom, Absalom!* structured around a racial secret—narrates southern racial and environmental exploitation as related aspects of a single crime. Although Faulkner produced a considerable body of work in the years following the appearance of the *Portable* and the receipt of the Nobel Prize, critical judgment on the quality of these novels is unsettled.

FAULKNER'S LEGACY

Rather than attempt to directly adjudicate the value of Faulkner's late work, I would like to approach the issue obliquely through consideration of what might be meant by successful "late" modernist work in a Faulknerian vein, concluding with a gesture back toward the observations with which I began this chapter on the lability of Faulkner's reputation. For even as contemporary literary *scholars* work to establish some method for judging the worth of Faulkner's challenging oeuvre, *writers* read Faulkner, and use him, in ways that complicate efforts to ground his work in a singularly (or single) American frame of reference.

Schwartz's assessment of the ideological valences of the Cold War renovation of Faulkner's reputation does not attend in any systematic fashion to the shape of that reputation outside of the United States. But as Sartre's review of *The Sound and the Fury* indicates, Faulkner's work was read with interest in France well before the onset of the Cold War; and as Pascale Casanova has made clear, the rise of "global Faulkner" can be viewed as a prewar French phenomenon as much as a Cold War American one. Maurice Coindreau's *Nouvelle revue française* essay, which marked the beginning of serious critical attention to Faulkner in France, came out in June 1931, shortly before the appearance of his translation of *As I Lay Dying,* the first of Faulkner's novels to be published in French. It was the French translations of Faulkner published through the 1930s and 1940s that impressed authors as various as Juan Benet, Gabriel García Márquez, Carlos Fuentes, Ricardo Piglia, Juan Carlos Onetti, Juan José Saer, Jorge Luis Borges, Rachid Boudjedra, and Kateb Yacine. According to Casanova, these authors found in Faulkner's formally daring approach to intransigent historical problems literary "tools of liberation":

> Faulkner's work ... reconciles properties that normally are thought to be incompatible. As a citizen of the most powerful nation in the world, and as a writer consecrated by Paris, Faulkner nonetheless evoked in all his books ... characters, landscapes, ways of thinking and stories that exactly coincided with the reality of all those countries said to lie in the "South"—a rural and archaic world prey to magical styles of thought and trapped in the closed life of families and villages....
>
> Faulkner thus helped a primitive and rural world that until then had seemed to demand a codified and descriptive realism to achieve novelistic modernity.[21]

However, and to return to the American frame, it is Black authors who provide the most complicated and interesting testimony regarding Faulkner's legacy. In his famous essay "The World and the Jug," Ralph Ellison sought to distinguish between those authors he considered "relatives" and those he considered "ancestors": "while one can do nothing about choosing one's relatives, one can, as an artist, choose one's 'ancestors.' [Richard] Wright was, in this sense, a 'relative'; Hemingway an 'ancestor.' Langston Hughes ... was a 'relative'; Eliot ... and Malraux and Dostoievsky and Faulkner were 'ancestors'—if you please or don't please!"[22] A little more than twenty years after Ellison claimed Faulkner as a literary ancestor, Toni Morrison, who took considerable pains to make clear that she did not regard herself as an author "influenced" by Faulkner, reported that his work nevertheless had "an enormous effect" on her:

> There was in Faulkner this power and courage—the courage of a writer, a special kind of courage. My reasons, I think, for being interested in and deeply moved by all his subjects had something to do with my desire to find out something about this country and that artistic articulation of its past that was not available in history.... And there was something else about Faulkner which I can only call "gaze." He had a gaze that was different. It appeared, at that time, to be similar to a look, even a sort of staring, a refusal-to-look-away approach in his writing that I found admirable.[23]

In other words, the importance Faulkner had for Morrison lay not in his public prescriptions for social change. And how could it, given the tortured nature of those prescriptions, delivered late in the life of a man who, however aghast and ashamed, accepted a certain definition of what it meant to be a white man in Mississippi? Rather, the importance lay in Faulkner's willingness to attempt a particular kind of "artistic articulation" of American history—an articulation grounded in the understanding that if one may not awaken from history's nightmare, the least one can do is acknowledge it as one's own.

Postscript

This chapter originally was written with the aim of providing an overview of Faulkner's work that places it in the overlapping contexts of international literary modernism and US literary history. Presented here, it offers preliminary soundings of themes, issues, and events that are more fully engaged in the following chapters, among them the Russell Warren Howe interview; Toni Morrison's critical engagement with the fiction; the mutability of Faulkner's literary reputation and the role of cultural politics in effecting those reassessments; and the use of modernist literary techniques in representations of gruesome or unsettling narrative content. These in turn underpin the broader investigation into the disjunctions and incommensurabilities of the Faulknerian text that are central to my overall interpretive project.

Biography has a role to play in this chapter, but it should be clear that it is not a central concern. Still, I would be remiss if I failed to mention important biographical studies by Jay Parini, Judith Sensibar, and Michael Gorra that have appeared in the years since its first publication. Parini's unsparing yet dispassionate description of Faulkner's alcoholism and its consequences, Sensibar's thoughtful, astute attention to the women in Faulkner's life and their influence on his writing, and Gorra's Civil War recontextualizing of Faulkner's work all substantially forward our understanding of Faulkner.[24] While the chapters that follow do not directly engage with these fine studies, I am grateful for the ways they have enlarged and enhanced my appreciate for the connections between the work and the life.

2

Pulp Fictions

It's fall 1995, and I am teaching an upper-level undergraduate course called "Southern Modernists" at the small liberal arts college in upstate New York where I'd had the good fortune to land a full-time, tenure-track assistant professorship. It's my first semester at the college and my maiden voyage in the course itself, which resembles any number of courses in any number of US colleges both north and south of the Mason-Dixon Line: a survey of modern southern literature featuring most of the usual (and a few unusual) suspects. Beetling over the syllabus is William Faulkner, who appears in triplicate: *The Sound and the Fury, Absalom, Absalom!,* and *Go Down, Moses.* I'm pleased with the way my students approach these texts. Early in the semester it became clear to me that most of them had come to the course with the expectation that they would read a lot of Faulkner and that it would be challenging; indeed, this expectation was actually a hope, and the realization that Faulkner was in truth a demanding author gave an added luster to their pride in reading and understanding him.

It was midway through the semester, and midway through *Absalom, Absalom!,* that I realized how central Faulkner was not only to my course but also—in an unexpected yet profound way that I explore in this chapter—to my students' understanding of contemporary culture. "You know," a young man said during a moment of classroom silence, "Quentin Tarantino ought to direct this." Why, I asked, did he think so? "Because," he shrugged, "there's this time thing."

For the student, "this time thing" pointed chiefly to a certain homology in narrative structure between Tarantino's films and Faulkner's novels—but it ramifies much more broadly. For starters, there is a "time thing" embedded in the very premise of the course itself. What does it mean to read and teach Faulkner now? How is that different from, or similar to, what it meant to read and teach Faulkner a generation ago? How does our experience reading and teaching Faulkner today prepare us (or fail to prepare us) for the task of teaching and reading him a generation hence? It's worth considering the possibility that contemporary cultural artifacts like Tarantino's films show us that we have reached the point where we must begin to theorize not only ways of reading Faulkner's narrative but also of reading the narrative of "Faulkner."

One thing reading Faulkner teaches us (over and over again, of course) is that, to a significant and sometimes maddening degree, looking ahead means looking back. In one (admittedly flippant) sense, applying this insight might invite the assertion that reading Faulkner thirty years from now may not, in any significant way, be different from the experience of reading him thirty years ago. This most likely is the view that fuels views of Faulkner's fiction as "a sort of privileged male retreat,"[1] the work of a writer who speaks too regressively about women and Blacks to be of much contemporary or future use. Faulkner's liabilities on this front are further compounded by a certain style of historicist scholarship, one where the heavy emphasis on context reduces the work to something like a political/social time capsule or symptom. As student time becomes more and more remote from Faulkner time, the pressure may increase on literary scholarship to establish a single context of literary production (simply and obviously, the white American South from the 1920s into the early Cold War) as the ground stabilizing Faulkner's elusive figure. A good example of how this phenomenon plays itself out critically is the recent proliferation of "keys" to Faulkner's work, both those with fairly pragmatic aims (i.e., raising and answering questions such as what is a fyce, how is Jefferson both like and unlike Oxford) and those with more expansive cultural aspirations.[2] These "keys" are, of course, not unique to our moment, not peculiar to Faulkner, and not exactly *bad* for literary study; my point is rather that it is increasingly possible to envision a time when they will become *crucial* to the study of Faulkner, not simply supplementary. This is to say, in other words, that reading Faulkner may become an increasingly *academic* exercise, incurring all the benefits and liabilities such a reading practice entails.

I don't see anything unredeemedly crippling in our current fascination with contextualizing Faulkner; yet, if we still have an interest in what "art and fiction can do but sometimes history refuses to do," we must turn to the other possibility inherent in this marriage of past and future.[3] Here, the future is licensed to revise our understanding of the past; we read our history as we do because our present knowledge (which, at the time of the text's creation, was future knowledge) demands that we do so. It is more difficult to talk about how *this* linking of past and future would work as a reading strategy thirty years hence—such talk would be so speculative as nearly to be useless—but the collection *Unflinching Gaze: Morrison and Faulkner Re-Envisioned* gives one idea of what this sort of reading might entail: there, critical attention is focused on exploring the ways Faulkner's fiction speaks to what comes later—specifically, the fiction of Toni Morrison.[4] The interpretive work undertaken is concerned less with establishing how Faulkner's texts mirror their moment of production than in how generations later they call up responses, both those that might be expected and those that couldn't have been anticipated.

Repetition is the pedal point of this discussion of past and future; since enough has been said about repetition in Faulkner to make us suspect that the inexhaustible voice, still talking, is largely repeating itself, it's a question whether anything novel might be offered to the discussion.[5] But it's hard to resist taking one more turn of that screw, knowing that repetition can propel us forward—after all, it's one way that we learn—even as it seems to hold us back. Among other things, this is what it means to be a *profess*-or of Faulkner: every year a new class, but every year the same texts. Certainly we learn, as our students do, but in all of our repeating we cannot reproduce for ourselves what I suspect many of us most cherish in our own experience of Faulkner and so hope to pass on to our students: that shock of pleasure and astonishment and eager confusion that thrilled us when our eyes first fell upon the words *Through the fence, between the curling flower spaces, I could see them hitting.... Memory believes before knowing remembers.... I dont. I dont! I dont hate it! I dont hate it!*[6] Registering the experience of that "emotion definite and physical and yet nebulous to describe," and its necessary loss, is one accomplishment of Faulkner's posthumously published introduction—elegy, really—to *The Sound and the Fury*.[7] For as much as we love the books, and as many times as we may read them—to be sure with a deepened appreciation, a more mellowed affection—"that ecstasy, that eager and joyous faith and anticipation of surprise ... will not return."[8] Not only not for him, but not for us, too.

Still. The examples of Benjy and Quentin (Compson, not Tarantino) remind us that repetitively mourning this loss cannot pass as a mature literary experience. And as much as we may like to bestow the gift of an enchanted first reading upon our students, I suspect that we should simultaneously be teaching them to be wary of geeks bearing gifts. This is not to deny the sensual pleasure of Faulkner's text; it is simply to warn against an approach that takes the semesterly reproduction of that pleasure as its primary purpose. In the present moment that opens up the space for repetition—that crowded, breathless, bleared conjunction of past and future where we may feel fated to repeat ourselves—we need to inculcate a critical self-awareness of just what is happening *in* that moment, of what is being affirmed in repetition, of what it is in the larger culture that insists upon repetition. It is important that our students "own" Faulkner, certainly, but it is equally important that they understand how Faulkner—and here I mean Faulkner as the sign of a certain activity of cultural accumulation and ensuing cultural authority—owns them. It is by recognizing this cultural exchange staged in Faulkner that students become self-aware and culturally aware: it takes time to read Faulkner, and it is precisely in investing the time that readers gain entry into a particularly heady, and seductive, discourse of cultural power.[9] I do not mean to suggest here that all readers who understand and like Faulkner (or even those who like him without understanding him) are cultural conservatives warming themselves in the pale fire of Dead White Male Authors—though, to be sure, such is one angle on what it means to persist in reading Faulkner. Rather, we do well to encourage careful reading of Faulkner that entails both a recognition of how cultural authority is created and a critical reckoning of how such an authority, once created, operates.

This is a reading of the past in the future with an edge. And while other authors probably offer similar opportunities for such reflection, I find it striking that Pierre Bourdieu devotes the penultimate pages of *The Rules of Art* to a reading of "A Rose for Emily," thereby bringing a mammoth study of modern literary culture and its role in the creation of cultural capital (a study that begins with the example of Flaubert) to rest squarely on Faulkner's shoulders. Bourdieu demonstrates how Faulkner constructs his story for "the *meta-reader* who will know how to read not only the narrative, quite simply, but the ordinary reading of the narrative, the presuppositions engaged by readers in both their ordinary experience of time and action, and in their experience of reading a 'realist' or mimetic fiction."[10] Faulkner's story, Bourdieu explains, "calls for repeated reading, but also the *divided reading* which is needed to combine the impressions of the first naïve reading, and the revelations it arouses, with the second reading, the retroactive illumination that the knowledge of the ending (acquired at the end of the first reading) casts on to the text" (325). Bourdieu demonstrates how the reader who successfully negotiates all of the text's demands nevertheless is caught in a "trap . . . [in which] the reader is forced to acknowledge everything . . . customarily and unwittingly grant[ed] to authors" (325). The divided reading, then, is one that reads both the demands of the text and the expectations of the reader—as those expectations have been formed through prior reading.

Faulkner draws on several narrative strategies to set this trap, but Bourdieu stresses how the story relies on a retrospective "time thing" to achieve its most unsettling effects, a "reflexive writing . . . [that] calls for a reflexive reading which, in contrast to the rereading of a crime mystery whose solution is now known, makes for a discovery not only of a set of misleading clues but of a *self-deception* into which the trusting reader has been led" (326; emphasis in original). This temporal aspect of drift toward self-deception is, we recall, highlighted in the story itself via the Confederate veterans who reminisce about Miss Emily Grierson on the day of her funeral, "confusing time with its mathematical progression" in their desire to feel Miss Emily "had been a contemporary of theirs."[11] The story makes clear, though, that this motivated confusion occurs simultaneously with the recognition that "there was one room in that region above stairs which no one had seen in forty years, and which would have to be forced" (129). The story dwells upon both the difficulty of opening up this past—the door is "forced" with "violence"—and its necessity (even as Miss Emily is being eulogized "we knew" it "would have to be" done). This double urgency is both expressed and contained though social convention: "They waited until Miss Emily was decently in the ground before they opened it" (129). The story thus insists on using and exposing mechanisms of self-deception that structure both memory and action—in addition to reading.

Bourdieu believes that this recognition of the ways in which we perpetually deceive ourselves about the manipulation of time in narrative structures forces us to recognize how similar deceptions inform and shape our social structures as well. This is why he is able to conclude *The Rules of Art* with a remarkable "Postscript" that calls for a true autonomy of intellectuals that yet manages to operate collectively: "a veritable *Internationale of intellectuals* committed to defending the autonomy of the universes of cultural production" (344; emphasis in original). This move from a close reading of temporal manipulations in "A Rose for Emily" to a demand for battle against capitalist expropriation of art into culture industry is breathtaking, but not illogical. Since it is Faulkner who simultaneously deploys and interrogates the coin of cultural capital (Miss Emily is "a tradition, a duty, and a care" [119]), it is not surprising that close attention to Faulkner's text would result in an equally shrewd analysis of a contemporary cultural climate that relies on texts like Faulkner's to establish and maintain its authority.

A sly reenforcement of Bourdieu's reading can be found in Faulkner's now-infamous biographic sketch sent to *Forum* magazine and published simultaneously with "A Rose for Emily" in April 1930. "Born male and single at an early age in Mississippi," Faulkner's note bumptiously begins, continuing with the evasions and outright lies that would characterize his authorial self-descriptions up to the appearance of *The Portable Faulkner* ("Got commission R.F.C., pilot. Crashed. Cost British gov't £2000. Was still pilot. Crashed. Cost British gov't £2000. Quit. Cost British gov't $84.30. King said, 'Well done'").[12] The need for a "divided" reading flows without interruption from fiction to autobiography and back, as we are forced to reckon not only with the authority we grant writers in their fiction but also with the power invested in the romance of the author as such: "Now flying again," the sketch informs us, after listing the four novels published since 1926 (47). The author's fiction of flying, it's suggested, reads the author's flights of fiction. Both are called into being by a particular social authority (a world in which writing novels means you "won't have to work" [47]) only to fully realize their power by resisting that authority: *Soldiers' Pay*—crashed; *Mosquitoes*—crashed; *The Sound and the Fury*—quit, and so, finally, well done.[13]

It is this simultaneous engagement with and repudiation of the conventions of narrative and cultural authority, a repudiation figured partly in narratives that flout conventional temporal organization, that structures my student's recognition of some common currency circulating between the novels of Faulkner and the films of Quentin Tarantino. As Bruce Kawin has pointed out, Faulkner "is one of the central figures in the cinema's rediscovery of its own narrative—and *anti*-narrative—potential"; Kawin traces this rediscovery to the work of Jean-Luc Godard, who read Faulkner, quoted him in his first feature film, and maintained a deep interest in his work throughout the early part of his career.[14] It is most clearly in contemporary commercial film and television—the first influenced in varying degrees by Godard, the second influenced by the first—that we can see the dominant culture's redaction and subsequent circulation of the renunciatory charge of the Faulknerian text, in the by-now-widespread use of self-conscious montage both to entertain and to sell. Tarantino's contribution to contemporary cinema, such as it is, lies in his decision to make the microcosmic temporal disruption central to montage—the jump cut—into a macrocosmic principle of narrative organization. And while Tarantino has yet to identify Faulkner as a direct influence on his work, he has (somewhat tautologically) described his own method of storytelling as literary: "I always felt that if you were to adapt a novelistic structure to cinema, the result would be extremely cinematic."[15] We can gain some purchase on the question of the role of Faulkner in contemporary culture through a discussion of the work of this filmmaker, who, as it turns out, was indeed named for Faulkner's "fatherless" Quentin—"the heroine," in his mother's words, of *The Sound and the Fury*.[16] Like Faulkner's novels, Tarantino's films are structured through temporal disjunctions that invite us to consider time and authority themselves as subjects. This is clearest in the opening minutes of "The Gold Watch," the central story of the 1994 film *Pulp Fiction* and the place where the retrospective structuring of authority and the concomitant formation of cultural capital are most strikingly figured.

The scene begins with a disorienting shot of *Clutch Cargo,* a Vietnam-era cartoon show that mixed animation and live footage to feature cartoon figures speaking with human mouths. The television screen briefly fills the frame; then the camera pulls back to show us the TV, a portion of a middle-class den, and the small boy, around seven or eight years old, who is watching the program. At the sound of a woman's voice—"Butch, stop watching TV a second"—the camera shifts to adopt the child's point of view, maintained throughout the remarkable scene that follows, in which a boy comes into his patrimony.

The father's legacy is the gold watch of the title, and it is given to Butch by Captain Koons, played by Christopher Walken. Koons effects the transfer of the father's legacy with a remarkable speech that outlines both the history of the watch ("This watch I got here was first purchased by your great-granddaddy. It was bought during the First World War in a little general store in Knoxville, Tennessee") and its transmission.[17] Despite the manufactured and highly modern nature of the watch itself ("it was . . . made by the first company ever to make wristwatches. You see, up until then, people just carried pocket watches" [85]), the process of father-to-son transmission is invested with what could plausibly be described, via Walter Benjamin, as an aura.[18] The investment here is in the passage of time *through* the watch (as it is handed down from father to son); the watch's function as a time-keeper is a metonym of this process. From great-grandfather Coolidge, World War I veteran, the watch passes to the grandfather fighting in the second World War. This Coolidge is killed in the battle of Wake Island; nevertheless, he manages to pass the watch along to "a man he had never met before in his life, to deliver to his infant son, who he had never seen in the flesh" (Tarantino 86).

In Captain Koons's speech describing the movements of this legacy, the death of the grandfather in World War II marks the beginning of a generic shift in the narrative, from heroic, to tragic, then finally to scatologically satiric, when Butch's father, a prisoner of war in Vietnam, hides the watch "in the one place he knew he could hide somethin'. His ass." The father dies of dysentery (!) and the watch passes to Captain Koons, who, he tells Butch, "hid this uncomfortable hunk of metal up my ass for two years. Then, after seven years, I was sent home to my family. And now, little man, I give the watch to you" (86). The "little man" accepts the watch, which then becomes the centerpiece of the drama in which the adult Butch (played by Bruce Willis), fleeing from danger, chooses to risk everything in order to preserve this legacy.

In a speech cut from the finished film, Butch convinces himself to return to his apartment—most certainly now invaded by hitmen working for the gangster Marsellus Wallace—to retrieve the watch his girlfriend forgot to pack through an appeal not only to the memory of his father but also to a repetition that replaces the father:

> You see, Butch, what you're forgettin' is this watch isn't just a device that enables you to keep track of time. This watch is a symbol. It's a symbol of

how your father, and his father before him, and his father before him, distinguished themselves in war. And when I took Marsellus Wallace's money, I started a war. This is my World War Two. That apartment in North Hollywood, that's my Wake Island. In fact, if you look at it that way, it's almost kismet that Fabienne left it behind. And using that perspective, going back for it isn't stupid. It may be dangerous, but it's not stupid. Because there are certain things in this world that are worth going back for. (114–15)

As Butch tells us, there are certain things that are worth fighting for because they are worth "going *back* for" (emphasis added). And the "going back" is itself so compelling that other considerations—of perspective and historic scale, for example—pale in comparison. Butch's moment of retrospection is entangled in a drive to repetition: he goes back because he believes it's how he can repeat, and in doing so recapture, a lost man's time. That this golden time has come to him as an "evacuated" symbol—and here I simply point to Norman O. Brown's work connecting time, gold, excrement, and the Oedipal crisis[19]—simply makes it all the more emotionally resonant. In a move that readers of Faulkner (and Freud) will quickly recognize, Butch identifies with his grandfather ("this is my World War Two," not "this is my Vietnam") and thereby articulates his desire to displace his father—to assume the authority of the father—by revisiting an older heroic past.

As I indicated, this speech does not appear in the film itself; yet what is manifest in the screenplay remains readable as a latency in the film. By removing the speech, in fact, Tarantino casts the watch more clearly as a fetish, the mark of a perpetual effort to recuperate a loss. It is the sign of temporal retention *par excellence,* and as such it becomes more than a little ridiculous. Just as the story of the transmission of the watch slid from tragedy to satire, so the narrative of the recovery of the watch moves from tragedy (the murder of Vincent Vega, played by John Travolta) to gross and outrageous comedy. Further, the comedy emerges in the use of filmic quotation, which is to say, through a species of repetition: Tarantino has described the effect of this section of *Pulp Fiction* working as if "you're watching the boxing movie *Body and Soul* and then suddenly the characters turn a corner and they're in the middle of *Deliverance.*"[20] One example of repetition through quotation appears in the prolonged moment in which Butch chooses his weapon before returning to rescue Marsellus. As Tarantino explains:

He picks up the hammer and that's almost realistic, that's almost like him. . . . But then he picks up a baseball bat and it's like he's gonna be Joe Don Baker as Buford Pusser in *Walking Tall* going down there. No, I'm not gonna be *Walking Tall*, I'm gonna be Leatherface in *The Texas Chainsaw Massacre*. No, I'm gonna be Tanakura Ken in *The Yakuza*, I'm gonna be a samurai going down there. (Woods 120)[21]

Butch's climactic rescue of Marsellus Wallace is preceded by a moment of musing retrospection in which choosing the correct *quotation* (rather than reinhabiting the proper historic moment, the approach Butch toys with in the speech that was cut) is what determines both the dimensions and the success of his "heroic" action. Thus the task of recovering the sign of temporal recuperation (the watch) is shown to hinge on the proper use of quotation, a form of repetition. In other words, the point of "The Gold Watch"—in some ways, the point of *Pulp Fiction*—is to validate repetition (and the ensuing temporal disruption in narrative) for its own sake. Some things are worth going back for simply because you get to go back for them.

For Tarantino, this quotation/repetition compulsion amounts to a strategy for blocking investigation not only of concerns about originality but also of derivation, and, by extension, of authority. All of the magazine interviews and fan paperbacks about Tarantino dwell on his background as a high school dropout and "video store geek" whose film education came through the small screen. The emergence and proliferation of VHS editions of cinematic work during this period has proven, in Tarantino's case, to be both an unbelievable boon—in any interview with him it quickly becomes clear that he has seen almost everything—and a severe handicap, given the sometimes dramatic damage than can be done to a film by inattentive reformatting, colorization, and contemporary remakes. Tarantino has seen everything, yes, but largely at a distorted remove, an education that has resulted in a similarly distorted understanding of film history. Though he dedicated *Reservoir Dogs* to Jean-Luc Godard, and though he's named his production company A Band Apart (in homage to Godard's 1964 film *Band à part*), Tarantino's introduction to the French New Wave was Jim McBride's 1983 remake of *Breathless;* all accounts are that Tarantino hugely admired the film and has continued to champion it even after seeing the original.[22] The historic reliance of film on literary classics (the recent *Moll Flanders*es, Kenneth Branagh's *Hamlet,* Jane Campion's *Portrait of a Lady,* and the Jane Austen explosion have heightened our sense of this phenomenon) is simply one aspect of a long-established practice of paraphrase and quotation in the modern circulation of cultural capital that is perhaps rather more obviously apparent to directors of Tarantino's age than to filmmakers of past generations (and this awareness operates as a clear subtext in McBride's film).[23] It would not be hard for a member of Tarantino's generation to conclude, then, that repetition is much more than a technique for reinforcing cultural norms or values: in a fundamental way, it *is* culture value itself. The path to authority thus lies not through originality (a concept under significant pressure well before Faulkner's time); rather, one gains cultural authority by a direct appeal to the technologies of repetition that ensure the transmission of authority through time. One gets to speak not because one has something to say, but because one has something to say that has been said before.

The implications of the emergence of this sort of repetition in contemporary film—and its important differences and similarities to Faulknerian repetition—become clearer when we place "The Gold Watch" next to the opening pages of Quentin's section in *The Sound of the Fury,* where the grandfather's watch—"the mausoleum of all hope and desire" (*SF* 76)—figures so prominently. While this pairing yields many surface similarities—the watch as legacy, even the connecting of watch and feces ("Excrement Father said like sweating" [*SF* 77])—the differences are acute. While Butch murders, is nearly raped, and finally rescues his sworn enemy in order to save his patrimony, Quentin tries to destroy his grandfather's watch. Quentin's desire to stop time culminates in his suicide; this desire arises from a parallel, contradictory wish to repeat time, figured in the drive toward incest as well as in the narrative's temporal disruptions.[24] Much as Faulkner's narrative itself is analeptically punctured and torn, shredded by temporal pressures, so too is Quentin slain by time. Like Butch, Quentin makes use of quotation, but what he hears are not the pronouncements of an empowered and empowering larger culture: His father's nihilistic words are never far from his consciousness, and, far from propelling him into heroic action, these quotations goad Quentin on toward the banks of the Charles River. While many of the differences between Butch and Quentin may be tied to genre (*The Sound and the Fury* is essentially tragic, whereas *Pulp Fiction* is largely satiric), most of them are also thematic, clustering around the question of authority. In his culture, Butch accepts and celebrates the ways in which repetition guarantees his continued potency; for Quentin, that potency has been lost, and he despairs of it ever being restored. And both Butch's confidence, on the one hand, and Quentin's sorrow, on the other, arise from their interactions with Black characters; it is those interactions that condition Butch and Quentin's self-assessments as culturally potent subjects.

The question Quentin poses to the clock repairman near the opening of his section is a question about authority. Faced with a window display of "about a dozen watches" showing "a dozen different hours," each with an "assertive and contradictory assurance" (*SF* 85), Quentin asks the repairman, "would you mind telling me if any of those watches in the window are right?" (*SF* 84). Quentin does not want to know *which* watch has the right time, just if *any* of them are right. As it turns out, none of them are. Immediately after this exchange, Quentin buys the "two six pound" flatirons with which he plans to ensure his death by water, then boards the streetcar on which "the only vacant seat was beside a nigger" (*SF* 86).

The fact that he must sit next to a Black man on the streetcar occasions Quentin's first sustained meditation on race, inaugurated by the now-famous observation that "a nigger is not a person so much as a form of behavior; a sort of obverse reflection of the white people he lives among" (*SF* 86). This observation summons forth the recollection of that time, for Quentin, when the obverse reflection appeared most flattering: "that morning in Virginia" when, on the train home for the Christmas holidays, Quentin sees "a nigger on a mule in the middle of the stiff ruts" of a road crossing, "as if they had been built there with the fence and the road, or with the hill, carved out of the hill itself, like a sign put there saying You are home again" (*SF* 86–87). Quentin calls the Black man "uncle"; he responds with "boss"; as the train pulls away, Quentin is moved to describe the rapidly fading scene as "motionless," "static," and "serene" (*SF* 87). This extended recollection closes with yet another memory before Faulkner returns the reader to the streetcar: Quentin recalls his effort to "come out even with the bell" at the end of the school day, counting out the class's remaining fifteen minutes and always failing to finish exactly in time (*SF* 88).

The question about the watches (which foregrounds a modern notion of time as arbitrary and so always "wrong") and the anecdote about the final minutes of the school day (when, Quentin recalls, the anticipated but still startling ringing of the bell would make his "insides... move, sitting still" [88]) are parables about missed, or wrong, time that frame the moment Quentin recognizes as his "right" time: that instance when the "obverse reflection" of the "nigger" felt eternal, the naturally ordained "uncle" to the white "boss," placed not simply near the fence and the road but carved out of the very landscape itself: a natural phenomenon. It is worth remembering, in this connection, that the class in which Quentin always fails to "come out even with the bell" is US history: "'Tell Quentin who discovered the Mississippi River, Henry,' 'DeSoto'" (88). His disgust with the northern Black Deacon, combined with what Faulkner elsewhere in the novel invites us to see as the status free-fall of the Compsons, leads Quentin to anticipate a cultural impotence of the white male that he would rather die than face (his decision to leave his bloodied clothes to Deacon is itself something of suicide note here).

However, it takes only a minute's reflection on the historical arc leading from Quentin to Butch to realize this imagined and feared cultural impotence never happened. Tarantino's unapologetic, nearly obsessive deployment of the N-word throughout *Pulp Fiction* is perhaps the clearest signal of this uninterrupted white potency. As Sharon Willis has noted: *"Pulp Fiction* depends ambiguously and ambivalently on the very racism it wishes to distance itself from.... Tarantino's universe seems to depend intimately on ... an iconic [i.e., stereotyped] construction of African-American masculinity. This is the universe in which *Pulp Fiction* posits that the term, 'nigger,' can be neutralized through a generalized circulation in which it designates anyone at all, of whatever race" (60–61).

Willis refers here to a much-quoted interview in which Tarantino claimed that he seeks, through the force of sheer repetition, to strip the word of its cultural power.[25] My discussion of the work of repetition within *Pulp Fiction* should significantly problematize, if not completely discredit, Tarantino's rationale for keeping the epithet in such prominent circulation in his films. The justification is as inadequate (and thereby suggestive) as the equally oft-cited explanation that the "flesh-colored" Band-aid (the most salient feature of Marsellus Wallace when we first see him in the film) was put there to hide a "distracting" scar on the back of actor Ving Rhames's head.[26] The virtue (such as it is) of this entirely implausible explanation lies in the way that it literalizes the poverty of the claim that the scars of Blacks are "distractions": the effort to conceal evidence of past injury only draws greater attention to it. So, too, with Tarantino's use of the N-word. As Todd Boyd has pointed out, "Tarantino sees his use of the N-word as proof that he is conversant in the nuances of Black culture in the most sophisticated way.... In the sense that Blackness always has been the model for what was hip in American society, Tarantino has simply added himself to a long list.... For a white person who subscribes to this theory, being called the N-word affirms one's hipness; being able to say it simultaneously allows the user to reference one's own whiteness without fear of compromise."[27]

To put it another way: Tarantino wishes to quote the N-word in much the same way that Butch quotes action films: to conjure power. In the world of *Pulp Fiction*, then, the epithet remains the "obverse reflection" of a now nominally liberal, idealized, "color-blind" whiteness, solely by virtue of its repeated circulation: a referencing of white cultural authority that, in posing as its evacuation, actually work as its enforcement.

In concluding her analysis of Tarantino's work, Willis returns to the story of Butch's watch to propose that, like Quentin at the end of the school day, the world of *Pulp Fiction* fails to attend to history: "Tarantino's films seem to posit that we might read history by sifting through the father's waste. But then they do not go on to read what they find there" (67). Placing Tarantino's work next to Faulkner's certainly amplifies this proposition. Yet it seems to me that another way to read the problem of history as it appears in these works is to acknowledge that, while operating with quite different premises, both Tarantino's films and Faulkner's novels force us to reckon with the ways in which contemporary cultural authority is constituted and circulated: not by actually *reading* history but rather by quoting or referencing it. There is no question, after all, that the establishment of Faulkner—an author whose best work probes the painful fault lines of American apartheid—as prized cultural coin fortifies, on some level, the continuance of white male cultural potency. "This time thing" is indeed the shared instrument to that end in the work for Tarantino and Faulkner: both author and *auteur* are engaged in projects that mobilize and deploy cultural capital in ways that force us to explore the implications of investing in that capital in the first place.

Another, closing word on quotation and cultural capital: Faulkner is quoted twice in Ken Burns's 1989 television miniseries *The Civil War,* first by novelist Shelby Foote about midway through the series, then by historian Barbara J. Fields near the very end. In the episode about the battle at Gettysburg, Foote recalls Gavin Stevens's remark, in *Intruder in the Dust,* that "for every Southern boy fourteen years old, not once but whenever he wants it, there is the instant when it's still not yet two o'clock on that July afternoon in 1863."[28] Foote chuckles as he recalls this line, looking down with a genially bemused expression—marveling at Faulkner's ability to so accurately capture the experience of "every" southern boy.[29] Fields, on the other hand, chooses to reference Faulkner to a different end: "William Faulkner said once [that] history is not *was.* It's *is.* What we need to remember about the Civil War is that the Civil War *is,* in the present. . . . If some citizens live in houses while others live on the street, the Civil War is still going on. It's still to be fought, and regrettably it can still be lost."[30]

Here are two possible ways of citing Faulkner, both of them emphasizing his insistence on the living past; yet the first casts the author as a white supremacist nostalgic, while the other presents him as cryptic, demanding, and impatient with the world as he found it. Faced with quotations that produced such opposed readings not only of the Civil War but of the very use and meaning of history as well, Burns abandoned the attempt to frame history through Faulkner and instead closed the series with Foote reading a passage from the final volume of his own Civil War narrative, lines quoting the expressed desire of a Confederate veteran, Sergeant Berry Benson of South Carolina, to revisit the war. This televised history of the war, then, concluded with a heartfelt wish that the Civil War may yet be fought again, "after this life," when "after the battle, then the slain and wounded will arise, and all will meet together under the two flags, all sound and well, and there will be talking and laughter and cheers, and all will say: Did it not seem real? Was it not as in the old days?"[31]

In quoting Faulkner, both Foote and Fields sought to claim authority for their quite different views of the meaning of the Civil War. But as their chosen quotations show, Faulkner's authority is a riven thing. In deciding to close the series with a Confederate wish that the war continue forever in heaven, Burns chose to end his project on a single, less fraught, authoritative note, a move that sought to turn us away from the uncomfortable oscillation set up in the center of the narrative by those competing Faulkner citations. Yet that very oscillation—that structure of tension and antagonism—is the heart of the Faulknerian reading experience. It's what fuels the multiple negatives and the temporal ruptures that so uniquely texture his fiction. And it's an oscillation that has moved outward to inform some of the most compelling expressions of contemporary culture, from Godard's *A bout de souffle* (in which *The Wild Palms* is directly quoted) to Tarantino's *Reservoir Dogs.* Even without Kawin's remarkable claim that "Godard has been putting Faulkner on film throughout his career" (153), we would recognize, as my student did, the deep connections between Faulkner's investigations in narrative time and the ensuing cinematic versions of those investigations. These are investigations worth pursuing, despite the inherent paradox: reading Faulkner means investing in the structures of cultural capital, which means entering the culture's vexed system of repetition in service to maintaining white, patriarchal authority within the status quo, but it also means seeing those structures for what they are, and what they do. For the long term this is not enough—as bell hooks complains of *Pulp Fiction,* such a practice seems to "titillate with subversive possibility . . . but then everything kinda comes right back to normal."[32] But for now, the need for some sort of critical purchase on the mechanisms of cultural power gives us one good reason to keep on reading Faulkner—into the twenty-first century, at least.

Postscript

The focus in this chapter, both when it was written in the late 1990s and as I offer it here, is on the approach to narrative structure Faulkner's fiction and Tarantino's films hold in common and how a similarly shared content (the patronymic watch) both interrogates and serves the interests of white male supremacy. Another shared aspect, obvious now in retrospect, is the interest in pulp fiction itself. Like Tarantino, Faulkner was a student of pulp, scouring popular magazines of the 1920s and 1930s like *Black Mask* (Tarantino's avowed inspiration for his film), *Gangster Stories,* and *Gun Molls* for themes and techniques. Unlike Tarantino, Faulkner was quick to disparage this material (his introduction to the Modern Library edition of *Sanctuary,* which seeks to actively separate that novel's low ambitions from the higher aims of *The Sound and the Fury,* is exhibit A here),[33] but recent scholarship has well and amply shown the depths of his engagement with it. In truth, Faulkner had a habit of publicly bad-mouthing those media and genres that he assiduously mined both for content and form, and not only when he was financially strapped.

In the years since "Pulp Fictions" was first published, important work by Sarah Gleeson-White, David M. Earle, and Jaime Harker has greatly expanded our understanding of this particular Faulknerian tic, revisiting the subject of Faulkner's literary reputation pre–*The Portable Faulkner* and prompting fresh critical reflection on how, exactly, the "corn cob man" became a Nobel laureate. Their research makes abundantly clear that the separation between "high" and "low," art and commerce, was never as strict as Faulkner made it out to be.[34] Of course, this attitude was not unique to Faulkner; it was a well-worn refrain in the period's "high" modernist discourse, and it is not surprising that Faulkner would sing along. As this avowed structure of opposition has a key interpretive role to play in several of the chapters that follow, I want to make clear here that it should be understood as a dominant rhetorical trope of the time and not as an accurate description of Faulkner's literary habits, either as a writer or a reader.

3

Writing *A Fable* for America

> O righteous God! Thou hast directed
> how everything must befall.
> Then to whom is the reward presented: him who wants,
> or cannot want, things otherwise?
>
> —ARNOLD SCHOENBERG, *Moses und Aron*

In *Creating Faulkner's Reputation,* Lawrence H. Schwartz sets out to explain the early Cold War "inflation" of William Faulkner's literary stock, a transformation that, despite being both widely acknowledged and even dateable (it occurred between 1946 and 1950), had yet to be examined "in a serious, thorough, or scholarly way."[1] Truly, the story deserves analysis; Faulkner's triumph after years of disparagement and neglect is as remarkable as it is well-known. Author of thirteen novels published between 1926 and 1942, Faulkner had been dismissed by the bulk of the US literary critical establishment as a talented but crude purveyor of gothic, politically retrograde, willfully recondite fictions before the 1946 publication of Malcolm Cowley's *The Portable Faulkner* ushered in a near-total *volte-face.* For Schwartz, a "serious, thorough, scholarly" approach to the question of literary recognition is one that bypasses discussion of formal or technical accomplishment (such discussion, he implies, is beside the point: "in every era, there are many excellent writers who never achieve widespread recognition" [3]) in favor of an investigation into the political and economic conditions in place when recognition is granted, since these conditions not only set the terms for reception but also constitute, in however condensed or displaced a manner, whatever is meaningful in the work itself. This move to uncover the political unconscious of art (or of a given artist's career) is by now as well-established as earlier endeavors to demonstrate a work's "organic unity" or uncover its mythical archetypes, and while it has produced brilliant readings of texts, it is no more immune to encumbering assumption than the methods it supplanted.[2] *Creating Faulkner's Reputation,* which has wielded enormous influence on a generation of Faulkner scholars, is encumbered in two ways. The first involves Schwartz's approach to Faulkner's texts, which he characterizes but does not analyze. The second has to do with the narrow, even parochial, quality of the study's contextual frame: Schwartz assumes that because Faulkner is an American author, his international reputation can only be a function of his standing in the United States. Taken together, these assumptions constitute the parallel tracks on which many discussions of Cold War culture have proceeded for the past forty or so years: context matters more than text, and the US context matters most of all.

In Schwartz's view, Faulkner's "remote, complex, iconoclastic" novels are so fundamentally "inaccessible" as to be virtually unreadable without scholarly assistance (5). Luckily for Faulkner, the anticommunist "postwar cultural readjustment" in the United States during the late 1940s conjured that assistance into being via a sustained, well-funded campaign to repudiate "the socially conscious literary traditions of naturalism/realism" in favor of an "elitist aesthetic" exemplifying "the same values that Western intellectuals saw in capitalism which made it morally superior to communism" (5, 4). While Schwartz grants that there "was no conspiracy to launch" Faulkner *per se* (5), he does seem to believe that something resembling a conspiracy was needed to relaunch literary modernism in the United States. Accordingly, he takes pains to explain how a particular postwar liberal political consensus made itself felt in literary circles through a conflation of the formalist values of the rightist New Critics (chiefly the southerners Allen Tate, Robert Penn Warren, and John Crowe Ransom) with the leftist anticommunism of the New York intellectuals (Philip Rahv, William Phillips, and Lionel Trilling). This conflation was hastened along by a timely and politically motivated series of Rockefeller Foundation grants to the *Sewanee Review* (for the southerners) and the *Partisan Review* (for the New Yorkers) designed to further scholarship promoting literary modernism, whose aesthetics, Schwartz claims, "not only reflected [an anticommunist] political ideology but helped to legitimize it as well" (201).[3] What emerged was "a closed community of enforced conformity where dissent was suppressed and oppositionist literature and criticism were displaced" (202), and it was the members of this newly empowered interpretive community who, by way of forwarding their politico-aesthetic agenda, championed the critical revaluation of Faulkner. "Had the aesthetic values of the 1930s persisted or had anti-Communism not become prevalent," Schwartz asserts, "Faulkner could not have achieved renown.... Earlier efforts to launch Faulkner met with failure until the demands of the Cold War propagated a new aestheticism. Without that change in aesthetic sensibility it seems unlikely that such a difficult writer would have achieved the wide recognition he did" (5, 7–8).

Since this "change in aesthetic sensibility" was entirely politically motivated, it is ultimately the Cold War, not the novels, that created Faulkner's reputation, and Schwartz accordingly reads the Cold War (or, to be precise, the various cultural skirmishes in the United States during the early Cold War years as recorded in philanthropic foundation memoranda and scholarly essays), not the literature. Faulkner's reputation thus emerges as something that, once shaped, hardened into a structure impervious to any effects released by the texts themselves, a postulate that doesn't serve Schwartz well when his analysis moves into the proximity of the 1954 publication of *A Fable*, the first novel of Faulkner's to appear after he was awarded the Nobel Prize for Literature and arguably his most keenly anticipated and sorely disappointing work. Schwartz acknowledges the anticipation, since it is an important aspect of the history he wants to explain—*A Fable* could plausibly be described as the first eagerly awaited novel of Faulkner's career—but he makes no mention of the widespread critical disappointment; indeed, in closing his narrative with the awarding of the Nobel, Schwartz invites his readers to assume that Faulkner's work thenceforth enjoyed unalloyed critical praise, which was hardly the case. This neglect of *A Fable* and its reception points to two larger lacunae in Schwartz's argument: a disinterest in addressing Faulkner's shifting reputation in the Cold War years after the Nobel, and an unwillingness to take seriously the possibility that the novels themselves might invite readings beyond the control of the author's ideologically motivated literary-critical Cold War American handlers. Yet both the reception of *A Fable* and the novel itself have a good deal to tell us about the entangled relationships of Cold War commerce, politics, and art that cannot emerge in a discussion of Faulkner's work limited to describing how a group of scholars and foundation trustees sought to turn the literature into "a cultural weapon in the early years of the Cold War" (210).

Schwartz's unwillingness to directly engage Faulkner's fiction imposes certain limitations to his argument, but it is his overvaluing of Faulkner's American reputation that defines it, an overvaluing that went mostly unnoticed by the study's early reviewers, themselves operating within a late Cold War literary-critical imaginary. *Creating Faulkner's Reputation* was published in 1988, and Schwartz describes his findings as "not sympathetic to the main tendencies in Faulkner scholarship" (6). Those tendencies are not described, and Schwartz seems to encourage his readers to assume that they remained largely unchanged since the late 1940s, when Faulkner "was presented by Cowley, Warren, and others as an important novelist, a literary genius, and a serious moralist" (4). In reality, though, *Creating Faulkner's Reputation* found many appreciative readers: shifts in the "main tendencies in Faulkner scholarship" had been underway for some time, and Schwartz's interests resonated with those of a generation of critics similarly inclined to undertake more theoretical, political, or sociological investigations of the work than previously entertained, bringing feminist and deconstructive analytical tools to the novels and being particularly keen to interrogate racial representations in the works.[4] Only two reviewers—neither of them especially representative of "the main tendencies"—paused to worry over the way Schwartz finessed what should have been the most carefully plotted move in his argument: how, exactly, Faulkner's Cold War US makeover translated into a Nobel Prize (which Schwartz identifies as the "keystone" of the anticommunist "public affirmation of American culture" [210]). In an otherwise positive review, Michael O'Brien writes that "the book's most serious omission is an adequate explanation for the awarding of the Nobel Prize."[5] Fred Pinnegar not only notes the "omission" but also (perhaps unintentionally) casts it as symptomatic of a more thoroughgoing critical oversight: "Schwartz acknowledges at several points that this award was an essential element in the creation of Faulkner's literary reputation . . . but he tells us nothing about the politics associated with it, such as why, how, and by whom he was nominated. Faulkner may have been ignored at home in the 1930s and 40s, but in Europe (especially France) he had a loyal and critically astute following."[6]

As Pinnegar observes, while it is possible to construct the narrative of the rise of Faulkner's reputation by starting in the United States in the late 1940s, it is also possible to tell a story that begins earlier and elsewhere. What happens to the nationalistic shape and ideological force of Faulkner's redeemed reputation if one grants the possibility that this redemption may be the result not only of a postwar American campaign to recruit culture to the anticommunist cause but also of the painstaking work of translators laboring in 1930s Paris or Buenos Aires or Budapest? Schwartz's discussion of Faulkner's European reputation is mostly limited to his reception in France after World War II; he describes Henri Peyre's 1947 essay "American Literature through French Eyes" (written not for the French but for Americans and published in the *Virginia Quarterly Review*) as "one of the first attempts to explain . . . the *new* international importance of contemporary American literature" in France (143; emphasis added). However, Maurice Edgar Coindreau's *Nouvelle revue française* essay about Faulkner was published in June 1931; his translations of "Dry September" and "A Rose for Emily" appeared during the winter of 1931–32; and René-Noël Raimbault's translation of *Sanctuary*, the first Faulkner novel published in French, came out in 1933.[7] Faulkner's work first appeared in Spanish via the 1934 publication of *Sanctuario* (*Sanctuary*), translated by the Cuban writer Lino Novás Calvo; Jorge Luis Borges reviewed Faulkner's novels in the 1930s and was the translator responsible for the 1940 Argentinian publication of *Los palmeras salvajes*. Faulkner's work did indeed come to play an important symbolic role in Cold War Hungary (the nation's first post-1989 president, Árpád Göncz, was admired not only for his support of Imre Nagy in the 1956 revolution but also for his Hungarian translations of *Sartoris, The Sound and the Fury,* and *Absalom, Absalom!*), but Hungarians had been introduced to his work in the early 1930s through a translation of "That Evening Sun" by the modernist writer Desző Kosztolányi.[8] It's possible, then, that the international circulation of, and interest in, Faulkner's work grew out of something other than, or in addition to, US Cold War efforts to establish cultural supremacy: Faulkner may have won the Nobel Prize in part because Europeans had been reading him with interest since before the start of World War II.[9] Seen this way, Faulkner's Cold War critical revaluation emerges as a chapter in a much longer-running narrative of the global spread of literary modernism—a narrative not without politics, to be sure, but also a narrative more international than Americanist.[10]

This is not to say that various extraliterary factors did not work together to give Faulkner's reputation a boost in the early years of the Cold War. However, acknowledging these efforts tells us little about the vagaries of Faulkner's reputation *during* the Cold War. Bringing that historical lens into focus requires attention to Faulkner's activities after the Nobel, to the work published in its wake, and that work's reception. And there is no better place to start this inquiry than with the book Faulkner called his "magnum O," the 1954 novel *A Fable*.

* * *

In the past four decades the world of Faulkner scholarship has seen several campaigns on behalf of what might be termed the author's "second drawer" works, perhaps none more vigorous than that mounted on behalf of *A Fable*.[11] And vigor is needed, as even the novel's most ardent advocates must consider the commentary that greeted *A Fable* when it was first published. Initial critical reaction ran a rather narrow gamut: sympathetic readers called the book "a heroically ambitious failure," while those with less patience termed it "a calamity." A little over a year after its appearance the novel was the subject of a savagely apt parody in *Punch;* Ernest Hemingway, never one to mince words (or concede a rival), termed it "not pure shit but 'impure diluted shit'" (Blotner 2:1502, 1644).[12] Since then, scholars have described *A Fable* as "troublesome," a "failed political novel," "a book of badness simply astonishing for Faulkner." André Bleikasten grouped *A Fable* with a cluster of misbegotten literary productions from Faulkner's later years, all of them offspring of the post-Nobel conjugation of Faulkner "the writer" with Faulkner "denizen of the world." "For a long time a watchful angel kept" these two Faulkners apart, Bleikasten writes. "I wish they had never met."[13]

It is tempting to hypothesize that this last characterization of *A Fable* as a peculiarly Faulknerian "hideous progeny" actually forecasts a hopeful future for the work: like *Frankenstein,* maybe all *A Fable* needs for its redemptive transvaluation of critical value is the appropriate interpretive paradigm shift. Faulkner himself hinted as much, predicting that it would take "maybe 50 years before the world can stop to read" *A Fable*.[14] But Bleikasten's sly description of the novel as the product of two aspects of a single "Faulkner" forces us to recognize the interpretive paradoxes presented by Faulkner's self-divided art, and to acknowledge that, as monsters go, *A Fable* is more like Dolly the sheep than Victor Frankenstein's creature—a lavishly tricked-out, scandalously expensive yet withal fundamentally conservative reproduction of the (wooly yet ultimately comforting) known, not an impassioned, terrifying effort to transform moribund matter into some unprecedented living thing.[15] For all its complication, the problem with *A Fable* lies not in an ungainly variousness but in a fundamental predictability: from its allegorical importunity to its local textual aspects (as Bleikasten notes, the narrative voice itself "all too often sounds like a mocking echo . . . Faulknerian to the point of self-travesty"), *A Fable* sets its readers on edge largely through its insistence on going over (and over) narrative ground already better covered elsewhere.[16] For readers who admire the work of the 1930s, Faulkner's insistent self-referentiality in *A Fable*—a self-referencing that seems to signal a certain imaginative exhaustion and that approaches a rather gruesome self-consumption—is among the text's most painful qualities. As was noted at publication, *A Fable*'s near-parodic borrowings include Faulkner's own Nobel Prize speech—probably the text most widely cited by his early Cold War champions eager to prove that the critics of the 1930s had failed to sufficiently appreciate the author's humanism—reproduced in a manner that seems reckless, if not cynical.[17]

This near-compulsive self-repetition finds its external corollary in *A Fable*'s multiple borrowings, a baroque accretion of allusion and allegory whose extratextual targets are so multiple and various as to border on the hysterical.[18] In an unprecedented gesture, Faulkner opens *A Fable* with a paragraph of acknowledgments in which he thanks William Bacher, a producer, and Henry Hathaway, a director—acquaintances from his Hollywood days—for "the basic idea from which this book grew into its present form" and credits James Street's *Look Away!* (a 1936 gallimaufry of news and feature articles about the South) with providing "the story of the hanged man and the bird" (*A Fable* 667).[19] Following the path laid down by his modernist predecessors, Faulkner unapologetically made allusion and revisionary repetition (or, as he sometimes joked, theft) practically into an aesthetic creed ("An artist is a creature driven by demons. . . . He is completely amoral in that he will rob, borrow, beg, or steal from anybody and everybody to get the work done"), but even by his own capacious standard the material that went into the making of *A Fable* came to him "ready-made" (to cite a crucial term in Max Horkheimer and

Theodor Adorno's critique of mass cultural productions) to an unusually high degree.[20]

My favorite description of *A Fable* appears in the "Chronology of William Faulkner's Life and Works" at the beginning of *The Cambridge Companion to William Faulkner*. There, Philip M. Weinstein describes it as Faulkner's "most premeditated novel," and that single word, "premeditated"—implying, as it does, that the book is a sort of crime, with a perpetrator who knew exactly what he was doing—informs my own view of *A Fable*.[21] For I share the misgivings of the novel's detractors, misgivings that arise primarily from what it feels like to read the book. One might not expect the experience to be wholly pleasurable, but neither is it invigorating or productively challenging. *A Fable* makes all of the demands of a Faulknerian text (multiple intersecting plots, abstruse references to literary and social history, a scrambled chronology, periodic sentences running a page or more in length) but offers none of the usual compensations (a moment in which those seemingly unrelated plots crystallize into a complex pattern of meaningful interdependence; an unexpected yet apt intervention in the *uses* of literature and history; breathtakingly beautiful language). *A Fable* takes all of the achievements of the Faulknerian vision and hollows them out. Now scholars and critics can (and have) argued that this hollowness, understood metatextually, is precisely the point of the book, but that interpretive sleight of hand does little to make up for feeling, after finishing *A Fable*, that one has been rather cold-bloodedly toyed with.[22] In fact, it was partly an effort to mute such an impression that led Saxe Commins to withhold Faulkner's prepublication statement about *A Fable*, which begins with the assertion that, appearances to the contrary, the novel "is not a pacifist book" and goes on to insist that it has no "aim or moral."[23]

Nevertheless, this experience of reading *A Fable* and coming away with the sense of having been dallied with, of having overinvested oneself in a text that finally never moves beyond the *promise* of fulfillment, is key to understanding the novel's method and meaning, both of which arise from Faulkner's engagement with the manipulations of American mass cultural entertainment during the early years of the Cold War, when US cultural hegemony first clearly emerged as a historical possibility. Faulkner called *A Fable* his "big book" not because of its length (437 pages) or the amount of time he dedicated to writing it (ten years) but rather because he believed it would be his "cross-over hit," the text that would bring modernism to the masses by rigging out a well-known "uplifting" story with the abstruse tackle of modernist literary technique. It is useful to remember that *A Fable* was born in Hollywood, not Yoknapatawpha. The story of the second coming of Christ in the trenches of World War I was conceived as a money machine adaptable to multiple media outlets, and it is exactly the imbrication of the novel's "primer-like biblical references and explanations" (which, in an early letter to his agent, Faulkner pledged to tone down but in fact made only more obvious and detailed) with its modernist "special effects" that mark its provenance in culture industry.[24] Hathaway, the director (and World War I veteran) who came up with the idea of making a movie about the enigma of the Unknown Soldier, was "the consummate Hollywood professional"; Bacher was "a nonstop talker and a hypnotic salesman."[25] Joseph Blotner suggests that, when the two of them approached Faulkner in 1943 with the idea that "the three of them would make the picture together and share alike in the profits," Faulkner agreed to the project largely because he believed it would ensure that he "might never have to return to Hollywood" again (Blotner 2:1149).

In yoking together modernist sophistication and commercial cultural pandering, *A Fable* lays bare the interconnections and interdependencies of "high" modernism and consumerist mass culture, and it is this persistent, deliberate double-voicedness, this sentimental modernism, that produces the text's disquieting effects. In a famous letter to Walter Benjamin, Theodor Adorno writes that both modernist artworks and mass cultural productions "bear the stigmata of capitalism. . . . Both are torn halves of an integral freedom, to which however they do not add up"; I want to suggest that one way to think of *A Fable*'s textual shortcomings—and by far the best way to grasp its signal importance as a cultural document of America in the early years of the Cold War—is to see how the novel's flaws demonstrate the ways in which these "torn halves" of modern life fail to "add up."[26] Like Arnold Schoenberg's twelve-tone compositions, *A Fable* seeks to articulate the lures and structures of modern commodification even as it transcends them. It is not surprising that reading Faulkner's novel turns out to be about as easily enjoyable as listening to *Moses und Aron*.[27] Unlike Schoenberg, however, Faulkner could not content himself with the abstract integrity of modernist negation; unlike *Moses und Aron*, *A Fable* truly seeks to please—and to sell.

I want to propose that, despite the novel's primarily European setting, the frustrating and ungainly aspects of *A Fable* are best accounted for when we read the novel as a book about America, a text that offers Faulkner's most sustained meditation on the quality of American political and artistic life at the moment of the United States' postwar emergence as a global power via the twin forces of military victory and mass cultural expansion—an emergence absolutely coincident with the years that Faulkner dedicated to writing *A Fable*. In its exploration of the rhetoric of freedom and equality via ideologies of brotherhood (through the resistance of the corporal and his twelve followers, through the secret fellowship of Masonry, and through the global fraternity of officers and generals); in its recognition of the continuing importance of a related sentimental Christianity as a crucial element in US national identity formation and a useful means of shoring up domestic support for diplomatic adventuring in the fight against "godless" communism; and in its anticipation of the ways in which the modernist negation of "unfreedom" (to use an Adornian term) would be increasingly and indiscriminately linked, in service to the US pursuit of a capitalist global hegemony, with mass cultural phenomena like Hollywood films and major league sports (even Eisenhower's golf stroke was fuel for the propaganda work of the United States Information Agency), *A Fable* registers the peculiarly American-inflected triumph of consumerist mass culture and a related "modernist conformism" in the aftermath of World War II.[28] *A Fable* is mostly of a piece with the politico-cultural imaginary of the early Cold War United States, and Faulkner was right to title the novel as he did: as Susan Stewart has pointed out, the fable is "a genre revered precisely for stasis, eternity, and closure, . . . revived with the emergence of the neoclassical or whenever a desire for ideological completeness appears."[29] Yet *A Fable* is an importantly problematic text of the new "American century," presenting a peculiar set of interpretive challenges. The novel demands readers skilled in *allegoresis* and the related contemporary techniques of cultural symptomatology even as it renders these methods inadequate to the task of capturing the full range of its textual effects. Thus the interpretive course I chart here is not a straightforward one; what I offer is less a royal road through the novel than a mapping of its constitutive tensions, and I make no attempt to harmonize this discordant text by transmuting its Christian allegory into politico-materialist terms, as some recent readings of the novel have done.[30] This is not to claim that *A Fable*'s method is unprecedented. It is not, as Faulkner predicted, his "War and Peace close enough to home, our times, language, for Americans to really buy it" (*Selected Letters* 238), but it is, perhaps, his *Uncle Tom's Cabin*.

Stowe's text provides a useful comparison here, for, like *A Fable,* it employs aspects of the Christian myth as crucial allegorical scaffolding. And, also like *A Fable,* it is not a text that goes down easily, though its importance to American literary history is impossible to deny. A proper accounting of the long-running analysis of literary sentimentalism occasioned by the recanonization of *Uncle Tom's Cabin* requires more space than I have here, but I would like to visit some aspects of that analysis in order to more clearly fix my claim that the allegorical and rhetorical mode of *A Fable* is best understood as a sentimental modernism. A good starting point would be Shirley Samuels's comment that sentimentality in the United States is "a national project: in particular, a project imagining the nation's bodies and the national body"[31]—which is to say, a project grounded in allegory, wherein abstraction is made flesh. Samuels's formulation also usefully reminds us that, as a political and social project as well as an artistic one, sentimentalism deploys an expressive register that was not limited to, or invented by, women writers. Elizabeth Barnes has traced the tradition of the American sentimental back to the founding of the Republic and concludes that representing structures of sympathetic relations became an important way for our earliest citizens to imagine themselves as interconnected members of a single social enterprise, such that "a sentimental vision of union . . . eventually becomes the ideal for both men *and* women."[32] In Barnes's reading, the Declaration of Independence emerges as "a definitive example of American sentimental politics," deriving its power from "a surprising conflation of the personal and the political body—a vision of 'the people' as a single and independent entity, asserting its liberal privilege in a body at once collective and individual" (ix). As Barnes explains, the Declaration's assertion that all men are created equal "epitomizes the power of sentimental representation—a power to reinvent others in one's own image" (2). This is a power at once liberating and appropriative, a notion of equality in which the assertion of a fundamental sameness blurs the distinction between attachment and annexation. And as an allegorical project positing a system of sustained equivalences between terms, such that one translates into, and interprets, the other, sentimentality also has within it an almost limitless potential for expansion.

As Maureen Quilligan has observed, "one never knows where to stop" with allegory: "the process of interpretation can go on indefinitely, as it is in fact supposed to."[33] Sentimental allegory, then, is a mode of reading the world, and one's place within it, that promises a virtual monopoly on signification, a truly imperial command of sympathetic insight. Understood as an allegorical discourse of identification, "sentimental fiction essentially puts self-interest to affective work, reconciling the seemingly irreconcilable division between internal and external authority, between individual rights and the needs of the community to which the individual belongs" (Barnes 18). According to Barnes, sentimental fictions accomplish this affective work in several ways. For the purposes of discussing *A Fable,* it is necessary to note only two: the invocation of familial structures and the celebration of vicarious feeling.[34]

Sentimental narratives "stage political issues as personal dramas" largely through an appeal to familial structures, in which "sameness, rather than difference, offers the key to democratic equality and, hence, to national identity" (Barnes 16). In sentimental narratives, families are as families do: acting *as if* someone is your brother is enough to make him so; feeling comes to stand for being. Similarly, "vicarious relations, like the sentimental construction of sympathetic identification, blur the boundary between action and emotion to suggest that sympathetic feeling itself is an act that holds society together" (Barnes 116). The substitution, through an appeal to a recognition of sameness, of feeling for being and acting thus becomes the hallmark of the sentimental text. Barnes is careful to explore how the sentimental reconciliation of differences has difficulties as well as virtues: as already noted, the transformation of self-interest into an engine of social cohesion can as easily become a model of appropriation and consumption as of universal brotherhood. An appreciation for these aspects of sentimental discourse goes a long way toward explaining both its messy political effects—sentimental appeals can be as productive of complacency as of critique—and its fit with capitalist consumerism. Barnes's analysis thus refines and clarifies a point made many years ago by Ann Douglas in her study of sentimentality in American culture, a point that is worth keeping in mind when thinking about *A Fable:* "There is an enormous and vital distinction between an interested, respectful acceptance of the full human condition and a glorification of the death of the critical instinct— between acknowledging human limitations and celebrating them.... The first is a religious impulse, the second is finally a commercial one, and eventually involves the preparation of the individual for the role of consumer."[35] While Douglas sees religious and commercial impulses occupying separate spheres that need to be kept far apart, however, Barnes suggests—correctly, I think—that religion and commerce are better understood as *recto* and *verso* of a single American document.

I invoke the nineteenth-century bestseller *Uncle Tom's Cabin* in my analysis of *A Fable* chiefly so as to make explicit the importance of Christianity to the sentimental American discourse of "fellow feeling." The mystical body of Christ emerges as the place that equates feeling and action. Through Christ, we become members of one family; Christ's suffering for our sins presents a model of the virtue of vicarious action. Barnes's discussion of Thatcher Thayer's *The Vicarious Element in Nature and Its Relation to Christ*, a religious tract published thirty-six years after Stowe's novel, makes clear the importance of the Christ myth to American efforts to form a more perfect union:

> Thayer simultaneously depicts the individual body—and the senses attached to it—as the epistemological center of a national universe and yet dissolves the individual body into a larger body, a body constituted "more for others" than for oneself.... It is the individual body writ large, producing, as if of one accord, a "national sentiment." Thayer's rhetorical transition from the political to the spiritual, from the vicarious element in nature to its supernatural incarnation in Christ, marks the crowning achievement of sympathy's sociopolitical work. For Christ becomes the representative whose ability to identify completely with all humanity signifies the unifying power of sympathy. In Christ we get not only a theological but a *political* model for the unification of diverse individuals into one corporate body—Christ's own. (118–19)

Following Barnes's linking of the Christian body with the corporate body points us back to *A Fable,* where the Christ figure is known throughout the text primarily (and symbolically) as "the corporal," in the first instance a naming likely intended, via its relative "corporeal," to summon up associations of the Word made flesh. But "corporate" is also tucked into that nomination, and it, too, matters in *A Fable.* The corporation of which "the corporal" is the chief representative body is the twelve who, in turn, represent the entire regiment that refuses an order to go over the top in the spring of the last year of World War I. The furious and humiliated division commander Charles Gragnon wishes to execute the entire regiment for this mutiny, but Christian allegory dictates that the execution of the corporal will stand vicariously for the punishment of all. This sentimental appeal to the vicarious is complemented in the narrative by the familial structure the corporal is able to impose upon the twelve: they are as brothers, and it is out of loyalty to his brothers ("There are still ten" the corporal replies to the marshal's claim that "the brotherhood of your faith and hope" has been shattered by the betrayals of Pierre and Polchek [*Fable* 986–87]) that the corporal goes to his death.

Readers of *A Fable* have seen fraternity in action well before the old marshal named the corporal's band a "brotherhood." The section Faulkner sought to sell to *Partisan Review* as "Notes on a Horsethief" relies heavily on the unifying power of American Freemasonry in order to make convincing its tale of common-man resistance to the commercialization of "the best, the brave" (*Fable* 816). In Steven C. Bullock's study of Freemasonry in the United States, the fraternity emerges as an important instance of American sentimental discourse. In the creation of "the American social order," Freemasonry "played an important role in shaping the momentous changes that first introduced and then transformed the eighteenth-century Enlightenment in America, helping to create the nineteenth-century culture of democracy, individualism, and sentimentalism."[36] Bullock's interest is in the golden years of Masonry, when the fraternity was called upon to solemnize the dedication of the Capitol and when George Washington made it a point to stand for a portrait wearing his Masonic regalia, and he convincingly demonstrates the importance of Masonic ideals (which, among other things, promised a future wherein all the world would "rejoice together as brethren of one common family") to the founding of the republic—even as (or especially as) he outlines Masonry's habits of exclusion: only freeborn men could join, and the dues structure made membership nearly impossible for the lower classes (1). By the time Faulkner was writing "Notes on a Horsethief," however, the glory years of Masonry were long over; the organization was nearly destroyed in the national anti-Masonic movement that emerged in the wake of the 1826 disappearance of a member who had threatened to publish a pamphlet revealing Masonic secrets. When Masonry reappeared in the 1850s, it was largely as a social order devoted to "moral uplift and self-improvement, inculcating the traditional virtues of sobriety, thrift, temperance, piety, industry, self-restraint, and moral obligation"; Masons imagined their lodges as second homes promising peaceful asylum from the outside world.[37] A masculine organization, Freemasonry successfully translated its public mission into a private one by claiming to inculcate many of the same values prized by the contemporaneous and similarly sentimental, though feminized, cult of domesticity.

A final observation about Freemasonry before returning to the issue of brotherhood in *A Fable:* fraternalism is concerned ostensibly with the promotion of universal amity, but it is crucial to remember—as Mary Ann Clawson points out in a study tracing the history of the fraternal ideal from the guilds of medieval Europe to the trade unions of nineteenth-century America—that fraternalism has important economic as well as political and religious registers, and it is in this economic register that the "corporate" aspects of the "corporal" become especially audible. As Clawson explains: "A corporate concept of society assumes that groups, not individuals, are the basic units of society, and that people act, not primarily as individuals, but as members of collectivities. It assumes, moreover, that social institutions are governed not only collectively, but hierarchically. Corporatism is the social metaphor that most forcefully asserts that unity of interest is compatible with hierarchy and inequality."[38] As Clawson notes, modern Freemasonry emerged in eighteenth-century England largely through the desire of members of the British elite to take on the symbolic trappings of craftsmen, thus expressing "their commitment to the emerging market economy and to the social value of craft labor and material productivity" while retaining their own privileged position in that new economy (16). By a process of vicarious identification with the craftsman, members of the gentry sought to paper over the class conflicts of the new industrial order so as to maintain their high status within that order. Another important function of modern American fraternalism thus can be described as an effort to simultaneously articulate and contain the contradictions of democratic capitalism: "Fraternal forms of association have reached across boundaries, tending to unite men from a relatively wide social, economic, or religious spectrum. At the same time, fraternalism bases itself on a principle of exclusion, from which it derives much of its power" (Clawson 11). Or, to put it another way: through Masonry, sentimental assertions of "fellow feeling" provide the cover story that enables exploitative economic relations to continue unchecked.

Faulkner's Masons in the story of the racehorse manifest all of the complications and contradictions I have just described; indeed, this section of *A Fable* uses the Masons in order both to endorse and critique sentimental notions of the benignity of brotherhood. How much Faulkner knew of the history of US Masonry remains an open question, but it is not likely that he missed the one Masonic cultural retention still recognized by all Americans: the eye above the pyramid on the Great Seal of the United States adorning the back of the dollar bill. The brotherly impulses of the Masons in "Notes on a Horsethief" are motivated not only by sympathy for the efforts of Tobe Sutterfield and the sentry to honor the racehorse's heroic desire simply to run but also by a corporate desire to guarantee "that everybody . . . had a share in what it won" (*Fable* 843). We could take Sutterfield's insistence that, in racing the horse, he, his grandson, and the sentry had no interest in wealth ("There wasn't no money.... There never was none, except just what we needed, had to have.... We never had time to bother with winning a heap of money to have to take care of. We had the horse" [849]) as signaling an untainted (autonomous and aestheticized, perhaps) core mission whose transcendent aim redeems the compromising activities of the Masons. In this sense, then, the saga of the crippled racehorse can be read as an allegory of one type of heroic modernist negation-in-abstraction; in the novel's terms, "the mark of a free man . . . to say *no* for no other reason except *no*" (825–26; emphases in original), a kind of deliberate looking away.

Yet it is also the case that, by the time of *A Fable*'s publication, "the right to say no" was a phrase carrying no small ideological weight: it had become something of a slogan for the CIA-funded anticommunist Congress for Cultural Freedom (CCF), the self-described "international meeting of writers, scholars and scientists . . . [working] to dispel the intellectual confusion created by the totalitarian campaigns under the slogan of peace."[39] In a manifesto written for the CCF's inaugural meeting in Berlin in 1950, Arthur Koestler described refusal as a key feature of "intellectual freedom": "Deprived of the right to say 'no,' man becomes a slave" (180). As the CCF itself demonstrated, however, "saying no" to one compromised authority (the Communist International) may entail saying yes to another (the CIA): men need to be free to refuse the explicitly political coercions of "the totalitarian state" (Koestler 181), but they should give careful thought before saying no to cash—or to the corporate and/or governmental entities ensuring its flow.[40] And it is, of course, largely thanks to the corporate protection—one might even say the patronage—of the Masonic brotherhood that the sentry, the reverend, and his grandson are able for a time to pursue their dream of freedom for "the best, the brave."

After the death of the horse, a Tennessee "lodge room" serves as shelter for the sentry (Mister Harry, or "Mistairy" [mystery] in his cockney accent [804]), the place where he takes "his last degree in Masonry" before leaving for the war in Europe (*Fable* 847, 849). It is in warfare that the sentimental practice of Masonic-style brotherhood reaches its apotheosis in the corporatist proliferation of capital. The sentry's loan sharking succeeds largely because he transforms his debtors into brothers (through his "Association" [798]), successfully mystifying the nature of their relationship (even though all parties know, as an exchange between the runner and another soldier indicates, that it is the money, not the men, that makes "the Association" [798]). And so with the loss of the creature it ostensibly supported and protected, corporate brotherhood and its blandishments themselves come to substitute for the heroic vision "to save that horse that never wanted nothing and never knowed nothing but just to run out in front of all the other horses in a race" (849).

* * *

In a study published during the waning years of the Cold War, Andreas Huyssen made clear the interdependence of so-called "high modernism" and popular mass culture; the mass productions of the culture industry are, in truth, "the repressed other of modernism, the family ghost rumbling in the cellar," while modernism itself emerges as "the strawman desperately needed by the system to provide an aura of popular legitimation for the blessings" of mass culture.[41] John T. Matthews has drawn on Huyssen's work to examine Faulkner's early critical participation in the Hollywood film industry, focusing in particular on the screenplays and short stories of the early 1930s, when Faulkner was new to Hollywood, his contempt for commercial culture was at its sharpest, and his willingness to express that contempt was least checked.[42] Matthews's analysis is convincing; the Faulkner of the 1930s seems well aware of, and well equipped to take on, the contradictions of both modernism and the culture industry. But the Faulkner of the 1930s is not the Faulkner of the 1940s or of the Cold War, years that saw not only a dramatic renovation of his artistic reputation but also a steady decline in his creative powers. Faulkner's increasingly parlous negotiations of the artistic demands of those later years (and his letters testify to the difficulties with which he struggled), acknowledged to some degree by all but the most die-hard fans, are usually attributed to the combined effects of marital dissatisfaction, alcoholism, and distress at being forced to live increasingly in the public eye. *A Fable,* however, suggests that the slow fading of Faulkner's talent should be read as stemming from more than personal difficulties: the novel testifies to the collapse of the exquisitely sustained, and mutually sustaining, tensions between art and commerce that mark not only Faulkner's finest work but much of prewar American literary modernism. Or to put the issue another way: while close attention to the popular productions that Faulkner wrote in the 1930s reveals his insistent, if covert, efforts to make those productions accommodate some form of self-critique (and *Sanctuary* is exhibit A here), attention to the serious work of the later period forces us to reckon with the ways in which modernism as Faulkner understood it was "held hostage by the culture industry" (Huyssen 42). *A Fable* is an escaped hostage, come back with the news that "in the vortex of commodification there was never an outside" (Huyssen 42).

We have already seen how, like Poe's purloined letter, *A Fable* hides its mass cultural origins out in the open in its acknowledgment page, which fixes the provenance of the text in the American film industry and daily newspaper journalism. The acknowledgment also registers, however obliquely, Faulkner's frustrations in attempting to reshape this commercial material into something approaching a high modernist production (as well as his conviction that such work was going unappreciated) by memorializing his unsuccessful effort, via *Partisan Review,* to reproduce James Joyce's 1927–29 publication of sections of *Finnegans Wake,* under the title "Work in Progress," in *transition* ("to Hodding Carter and Ben Wasson of the Levee Press, who published in a limited edition the original version of the story of the stolen racehorse" [667]). Along these lines, Faulkner's complaints in letters to Harold Ober and Robert Haas that "movie scripting" had "corrupted" his writing are best understood less as efforts to find a reason for his increasing difficulties with *A Fable* than as a sign that the previously sublimated (and so imaginatively potent) relationship between commerce and art had begun to move forcefully into the open, where its generative power began to dissipate (*Selected Letters* 248). Faulkner's letters make clear his struggle to continue the modernist project by popularizing it via established Hollywood techniques. The 1947 rejection from *Partisan Review* prompted a remarkable note to Ober in which Faulkner expressed both serious doubts about the project ("I have never had an opinion from you . . . about it. . . . What is your opinion of this section in question? Dull? Too prolix? Diffuse?") and his conviction that current times were too "beat and battered" (and, as his language makes clear, too industrial and commercial) to appreciate his work: "That magazine does not exist now which would have printed sections from Ulysses as in the 1920s. And that man crouching in a Mississippi hole trying to shape into some form of art his summation and conception of the human heart and spirit in terms of the cerebral, the simple imagination, is as out of place and in the way as a man trying to make an Egyptian water wheel in the middle of the Bessemer foundry" (*Selected Letters* 261).

Though the choice of text may seem arbitrary, I find Arnold Schoenberg's *Moses und Aron* to be a useful companion to my reading of Faulkner's fable of modernism in commercial Cold War America. As is well known, Faulkner was not the only modernist in Hollywood during the 1930s and 1940s—the Central European émigrés "driven into Paradise" included not only Schoenberg and Adorno but also Igor Stravinsky, Thomas Mann, Ernst Krenek, Hanns Eisler, and Ernst Toch—though few have drawn any parallels between the Mississippian's experiences in culture industry and those of these other modernist exiles.[43] Certainly parallels are there to be drawn, and aspects of Schoenberg's experience, in particular, are worth considering. Schoenberg conceived *Moses und Aron* in 1930, at the opening of the decade that should have seen the fulfillment of his career. The work arose during what has been termed his "Jewish identity crisis": by 1933 Schoenberg had abjured his conversion to Protestantism, returned to the faith of his fathers, and fled Germany for the United States, where he settled in Southern California and taught, first at USC and then at UCLA, amid increasing poverty and professional underappreciation. Schoenberg intended *Moses und Aron* as an homage to his Judaism and a testament to his unshaken belief in heroic modernist abstraction; this latter theme emerges in the opera through the mutually constitutive relationship of Moses and his brother Aaron. The powerful yet inarticulate Moses, who seems to speak for Schoenberg himself, insists that God is invisible and unrepresentable, while the popularizer Aaron advises his brother that it is best to "be understood by all the people in their own accustomed way."[44] *Moses und Aron* remained unfinished, "a magnificent torso," chiefly because Schoenberg found no time to complete it. What had been a promising career in Germany collapsed in the United States, where he was forced to support himself largely through his teaching.[45] Like Faulkner, Schoenberg too found himself "sharecropping in the Golden Land"; as Faulkner complained of the damage caused by writing for the films, so Schoenberg repeatedly deplored the pedagogical frittering away of his creativity.[46] Unlike Faulkner, however, Schoenberg would not let Aaron speak for Moses; though his atonal style eventually found its way into American film scores, Schoenberg himself never wrote for the pictures (though it was not for lack of trying).[47] Six years after his 1945 Guggenheim application was rejected, Schoenberg was dead, and the two works he saw as his greatest contributions to modern music, *Moses und Aron* and the oratorio *Die Jakobsleiter,* remained in fragments.

As Moses speaks for Schoenberg, so the runner in *A Fable* speaks for Faulkner, not only because he articulates the antinomies that so characterize the Faulknerian imagination but also because his project in the battlefield echoes Faulkner's in the novel.[48] The runner recognizes the hidden connections binding heroic individualism (modernism) and modern military/corporate life (mass culture); he believes, further, that purposefully making this connection overt represents humanity's best chance to honestly fulfill the seemingly opposed promises of individual autonomy and human fellowship. In acting on this belief, however—in forcing the sentry to mobilize the members of the Association to say no to the war (*Fable* 959-64)—the runner precipitates the barrage of fire that leaves him "a mobile and upright scar," divided exactly down the middle so that "one entire side of his hatless head was one hairless eyeless and earless sear" (*Fable* 1070). He becomes, in effect, the living sign of the catastrophic effort to add up the two halves of a torn freedom. In rendering the runner monstrously mutilated as a result of his attempted reconciliation, Faulkner registers the mutilated status of *A Fable* itself. I have already described the reactions of the literary community to the novel; I should add that Hollywood, too, found the book baffling and repellent. William Bacher wanted nothing to do with it as a possible film project; after Henry Hathaway read *A Fable* he remarked, "I couldn't find my story. I didn't recognize anything" (Blotner 2:1503).

* * *

Joseph Blotner has observed that, while Faulkner "had no alternative" to working as a screenwriter, "it had been only himself who had driven him to complete the struggle to finish *A Fable*" (Blotner 2:1503). While it is true that Faulkner tended to recycle material rather than abandon it, he had set aside unpromising work before ("A Portrait of Elmer" is a case in point), so his in many ways baffling dedication to finishing *A Fable* is worth noting and, if possible, explaining. The simplest explanation ties the novel to the Nobel Prize: As the chief work in progress when Faulkner received the award, *A Fable* was immediately invested with bestseller potential. There is also the fact that Christian-themed book-and-movie packages tend to do extremely well in the United States: in 1942, the year before Faulkner signed on to Bacher and Hathaway's project, both Franz Werfel's *The Song of Bernadette* and Lloyd C. Douglas's *The Robe* had places on the then-newly created *New York Times* bestseller list. *Song of Bernadette* was made into a film that won Jennifer Jones a best actress Oscar in 1944; in 1953 *The Robe,* too, became a successful picture.[49] The temptation of finally striking it rich, then, may have provided Faulkner with sufficient motivation to stick with the project. It would be a mistake, however, to attribute Faulkner's dedication solely to commercial calculation, for it seems clear that he did believe in *A Fable*—and in the same way, it seems to me, that he believed in America as it entered the Cold War: with a desperate sincerity equal parts genuine and manufactured.

Faulkner almost did not make the trip to Stockholm to receive the Nobel Prize. As he told the first reporter who called him for reaction to the news that he had received the 1949 award for literature, "I won't be able to come to receive the prize myself.... It's too far away. I am a farmer down here and I can't get away." Faulkner left on a hunting trip with friends a week after learning he had won the award, and while away began a bender that continued into his return to Oxford (Blotner 2:1338, 1346–50).[50] His idiosyncratic response to receiving the Nobel—we might say, his insistence on the right of a free man to say no for no other reason except no—collapsed in the face of intense governmental pressure brought to bear in the guise of the poet, fellow-Mississippian, and Foreign Service officer Muna Lee, who would come to play a major role in arranging Faulkner's later service for the State Department. The details of Lee's campaign to get Faulkner to Stockholm, which conscripted Faulkner's friends and family as well as high-ranking government officials, appear in the second volume of Blotner's Faulkner biography and do not require much elaboration here beyond noting that what Blotner coyly terms "the process of persuasion" included lying, emotional blackmail, and near-constant flattery.[51] That Faulkner continued to drink heavily even after agreeing to the trip indicates that his acquiescence was less than total. But he went, and in doing so became one of America's first Cold War cultural celebrities. Schwartz is right, then, to see the awarding of the Nobel as an important event. It marks not only the fulfillment of the revaluation of Faulkner's writings begun years before but also a new level of play in US cultural diplomacy.

Faulkner is usually described as a reluctant (or resistant) cultural diplomat, and while there is much to support this view (starting with his propensity for crippling binges while traveling on State Department business; Faulkner's lifelong habit of falling into debilitating alcoholic bouts when he felt emotionally cornered was a particular kind of passive-aggressive defiance), the intensity of his participation, which was extreme on all counts, is less easily explained.[52] Following his December 1950 trip to Stockholm, Faulkner—the shy farmer who could not bear to leave his land—made overseas journeys every single year in the next five years, to destinations as various as Paris, Cairo, Lima, São Paulo, Tokyo, Manila, Rome, London, and Reykjavik. All but three of those trips were undertaken for the State Department.[53] We cannot discount the importance of government pressure, and his own odd brand of patriotism, in bringing Faulkner to agree to participate in these ventures, but neither can we ignore the possibility that he also came to enjoy the "coercive seductions" they offered—the adulation, the good food and plentiful liquor, the pretty, attentive women—and to pursue them much as he pursued (even as he claimed to despise) the pleasures offered him in Hollywood.[54] It is also quite possible that Faulkner viewed his international State Department "service" as a kind of displaced substitute for the World War I overseas military service that for years he falsely claimed. Like finishing *A Fable,* then, traveling for the State Department was a deeply ambivalent undertaking for Faulkner, something he both wanted yet also had to force himself to do. And, also like *A Fable,* Faulkner's career as Cold War cultural diplomat came to pieces over his belief that he could enjoy the fruits of a rapidly expanding capitalist imperium even while attempting to inscribe its negation.

We get some sense of the difficulties and tensions involved in Faulkner's diplomatic project through an extraordinary letter he wrote Harold E. Howland, the official in the State Department's International Educational Exchange Service who had asked Faulkner to join the August 1955 seminar on American literature in Nagano, Japan (Faulkner's participation in the seminar swelled into an eleven-week around-the-world journey involving stops in nine cities). "I want to do this job right," Faulkner wrote, "and will of course follow the judgment and plans of the Department":

> If I go anywhere as simply a literary man or an expert on literature, American or otherwise, I will be a bust. I will do better as a simple private individual, occupation unimportant, who is interested in and believes in people, humanity, and has some concern about man's condition and his future, if he is not careful.
>
> About rights to any read or spoken material being property of the Dept. I have in progress a book composed of chapters, the subject being What has happened to the American Dream. I read one chapter at Univ. of Oregon and published it in Harper's magazine. I have another chapter which I could read in Japan; I may even compose still a third one to read there. I would expect to retain rights to these, to include in the book. Though naturally I should consider the Dept. had rights to use them in any way it saw fit to further whatever work in int. relations they might do, once I had used them under Dept. auspices. Can this be done? All other material coming out of my visit, will be the Dept's, with me to have the privilege of using any of it to build further chapters on this theme for the above purpose, by notifying the Dept. that I wished to do so. That is, I would like the privilege of clearing with the Dept. in advance any speech etc. which I saw I could later use, to reserve this right.[55]

The speech Faulkner delivered in Oregon was titled "Freedom American Style"; it appeared in the July 1955 issue of *Harper's* as "On Privacy: The American Dream: What Happened to It." Its proximate cause was the fall 1953 publication, in *Life* magazine, of a two-part essay on Faulkner's life and work by the reporter Robert Coughlan, a public airing of private material that Faulkner deeply resented and that he saw, not incorrectly, as a sign that the pursuit of profit in culture industry organs could, "simply by functioning under a phrase like Freedom of the Press," render superfluous other, less fungible freedoms.[56] "On Privacy" is clear enough in its scorn for the haste with which Americans have abandoned their "Dream" of creating "a sanctuary on the earth for individual man" in favor of the dubious security of life as "one more identityless integer in that identityless anonymous unprivacied mass" (62, 71). But a full appreciation of "On Privacy" as a testament of Faulkner's Cold War fate emerges only when we read the essay with attention not only to what it says but also to the venues Faulkner considered for its dissemination. Faulkner tells Howland that "On Privacy" is part of a projected book, but when he finished the piece he described it to his editor as a "lecture"—that is, a public performance: "It is a section of a kind of symposium, maybe 5 or 6 lectures . . . I have more and more offers to lecture, my price is up to $1000.00 from colleges now, and I may take it up, use this one for the first of a series, to be a book later" (*Selected Letters* 372). "On Privacy," then, is a deliberate, if defensive, attempt on Faulkner's part to profit from his fame—as with *A Fable,* to manipulate the structures of culture industry to his benefit—even as the lecture's two verdicts on the role of the artist in America make plain the acrimony, even cynicism, informing such a project. "Artists have no more place in American life than the employers of the weekly pictorial magazine staff-writers have in the private life of a Mississippi novelist," Faulkner writes in a sardonic formulation equally informed by disdain and despair (70). "America has not yet found any place for [the artist] . . . except to use his notoriety to sell soap or cigarettes or fountain pens or to advertise automobiles and cruises and resort hotels"—or, as Faulkner was beginning to realize, to sell the United States itself (75). The gesture of offering a text like "On Privacy" to the State Department as the centerpiece text of his trip to Japan, for the government "to use . . . in any way it saw fit to further whatever work in int. relations [it] might do" adds a certain measure of underhanded spite to the bitterness—but this bitterness never rises to the level of a thoroughgoing critique. For when State said "Go," Faulkner almost always went.

Reading "On Privacy" as a manifestation of the antagonistic logic of going public to ensure one's privacy (like the logic of waging war to end war or ensuring the peace through Mutually Assured Destruction) brings into sharper focus Faulkner's effort not only to ride two horses at once but also to coordinate their seemingly opposed trajectories—as in *A Fable,* to add up the torn halves of freedom. The strenuousness of this project is signaled in the tortured passage about "rights" in his letter to Howland: who has the final claim on a work embedded in the very system it seems to want to disrupt? Whose interests does such work serve? If we are willing to credit Faulkner's seeming belief that, given the American effort to make the right to privacy serve the right to profit, there should be at least the theoretical possibility that one voice can talk back in two channels, we need also to acknowledge the hubris informing that belief. And it is, finally, this hubristic faith in limitless possibility—the conviction that one can, in the phrase Faulkner used to describe his own ambition as a writer, "say it all"[57]—that links *A Fable* and Faulkner's adventures in diplomacy as related articulations of a globally imagined postwar American project, and that structures their similar failures. For Faulkner's diplomatic forays were not the thoroughgoing successes that governmental and scholarly folklore claim.

Much of the scholarship examining the growth and effects of US cultural diplomacy during the Cold War proceeds from the assumption that the State Department's propagandistic *intentions* for these programs provide the interpretive key: because the government expected American artists, writers, musicians, and dancers to present a happy national picture to the citizens of countries indifferent, or hostile, to US foreign policy, they did so. This governmental fantasy of "who pays the piper calls the tune" has set the terms of the discussion of Faulkner's work for the State Department, where the judgments recorded in internal State Department memoranda (the so-called "Progress Reports") are taken as proving the success of his work as propagandist. These memoranda do indeed paint glowing pictures: for example, one describing Faulkner's 1957 trip to Greece claims that in "many Greek homes . . . there are prominently displayed beside the autographed pictures of the King and Queen, Ambassadors and other notables, the autographed photograph of William Faulkner."[58] The fulsomeness of this particular example of the rhetoric these memoranda routinely employ reminds us that these documents are, first and foremost, exercises in bureaucratic self-perpetuation. Like most internally administered official "assessments," they function chiefly to generate and keep in circulation narratives flattering to the bureau and its mission. But beyond this, it is tremendously naïve to assume that admiration for Faulkner's novels straightforwardly translated into admiration for the United States. As Deborah N. Cohn has pointed out, Faulkner's "profound" influence on the writers of the Latin American "boom" did not stop them from supporting the Cuban revolution—not, one supposes, the kind of outcome the State Department had hoped would result from Faulkner's diplomatic work.[59]

Without doubt, the State Department was eager to cultivate international interest in Faulkner during the Cold War, seeking both to deepen and expand the many prewar engagements with his writing abroad and to capitalize on the novelty his work and person presented to those who had never heard of him before the Nobel. And to a certain degree their energetic marketing was lastingly successful. The high esteem for Faulkner held to this day in Japan is clearly an outgrowth of his three-week-long department-sponsored visit to the country in 1955. It is also true that, in certain nations, admiration for Faulkner during the Cold War had a political function. Árpád Göncz, the lawyer, writer and, in 1990, first democratically elected president of the Hungarian republic, taught himself English while imprisoned for his participation in Hungary's 1956 anti-Soviet uprising; his 1970 translation of *The Sound and the Fury,* released seven years after his amnesty, carried a certain dissident *frisson* even though publication of the novel signaled that Faulkner, a proscribed writer in the Hungary of the 1940s and 1950s, had won government sanction during the 1960s "thaw."

Still, it would be incorrect to read the growing regard for Faulkner's work in Japan, Hungary, or elsewhere during the 1950s as nothing but a product of Cold War diplomatic opportunism—especially considering that State's eagerness to promote Faulkner, an extraordinarily high-maintenance "diplomat," was actually rather short-lived. In retrospect, the difficulties were predictable. The first signs that Faulkner would prove a problematic ambassador emerged in Paris in 1952, when he attended the CCF-sponsored festival *Oeuvres du XXe Siècle.* Faulkner's formal appearance at the festival was deemed a success, at least officially (Blotner 2:1412), but the days leading up to it were harrowing. As W. H. Auden, who also attended, wrote to friends afterward, Faulkner created "an anxious time . . . for he went into a bout on arrival, shut up in his hotel throwing furniture out of the windows and bottles at the ladies and saying the most *dreadful* things about coons [sic]. However we managed to get him sober and onto the platform on the last day to say that the Americans had behaved badly but that he hoped they would behave better in the future and sit down."[60] Drinking precipitated a collapse in South America during Faulkner's very first State Department outing; he required medical care, paid for by the government.[61] For his 1955 diplomatic "grand tour" (following the three-week stay in Japan, he made visits to the Philippines, Italy, Germany, France, England, and Iceland), Faulkner started drinking before he left Washington. By his second day in Tokyo, the US ambassador was ready to send Faulkner home; Blotner's account makes clear that the trip went from a disaster-in-the-making to runaway success almost entirely thanks to the extraordinary dedication and creative interventions of Leon Picon, the head of the embassy's book program (Blotner 2:1541–67). A 1957 trip to Athens went fairly smoothly, but by 1960 most in the State Department had had their fill of Faulkner. Government files indicate disagreement within the agency about the merits of continuing the relationship with him, disagreement sharp enough to lead State to withhold sponsorship of his final "diplomatic" mission to Caracas in April 1961, for the sesquicentennial of Venezuelan independence. This trip was arranged by the North American Association, a privately funded concern representing US firms doing business in Venezuela, after State refused the embassy's request for government sponsorship; though embassy personnel did assist with various aspects of the visit, Faulkner was not on the American Specialists payroll. A bluntly worded internal memo urged frank talk "about the facts of life on this one"; State's official reply is uncompromising and, with its unusual reference to undocumented back-channel discussions, no more discreet than strictly necessary:

> Mr. Faulkner is very well known to us in this office as he has had three previous American Specialist grants, besides personal contact from time to time with officers of the Staff. Except for certain problems which working with him entails, he would undoubtedly be one of the best representatives of American letters that could be sent to participate in the Venezuelan Independence Sesquicentennial.

We believe, however, that for reasons which Mr. Colwell recently discussed with you, the possible difficulties outweigh the very considerable advantages that might accrue from the grant. We recommend, therefore, that no further action be taken regarding this proposal.[62]

State's disenchantment with Faulkner's performance presages the awkward and persistent difficulties the government would face in managing the often strong-willed and independent artist "pipers" it had recruited as "ambassadors"—difficulties that, with the end of the Cold War, led to the rapid abandonment of all but the most obviously propagandistic and easily manipulable cultural programs.

Faulkner, too, quickly soured on cultural diplomacy. In 1958 he turned down an invitation to travel to the Soviet Union, a trip made possible by the recently signed bilateral exchange agreement and one that would have subjected him to a degree of public scrutiny similar to that attending the awarding of the Nobel. Faulkner framed his refusal in distinctly anticommunist terms ("If I, who have had freedom all my life in which to write of truth exactly as I saw it, visited Russia now, the fact of even the outward appearance of condoning the condition which the present Russian government has established, would be a betrayal"),[63] but his experience two years earlier in Eisenhower's ill-fated People-to-People program points to an additional factor: his growing awareness not only of the constitutive incoherence of US efforts in public diplomacy but also the degree to which the government sought to resolve the incoherence by stage-managing its international exchanges (Blotner 2:1691). Faulkner cared little for the Eisenhower administration—following Ike's re-election, he quipped that Adlai Stevenson "had three strikes against him: wit, urbanity, and erudition" (Blotner 2:1624)—but Eisenhower had contacted him personally in June 1956 with the request that he serve as chairman of the writers' group of the newly proposed People-to-People program, and it was Faulkner's belief, as he later told *New York Times* book reviewer Harvey Breit, that "when your president asks you to do something, you do it" (Blotner 2:1629). Faulkner got the ball rolling in late September by sending out a form letter over his signature to some fifty authors soliciting their involvement in the program. "Pending a convenient meeting, will you send me in a sentence, or a paragraph, or a page, or as many more as you like, your private idea of what might further this project?," Faulkner wrote. "I am enclosing my own ideas as a sample. 1. Anesthetize, for one year, American vocal cords. 2. Abolish, for one year, American passports" (*Selected Letters* 404). Though the letter straightens up in its postscript ("In a more serious vein, please read the enclosed one-page description of Mr. Eisenhower's purpose"), subsequent events make clear that Faulkner never cared much for the president's scheme. In November writers who had replied to Faulkner's letter gathered at Breit's New York City home to hear discussion open with Faulkner's observation "that most committees, maybe all, are the last despair and cry of impotence . . . we have spent all our lives already doing this very job which President Eisenhower discovered last year is a critical necessity. So there is not much more we can do" (Blotner 2:1623). From this compromised beginning, the meeting ambled through a "strange, confused, and inconclusive" mix of proposals (Blotner 2:1622). The presence of the Anglo-Hungarian playwright George Tabori led Faulkner to condemn the United States for its irresponsibility in fomenting the Hungarian rebellion, crushed only weeks earlier by the Soviet Union ("Think of the fiasco that came from the Voice of America which told people in other countries that they could be free . . . that this country would help people. But we never did" [Blotner 2:1623]). William Carlos Williams pleaded for a writers' campaign to free Ezra Pound, still interned at St. Elizabeth's Hospital; Saul Bellow, angry at both Faulkner and Williams, left in a rage; and John Steinbeck, after noting that "the whole Person-to-Person thing is illegal under the law as it stands today, [so] not a thing can be done," suggested that "the best propaganda would be a mail order catalog" (Blotner 2:1623–24).

By February 1957, when he and Breit were to give some accounting of their work at a New York City gathering of the various committee chairs of the People-to-People program, Faulkner's disaffection was acute. Over whiskey the night before the meeting, he frankly voiced his doubts. "I don't go along with that stuff," Faulkner told Breit. "We don't need any foreign writers here, and our writers don't have to go anywhere. Writers all over the world understand each other. What we need is an exchange of plumbers and carpenters and businessmen." The next day, a shaky, hungover Faulkner and a nervous Breit arrived late at the Metropolitan Club, sat in the back of the room, and left early, without making any report at all (Blotner 2:1629–31).

Faulkner was joking when he proposed launching the People-to-People program with a year of American silence, but by 1959, when the State Department came asking another favor—this time, Muna Lee sought to persuade Faulkner to give an address in Denver at the 7th National Conference of the US National Commission for UNESCO—he seemed ready to put the plan in action. He was fed up with lecturing; he found it not only personally trying but also of dubious political value. "Of course I will do whatever I can," he wrote in reply to her request. "But I am the wrong one to be the official speaker here":

> For the reason that I believe that speech is mankind's curse, all evil and grief of this world stems from the fact that man talks. I mean, in the sense of one man speaking to a captive audience. Except for that, and its concomitants of communication—radio, newspapers, such organs—there would have been no Hitler or Mussolini. I believe that in the case of the speaker and his captive audience, whatever the reason for the captivity of the audience, the worst of both is inevitably brought out—the worst of the individual, compounded by the affinity for evil inherent in people compelled or persuaded to be a mass, an audience, which in my opinion is another mob. (*Selected Letters* 424–25)

The parallels between Faulkner's analysis of the usefulness to fascism of mass "concomitants of communication" and that of Horkheimer and Adorno (and, before them, Walter Benjamin) are striking. More noteworthy is Faulkner's near-total loss of faith in a program he had willed himself to embrace just five years earlier. At Nagano in 1955 he had put himself entirely in the hands of State, dutifully (if often reluctantly) appearing at various prearranged and prepopulated press conferences, photo opportunities, and seminars. Now, "speaking to a captive audience" was worse than ineffective: it was dangerous. Faulkner's resistance proved weak, however; though he went to Denver vowing not to speak, ultimately he was cajoled onto the platform by Foreign Service officer Abram Minell, almost certainly sent by Lee for just that purpose (Blotner 2:1744). Over a bottle of Cutty Sark, and with Minell at the typewriter, Faulkner dictated a page's worth of commentary. Minell rearranged the conference program to get Faulkner onto the last plenary session, where the author delivered what turned out to be a variation on the themes articulated in his Nobel Prize speech. By this point in his career as a public intellectual Faulkner's repetitive nostrums regarding individual man's capacity to endure and prevail had begun to resemble trademarked, assembly-line products; in truth, Faulkner's increasing recourse, in his public pronouncements, to the rhetoric of the Nobel speech came to resemble the kind of "highlights" performance that, thanks to Adorno's analysis of "classical" music radio, we recognize as a hallmark of culture industry.[64] The "quality-controlled" production of the known and easily recognized, first signaled in the rhetoric of *A Fable,* reaches its apotheosis—finds its market niche, as it were—here, as cultural diplomacy aligns with culture industry.[65]

Beyond these mutual disenchantments, a further—and more consequential—explanation for both Faulkner's unwillingness to continue his service as goodwill ambassador and State's eagerness to bring the relationship to a close lies in the increased degree of critical engagement with Faulkner's work that worldwide approbation and cultural diplomacy made possible. *Creating Faulkner's Reputation* leaves out this important aspect of Faulkner's Cold War reputation, in part because, as I've already indicated, Schwartz is eager to present his reading of literary history as the first serious revisionary assessment of Faulkner since the awarding of the Nobel Prize. In fact, however, the skeptical view of Faulkner's art that Schwartz claims to be newly putting into play had already emerged during the author's lifetime, in part thanks to the heightened international profile US government efforts to exploit him had created.

With the publication of *Light in August* in 1932, Faulkner had begun the imaginative interrogation of southern racial history that would inform some of the best work of his career, but he did not see himself as having a mandate to speak publicly on racial injustice in the South until after 1954—the year of the Supreme Court's *Brown* decision (May 17), the publication of *A Fable* (August 2), and his first State Department trip (August 6–16). Faulkner's earliest public statements on desegregation were brief, blunt, and, among supporters of the court's decision, successful. His March 20, 1955, letter to the editor of the *Memphis Commercial Appeal* mocking the efforts of some Mississippians to maintain segregated schools was reprinted in *the New Leader* and applauded in *Masses & Mainstream*.[66] Later that year his reaction to the Emmett Till murder—written on a stopover in Rome during the Japan-to-Iceland State Department tour and distributed worldwide by United Press International—was similarly praised. However, and as Carol Polsgrove has noted, "in the longer span of his life, Faulkner's political statements of the mid-1950s would appear ... an aberration" (8)—not so much (at least at first) for what he said (though that would become an issue) as for the way he said it. Faulkner initially took pains to make his early public comments fit within the larger Cold War rhetoric; they sound what Polsgrove calls the note "of apocalypse: the undercurrent of final struggle between the democratic countries and the communist world" (8–9). University of Mississippi professor of history James W. Silver, a friend of Faulkner's, would later assert that the author, during his travels for State, "became alarmed at the powerful influence of racism in the propaganda of the Cold War" and tailored his civil rights statements accordingly (9).[67] Contemporary historians have demonstrated the importance of the civil rights movement as a diplomatic and strategic challenge for the United States during the Cold War; Faulkner was clearly reading the signs right.[68] However, desegregation and civil rights were fundamentally personal issues for Faulkner, bound up with his deepest feelings about himself and his region. He could not sustain the emotional detachment that a properly diplomatic approach to the problem demanded, and the polished Cold War rhetoric soon gave way to something much more raw.

On February 21, 1956, Faulkner sat down to an interview with London *Sunday Times* correspondent Russell Warren Howe. The days leading up to this interview, which would produce Faulkner's most infamous statement on desegregation, had been filled with anxiety. Earlier that month riots had erupted at the University of Alabama when Autherine Lucy, an African American woman admitted to the graduate school program in library science, arrived on campus.[69] The white mob was large, ugly, and violent, and Lucy needed a police escort to get to class. On the evening of the third day of the term she was suspended from the university. The board and administration claimed she was being turned away for her own safety (it had been reported that members of the mob shouted "let's kill her!"), but lawyers for the NAACP, who had earlier won a court order preventing the university from denying Lucy admission on the basis of race, charged the university with contempt of court. Faulkner was convinced that NAACP would win their case, and that Lucy's return to the university would result in her murder.[70]

Faulkner's own moderate support of civil rights had made him a target of hometown harassment; according to Blotner, the situation at the University of Alabama was making him "almost frantic" with worry (2:1590). He had been drinking "steadily"—but, Blotner notes (in an odd formulation), "not enough to prevent his making comments more desperate and provocative than any he had thus far uttered" (2:1590). Desperate and provocative, indeed: Howe quoted Faulkner claiming that "if it came to fighting I'd fight for Mississippi against the United States even if it meant going out into the street and shooting Negroes."[71] However, while these comments are the ones most remembered today—and the ones Faulkner explicitly repudiated—they were not, in fact, the only words to draw critical attention. Faulkner's alcoholism was something of an open secret by the time of the Howe interview, so when he wrote, in a letter to the editor of the *Reporter,* that his comments about armed resistance were "statements which no sober man would make, nor, it seems to me, any sane man believe," the implication was clear enough (*Essays* 225). Less clear, and less excusable, was Faulkner's insistence in the interview that the white South needed to be left alone to work out integration in its own way and on its own schedule. His statements to this effect are disturbing enough ("In the long view, the Negro race will vanish in three hundred years by intermarriage"; "things have been getting better slowly for a long time. Only six Negroes were killed by whites in Mississippi last year"; "Ninety per cent of the Negroes are on one side with the whites, against a handful like me who believe that equality is important" [Howe 18–19]), but the presumably more calculated formulations of two essays published within months of the *Reporter* piece—"A Letter to the North," in *Life,* and "If I Were a Negro," in *Ebony*—are not much better.[72] In these pieces, Faulkner elaborates a thesis that came to be derided as "go slowism," a recommendation that Blacks adopt an attitude of saintly forbearance toward white southerners that would, over time, allow whites to redeem themselves through voluntary action. "If I were a Negro in American today," Faulkner wrote in *Ebony,*

> this is the course I would advise the leaders of my race to follow: to send every day to the white school to which he was entitled by his ability and capacity to go, a student of my race, fresh and cleanly dressed, courteous, without threat or violence, to seek admission; when he was refused I would forget about him as an individual, but tomorrow I would send another one, still fresh and clean and courteous, to be refused in his turn, until at last the white man himself must recognize that there will be no peace for him until he himself has solved the dilemma. (*Essays* 109)

What Faulkner offers here is less a model for nonviolent resistance than a variation on the classic sentimental American narrative of white redemption through Black suffering, and while it may induce stirring emotional effects in some (think, again, of *Uncle Tom's Cabin*), it hardly stands as a desegregation program more effective (or more humane) than the NAACP initiatives already underway. Nor did it help Faulkner's case that he couched his recommendation in assertions of white victimization, terming the *Brown* decision "the first implication . . . even promise, of force and violence" (*Essays* 88).[73] Faulkner's inability to embrace full integration in his lifetime has been described as a function of his anguish over the rapid disappearance of the racial "middle road" of the white southern liberal, who managed questions of racial inequality largely by subsuming them into "other discourses," most especially class discourses.[74] Faulkner was well-practiced in this rhetoric (it is the primary mode of a third civil rights essay published during this period, "On Fear: The South in Labor"), but it was thoroughly exhausted by 1954.[75] "Black civil rights activists, leaving behind the middle ground . . . would make white Southerners like Faulkner irrelevant in the new politics of the region," Grace Elizabeth Hale and Robert Jackson have noted. "The history African-Americans created in the fifties and early sixties would force white Southern liberals to abandon their peculiar middle and to side, finally, with segregation or integration. White violence simply gave Faulkner something to agonize over as he put off making his choice" (33).

While Faulkner temporized and pleaded for others to do the same, his readers were actively choosing. Reaction to his comments was swift and sharp. A parody of Faulkner's remarks was published in *The Nation* within weeks of Howe's interview.[76] Ralph Ellison, starstruck when Saxe Commins had introduced him to Faulkner four years earlier, pulled no punches in a letter to his friend Albert Murray:

> For one thing he forgets that the people he's talking about are Negroes and they're everywhere in the States and without sectional allegiance when it comes to the problem. The next thing that he forgets is that Mose isn't in the market for his advice, because he's been knowing how to "wait-a-while"— Faulkner advice—for over three hundred years, only he's never been simply waiting, he's been probing for a soft spot, looking for a hole, and now he's got the hole. Faulkner has delusions of grandeur because he really believes that

he invented these characteristics which he ascribes to Negroes in his fiction and now he thinks he can end this great historical action just as he ends a dramatic action in one of his novels with Joe Christmas dead and his balls cut off by a man not nearly as worthy as himself; Hightower musing, the Negroes scared, and everything just as it was except for the brooding, slightly overblown rhetoric of Faulkner's irony. Nuts! He thinks that Negroes exist simply to give ironic overtones to the viciousness of white folks, when he should know very well that we're trying hard as hell to free ourselves; thoroughly and completely, so that when we got the crackers off our back we can discover what we (Moses) really are and what we really wish to preserve out of the experience that made us.[77]

Even more emphatic, Murray's reaction singled out for special contempt Faulkner's work in cultural diplomacy: "Saw that Faulkner thing in *Life.* Sad, pitiful, stupid thing for a writer like that to do. That underdog shit makes me puke. . . . Son of a bitch prefers a handful of anachronistic crackers to everything that really gives him a reason not only for being but for writing. I'm watching his ass but close forevermore. Imagine a fatass travelling all around the world selling humanity for the State Dept and then going back home pulling that kind of crap at the first sign of real progress" (*Twelves* 125).

While Ellison and Murray expressed their dismay mostly to each other, James Baldwin made his exasperation known publicly. "Faulkner and Desegregation" appeared in the fall 1956 issue of *Partisan Review.* This is one of the journals whose editors (William Phillips and Philip Rahv) are described by Schwartz as having been particularly eager to promote Faulkner's fiction as "a cultural weapon in the early years of the Cold War" (Schwartz 210), even though, as we have seen, they had no compunction in rejecting "Notes on a Horsethief" in 1947. Nor, less than ten years later, did they scruple to print Baldwin's essay, then and still a devastating response to Faulkner's southern gradualism.[78] Baldwin opens on a vaguely sympathetic note—"Any real change implies the breakup of the world as one has always known it, the loss of all that gave one an identity, the end of safety"—but swiftly moves to condemn Faulkner's position, which he characterizes as "a species of defiance most perverse when it is most despairing" arising from a mind that "concedes the madness and moral wrongness of the South but at the same time . . . raises it to the level of a mystique."[79] His merciless climactic dissection of Faulkner's position combines a reading of southern history with a deep understanding of Faulknerian rhetoric. As Baldwin explains, Faulkner

> is at his best, and is perfectly sincere, when he declares, in *Harper's* "To live anywhere in the world today and be against equality because of race or color is like living in Alaska and being against snow. We have already got snow. And as with the Alaskan, merely to live in armistice with it is not enough. Like the Alaskan, we had better use it." And though this seems to be flatly opposed to his statement . . . that, if it came to a contest between the Federal government and Mississippi, he would fight for Mississippi, "even if it meant going out into the streets and shooting Negroes," he means that, too. Faulkner means everything he says, means them all at once, and with very nearly the same intensity. (570)

For Baldwin, and many others, Faulkner's belief that he could "say it all" had finally caught up with him.

However, we should not imagine that Faulkner's writing consequentially lost all salience to these and later authors (or, to put it another way, to conclude that Faulkner's late-1950s collapse gives the lie to the work of the 1930s). To the contrary, Cold War readers and writers maintained an active creative engagement with Faulkner, picking and choosing their way through his *oeuvre*, keeping what was useful, setting aside what was not, and frequently taking issue with both his claims and his techniques—habits of critical reading practiced especially skillfully by African American authors who came of age during the civil rights movement. Murray's 1956 vow to keep a close watch on Faulkner's nether regions did not preclude his participation some forty years later in a celebration of the author's centenary at the University of Mississippi. "He may have misled us a few times in public utterances," Murray remarked, "but that was not his actual literary work. . . . I mean he was right on the verge of being a very pathetic person. But many great writers are."[80] Ellison refused to deny "the meaning which [Faulkner's] works hold for me," pointedly including Faulkner in the list of literary "ancestors" that concludes his 1964 riposte to Irving Howe.[81] Baldwin never backed away from his shrewd and thoroughly justified criticism, even as, in later years, his defense of William Styron's *Confessions of Nat Turner* moved him to acknowledge what he had found praiseworthy in Faulkner's work.[82] In 1955 Chloe A. Wofford, a candidate for a master's degree in English at Cornell University, filed a thesis comparing "Virginia Woolf's and William Faulkner's Treatment of the Alienated"; thirty years later Wofford—by then nationally known as Toni Morrison—described herself as a reader "deeply moved by all [Faulkner's] subjects" in part because of the author's ability to "infuriate you in such wonderful ways."[83]

It was Faulkner's extremely high, State Department–inflated, post-Nobel profile—we might say, his "created reputation" as a specific type of cultural spokesman for Cold War America—that made this intense, and intensely public, critical engagement possible, but it was Faulkner's *writing* that made it a critical *engagement* rather than a summary dismissal. An appreciation for this Cold War reaction to, and sustained interrogation of, Faulkner's work highlights the insufficiency of claims that Faulkner's Cold War reputation was uniformly exalted, that his readers (too dull or impatient to comprehend his "remote, complex, iconoclastic" prose) unquestioningly accepted the critical judgment of a small cadre of ideologically motivated scholars, or that "dissent was suppressed" in discussions of Faulkner's work after 1946.[84] Then, too, this fuller understanding of Faulkner's Cold War years proves neither the absolute worth of his work nor the fundamental integrity of his detractors. A strictly allegorical reading of a text's relationship to its context necessarily limits its analysis to the immediate circumstances of textual creation and circulation. By contrast, I've aimed here for reading of *A Fable* less symptomatic than symplastic (to borrow a term from botany), one conducing an enlarged understanding of the networks linking text, politics, author, and readers and inviting a *continuing*, historically expanding, appreciation of the relationship between the work and the evolving cultural whole of which it is simultaneously constitutive, representative, and critical. In using his Cold War "moment as a pinnacle from which [he] might be listened to" (*Essays* 119), Faulkner exposed his work, and himself, to a degree of careful reading, and a level of public criticism, he likely never would have faced had he stayed down on the farm. Like the Cold War United States itself, Faulkner took his postwar ascendancy as a license to preach; *A Fable* is his first effort to cast that hubristic faith into literary form. It may be that the heroic impulse to say no to things as they are is "not going to die. Never" (this is the runner's pledge at the end of

A Fable), yet it is also the case that *A Fable* shows us how, through its own outrageous presumption, that impulse can come to grief: in the final words of the novel, "What you see are tears" (*Fable* 1072).

Faulkner believed *A Fable* would be his "big book" because it would bring him his largest readership ever. Americans would "really buy it" (*Selected Letters* 238), but the novel would also win him new intellectual respect, and it would do this by giving a mass readership both what it already wanted and what it did not yet understand. Turning the twin engines of culture industry and cultural diplomacy against themselves proved beyond Faulkner's capacity, however; he could not negotiate the final ironizing curve. Still, *A Fable* remains important for what it tells us about one of the many paths taken by the heroic high modernist project in the postwar United States. Modernist art, and modernist artists, were indeed recruited as cultural foot-soldiers in the Cold War—though with consequences few anticipated. Faulkner not only participated in this attempted co-opting of modernist negation (first via culture industry and then through cultural diplomacy): in *A Fable,* he registered some of its effects. Once we recognize the novel as the guilty testimony that it is, we understand why an assertion that the Cold War made William Faulkner's reputation tells only half of the story, since it leaves out the part about how the Cold War unmade it, as well.

Postscript

In bringing together two essays written fifteen years apart, this chapter offers a critical rethinking of the widely held notion that the global, midcentury elevation of Faulkner's reputation was a thoroughly manufactured phenomenon made possible by the opening of a "cultural front" in the Cold War. According to this notion, Faulkner never would have attained canonical status without the efforts by philanthropic agencies and ideologically motivated literary critics to pitch Euro-American modernism as an avatar of capitalistic freedom. More than anything, it was this politically driven transformation of the US aesthetic sensibility—from the "democratic" realism of the 1930s to the "elitist . . . and inaccessible" methods of modernism—that created "the sudden inflation of William Faulkner's literary reputation" (Schwartz 5, 1).

My engagement with this knotty subject began with an essay, written for the 1998 Faulkner and Yoknapatawpha conference, on *A Fable*'s place in the Cold War US cultural imaginary.[85] Cold war cultural diplomacy was lightly touched on in that piece; Faulkner's State Department trips were only obliquely mentioned. Realizing there was a much larger landscape to explore, I embarked on a research project that, nearly twenty years later, resulted in the publication *Don't Act, Just Dance,* a monograph critically examining the premise, central to Schwartz's study (and to the work of Serge Guilbaut before him), that modernist art was recruited into US cultural diplomacy thanks to its unique capacity to "speak" for capitalist freedom.[86] In showing there was a great deal more to the subject than this formulation allows, I ranged well beyond the example of Faulkner to works in dance, film, and music, framing those readings with a discussion of the history of cultural diplomacy (and its relationship to US funding for the arts) couched in theoretical insights into the relationship between art and politics.

While Faulkner was not the focus of that study, his experience as the country's first Cold War cultural ambassador deserved its own analysis. "Unsteady State: Faulkner and the Cold War," published the same year as *Don't Act,* is my reply to Schwartz's original thesis.[87]

In bringing these two pieces together in this volume, I provide a more capacious frame for understanding the effects of the Cold War on Faulkner's writing and reception. The work of Greg Barnhisel, Deborah Cohn, Alan Nadel, Helen Oakley, and Harilaos Stecopolous also has expanded both the types of questions posed and the range of texts examined in exploring this topic.[88] Though the notion that the Cold War "created" Faulkner's reputation seems increasingly far-fetched, Schwartz's study remains a useful point of contact for a continuing and growing body of work around the question of late-stage Faulkner and the role he and his fictions came to play in the Cold War American cultural imaginary.

4

A Postmodern *Absalom, Absalom!*, a Modern *Beloved*

THE DIALECTIC OF FORM

I have a title for it which I like, by the way: ABSALOM, ABSALOM; the story is of a man who wanted a son through pride, and got too many of them and they destroyed him.

—WILLIAM FAULKNER, *Selected Letters*

I don't know if that story came because I was considering certain aspects of self-sabotage, the ways in which the best things we do so often carry seeds of one's own destruction.

—TONI MORRISON (in reference to *Beloved*)

It may seem ironic to open a chapter concerned with formal issues in *Absalom, Absalom!* and *Beloved* with a pair of epigraphs better suited to setting the tone for a discussion of thematics. But since irony—both the Western "high modernist" variety and the uniquely African American style known as signifying—will be an item under discussion here, it is perhaps not a bad way to start.[1] I want to begin my examination of *Beloved* and *Absalom, Absalom!* with a brief foray into matters of content in order to emphasize the generally acknowledged point that formal issues are important precisely because our approach to the literary subject is so thoroughly mediated by structure, diction, and tone. There is, of course, the history of Cold War formalist criticism in the United States, which saw undue (and often ideologically vested) emphasis on this mediation; we have all learned that the excesses of the old New Criticism are to be avoided. By the same token, however, contemporary efforts to discuss a text's content and context that treat issues of literary technique as givens run the risk of a different sort of ahistoricizing move, one that fails to read how an author's approach to formal problems is likewise grounded in history and social context.[2] So I back into form via content in order to point out that, in addition to many striking similarities (deploying the Gothic in describing a family tragedy; positing one family's tragedy as synecdoche for a larger social cataclysm; representing this country's slaveholding past via historic romance), *Absalom, Absalom!* and *Beloved* share a theme, which Morrison identifies as "self-sabotage" (Rothstein C17). To take "self-sabotage" as a central theme in both *Beloved* and *Absalom, Absalom!* is to hazard the charge of universalism, but it is a hazard worth chancing here, as a brief look at the geneses of the two novels shows.

Tracking Morrison's comments about *Beloved* as it was being written (and even in the few weeks after it was first released in the early fall of 1987) reveals that the historic, lived experience of slavery first appeared to her as a *backdrop* for the (seemingly) larger, universal question of what she calls, in one interview, "self-murder."[3] It is worth remembering that Morrison initially envisioned *Beloved* and *Jazz* as one novel, inspired by a pair of events she uncovered through her editing work at Random House.[4] A 1985 interview with Gloria Naylor, given as Morrison was in the midst of writing *Beloved* (and, importantly, when she still saw *Beloved* and *Jazz* as one work), helps us identify the impulse responsible for the novel's shift in emphasis from the universal to the historic particular:

> What made those stories connect [Margaret Garner's history and the 1920s Harlem murder that became the basis for *Jazz*], I can't explain, but I do know that . . . both of those incidents seem to me, at least on the surface, very noble . . . generous, wide-spirited. . . . And I thought . . . the best thing that is in us is also the thing that makes us sabotage ourselves. . . . So . . . I just imagined the life of a dead girl which was the girl that Margaret Garner killed. . . . I just imagined her remembering what happened to her, being someplace else and returning, knowing what happened to her. And I call her Beloved. . . .
>
> I have about 250 pages and it's overwhelming me. There's a lot of danger for me in writing it, which is what I am very excited about. The effort, the re-

sponsibility as well as the effort, the effort of being worth it, that's not quite it. The responsibility that I feel for the woman I call Sethe, and for all of these people; these unburied, or at least unceremoniously buried, people made literate in art. But the inner tension, the artistic inner tension those people create in me; the fear of not properly, artistically, burying them, is extraordinary.[5]

Imagining the dead girl gives rise to a sense of responsibility and a fear of not "properly, artistically" burying those summoned forth in service to the larger theme. It is in the effort to *embody* the theme of self-sabotage—to flesh out the ghost, to give form to the idea—that Morrison confronts the specific, the historical, and "the responsibility."[6] It is in this dialectic of content and form that the moment of historical consciousness emerges for Morrison.

Recalling the more thoroughly reported details of the writing of *Absalom, Absalom!* shows us that this dialectical model holds for Faulkner, as well. Indeed, the search for a proper form in which to express a historicized content is explicitly thematized in that novel, as the effort to reconstruct the Sutpen saga replaces the saga itself as the work's central concern; Joseph Blotner notes that it was "not the events in the lives of Sutpen and his children, but how to relate and interpret them" that "perplexed [Faulkner] from the start."[7] Keeping this dialectic uppermost in mind is what enables the production of a formalist criticism that remains deeply engaged in questions of historical context and content. And Theodor Adorno's notion of a negative dialectics, wherein the dream of synthesis is always blocked by some residue, some surplus, some haunting, has enormous ramifications for a text like *Absalom, Absalom!,* in which, finally, the ledgers don't balance out. For Adorno, this "sense of nonidentity" in the dialectical moment, of something left over and unaccounted for, is in some ways constitutive of thought itself; the modernist turn arrives, he believes, with the recognition and explicit acknowledgment of this truth.[8] In Faulkner's high modernist text, the acknowledged inassimilable surplus is African American history itself; first invoked as adjunctive to the story of Sutpen, it gathers force and momentum, sweeping all else before it by the novel's conclusion.

It is this remainder haunting the mediation of form and content that makes it possible to read *Absalom, Absalom!* and *Beloved* together and helps to explain the similar effects the texts have on their readers. Both novels force us to struggle with that which is most resistant to expression (the nature and purpose of Beloved herself, the ultimate ramifications of Sutpen's design) and which, in its resistance, fuels some of the novels' most breathtaking technical accomplishments. Morrison and Faulkner do this by adopting formal strategies that invite us to hear "unspeakable thoughts, unspoken," that offer tales of telling which are "true enough" yoked to others which are clearly historically impossible (Sutpen's Haiti adventure, for example),[9] and that make narrative choices scarred by "*the lost irrevocable might-have-been.*"[10] For Faulkner, this meant producing a postmodern text that, to paraphrase Fredric Jameson, draws its power from its effort to represent the attempt to think historically in an age that believes it has forgotten how to do so.[11] *Absalom, Absalom!* figures this effort to think historically as a dialectical residue in the work's *content:* Jim Bond remains at large in the novel's conclusion, where the memory of his anguished howling sets Quentin shuddering in his Harvard dormitory bed. Morrison, on the other hand, produces a narrative that deposits its excess in the realm of *form: Beloved* critically deploys "high modernist" techniques in order to reveal the Africanist remainder at the center of modernism's enterprise. Thus, *Absalom, Absalom!* and *Beloved* not only represent African American history artistically: they engage the history of artistically representing African Americans. While it is possible to arrive at these observations by examining each text independently, it is only through reading them together that we gain a historical perspective on the importance of African American *forms* in the emergence of American literary modernism.[12] Reading the two works together also opens up a way toward thinking of the distinction between modernism and postmodernism as a phenomenon of reader reception—in which an examination of the social, political, and aesthetic uses to which texts are put becomes an important factor—rather than a question of formalist periodization.

If there is resistance to reading American literary modernism as deeply indebted to both Africanist aesthetics and the strategies of indirection born out of the enslaved's response to slavery, it is because we have been trained to read a haunted space as an empty place. The period that gave us the New Criticism and the humanist Cold War Faulkner also gave us the dominant ideological reading of modernism, in which various strategies of indirection—difficult syntax, highly stylized structure, and ruptures in narrative sequence—were held to serve the overall aim of making, to paraphrase Joseph Frank, history ahistorical. In this view, the empty horror at the center of industrialized life fueled an effort on the part of modern literary artists—Frank selects James Joyce, Marcel Proust, T. S. Eliot, and Djuna Barnes as his primary examples— to transform "the time world of history into the timeless world of myth."[13] Allen Tate seconded Frank's formulation when he argued that literary modernism sought to "arrest the naturalistic flux of experience at an instant of time that . . . [has] neither temporal antecedents nor temporal consequences."[14] It is this idea of modernism as a flight from history that fueled much of the literary Left's criticism of the movement, beginning with Georg Lukács and continuing up to Houston A. Baker Jr.[15]

Yet modernism appears forcefully in *Beloved,* when, in the novel's middle section, Morrison offers the reader four chapters of direct discourse in which Sethe, Denver, and Beloved give voice to their histories, fears, and desires, first singly, and then together. Starting with Sethe's recollections of her childhood, her life at Sweet Home, and the murder of her daughter, the chapters become progressively more technically challenging and culminate in a dense fugal interplay of all three voices that achieves its effects through liberal use of verbal compression, fragmentation, and juxtaposition. Before this choral moment, each woman speaks her past directly to the reader; Sethe and Denver reveal their personal pasts, already partly shown in the novel, while Beloved's section reveals the hitherto hidden deep past of the Middle Passage. The eight pages comprising Beloved's speech and the ensuing chorus with Sethe and Denver are among the most technically dazzling and reader-resistant pages in all of Morrison's work. What most concerns me here is *why* Morrison decided to shape this language as she did, and why she chose to use a fragmented narrative method overall: given *Beloved*'s effort to reclaim a lost history, why would Morrison decide to use a technique so closely identified with the effort to escape history?[16]

Morrison's many pronouncements on how she would like to be read and critiqued are enough to give pause to anyone attempting to place her work next to that of a white, Western, male author.[17] Yet she herself, in fact, provides some precedent for reading *Beloved* with *Absalom, Absalom!:* her master's thesis at Cornell University tackled the problem of "Virginia Woolf's and William Faulkner's Treatment of the Alienated." "It can be inferred from contemporary literature that a great part of the uniqueness of our time has its roots in the widespread concept of man as a thing apart," Morrison writes, "as an individual who, if not lost, is impressively alone."[18] Morrison decides that for Woolf "isolation is inevitable but, because of the world's disorganization and despair, it can be an advantage" (Wofford 2). Faulkner, on the other hand, "believes it possible to establish complete harmony between man and his position by a return to the old virtues of brotherhood, compassion and love. He believes, too, that man has a responsibility to the future and must be reconciled to it. Alienation is not Faulkner's answer" (3). It seems clear from this and other remarks Morrison has made about Faulkner that it would be fair to characterize her view of his work as a patient, even perhaps a sympathetic, one, and to see the seeds of that view emerging from the opinions expressed in the thesis. Certainly, her discussion of Faulkner is more admiring than her discussion of Woolf, whose very style, Morrison argues, "suggests ... that by isolating oneself into the fragmentary experiences and sensations as they come, the dread of time eating at the edges of life can be avoided. One can live outside time, as it were" (23). For Morrison, living outside time is ultimately undesirable: "In death only the alienated find freedom and refuge from time—a solution Virginia Woolf may well have believed in to end her life as she did in 1941" (23). Morrison's examination of Faulkner comes on the heels of this criticism of Woolf's vision, in which (Morrison seems to say) one type of modernistic style emerges out of an escapist, nihilistic, and finally unacceptable world vision.

In her thesis, Morrison reads *The Sound and the Fury* and *Absalom, Absalom!* together in order to argue that Faulkner, through Quentin Compson, "provides us with an example of a tragic failure brought about by isolation. Faulkner's belief [is] that isolation is self-imposed, contrary to nature and morally destructive" (25). Like Sartre, Morrison is drawn to consider Quentin as the absolute center of the two novels in which he appears; her readings of *The Sound and the Fury* and *Absalom, Absalom!* see Faulkner filtering his most important concerns through Quentin's consciousness.[19] Morrison views the two novels as halves of an artistic whole: *The Sound and the Fury* is a psychological drama—"Faulkner provides the reader with information about Quentin's childhood and family and shows the effects of both on him" (23)—whereas *Absalom, Absalom!* is a historical one (the novel "becomes for Quentin a lesson about the South, for the story is, in addition to being the story of a man, the story of what the South can make of a man" [23]). Morrison decides that Quentin, because of his psychological inadequacies, fails to learn his lesson: "His feeling of detachment prevents a clear understanding of the South's need, for he lacks human sympathy" (29). Her decision to cast Quentin as emotionally impoverished and unable to sympathize with "the people involved in the Sutpen story" indicates that she sees in Faulkner's novel a way of reading the fates of Judith, Henry, Charles Bon, Ellen, and Sutpen that portrays them as "people suffering and needing pity," as ghosts who were once human flesh.[20] Morrison uses Faulkner's Nobel Prize speech to argue that he repudiates Quentin's self-involved alienation and final suicide as a "victory without hope and worst of all without pity or compassion" (35).

Morrison concludes her thesis by noting that Faulkner and Woolf have "approaches to isolation [that] differ greatly, [but] they have this important value in common: each treatment is an effort to discover what pattern of existence is most conducive to honesty and self-knowledge, the prime requisites for living a significant life" (39). Morrison rejects one modernist approach—what she describes as Woolf's belief that "isolation . . . [provides] the means for acute self-analysis"—while embracing another that, in her formulation, emerges as a dialectical negation of the Woolf view: "William Faulkner's Quentin Compson never attains self-knowledge *because* he is alienated" (39; emphasis added). Alienation is cast as both a product of modern life and as an obstacle in the effort to live a "significant" life in the modern period. It is thus simultaneously an injury and a defense mechanism, and—to the extent that a modernist literary practice treats it as such—an indictment of the material conditions from which it emerges.

While it would not be fair to characterize Morrison's mature view of Faulkner as progressing unchangingly from one formed when she was twenty-four years old, it is clear, in this conclusion to her thesis, that she already is viewing literary modernism with a careful eye, sifting its themes and techniques and selecting for praise those that seem more likely to contain within themselves some seed of self-critique. And if we look closer to the present day, we find Morrison again talking about Faulkner in sympathetic (if somewhat more guarded) tones. Morrison appeared at the 1985 Faulkner and Yoknapatawpha Conference at the University of Mississippi and read from *Beloved*, then a work in progress. Before she began reading her fiction, Morrison offered these brief remarks about Faulkner:

> In 1956 [sic] I spent a great deal of time thinking about Mr. Faulkner because he was the subject of a thesis that I wrote at Cornell. Such an exhaustive treatment of an author makes it impossible for a writer to go back to that author for some time afterwards until the energy has dissipated itself in some other form. But I have to say, even before I begin to read, that there was for me not only an academic interest in Faulkner, but in a very, very personal way, in a very personal way as a reader, William Faulkner had an enormous effect on me, an enormous effect.[21]

After her reading, Morrison accepted questions from the audience, and she was asked what effect reading Faulkner had had on her writing. This was her reply:

> Well, I'm not sure that he had any effect on my work.... But as a reader in the '50s and later, of course ... I was concentrating on Faulkner. I don't think that my response was any different from any other student at that time, inasmuch as there was in Faulkner this power and courage—the courage of a writer, a special kind of courage. My reasons, I think, for being interested and deeply moved by all his subjects had something to do with my desire to find out something about this country and that artistic articulation of its past that was not available in history, which is what art and fiction can do but sometimes history refuses to do.... [T]here was an articulate investigation of an era that one or two authors provided and Faulkner was certainly at the apex of that investigation. And there was something else about Faulkner which I can only call "gaze." He had a gaze that was different. It appeared, at that time, to be similar to a look, even a sort of staring, a refusal-to-look-away approach in his writing that I found admirable.... In an extraordinary kind of memorable way there are literary watersheds in one's life. In mine, there are four or five, and I hope they are all ones that meet everybody's criteria of who should be read, but some of them don't. Some books are just awful in terms of technique but nevertheless they are terrific: they are too good to be correct. With Faulkner there was always something to surface. Besides, he could infuriate you

in such wonderful ways. It wasn't just complete delight—there is that other quality that is just as important as devotion: outrage. The point is that with Faulkner one was never indifferent. (296–97)

In the midst of writing her first historical novel, Toni Morrison found that what she had been drawn to in Faulkner "as a reader" was an "admirable . . . refusal-to-look-away," an approach to representing "an era" that exemplified for her "a special kind of courage" in an "artistic articulation of [this country's] past that was not available in history," something that only "art and fiction can do." While denying Faulkner any direct influence on her work, Morrison's reply indicates an awareness that he had attempted something similar to her current project, and that his effort produced something worthwhile—if also imperfect or incomplete (Morrison leaves us to guess at the source of the outrage).

Past efforts to read *Beloved* in the context of the white Western canon largely have focused on the text's relationship to nineteenth-century romance, and especially its relationship to *The Scarlet Letter*. *Beloved*'s engagement with that prior text, it has been argued, produces, among its effects, a revision and rearticulation of the notion of literary mastery (Stryz); a challenge to Hawthorne's cultural authority (Woidat); a criticism of contemporary criticism (Lewis); or a realization that both it and the nineteenth-century text remind us how "that which the past has taken from us no present or future reality can restore."[22] All of these judgments are useful to any effort to read Morrison in and against the white American canon; but reading these critiques, and then turning to Rafael Pèrez-Torres's essay on *Beloved* as a postmodern novel, would lead one to believe that, as far as contemporary scholars are concerned, *Beloved*'s relationship to twentieth-century modernism is a nonissue, a dead end, a nothing.[23] But just as Morrison seeks, through her novel, to reclaim a lost history—to "call them my people, which were not my people; and her beloved, which was not beloved"—so she also seeks to reclaim an entire artistic movement, to uncover "the ghost in the machine" of modernism by pointing out the ways in which that movement owed its emergence to what she has elsewhere called "a dark, abiding, signing Africanist presence."[24] In a 1988 speech, Morrison remarked that she was "always amazed by the resonances, the structural gear-shifts, and the uses to which Afro-American narrative persona and idiom are put in contemporary 'white' literature. . . . The most valuable point of entry into the question of cultural (or racial) distinction, the one most fraught, is its language—its unpoliced, seditious, confrontational, manipulative, inventive, disruptive, masked and masking language. Such a penetration will entail the most careful study, one in which the impact of Afro-American presence on modernity becomes clear and is no longer a well-kept secret" ("Unspeakable" 11).

This emphasis on the language (rather than on the "story") is, I would argue, an effort to direct the excavation of the "Afro-American presence on modernity" along formalist lines. Four years later, Morrison made her point (and claim) again, this time drawing a parallel between American political habits and American literary conventions: "It has occurred to me that the very manner by which American literature distinguishes itself as a coherent entity exists because of this unsettled and unsettling population. Just as the formation of the nation necessitated coded language and purposeful restriction to deal with the racial disingenuousness and moral frailty at its heart, so too did the literature, whose founding characteristics extend into the twentieth century, reproduce the necessity for codes and restriction" (*Playing* 5–6). For the purposes of exploring a materialist formalist refashioning of modernism in *Beloved*, I'd like to draw attention to Morrison's assertion that the creation of the American nation depended on "coded language and purposeful restriction." In addition to being an exact description of white America's legal and social relationship to its Africanist roots, it is also a strikingly apt and economical description of the formal properties of literary modernism *and* of the African American rhetorical practice, signifying, that Henry Louis Gates Jr. has seen as a paradigm for African American literary expression.[25] The difference between signifying and high modernism lies in the intensely reflective nature of the Africanist literary practice: it reads both itself reading (the usual modernist turn) *and* the dominant culture's effort to read it (as it reads itself). Morrison's modernism is both of the earlier Anglo-American movement and apart from it, a relationship established through a critical turn on double consciousness that, in *Beloved,* underscores the vested nature of the desire to forget at the center of Western modernity. In its fragmented and recursive narrative, *Beloved* dramatizes the *survivalist desire* to forget and, through this critical yet critically interested dialogue with literary modernism, forces a reconsideration of the charge that modernism, in its flight from history into myth, seeks to ignore or somehow naturalize social injustice.

Morrison's effort to connect Africanist values and modernist values comes to the fore in *Beloved,* where knowledge that we have all "forgotten" comes back to haunt us and demand some reckoning; in Morrison's novel, Faulkner, the apotheosis of American literary modernism, and *Absalom, Absalom!,* the crowning achievement of that apotheosis, become the chief targets for exhumation and reburial. Before *Beloved,* one could argue, *Absalom, Absalom!* was a text whose *content* appeared dis(re)membered and scattered throughout Morrison's work: Clytie revised as Circe in *Song of Solomon,* Charles Bon as Son in *Tar Baby.* In *Beloved,* Morrison realizes that the real target for revision and reclamation is not the author's use of individual Black characters, but the very literary language itself. *Beloved* remembers that prior text's most striking formal properties—its recursiveness, its use of multiple voices, its fragmentation, even its acknowledgment that some stories never can be properly told or forgotten—in order to respectfully, but nonetheless thoroughly and without regret, bury the notion of a "pure" white American modernism. Reading *Beloved* through *Absalom, Absalom!* helps us to see how, in her novel, Morrison "properly, artistically," places the Africanist body in that grave where "*we had no corpse*" (*AA* 123); *Beloved* suggests that modernism's "empty hall echoing with sonorous defeated names" ultimately housed not many ghosts, but one (*AA* 7).

Morrison's notion of "purposeful restriction" would seem to coincide philosophically with Tate's "arrest" and Frank's "timeless world of myth," insofar as it implies a concerted effort to refuse narrative entry to certain (undesirable) elements.[26] I would like to approach the notion of "purposeful restriction" in another sense: how it describes what an author does in seeking to transmute "content" into "form." Morrison's approach to *Beloved* is perfectly suited to this inquiry, since the seed for the novel was the true story of Margaret Garner, a fugitive slave who, finding herself in imminent danger of being returned to slavery, chose to kill one of her children rather than see the child reenslaved. In the many interviews given on the publication of *Beloved,* Morrison was careful to point out that the book was only *inspired* by Garner's story; it was not an effort to retell it. In nearly every interview, she emphasizes the notion of inspiration by insisting that, after all, she didn't know much about the story—and deliberately so, for compelling artistic reasons:

> I was amazed by this story I came across about a woman called Margaret Garner who had escaped from Kentucky, *I think,* into Cincinnati with four children.... And she was a kind of *cause célèbre* among abolitionists *in 1855 or '56* because she tried to kill the children when she was caught. She killed one of them, just as in the novel. I found *an article* in a magazine of the period....
>
> Now, I didn't do any more research at all about that story.... I did a lot of research about everything else in the book—Cincinnati, and abolitionists, and the underground railroad—but I refused to find out anything else about Margaret Garner. I really wanted to invent her life. (Rothstein C17; emphasis added)

Morrison's remarks here are representative of claims she made whenever she was asked about the genesis of the story of Sethe, complete with the hedging ("I think," "1855 or '56") and the emphasis on a minimal amount of research (*one* article in a magazine, not three or four). But in fact, Morrison knew quite a bit about Margaret Garner, as one interview shows. When, in an article published in the March 1988 issue of the *Women's Review of Books,* Marsha Jean Darling wonders "what difference it would have made if Halle had been there the day that the white men came across the yard to get Sethe," Morrison replies: "In fact it didn't make a difference, because in fact Margaret Garner escaped with her husband and two other men and was returned to slavery."[27] When Darling follows up this response by asking, "Despite the fact that she killed the child, she was returned?," Morrison replies:

> Well, she wasn't tried for killing her child. She was tried for a *real* crime, which was running away—although the abolitionists were trying very hard to get her tried for murder because they wanted the Fugitive Slave Law to be unconstitutional. They did not want her tried on those grounds, so they tried to switch it to murder as a kind of success story. They thought that they could make it impossible for Ohio, as a free state, to acknowledge the right of a slave-owner to come get those people.... But they all went back to Boone County and apparently the man who took them back—the man she was going to kill herself and her children to get away from—he sold her down river, which was as bad as was being separated from each other. But apparently the boat hit a sandbar or something, and she fell or jumped with her daughter,

her baby, into the water. It is not clear whether she fell or jumped, but they rescued her and I guess she went on down to New Orleans and I don't know what happened after that. (Darling 6)

In response to Darling's rather vague question, Morrison reveals a strikingly thorough knowledge of the particulars of Margaret Garner's sad history, including a familiarity with the legal maneuvers employed by the abolitionists who wanted to use Garner's infanticide as a test case for the Fugitive Slave Law. That Morrison remembers even the name of the Kentucky county from which the Garner family fled (Boone County, named nowhere in *Beloved*) indicates a familiarity with the history born of some research more thorough than a brief, emotionally bedazzled reading of a single magazine article. Morrison doesn't know what happens after Garner's accident on the riverboat not because she chose to cut off her research but because the historical record itself, in fact, fails to tell us what became of the woman.[28]

I bring this up not to complain that Morrison misrepresented her process in writing *Beloved* but to examine how she chose to exercise a "purposeful restriction" in fitting Margaret Garner's story to her artistic project. In shaping her story, Morrison was confronted with a conflicting series of accounts in both the popular press and scholarly journals; the very way in which the child died remains unclear.[29] But there is enough agreement in the general outlines of the event to highlight those points at which Morrison chose to depart from the historic record.[30] In these accounts, Garner was not alone with her children in the early summer in a woodshed behind a house situated at the outskirts of Cincinnati, but in the city home of a free kinsman in the middle of January (the fugitives walked across the frozen Ohio to freedom);[31] the Garner family was not owned by a single slaveholder, but split up between the owners of two plantations in Boone County (one man owned Garner's husband and his parents; another owned Margaret and the children). The fugitives were recaptured within hours of their escape rather than one month later as in *Beloved*. And, as Morrison tells Darling, Margaret Garner was never tried for the murder of her daughter. A federal judge remanded the enslaved back to Kentucky; efforts to try Garner for murder under state statutes were rendered superfluous when she was sold down the river despite pledges from Kentucky officials that she would be held to stand trial in Ohio.

Nearly all the areas of disagreement in the historical record appear—not surprisingly—in the realm of the act itself and the enslaveds' reactions to it. Some reports stressed that all four adults were in the room at the time of the murder and that the men "began to scream" when Garner attacked the child; other emphasized that the men were elsewhere in the building, armed and, in a desperate, manly effort to protect their women and children, shooting at (and wounding) the slave catchers. One report claims that, when Margaret asked her mother-in-law to "'help me to kill the children.'... the old woman began to wail ... and ran for refuge under a bed"; another states that the mother-in-law "neither encouraged nor discouraged her daughter-in-law,—for under similar circumstances she would have probably done the same."[32] Finally, according to one account, the murdered child was not "thunder black and glistening" (*Beloved* 261) but "almost white."[33]

There are two ways of looking at Morrison's "purposeful restrictions," and both are pertinent to a discussion of the novel's relationship to *Absalom, Absalom!* The first is Morrison's belief—expressed both in interviews and in the novel—that the historical record cannot be trusted to offer a true appraisal of Black history. As Morrison tells Christina Davis: "The reclamation of the history of black people in this country is paramount in its importance because while you can't really blame the conqueror for writing history his own way, you can certainly debate it. There's a great deal of obfuscation and distortion and erasure, so that the presence and the heartbeat of black people has been systematically annihilated in many, many ways and the job of recovery is ours."[34] The trail of newspaper clippings, the articles in historical journals written out of those clippings—in the last analysis, none can be trusted to tell Margaret Garner's story, because they are, to greater and lesser degrees, grounded in a racist enterprise. In *Beloved,* Morrison puts it this way:

> There was no way in hell a black face could appear in a newspaper if the story was about something anybody wanted to hear. A whip of fear broke through the heart chambers as soon as you saw a Negro's face in a paper, since the face was not there because the person had a healthy baby, or outran a street mob. Nor was it there because the person had been killed, or maimed or caught or burned or jailed or whipped or evicted or stomped or raped or cheated, since that could hardly qualify as news in a newspaper. It would have to be some-

thing out of the ordinary—something whitepeople would find interesting, truly different, worth a few minutes of teeth sucking if not gasps. And it must have been hard to find news about Negroes worth the breath catch of a white citizen of Cincinnati. (*Beloved* 155–56)

This rejection of the notion that "realist" descriptions of events are suitable to the effort of recovering African American history leads to the second way of looking at Morrison's revisions, one that sees her strategy as a reclamation of exactly those modernist methods of telling deployed in *Absalom, Absalom!* As first Rosa Coldfield, then Mr. Compson, then Rosa again, then Shreve and Quentin each strive to tell the story of the fall of Sutpen and the murder of Charles Bon, the reader is forced to recognize the ways in which each character invests his or her own psychological needs into the story. Thus the enraged, embittered Rosa Coldfield presents a nostalgic, Old South view of the tale, emphasizing romance and a Manichean ethics. The cynical, alcoholic Mr. Compson prefers a detached, ironic reading that suggests the cause of the fall of Sutpen in Bon's exoticism, Henry's prudish (yet voyeuristic and homoerotically charged) sexuality, and Sutpen's lack of breeding, but that collapses into paradox: "It's just incredible. It just does not explain" (*AA* 80).[35] In their turn, Shreve and Quentin seek to wrest a meaning from this history for themselves, first clearing a space for "play" that will permit their search for a deeper truth in "love, where there might be paradox and inconsistency but nothing fault or false" (*AA* 253). But even in their play Shreve and Quentin (and us) make use of what has gone before; their "overpassing" must launch itself from the scenes of those deeply vested versions of the story that they have heard. Faulkner thus simultaneously beckons toward and abjures a notion of narrative transcendence; however much it may be desired, there is no "overpassing" that does not start (and end) in some specific place.

In writing *Beloved*, Morrison was faced with a choice: to creatively deploy a "realist" narrative discourse so that its complicity with racial terror became clear, or to enter into a dialogue with "psychological" modernism that would, in a sense, complete the gesture begun in *Absalom, Absalom!* by exploring the ways in which modernism simultaneously inscribes and unmasks its complicity in social injustice. In fact, Morrison does both: revising realism through *Beloved*'s content (especially through the figure of Schoolteacher, the sadistic scientific racist) and modernism in its technique and form. And by invoking and repudiating past printed accounts of Margaret Garner's story, Morrison, like Faulkner, warns against a too-easy transcendence of a confusing, painful history. What she has given us, after all, is not a story to pass on.

This brings us to the conclusions of the two novels and back to the question of irony. As Quentin and Shreve settle for sleep in their dormitory room, Shreve describes the telling of the Sutpen story as a scene of incomplete compensations:

> "So it took Charles Bon and his mother to get rid of old Tom, and Charles Bon and the octoroon to get rid of Judith, and Charles Bon and Clytie to get rid of Henry; and Charles Bon's mother and Charles Bon's grandmother got rid of Charles Bon. So it takes two niggers to get rid of one Sutpen, dont it?" Quentin did not answer; evidently Shreve did not want an answer now; he continued almost without pause: "Which is all right, it's fine; it clears the whole ledger, you can tear all the pages out and burn them, except for one thing. And do you know what that is?" Perhaps he hoped for an answer this time, or perhaps he merely paused for emphasis, since he got no answer. "You've got one nigger left. One nigger Sutpen left. Of course you cant catch him and you dont even always see him and you never will be able to use him. But you've got him there still. You still hear him at night sometimes. Dont you?"
>
> "Yes," Quentin said. (*AA* 302)

All the past tellings—the fragmented circumlocutions and desiring displacements, the embracing and rejecting in turn of nostalgia and paradox as avenues of explanation—that have gone into this "overpassing," and the "overpassing" itself, stop dead at the agonized, howling remainder present in the figure of Jim Bond. He is what the novel cannot overpass, that lived and living piece of Sutpen history that prevents Quentin and Shreve from clearing the ledger and burning the pages. His presence reduces Shreve's smug amazement to an ironic anthropological fantasy; it renews in Quentin the gnawing, unreconciled nature of his own feelings toward the South.[36] If the narrative project of *Absalom, Absalom!* has been to show that nothing is ever told once and is finished, Jim Bond serves as the (racial, historical) sign of remainder that fuels the repetition. "You will never be able to use him," Shreve says, in a formulation that recalls the use to which Blacks were put in slavery. "But you've got him there still." If the Africanist body is the "nothing" at the center of Faulkner's text, then there is literally nothing that can be done with Jim Bond; Faulkner's novel closes with Jim Bond's howling ringing in Quentin's (and the reader's) ears.[37] Quentin's famous response to Shreve's question "Why do you hate the South?"—"'I don't hate it,' Quentin said . . . ; 'I dont hate it,' he said. *I dont hate it* he thought. . . . *I dont. I dont! I dont hate it! I dont hate it!*" (AA 303)—constitutes a desperate attempt to silence that howling through paradox.

This reading of the narrative project and conclusion of *Absalom, Absalom!* has been more suggestive than definitive, but it puts us in a position to see the second—and, I would say, more radical—way of viewing Morrison's recuperation of modernism via Faulkner's novel. *Absalom, Absalom!* is haunted by the ways in which an unfree Africanist presence conditions the modernist enterprise, and it shows us how irony and paradox may be deployed in an effort to contain that remainder. *Beloved*, too, is haunted by this presence, and Morrison, too, deploys irony and paradox in the conclusion of her novel. Having pieced together the story of the murder of Sethe Garner's child; having followed the disembodied haunting and consuming embodied presence of that child, and the final dis(re)membering and scattering of that body; having made the imaginative links between the spirit of Beloved and those of all Africans lost in the Middle Passage; having accomplished all this, the readers of *Beloved* are unequivocally told at the end of the novel that what they have "is not a story to pass on" (*Beloved* 275). Many critics have decided that Morrison simply can't really mean this, and have pointed to the fact that the story has, in fact, been passed on—through the novel.[38] In his respectful reading of the novel, James Phelan argues that Morrison's insistence on *Beloved*'s "stubbornness" in yielding up its meaning serves to uncover the reader's own desires for interpretive "mastery and possession."[39] Phelan's reading offers a fruitful way of exploring *Beloved*'s relationship to modernist paradox in general and *Absalom, Absalom!* in particular—a text about a master, by a (modernist) master, that in many ways owes its continuing aesthetic life to its readers' attempts to master its hidden meanings. To borrow terms from digital audio technology, Morrison samples and remasters Faulkner's text—both by critically redeploying its method and by reinhabiting the history it simultaneously evokes and abandons—and thus places into question the very notion of literary mastery.

But the conclusion of *Beloved* also reflects quite literally on the problems Morrison confronted in writing the novel. As she has remarked in several interviews, she was repeatedly surprised by how much slave history had been silenced—not only by the masters but also by the enslaved. "There was something untold, unsaid, that never came down," Morrison said in one postpublication interview. "There was some deliberate, calculated, survivalist intention, to forget certain things. [For example], there was almost no reference to the ships . . . I know no songs about it. I know no stories about it."[40] But while stories of the Middle Passage were not "passed on," the experience itself was not truly forgotten. As Morrison tells Paul Gilroy, "The struggle to forget, which was important in order to survive, is fruitless and I wanted to make it fruitless."[41] The irony lies in knowing how some things that are not "passed on" yet remain unforgettable; now our "weather," Beloved will be with us forever (*Beloved* 275).

Reading *Beloved* as a modern postmodern text and *Absalom, Absalom!* as a postmodern modern text raises the question, finally, of just what these terms—modern, postmodern—practically mean. It seems to me that examining the social, political, and aesthetic *uses* to which texts are put is perhaps a better approach to what frequently has been seen as a question of formalist periodization. A brief discussion of the public responses to *Beloved* and *Absalom, Absalom!* opens the way toward thinking about modernism and postmodernism as phenomena of reception. So as we began this discussion of formalism with content, let us end with context.

Over and over again, in the first reviews of *Absalom, Absalom!*, critics remarked (usually complaining, sometimes marveling) on the forbidding surface of Faulkner's text. Clifton Fadiman's infamous comment that "one may sum up both substance and style by saying that every person in 'Absalom, Absalom!' comes to no good end, and they all take a hell of a time coming even that far" represents an extreme view, but it is representative: Harold Strauss remarks that the novel is "strange chiefly because of the amazing indirectness with which Faulkner has managed to tell a basically simple story," and William Troy observes that "through neither the form nor the style do we escape from the closed universe of his intensely personal vision."[42] In these reviews, Faulkner's style and form were all; this remained the dominant view of Faulkner's craft even after his reputation was rehabilitated during the Cold War. In the 1930s, Faulkner was rejected because his forbidding style seemed to mark him as an author disinterested in, if not absolutely opposed to, the current effort to enlist the arts in building an equitable society (his post-*Sanctuary* notoriety as "the corncob man" didn't help). In the 1950s, Faulkner was embraced because his forbidding style seemed to confirm the then-ascendant notion of the modern heroic artist lionized for the completeness with which he realized his own (intensely personal, socially disengaged) aesthetic vision.[43]

Today, Faulkner is being read for his history—particularly for the ways in which his texts reveal how the southern modernist wish to "forget" history arises as much from the white ruling class's effort to remain in power during a period of social upheaval as from any psychosexual trauma.[44] This view of Faulknerian texts corresponds with notions of the postmodern outlined by both Jameson and Linda Hutcheon: it is the engagement with history, as opposed to the modernist flight from history, that marks the postmodern text. Certainly, much of this new Faulkner arises from his texts; but more than a small portion of it—in fact, a rather large portion of it, if the grounds for my claims here have warrant—arises from the echoes of Faulkner's themes and techniques in works like *Beloved,* echoes that lead us back to the older author with new eyes and an altered understanding.

From its first appearance, *Beloved* was hailed as a historical, politically engaged, redemptive novel. In the conclusion of his review, Thomas R. Edwards asserts, "I would suppose that in *Beloved* Morrison means to help thoughtful black people, especially women, to create or re-create an imagination of self that 'white history' or 'male history' has effectively denied them."[45] Margaret Atwood remarks that the novel invites us to "experience American slavery as it was lived by those who were its objects of exchange"; even Stanley Crouch, in his notorious dismissal of the work, latched onto its historic reach in order to enter the complaint that "*Beloved,* above all else, is a blackface holocaust novel."[46] The notable exception in this rush to privilege history is Judith Thurman's review, in which she observes: "Despite the richness and authority of its detail, "Beloved" is not primarily a historical novel. . . . [Morrison] treats the past as if it were one of those luminous old scenes painted on dark glass—the scene of a disaster, like the burning of Parliament or the eruption of

Krakatoa—and she breaks the glass, and recomposes it in disjointed and puzzling modern form. As the reader struggles with its fragments and mysteries, he keeps being startled by flashes of his own reflection in them."[47]

Thurman comes to this view because she reads *Beloved* in companion with other texts, starting with *The Cosby Show,* continuing with Shakespeare's *The Tempest* and Mary Shelley's *Frankenstein,* and concluding with selected insights drawn from Sigmund Freud and Friedrich Nietzsche; putting the "postmodern" *Beloved* in a historical cultural context leads Thurman to consider its "modern" impulses. This seems to me to indicate that, though we have made good postmodern use of Morrison's novel (reading it helps us think historically when we believe we have forgotten to do so), we do well to attend to the ways in which that use is predicated upon modernist assumptions that *Beloved* simultaneously distances itself from and fulfills. For some time now, literary modernism itself seems to have been the nightmare from which we've all been trying to awaken; *Beloved* and *Absalom, Absalom!* both remind us how it's the undigested histories that stick around to haunt us.

Postscript

Truly vintage work, this chapter was written for *Unflinching Gaze,* the 1997 collection of essays on the novels of William Faulkner and Toni Morrison that was one of the earliest entries into what has now become a crowded field of comparative analysis.[48] The collection initially was considered somewhat daring, appearing as it did at a time when there seemed to be but two models for considering questions of authors' engagements with the work of their predecessors: (1) Harold Bloom's oedipal "anxiety of influence," wherein junior writers seek to work out from under the oppressive influence of their forefathers through strategic (if often misguided) "misprisions" of the forebear's work; or (2) Sandra M. Gilbert and Susan Gubar's "anxiety of authorship," a direct response to Bloom's theory positing the search for voice and literary foremothers as key to understanding the work of women writers. Obviously, neither model offers an appropriate pathway into an exploration of the nature of the relationship between the novels of Toni Morrison and William Faulkner, especially after the publication of *Beloved.* This is not to say that these models lack utility in Black literary study. Ralph Ellison's perhaps excessive reverence for

Faulkner's achievement can be examined in a Bloomian framework; similarly, Alice Walker's recovery of the work of Zora Neale Hurston responds well to Gilbert and Gubar's thesis. It's rather to observe that, for a writer as powerful and confident as Morrison, the notion that she felt oppressed or overshadowed by Faulkner's achievement seems simply implausible, as does the notion that she found the lack of literary foremothers somehow daunting.

Henry Louis Gates Jr.'s theory of African American signifying pointed the way out of this methodological gridlock. It enabled a reading of Morrison's engagement with Faulkner that permitted both high-level overview (Morrison's take on literary modernism and then-dominant scholarly depictions of its techniques as bent to the work of historical evasion) and granular analysis (Morrison's critical repetitions and revisions of signature Faulknerian themes and tropes). And it did so in a way that remained true to Morrison's aesthetic credo: to write "for black people" without apology and without reference to some "little white man deep inside us."[49] Building a theoretical structure that would set the terms for a proper approach to the connections between Morrison's work and Faulkner's was particularly important given the fact of her 1955 master's thesis, which established the fact of her careful study of his work well before her own foray into fiction.[50]

In any case, these days the Morrison/Faulkner pairing feels more overdetermined than scandalous, and readings that mine formalist strategies for historical content, as I do in my chapter, have also become more common. As important as the growth of scholarship comparing the novels of Morrison and Faulkner is the expansion of the field of comparative readings within Faulkner studies to embrace a broad array of Black authors whose engagement with the work is similarly critical and revisionary—writers such as Édouard Glissant, Jessmyn Ward, Edwidge Danticat, Edward P. Jones, and Natasha Trethewey. The proceedings of the 2013 Faulkner and Yoknapatawpha conference, on the theme of Faulkner and the Black literature of the Americas, testify to the vitality and groundbreaking nature of this work, which includes bold explorations of Faulkner's indebtedness to the work of Black authors. We need only pair George Hutchinson's assertion that "the development of black modernism created a new environment for [Faulkner's] work, for his work's reception, and ultimately for his literary imagination" with Jay Watson's comparative reading of Zora Neale Hurston's 1933 story "The Gilded Six-Bits" and *Go*

Down, Moses's "Pantaloon in Black"—a reading making clear that Faulkner "actively harvested the story for material"—to grasp how far Faulkner studies has come in this regard.[51] This remarkable turn of the screw of authorial anxiety, in which past white scholarly assumptions of Black indebtedness to Faulkner are turned inside out, was made possible by the effort to come to terms with Morrison's critical engagements with his work. To be sure, Black critical engagement with Faulkner did not start with Toni Morrison (consider James Baldwin, for instance). But no one managed that critique with her particular brand of fierce and uncompromising respect—a respect that did not let the older author off the hook for anything. In that sense, one could describe Toni Morrison as a Faulknerista *par excellence*.

5

Posting Yoknapatawpha

> Writing is, after all, in its way, a *satori: satori* (the Zen occurrence) is a more powerful (though in no way formal) seism which causes knowledge, or the subject, to vacillate: it creates *an emptiness of language.* And it is also an emptiness of language which constitutes writing.
>
> —ROLAND BARTHES, *Empire of Signs*

During the late 1990s and early 2000s, the final page of the *New York Times Book Review* typically featured a column offering observations by guest authors or bookish staff writers on literary matters both contemporary (Oprah Winfrey's influence on bestseller lists, for example) and perennial (the difference between reading a play and seeing it). It was an American version of the European *feuilleton*, the newspaper arts essay that, at its best, aspires to combine erudition with accessibility. There was humor in this column (usually entitled "The Last Word," sometimes "Bookend," sometimes simply "Essay"), but the jokes were designed more to elicit the knowing chuckles of David Lodge readers than the guerrilla snorts of David Sedaris fans. So the February 6, 2000, edition of the column was somewhat out of the usual routine. First, it was not a column but a full-page illustration: In describing "Two Things That Depress Me When I Open a Novel," the writer Meg Wolitzer partnered with the artist Christopher Niemann to present her argument in graphic detail. Second, it was wickedly funny, infused with an atypical irreverence that refreshed even as it stung.

The first thing that depresses Wolitzer when she opens a novel is being confronted with "The Family Tree."[1] Niemann's cartoon shows us exactly what she means, offering a arboreal rendering of a genealogy that springs either illegitimately or parthenogenetically (no woman's name appears) from one Nelson Copious Bordeen ("The Patriarch") to wend its way through two main descending branches (via the offspring of children Figurine Oleanna and Half-Nelson) before concluding, three generations distant from old Copious, in Bastardine, the "unacknowledged," incestuously conceived offspring of Erik Fjordkvist, Jr. (great-grandson of Figurine), and Towelette Vespers (great-granddaughter of Half-Nelson) (31). The second thing that depresses Wolitzer when she opens a novel is finding "The Map of the Town"; Niemann obligingly provides a sketch of the main sights of "Opportunity Knox, Miss.," home of the Bordeen clan: "Bundt Bay (Where Karen, née Bastardine, sought her revenge on the townsfolk)"; the "Graveyard where Nelson Copious Bordeen's restless ghost often appears"; "Dagmar's Sewin' Shoppe"; and the "Dogwood Glade Rest Home (where Velveeta Scopes spent her remaining years)" (31). As the family tree already has informed us, Velveeta Scopes is the wife of Half-Nelson Bordeen and great-grandmother of the unfortunate Bastardine, and her names, both given and maiden—so closely resembling the names of certain denizens of a fictional world likewise marked by complex family trees, hand-drawn town maps, and improbable-sounding nomenclature—neatly let us know that Wolitzer found the inspiration for this "depressing" novel lying somewhere along an imagined axis linking the actual Dayton, Tennessee (home of the Scopes trial), to the apocryphal Frenchman's Bend, Mississippi.

Wolitzer and Niemann's column/cartoon is funny in the same way that the scores of entries in the now-discontinued "Faux Faulkner" contest were funny. It picks up recognizable Faulknerian tics—here the spatializations of time (genealogy and map) apotheosized in service to the exalted and deeply troubling Yoknapatawpha material of *Absalom, Absalom!* and *Go Down, Moses*—and resettles them on a clearly unworthy site ("Dock of the Bundt Bay [where Seven-Eleven Jones was found bludgeoned to death]") (Wolitzer and Niemann 31). And it's also funny because it's true. It's easy to understand why encountering such material leaves Wolitzer "depressed": those tics can be dismaying, and not only because they have been overworked by Faulknerian epigones. This accelerating, McMansion-esque proliferation of Yoknapatawphan literary architecture was brought home to me when a discussion of the genealogical material revealed in part 4 of "The Bear" led one of my best students to observe, "This is just all that Southern Gothic stuff, right?" For the encounter with map and genealogy can be seen as depressing not only in itself but also metonymically, as an aspect of the repetition that structures Faulkner's corpus, over which even the most devoted reader pauses before revisiting terrain that may surrender fresh treasures but that may also engender "a flagging attention which [is] almost distaste," as Faulkner himself once admitted.[2]

Sustained engagement with Faulkner's work makes it clear: there was little he didn't recycle, sometimes in wildly incommensurate contexts. Tropes, narrative devices, structural elements, and stock phrases reappear (sometimes strongly revised, sometimes minimally so, sometimes repeated whole cloth) from one work to another—not only, as in the example of Wolitzer and Niemann's cartoon, the genealogy (from *Absalom, Absalom!* to "Appendix: Compson") and the map (from *Absalom, Absalom!* to *The Portable Faulkner*), but style and structure, too: the synaesthetic imagery, the multiple negations, the periodic sentences. The scholarship has demonstrated, amply and well, the crucial role revisionary repetition plays in Faulkner's aesthetic vision; but, alas, there is no perceivable direct correlation between the excellence of the material and the number of passes through it. "Oh God," Temple Drake Stevens moans, "Again"—and only the most cultish Faulknerian doesn't feel a small identificatory shiver of self-pity (not least because it was Quentin Compson, in a text published twenty-two years earlier, who first made the word a token of despair).[3]

Wolitzer's column thus foregrounds an issue that is central to my discussion here: the status of the rebarbative in Faulkner's work and its relationship to the task of bringing Yoknapatawpha into being. I am not directly concerned here with issues of sexism and racism in Faulkner's treatment of his characters, the topics that most readily come to mind in discussions of offensive material in the work, topics that continue to receive their due in the criticism. Rather, I am concerned with the more general issue of the writing itself, its relative quality from work to work and over the course of the career. Because so much of what is awkward or repellent in Faulkner is connected to his habit of repetition, this can be seen too as a question about the relative merit of the late work, where his reliance not only on the repetition of character and event (crucial to the development of Yoknapatawpha as a fully imagined space) but also on a repetitive prose style comes under increasingly apparent strain—a strain most evident in the middle volume of the Snopes trilogy, *The Town*, where almost every importation of incident from *The Hamlet*, its precedent text, is confoundingly distorted, and which contains sentences like, "So she couldn't tell me because she could not."[4]

John T. Irwin's brief, seminal study makes clear the central role of repetition in Faulkner's *oeuvre;* Irwin does not, however, seek to account for those places where repetition overwrites or defaces the work it brings into being.[5] Perhaps because Yoknapatawpha has been subject to such relentless, ongoing critical development (a development that has made fresh prime plots increasingly hard to find), a growing trend in Faulkner scholarship has been to stake a claim for the merits of the less frequently studied work, and it is not hard to see why: recuperating previously neglected material strengthens the Faulkner market in much the same way that renovating a derelict building enhances the property tax base.[6] This is not to say that such reclamation efforts shouldn't be undertaken. Recent studies positing once-presumed mistakes as deliberate, thoughtful revisions and reframing some aspects of the late style as meaningfully baroque rather than self-indulgently rococo have revealed unsuspected virtues in the late novels even while acknowledging their flaws; the work of Michael Grimwood and Richard C. Moreland is relevant here.[7] It is, rather, to point out that such scholarship is influenced at least as much by the structure of the academic marketplace and the publication demands of tenure and promotion as by our ideal of disinterested literary analysis. And so, perhaps predictably, these initially cautious reassessments have been followed by studies claiming that the late Faulkner—even those works long held to be problematic (*A Fable, The Town,* and *The Reivers*)—is as good as, maybe even better than, *The Sound and the Fury, As I Lay Dying, Light in August,* and *Absalom, Absalom!* Rethinking Faulkner's relationship to Yoknapatawpha, the author's self-created "little postage stamp of native soil," the fictional "cosmos" traditionally regarded as the singular achievement of his career, has been crucial to this development.

The claim that Faulkner's late work, far from sounding a dying fall at end of day, should be viewed as his greatest, summative accomplishment is made perhaps most strongly in Joseph Urgo's 1989 study *Faulkner's Apocrypha*.[8] Taking as his foundation and point of departure a critically important 1987 essay by Cheryl Lester, Urgo argues that all of Faulkner's works after the Nobel were deliberate efforts to free his *oeuvre* from the interpretive frame Malcolm

Cowley had imposed on the novels in his introduction to *The Portable Faulkner,* a rationalizing, canonizing frame casting Yoknapatawpha as "a mythical kingdom . . . complete and living in all its details . . . [comprising] a parable or legend of all the Deep South."[9] Rather than acquiesce to Cowley's interpretation of his work as centered on an allegorical "mythical kingdom" of southern history, Urgo claims, Faulkner sought to produce an "apocrypha" that would undercut Cowley's plan to secure Faulkner's literary reputation through a homogenized, orderly development of Yoknapatawphan real estate. In the essay that set the initial terms of this revisionary view, Lester holds up for scorn the bumbling befuddlement (freely confessed in *The Faulkner-Cowley File*) induced in Cowley by the "errors" he encounters in moving from one Yoknapatawpha novel to another; she applauds Faulkner's disdain for Cowley's efforts to tidy up the texts and so create a unified, consistent Yoknapatawpha; and she reads Faulkner's "Appendix: Compson" as both a practical joke and a type of literary revenge. Far from providing the requested two- to three-page plot summary that would contextualize the excerpted final section of *The Sound and the Fury* for readers of *The Portable,* Faulkner produced an "appendix" that explodes the text both temporally and spatially, reaching back past the US immigration of Quentin MacLachlan Compson and forward beyond Caddy's liaison with a Nazi officer. In Lester's view, the "Appendix" amounts to "a critique, before the fact, of what has since become, in the United States, the canonical representation" of Faulkner's work (Lester 372). Urgo takes Lester's model and expands it to fit the last decade of Faulkner's life. In his view, Faulkner spent those years contentedly living the life of the feted Nobel laureate while pouring his perpetually enraged and rebellious spirit into his writing: fleeing Yoknapatawpha for Europe in *A Fable,* "rotating" narrative possibility through narrative discrepancy in the Snopes trilogy, and advocating youth's theft of authority from the old in *The Reivers.*

In calling Faulkner's final work an "apocrypha," Urgo draws on Faulkner's own famous description of his method in creating Yoknapatawpha: "Beginning with *Sartoris* I discovered that my own little postage stamp of native soil was worth writing about, that I would never live long enough to exhaust it, and by sublimating the actual into [the] apocryphal I would have complete liberty to use whatever talent I might have to its absolute top."[10] Though Urgo does not explicitly charge Cowley with reducing Yoknapatawpha to "the actual," it is true that Cowley's preferred view of Faulkner's "postage stamp" ("a parable or legend of all the Deep South"), combined with his anxiety over textual inconsistencies (did Quentin effect her escape via pear tree or rain spout?), indicates that he had fairly conventional notions of the relationship between reality and the creative imagination. On this point Urgo, following Lester, is right: Faulkner's creative imagination was far from conventional, and critical analyses of his novels that limit themselves, with whatever good intentions, to some version of "the actual" risk failing to rise to the work's interpretive demands.[11]

Urgo proposes a corrective, elevating assessment of Faulkner's achievement by approaching it as an "apocrypha": "a self-consciously 'other' interpretation of reality" that "aims to upset and to create a sense of *competing* accounts, not a single version of the real" (4, 14). This approach licenses an ingenious scheme of redefinition that not only permits smooth incorporation of what previously had been deemed problematic aspects of Faulkner's work—once transformed into manifestations of a deliberate narrative strategy, for example, all those discrepancies fall "into pattern like a jigsaw puzzle when the magician's wand touched it" (*Faulkner-Cowley File* 36)—but also entails a fairly radical redefinition of the Faulknerian literary universe. For Yoknapatawpha, in this new cosmology, far from being the summation of the apocryphal vision, emerges as just one place among many, an (admittedly heavily developed) literary subdivision best imagined as a rhetorical outpost in some greater, multivalent empire of signs: "Yoknapatawpha . . . is only a synecdoche for the writer's larger production of alternatives of self and place and time" (Urgo 4).

At first glance this appears to be a significant shift in interpretive approach—indeed, it's hard to imagine a more mutinously contrarian view of Faulkner's *oeuvre* than one claiming that Yoknapatawpha is not its most singular achievement—but in the end there may not be much difference between a view of Faulkner's chief accomplishment as the creation of a "complete and living" "mythical kingdom," a "parable or legend of all the Deep South," and one casting it as a kind of universalized rebel yell: "a political and ideological alternative to . . . the totalitarianism of modern society" (Urgo 4). Cowley and Urgo share a desire to see Faulkner as the writer/hero of the modern age (though the notion of what is properly heroic in the modern age changes from the mid-1940s to the late-1980s); Faulknerians both, they hold in common a critical agenda eager to present the author's body of work as a continuous, sustained whole, a lifetime achievement following near-metaphysical principles of organization and coherence.[12] Rather than debunk Cowley's Olympian ode to Faulkner, then, Urgo adds a new stanza and transposes it to a different key.

I am sympathetic to the sense that some common logic of creation connects Faulkner's post-Nobel work to that which preceded it, and I can understand how a drive to discover that logic might lead one to search beyond Yoknapatawpha—even as I am unconvinced that a common logic ensures a uniformity of literary quality. But though I don't share Urgo and Cowley's reverent approach to Faulkner, I do think their readings render the valuable service of illustrating the choice all readers must consider in making their way through Yoknapatawpha: whether to proceed latitudinally (that is, reading from text to text so as to construct a kind of "master text"; this is the choice made by Cowley in putting together *The Portable Faulkner*) or longitudinally (reading text by text, disarticulating each novel from its companions; this is the choice made by Urgo). This latitude/longitude paradigm is, to be sure, classically structuralist: it can be plotted along the same x-y graph and organized by the same relational tensions as the models of synchrony and diachrony, or of metaphor and metonymy, and it deconstructs itself in much the same manner. Cowley's latitudinal approach founders on Faulkner's imperfect, centrifugal repetitions; Urgo's longitudinal reading retains the holistic latitudinal impulse. To put the problem this way should, I hope, make clear the hazards awaiting readers who seek some kind of singular "royal road" through Yoknapatawpha: a working navigational geometry demands attention to both planes.

A more rambling peregrination through Faulkner's fictional county would attend to the transubstantiating points where latitude and longitude both arise and cross (points that permit the reading of a highly irregular, turbulent, and enigmatic geography by recoding that surface as rhythmic, predictable, and legible) and would take seriously the volatile method employed by Faulkner in translating actual into apocryphal: sublimation. For Freud, sublimation is the motor force propelling the artistic process, and it is fueled by sexual desire; as Jacques Lacan puts it, in a formulation that has consequences for my discussion of Yoknapatawpha: "Sublimation is . . . satisfaction of the [sexual] drive, without repression. In other words—for the moment, I am not fucking, I am talking to you. Well! I can have exactly the same satisfaction as if I were fucking. That's what it means. Indeed, it raises the question of whether in fact I am not fucking at this moment."[13] With Faulkner that question, if not posed in quite Lacan's manner, has nevertheless long haunted scholarly discourse, and not just among harried, baffled undergraduates whose first encounter with the ending of *As I Lay Dying* leaves them feeling, well, fucked with. There is ample evidence—in Faulkner's poetry as well as in the fiction, essays, and interviews—that writing for Faulkner was deeply sexual: passionate, orgasmic, and fundamentally unsettling. As many critics have pointed out (André Bleikasten most productively), the early work, in particular, is thick with observations linking writing and sex.[14] Indeed, a review essay written four years before *The Sound and the Fury* shows an author remarkably aware of the process taking place within him:

> I was not interested in verse for verse's sake then [in adolescence]. I read and employed verse, firstly, for the purpose of furthering various philanderings in which I was engaged, secondly, to complete a youthful gesture I was then making, of being "different" in a small town. Later, my concupiscence waning, I turned inevitably to verse, finding therein an emotional counterpart far more satisfactory for two reasons: (1) No partner was required (2) It was so much simpler just to close a book, and take a walk. . . .
>
> . . . Therefore, I believe I came as near as possible to approaching poetry with an unprejudiced mind. . . . Having used verse, I would now allow verse to use me if it could.[15]

What's remarkable about this passage is its anticipation of the sense of writing as bundling together a "masculine" drive toward erotic discovery and a "feminine" surrender to being discovered that would find its clearest articulation in one of the two 1933 prefaces to *The Sound and the Fury,* beginning with the second sentence in which Faulkner claims to have learned to approach language "with a kind of alert respect, as you approach dynamite; even with joy, as you approach women: perhaps with the same secretly unscrupulous intentions" and climaxing with the famous passage describing the writing of the novel as producing an "emotion definite and physical and yet nebulous to describe:

that ecstasy, that eager and joyous faith and anticipation of surprise which the yet unmarred sheet beneath my hand held inviolate and unfailing, waiting for release" ("An Introduction," *Southern Review*, 226).[16]

Though these two passages certainly merit attention via any number of feminist approaches, my interest in them at this moment lies in their ability to suggest that Faulkner well understood the Freudian sense of sublimation. Thus taking seriously Faulkner's description of the process driving both the discovery and the mapping of Yoknapatawpha involves thinking through how his little postage stamp releases sex into textual circulation; or, to be more exact, to considering how "writing" and "sex" might produce each other as passionate practices generated in, and generating, a public private space, a place both violated and inviolate. I should make clear that I am not simply rearticulating claims made well and elsewhere about sex as a constant yet multivalent subject in Faulkner's work (not only as a metaphor for artistic creation but also as a symbol of class and racial difference, a coefficient of a gendered power system, and a symptom of self-division), nor do I see my discussion as constituting a further chapter in the study of narrative as sexual allegory—though I will analyze an early thematizing of sex and writing in the fiction in order to make my point.[17] Rather, I am interested in seeing what happens to our understanding of Yoknapatawpha if we consider writing as a form of gratification, of release, that, for Faulkner, worked like sex, and that thus required the regular appearance—the repetition—of certain recognizable features if it were to come off satisfactorily.

The first fruit of Faulkner's sublimation into Yoknapatawpha, *Flags in the Dust* (identified by Faulkner as *Sartoris* in his description of the "little postage stamp of native soil"), deploys a transactional understanding of "writing sex" in the letters Byron Snopes sends to Narcissa Benbow; that this material was of some importance to Faulkner is indicated in his decision to return to it and continue working on it in short story form, through different versions and two titles, before finally publishing it in the January 1933 issue of *Scribner's* as "There Was a Queen."[18] The Narcissa/Byron material is thus an early example of the sublimation and repetition that inaugurated Yoknapatawpha as a creative entity and that provided the structural tension necessary to sustain this psychic geography over multiple articulations; it appears in the novel that is widely understood as Faulkner's last apprentice work (he himself called it "the germ of my apocrypha"), the one precipitating that "shutting" of one door and opening of another, ushering him finally into the realm of art.[19] I want further to propose that this material provides an opportunity for thinking through the relationship between two modes of writing sex—the erotic and the pornographic—that spiral through Yoknapatawpha as complementary and competing manifestations of the sublimation that drove Faulkner's art, and that a full appreciation of this spiraling (or "coiling," to use a favorite Faulkner term) is key for beginning to think through how Faulknerian repetition both seduces and repels.

Faulkner makes clear that, taken in the flesh, Byron Snopes, keeper of the books of the Sartoris bank in Jefferson, repels Narcissa Benbow. In their lone face-to-face encounter, mediated by the bars of the teller's window, Narcissa observes Byron's "forearms, from which the sleeves had been turned back, and the fine reddish hair which clothed them down to the second joints of his fingers; and . . . she remarked with a faint distinct distaste and a little curiosity, since it was not particularly warm today, the fact that his arms and hands were beaded with perspiration." These observations, however, are "not long in her consciousness," and she calmly accepts "the notes"—here, the banknotes produced as evidence of Byron's ability to correctly read and translate Narcissa's ciphered desires—that "he pushed under the grille to her." As Narcissa makes note, however absent-mindedly, of Byron, so Byron makes note of Narcissa: when she opens her pocketbook to put away the cash, he catches sight of his own letter lying secreted in the purse's "blue satin maw." It is not clear whether it is the sight of Narcissa herself or the glimpse of his letter in "her bag" that transfixes Byron, but he remains frozen and erect behind the bars of the teller window, sweating, head bowed, "his hand [making] a series of neat, meaningless figures on the pad beneath it" until Narcissa finally passes out of sight. Able to move again, he discovers that the pad of paper on which he had been doodling "adhered to his sweating wrist, so that when he removed his arm it came away also, then its own weight freed it and it dropped to the floor."[20]

Byron sweats; he writes; and his writing sticks: Narcissa cannot bring herself to discard the notes he sends her, despite her own misgivings and the advice of Jenny Du Pre. Clearly, Byron's letters lord it over her in ways "not . . . in her consciousness"—and neither can Byron free himself from the compulsion that drives his writing. Far from easing "his sleepless desire moiled in obscene shapes and images," writing only enlarges his obsession (*Flags* 225). Arguably, it is as much the sight of his letter in Narcissa's purse as the encounter with the woman herself that prompts Byron again to take up the pen and, in his "flowing Spencerian hand," write yet another letter. Readings of the relationship between Narcissa and Byron brought into being by the letters have drawn on critical modes both deconstructive and psychoanalytic to illuminate those aspects of Narcissa that make her susceptible to their lure, and Byron himself is no less vulnerable.[21] He is driven not only by his own "obscene" fantasies but by the relentless hounding of his juvenile amanuensis, Virgil Beard ("Got another business letter to write tonight, Mr Snopes? . . . Going to write another letter, Mr Snopes? . . . Got air other letter to write yet, Mr Snopes?"), whose "steadfast and unassertive" prodding ("like a mild but chronic disease" [255]) is driven by an epic greed and a canny understanding that the value of *his* writing (which is quite literally a rewriting, a cold and calculated repetition of once-passionate letters) derives from Byron's desire to disguise his hand. Faulkner makes this clear in an exchange that follows Virgil's copying of the letter Byron writes after the encounter with Narcissa in the bank, an exchange that turns on Virgil's threat to have his father visit the post office:

> The boy recapped the pen and thrust the chair back, and Snopes produced a small paper bag from his coat.
> The boy took it soberly. "Much obliged, Mr Snopes," he said. He opened it and squinted into it. "It's funny that air gun dont come on."
> "It sure is," Snopes agreed. "I dont know why it dont come."
> "Maybe it got lost in the post office," the boy suggested.
> "It may have. I reckon that's about what happened to it. I'll write 'em again, tomorrow."
> The boy rose, but he stood yet with his straw-colored hair and his bland, innocent face. He took a piece of candy from the sack and ate it without enthusiasm. "I reckon I better tell papa to go to the post office and ask 'em if it got lost."
> "No, I wouldn't do that," Snopes said quickly. "You wait; I'll 'tend to it. We'll get it, all right."
> "Papa wouldn't mind. He could go over there soon's he comes home and see about it. I could find him right now, and ask him to do it, I bet."

"He couldn't do no good," Snopes answered. "You leave it to me. I'll get that gun, all right."

"I could tell him I been working for you," the boy pursued. "I remember them letters."

"No, no, you wait and let me 'tend to it. I'll see about it first thing tomorrow."

"All right, Mr Snopes." He ate another piece of candy, without enthusiasm. He moved toward the door. "I remember ever' one of them letters. I bet I could sit down and write 'em all again. I bet I could." (*Flags* 117–18)

Virgil's hypothesis that his promised gun "got lost in the post office" has a special resonance for those familiar with Faulkner's own brief career as postmaster at the University of Mississippi, a job he refused twice before capitulating to the insistence of Phil Stone that he leave New York City and return to Oxford to take it, and one he filled with something less than distinction from December 1921 until his firing in October 1924.[22] In a three-page letter informing Faulkner of his imminent dismissal, US postal inspector Mark Weber wrote that his investigation revealed

> that you are neglectful of your duties, in that you are a habitual reader of books and magazines, and seem reluctant to cease reading long enough to wait on the patrons; that you have a book being printed at the present time, the greater part of which was written while on duty at the post-office [this was Faulkner's first poetry collection, *The Marble Faun*]; that some of the patrons will not trust you to forward their mail, because of your past carelessness. . . . That you are indifferent to interest of patrons, unsocial, and rarely ever speak to patrons of the office unless absolutely necessary; that you do not give the office the proper attention, opening and closing same at your convenience; that you can be found playing golf during office hours. . . . That you mistreat mail of all classes, including registered mail; [and] that you have thrown mail with return postage guaranteed and all other classes in the garbage can by the side entrance, near the rear door. . . . That you have permitted . . . unauthorized persons to have access to the workroom of the office . . . and have permitted card playing in the office. (Blotner 1:363–64)

As this litany makes clear, Faulkner enjoyed life at the P.O. insofar as it provided him with a base of personal, fraternal operations, serving as a kind of private clubhouse; he resented those aspects of the job connected to its status as "a public trust" (1:365). It was the occasion of his firing that prompted Faulkner's first use of the image of the postage stamp—that evidence that the tax has been paid enabling the public conveyance of private correspondence—as a symbol of his relationship to the world: "I reckon I'll be at the beck and call of folks with money all my life," Faulkner told his friend Skeet Kincannon, "but thank God I won't ever again have to be at the beck and call of every son of a bitch who's got two cents to buy a stamp" (1:365).[23]

But there is more going on here than a kind of personal inside joke (with Faulkner as model for postmaster, Virgil does well to suspect that his gun has "got lost"), for the author's experiences at the post office and Byron's life as a bookkeeper read each other in several ways. Both men are "jailed" in an interior landscape that frames community as something to be observed rather than lived (Byron behind the teller's grille in a bank filled with communal activity, Faulkner in the "cage" separating the public mailboxes from the private postal workroom); both men are employed in work that involves the care and handling of circulating "notes"; and both are engaged in writing projects that have no connection to the work they are being paid to do.[24] As his name suggests, Byron is a figure for the author/poet, but one as yet unsublimated and so a "desprate" man trapped in a repetition so compulsive and uncontrolled that it refuses redirection onto other paths (*Flags* 286).[25] Byron's writing is undertaken solely "for the purpose of furthering . . . philandering," and thus is pornographic in the sense articulated by Arthur Danto in his discussion of the work of Robert Mapplethorpe: it is a means to some other end rather than an end in itself.[26] Failing to attain its end, and having no intrinsic merit, it fails utterly (as the literary quality of the notes makes clear).[27]

My discussion of Byron's letters here is tailored to my point and so necessarily streamlined; I do not, for instance, explore the ways in which Byron's compulsions express not only sexual desire but also class antagonism, nor do I discuss Faulkner's further development of this material in "There Was a Queen."[28] It's clear that the letters exert a considerable power over Narcissa despite her "distaste" for their author and her insistence that they make her feel "dirty"—she keeps them in her lingerie drawer, perhaps a fate the young

Faulkner wished for his own poetry (at one point Narcissa "lightly" tells Miss Jenny that she is "saving them until I get enough for a book, then I'll bring them all out for you to read" [*Flags* 225])—but the source of this power remains obscure, and later portraits of Narcissa (most especially *Sanctuary*'s) as a sexual hypocrite seem compensatory, as if Faulkner were trying to account for something within the character that he himself barely understands. My point in drawing attention to Byron's letters is a fairly simple one: to indicate how, through an imaginative reconfiguration of his own groping toward literary art, Faulkner can be seen meditating on the relationship between sexual desire and writing, taking stock of his own early experiences and, through this first approach to the territory of Yoknapatawpha, preparing himself for the sublimation (which amounts to a kind of renunciation) that grants him, in his words, the "complete liberty"—the wide open spaces—to use his talent "to its absolute top."

If a meditation on an unsublimated, pornographic poetics has a role to play in the emergence of Yoknapatawpha, the erotic experience that was the writing of *The Sound and the Fury* made clear to Faulkner the many artistic gratifications such sublimation could bring about. The text seems "to explode on the paper before" him as Faulkner enters into his kingdom, experiencing aesthetic sublimation as the sublime: a rediscovery of the self as fundamentally other, a reconfiguration of a familiar land into an exciting *terra incognita*. *The Sound and the Fury* marks Faulkner's entry into Yoknapatawpha as that place where he is free to lose himself in writing such that he is reconstituted in writing, a reproductive "writing sex" in which no partner is required because the partner is the self. Bleikasten has observed that

> with Faulkner the autobiographical impulse is more elusive, more decentered, more disseminated. Had he completed "Elmer," the story of a young American painter he started to write before *Mosquitoes,* during his first visit to Europe, his second novel might have been a comic portrait of the artist. But the point is precisely that he did not finish "Elmer." Even in his first two novels it is fairly obvious that Faulkner does not belong with the confessional school of the Wolfes, Fitzgeralds, and Hemingways, those barely masked autobiographers who never ceased to embroider on their own life stories. (*Ink of Melancholy* 28)

This is in many ways true. Faulkner's work certainly was not "confessional" in the manner of a Thomas Wolfe. Yet I quibble with Bleikasten's implication that, at some definable point, Faulkner's fiction "ceased to embroider" his own life story. On the contrary, I would argue that Faulkner's writing was more deeply and thoroughly knotted into his psyche than that of Wolfe, Fitzgerald, or Hemingway: it was more intimately experienced and thus personally revealing in ways that transcend biographical narrative. Yoknapatawpha wasn't simply his creation ("William Faulkner, Sole Owner & Proprietor"; "a cosmos of my own . . . a kind of keystone of the Universe"; "Surveyed and mapped for this volume by William Faulkner")—it *was him.* "I am telling the same story over and over again," he told Cowley at an early stage in the process of assembling *The Portable Faulkner,* "which is myself and the world. . . . This I think accounts for what people call the obscurity, the involved formless 'style,' endless sentences. I'm trying to say it all in one sentence, between one Cap and one period. I'm still trying to put it all, if possible, on one pinhead. I don't know how to do it. All I know to do is to keep on trying in a new way" (*Faulkner-Cowley File* 14).[29]

It is this determination to "keep on trying" that brings us back to the problem of repetition. For if the two 1933 prefaces to *The Sound and the Fury* together comprise a description of the entry into Yoknapatawpha as a kind of ecstasy, they also confess to the evanescent nature of that ecstasy and describe attempts to recover it:

> I learned only from the writing of Sanctuary that there was something missing; something which The Sound and the Fury gave me and Sanctuary did not. When I began As I Lay Dying I had discovered what it was and knew that it would be also missing in this case because this would be a deliberate book. I set out deliberately to write a tour-de-force. Before I ever put pen to paper and set down the first word, I knew what the last word would be and almost where the last period would fall. Before I began I said, I am going to write a book by which, at a pinch, I can stand or fall if I never touch ink again. So when I finished it the cold satisfaction was there, as I had expected, but as I had also expected the other quality which The Sound and the Fury had given me was absent. . . . I said, It is because I knew too much about this book before I began

to write it. I said, More than likely I shall never again have to know this much about a book before I begin to write it, and next time it will return. I waited almost two years, then I began Light in August, knowing no more about it than a young woman, pregnant, walking along a strange country road. I thought, I will recapture it now, since I know no more about this book than I did about The Sound and the Fury when I sat down before the first blank page.

It did not return. ("An Introduction," *Southern Review,* 226)

Though "erotic" and "pornographic" are terms appearing nowhere in this passage, and though there is no reference to Yoknapatawpha as an imaginative geography, Faulkner's description of his effort to recapture the sublimity of writing *The Sound and the Fury* can be mapped onto a framework structured through those ideas. In attempting to account for the experience of writing his fourth novel, Faulkner comes to two related conclusions: writing *The Sound and the Fury* was "ecstasy" because he did not know where he was going, and this lack of narrative teleology meant that the writing itself—the process of discovery—was its own end. When he knows in advance the "end" of his writing (as he did with both *Sanctuary* and *As I Lay Dying*), that ecstatic loss and rediscovery of self in writing does not appear. Faulkner accepts this as a consequence of the careful plotting these novels required and imagines that he will recapture his love through a new project for which he has no narrative map.

But his love fails him. Not because he knows how the story will end (since he does not), but because even as he discovers his narrative he continues to treat the writing itself as a means toward some other end—though now that end is the recapture of "that eager and joyous faith and anticipation of surprise" that came unbidden in the writing of *The Sound and the Fury.* So long as he looks for that emotion, so long as he pursues it—wooing, through language, that orgasmic release *of* language, and much as he had once wooed women through verse—it will not come to him.

* * *

There is probably no other aspect of Faulkner's writing more commented on than its obsession with loss. The Faulkner of the 1933 prefaces is an author who seems to have resigned himself to the loss of his "heart's darling"—the loss of "the only thing in literature which would ever move me very much," which I would claim is not Caddy but the experience of surrendering himself to her discovery and so releasing her (and himself) into writing. Yet it's worth considering whether his return to *The Sound and the Fury,* prompted by service to Cowley's *Portable,* reanimated that abandoned project of recapturing the intensely private joy of writing it. Certainly, the letters Faulkner sends in those last dozen years of his life are marked, in what resembles a kind of midliterary life crisis, by a return to precisely the writing habits of his youth: wooing women through words (Jean Stein, Joan Williams), "being 'different' in a small town." That being different now meant speaking out on southern racial matters (rather than dressing as a dandy) and that the philanderings were now conducted under cover of marriage indicate the degree to which the stakes of repetition rose with age and respectability, but these surface differences do not disturb the underlying similarity. That the 1933 prefaces cut close to the bone is perhaps most clearly revealed in Faulkner's shamefaced reaction on the recovery of one version and its return to him in 1946. "Bless you for finding the introduction and sending it back to me," he wrote Robert Linscott. "I had forgotten what smug false sentimental windy shit it was. I will return the money for it, I would be willing to return double the amount for the chance of getting it out of danger and destroyed."[30] In the world of "sentimental windy" Faulknerian "shit," the introduction hardly holds its own against such later productions as *A Fable* and *The Reivers,* but Faulkner was right to feel embarrassed by the introduction. Not because it was "false" but because it was all too true, too revealing of himself and of his needs and desires as a writer.

My point here is not at all to diminish the significance for Faulkner, and for those of us who study his work, of the political and personal landscape of his final years. Quite the contrary: a sympathetic understanding of the creative and emotional challenges of that landscape helps us better understand the landscape of Yoknapatawpha, putting us in a position to view, analytically and disinterestedly, the flaws of the later work. This is perhaps to make the most obvious kind of point about the relationship between life and work. What is not so obvious, I think, and what I have tried to show here, is a connecting of the inner landscape ("the actual") and the work (the "apocryphal") that emphasizes the sexual aspect—the sublimation—of the *copula* linking the two, and that takes that thrilling dimension as one key to reading the arc of Faulkner's *oeuvre*. What I have offered here, then, is less a reading of the later work than a prolegomenon to such a reading. A pornographic approach to writing that sees it as a means toward a "concupiscent" end is abandoned once writing reveals its own ecstatic properties; initially acknowledged as a blessed if momentary moment of erotically charged enlightenment, this ecstasy becomes the object of an increasingly frantic effort to recapture lost glory that ushers in a return to the pornographic. Seen in this light, much of the late writing—most especially its bombastic and insistent revisiting of the scenes of past narrative, structural, and rhetorical triumphs—appears as a type of "desprate" letter, a lorn, pleading search that is a kind of writerly grief.

Yoknapatawpha was Faulkner's postage stamp in the sense that it legitimized and put into public circulation private letters to the world that may well otherwise have remained (like Byron's notes) subliterary. It is simultaneously Faulkner's place and space, in the relational sense that the geographer Yi-Fu Tuan has explained: "place is security, space is freedom: we are attached to the one and long for the other."[31] Lexically speaking, the word "post" is all over the map—not only the mail, it is also a pillar, a garrison or place of trade; it is also to hurry, to send a message, to delay, to publish; it is what comes after; and, according to at least one dictionary of English slang at the turn of the nineteenth century, it is sexual intercourse—and the map of Yoknapatawpha is all over postings: a space made of letters, in letters, for letters.[32] Like Roland Barthes's Japan—the locus that inspired the quotation that stands at the head of this chapter—it is an imagined space set upon a real place, where Faulkner experienced an ecstatic flash that brought him to writing and then abandoned him there, surrounded by the vast emptiness that language maps but never fills.

Postscript

What I see now in "Posting Yoknapatawpha," twenty years after it was first written, is how it made possible the work that followed. Thinking about Yoknapatawpha as both enabling and constricting; exploring the interpretive options that became available once Faulkner's sexualized understanding of writing was more firmly in focus: "Posting Yoknapatawpha" constituted my first foray into these themes. For those reasons, the piece is important to me.

Whether it's important to the larger Faulkner studies community is an open question. To be sure, the themes it engages have been explored by other scholars since its publication in 2004, if typically as separate projects rather than a conjoined endeavor.[33] It's possible that the chapter's thesis postulating a link between Faulkner's "secretly unscrupulous" approach to writing and the creation of Yoknapatawpha accounts for its low profile.

Be that as it may, "Posting Yoknapatawpha" also remains special to me for its directly declared interest in exploring the rebarbative in Faulkner not as a project for redemption (by reframing the problematic as transcendent, for instance) but rather as the excavation of the constitutive bones of a work. As I noted in the introduction, this step into interpretive disinterest, wherein Faulkner's work becomes a true subject of study rather than a cause to champion, is a step constitutive of the Faulknerista.

INTERLUDE

Chapters 1, 6, and 7 were written consecutively over the course of the 2004 Michaelmas term, when I had the good fortune to hold a research fellowship at the Rothermere American Institute at the University of Oxford. Though they share common themes—the relationship between sexuality and language; the marks Faulkner's encounters with extrasouthern material and aliterary media left on his fiction—the pieces were composed for different reasons and, accordingly, took different novels as opportunities to engage those themes. Chapters 1 and 6 were written in response to invitations to contribute to edited volumes that would be published by Cambridge (on the modernist novel) and Blackwell (a Faulkner edition in the *Companion* series). As noted in the postscript to chapter 1, "Putting It All on One Pinhead," for all its gestures toward the organizing principles of biography, chronology, and modernist literary history, lands on disjunction and incommensurability as key concepts for understanding Faulkner's literary project. That approach grew out of the thinking that informed "Posting Yoknapatawpha," written two years earlier, and it spilled into the writing of "'C'est vraiment dégueulasse': Last Words in *A bout de souffle* and *If I Forget Thee, Jerusalem*," appearing here as chapter 6 and the project I turned to immediately after completing chapter 1.

From its initial, fairly modest premise—an exploration of the phenomenon of mis- or non-represented last words in Faulkner's novel and Godard's film, a premise rooted in the by then well-established Faulkner studies subfield examining Faulkner's work in, and effects on, modern cinema—"C'est vraiment dégueulasse" quickly overflowed its banks, flooding into a broader discussion of the relationship between commercial value and artistic worth.

To be sure, Faulkner's years of Hollywood scriptwriting have not gone without scholarly notice, and Faulkner studies is currently seeing a welcome surge of renewed interest in the subject. Yet it's worth recalling that "C'est vraiment dégueulasse" appeared at a moment when that line of analysis was shifting away from a notion of "high" modernism and commercial film as aesthetic antagonists to today's more nuanced understanding of their interrelationship. Now well underway, this turn to a deeper, more open-minded approach to Faulkner's engagements with mass media productions is producing some truly fine work.[1] "C'est vraiment dégueulasse" was an absolute joy to write, and it has been a continuing pleasure to see how its then-uncertain interpretive propositions have come to inform many of today's operating critical assumptions.

For that essay, and for chapter 1, the work lay largely in fulfilling interpretive promises I'd made to editors in five-hundred-word abstracts. Revisions would be requested, to be sure, but the thesis for each piece had been established (or at least gestured toward) in advance, and it was certain that the work would see the light of day. By contrast, "Making Camp: *Go Down, Moses*" was drafted with no immediate prospect of publication. It was an exploratory and speculative project, written for myself in an attempt to formulate an answer—or two or three—to an interpretive question with which I'd become mildly obsessed: just what was Percival Brownlee doing in *Go Down, Moses?* The story of Brownlee had haunted me from my first reading of the novel, and in the way typical of hauntings: was there truly anything significant *there,* or was I seeing things? What was Faulkner's goal in folding the awkwardly comedic Brownlee escapades into the McCaslin ledgers' gruesome record of suicide and incest? Was Brownlee gay? If so, how did that matter?

In retrospect, it's easy to see the threads of past interpretive projects coming together in this piece: how my interests in Faulkner's approaches to race and sexuality, and my habit of comparative, cross-media reading, paved the way for this particular interpretive approach. It's also clear in hindsight that it was the writing of *this* piece, more than any other, that made me a Faulknerista.

That, and the experience of getting it published. Sent initially to one of the discipline's most competitive journals, where blind review was the standard practice, "Making Camp" received "revise and resubmit" reports from two readers who offered contradictory reactions and advice. The first reader, expressing admiration for the originality and strength of the overall argument, made specific, detailed suggestions for revision that would balance and streamline an essay that, in its early incarnation, was unquestionably distorted and overlong (the original draft was nearly fourteen thousand words). Closing on a note of confidence, this reader recommended that the revised essay be sent directly to the editorial board.

The second reader was less sanguine. Terming the piece "at once a bold and too-timid article" that, despite its length, was "unfinished by about five pages," this reader dutifully noted the essay's "carefully layered argument... about homosexuality, abjection, grief, and camp" and "nuanced originality" in reading "the homosexual function in *Go Down, Moses*" before voicing its primary complaint: a lack of "courage" in "naming the critical fathers to be slain." "I wonder who it is, mainly, this author is opposing," the reader mused, "since this essay would seem to occupy a position beyond the merely suggestive.... I mean to say that [while] it is useful to identify those who help enable this argument (Davis, Gwin, etc.), who's the bigger specter s/he won't name?" Unwilling to send the edited essay directly to the board, this reader stipulated that the revised essay be returned to them for further review.

Choosing to focus on the promise both readers saw in the piece and heartened at the prospect of publication in such a respected journal, I set to work on revisions that would tighten and streamline while also, somehow, expanding and enlarging. In the process, I quickly realized how problematic I found the second reader's insistence that the essay needed to engage in scholarly patricide if its claims were to be taken seriously. I suppose my resistance was gendered, in a manner overdetermined by the demand that I assume the role of Oedipus, but it was not rooted in some pseudofeminine dictum to "play nice": If there was one thing I had even less interest in than slaying "critical fathers," it was playing the part of a deferential, dutiful daughter. Rather, and as I sought to explain in the essay's final paragraph, my unwillingness was rooted in the conviction that, ultimately, efforts to advance understanding are not always well served by aggressive, categorical repudiation of past practices or beliefs. There's no question that righteous denunciation feels good. But its capacity to *do* good is hardly certain.

Revisions accomplished, I sent the piece off and awaited response. And waited. After many months, I hazarded an inquiry to the managing editor, who (after apologies for failing to follow up) informed me that the second reader—the one who saw scholarship as chiefly an oedipal *agon* and who had refused to send the piece on to the editorial board without a second review—had declined to read my revised submission. Faced with this development, the managing editor elected to reengage the first reader, who deemed the essay still publishable but now expressed "unease" with the revisions. "The essay is both (obviously) stronger and (subtly) weaker than when I first read it," they wrote. "It suffers perhaps (if I may put it thus) from its exacerbated self-consciousness as a strategic entry into a vexed discursive field." With this review in hand, the journal's editor in chief decided to request yet another round of revision before bringing "Making Camp" to the editorial board for decision. At this point, I decided to pull the essay and submit it to a different journal, where it was published.

A frustrating set of circumstances, to be sure—but, ultimately, a productive and even empowering one, since it was through this experience that I at last shed the "exacerbated self-consciousness" detected by that first reader. For while I did make a last set of revisions before publication, those edits focused on removing the hesitation and hedging that I now recognized as symptoms of speaking my piece *sotto voce*. I realized, in these final edits, that the point was not to "get it right"—that, I finally understood, was an impossibility rooted in a fantasy of absolute critical mastery. Rather, the point was to claim my voice, and to do so in a way that might clear a way for other voices, other scholars with similar questions; the point was not to slay some imagined paternal enemy but, rather, to build a community. Disagreement would follow, of course—no intellectual enterprise proceeds without it—but the disagreements would be driven more by curiosity and exploration than by the need to dominate and control. At least, such was the hope that informed the writing of the final draft, and it's one I still hold.

"Unhistoricizing Faulkner" was composed for the 2007 Faulkner and Yoknapatawpha conference, held on the topic of Faulkner's sexualities. Here, I sought to further develop two salient ideas from "Making Camp": first, the proposal that Faulkner's work offered prospects for queer theory that would provide fresh routes into the fiction while expanding our understanding of queer theory's applicability beyond its then-dominant biographically based approach; and second, the notion that historicist readings of Faulkner, powerful though they had proven to be, could not account for all the effects the fiction had on contemporary readers.

In the years since, historicist readings of Faulkner have continued to dominate, an unsurprising fact given the novels' relevance to the nation's ongoing racial trauma.[2] While not nearly as mainstream, queer readings of Faulkner—or readings exploring sexuality as textuality—have found a place in Faulkner studies, as evidenced by the 2020 publication of Phillip Gordon's *Gay Faulkner*—a work whose very title was unimaginable twenty years ago. I have a bit more to say about this development generally, and Gordon's work in particular, in the "postlude" following chapter 8. Here I will simply note that the relationship between historicist and queer readings of Faulkner may be understood as one manifestation of the relationship between the Faulknerian and the Faulknerista: at once reciprocal and resistant, contrasting and complementary.

6

"C'est vraiment dégueulasse"

LAST WORDS IN *A BOUT DE SOUFFLE* AND *IF I FORGET THEE, JERUSALEM*

> A plea for an America that is guilty gives me the chance of a better hearing.
> —ÉRIC ROHMER

About halfway through Jean-Luc Godard's *A bout de souffle*, Patricia Franchini, the American in Cold War Paris, asks her charming, thuggish French boyfriend, Michel Poiccard, if he's ever read *The Wild Palms*. The two are sitting on Patricia's bed in her tiny room, and their conversation up until this point has centered on love, so Michel's response—"Take your jersey off"—is not an *absolute* non sequitur, especially given that his answer to her earlier question ("Do you know William Faulkner?" "No, who is it? You've slept with him?") has already made clear to the film's viewers that Michel is not quite *un homme de lettres*. Undeterred, Patricia (played by Jean Seberg) reads aloud to her lover: "Listen," she says, "the last sentence [*la dernière phrase*] is beautiful. 'Between grief and nothing I will take grief.'" Having read the line in its original English, she turns to Michel (played by Jean-Paul Belmondo) and repeats it in French ("*entre le chagrin et le néant c'est le chagrin que je choisis*"), then asks him which he would choose. Michel's first response follows from his initial reaction to Faulkner's eleventh novel (and to Faulkner himself): "Show me your toes; a woman's toes are most important." When Patricia insists on an answer, Michel's reply is impatient and categorical: "Grief is idiotic. I'd choose nothingness. It's not any better, but grief's a compromise. You've got to have all or nothing."[1]

This intertextual moment—one of many in a film that also cites Louis Aragon, Guillaume Apollinaire, Lenin, Dylan Thomas, and Maurice Sachs—has received little attention in the body of work that has grown up around Godard's now-classic film (shot in 1959, released in 1960, and known to English-speaking viewers as *Breathless*), but it has not gone completely unnoticed. In his study on Faulkner and film, Bruce Kawin claims that the double-stranded novel of sex, death, flood, and imprisonment is centrally important not only to the meaning and structure of *A bout de souffle* but also to much of Godard's later work, though he avers that "in *Breathless,* [Godard] appears to have in mind only the title novella [the "Wild Palms" narrative] and not the entire work."[2] According to Kawin, *If I Forget Thee, Jerusalem* (as the novel has been known since the 1990 corrected text restored Faulkner's original title) has a plot that "clearly parallels" the film, even though *A bout de souffle* is "just as clearly at pains to render those correspondences as ironic as possible," and in much the same way that it renders ironic its correspondences to the movies of the American B-film company Monogram Pictures to which it is dedicated (Kawin 151). However, Kawin does not see the quotation itself functioning ironically in *A bout de souffle,* for, at the end of the film, "Michel gets 'nothing' and Patrice [sic] is left with the burden of remembering him, of trying to understand him, and of having caused his death." He names two of the novel's main characters to indicate how Faulkner's book, in his view, helps us interpret Godard's heroine: Patricia is "Harry with a difference, and Charlotte as a coward" (Kawin 151).

In his study of intertextuality in French New Wave cinema, T. Jefferson Kline takes a different approach. Though the quotation is useful for the light it sheds on the relationship between Patricia and Michel, that relationship is best understood not in terms of individual psychology but rather as a local example of the film's true subject: the post–World War II "*rapprochement franco-américain*" (as Michel jokingly calls sex with Patricia) that saw France flooded with American films, American books, and American music, all of which deeply influenced Godard's film practice. By citing the novel, Kline argues, Godard invites viewers to interpret the film not simply through the immediate quotation but also through the entire work, and he finds the "Old Man" narrative a fruitful, if silent, intertext. The tall convict, imprisoned after his failed attempt to stage a train robbery like those he'd read of in "the paper novels—

the Diamond Dicks and Jesse Jameses and such," "resembles no one so much as Jean-Luc Godard in his attempt to construct his own enterprise on the basis of literary and cinematic models.... Both convict and filmmaker have constructed their work on the basis of quotation, and in both cases the quotation has an uncanny way of betraying the erstwhile imitator."[3] Kline cites Godard's later repudiation of the film as evidence in support of his thesis: "*A bout de souffle* is a film that I just can't look at without beginning to perspire, to feel, I don't know, as if I'd been forced to strip naked at a moment that I didn't feel like it, and that's always seemed a bit strange to me.... It's a film that came out of fascism and that is full of fascist overtones" (Kline 185).

If Kawin sees Faulkner's contribution to Godard's artistic practice as largely enabling and liberatory (a perspective that repeats, on the literary critical level, the view Eisenhower-era Americans had of their relationship to postwar France), then, Kline is less sanguine, seeing *A bout de souffle*'s engagement with American modernism as signaling a dalliance with "fascist" aesthetics, a dangerous liaison with forms and modes of cultural expression more complacent than critical. That each scholar mounts his reading by privileging different aspects of Faulkner's novel—for Kawin, the crucial intertext is "Wild Palms," whereas for Kline it is "Old Man"—perhaps signals that the reasons for Godard's interest in Faulkner are less obvious, and more complicated, than might at first appear.

As contradictory as they are, Kline and Kawin's discussions of Godard's purposes in quoting Faulkner resemble each other in one revealing particular. They both fall silent on a rather obvious mistake Godard makes in his use of Faulkner: The line Patricia reads is not, in fact, *la dernière phrase* of the novel, but rather the last sentence of the "Wild Palms" narrative. It is true that "Wild Palms" ends with Harry's famous vow (and accompanying, if somewhat less frequently acknowledged, masturbation); but the novel itself goes on for another dozen or so pages, wrapping up the details of "Old Man" by explaining how the tall convict's heroic "escape" gets him an extended prison sentence. As we know, the actual last words of *If I Forget Thee, Jerusalem* contain an expletive—"'Women, shit,' the tall convict said" (*Jerusalem* 287)—that Faulkner's publishers refused to print, and Faulkner chose to accept the traditional sign of censorship rather than change the objectionable word. Thus the novel the journalist Van Doude gives to Patricia, and from which she reads aloud to Michel, almost undoubtedly concludes with "'Women,—!' the tall convict said," a last sentence that closes the novel on a "nothing" something other than the opposite of grief (unless, as may have been the case, Godard had in mind the 1952 French translation of the novel, which offers yet a third last sentence: "'—Ah! les femmes!' dit le grand forçat").[4]

The film's confusion (or disingenuousness: viewers can clearly see that Patricia is not at the end of the book as she reads the passage aloud) over the novel's true last words could be attributed either to Godard's indifference to the facts of his intertext (not impossible) or to the French publication history of the novel Godard knew as *Les palmiers sauvages,* a publication history that may have led him to believe he had accurately quoted *la dernière phrase*—were it not for the fact that mistaken last words (and women) have a crucial role to play in *A bout de souffle*, as well. Gunned down by the detective to whom Patricia has betrayed him, Michel looks up at his lover as he lies on a Parisian street and quietly mutters an assessment of his fate—"*C'est vraiment dégueulasse*" ("It's really disgusting")—before dying.[5] Patricia, though, doesn't quite hear him. "What did he say?" she asks the policemen gathered around the body, and Inspector Vital responds, "He said, 'You are really a bitch'" ("*Vous êtes vraiment une dégueulasse*").[6] Throughout the film, however, Patricia's American college French never has been quite the match for Michel's slangy argot, and the case is no different here. "What is '*dégueulasse*'?" she asks, ending the film with a final sentence that feels like more than a simple query about translation (Andrew 146).

This subject of improper, or misconstrued, last words matters because the questions it raises are linked to larger questions about the relationship between commercial value and artistic worth that are engaged in Faulkner's novel and in Godard's film, questions both texts address directly—indeed, the confluence of commerce and art is a concern central to both novel and film—but that neither is able to satisfactorily settle. My project here, then, is not simply to explain an intertext (that is, to interpret Godard's reasons for quoting Faulkner), but to uncover the common expressive practices and artistic interests subtending these two works: not only to read *A bout de souffle* through *If I Forget Thee, Jerusalem* but also to read Faulkner's novel through Godard's film. Both *If I Forget Thee, Jerusalem* and *A bout de souffle* articulate their concerns through references to expressive media similar to, and yet different from, their own: cinema and pulp fiction in the case of Faulkner's novel, literature and American genre movies for Godard's film. Faulkner wrote *If I Forget Thee, Jerusalem* after a stint of Hollywood screenwriting, his third (and at that point his longest) period of employment in the film industry and one that saw the beginning of an intense, highly erotic but also emotionally fraught affair with Howard Hawks's secretary and sometime "script girl," Meta Carpenter, an affair that lasted for more than fifteen years and that seems to have progressed along lines not all that different from a classic Hollywood melodrama ("'Bear with me, Meta,' he implored once again and I kissed him and put up a brave Irene Dunne-Ann Harding face").[7] Godard shot *A bout de souffle* after several years' apprenticeship as a film critic for *Cahiers du Cinéma*, where he and other future members of the New Wave group of filmmakers (François Truffaut, Éric Rohmer, Claude Chabrol) developed their *politique des auteurs*, essentially an assertion (it could not be called a theory) that great films, like great literature, were expressions of a single individual's artistic vision. Faulkner would later claim that he wrote *If I Forget Thee, Jerusalem* "to try to stave off what I thought was heart-break" over what he feared was the conclusive end of his affair with Carpenter (their relationship would see intermittent revivals in the years after the book appeared), but the novel is at least as much engaged with the vexed entanglements of mass and "high" art production and consumption as with the complications of illicit love.[8] In fact, and as Richard Gray has pointed out, relations between the sexes in *If I Forget Thee, Jerusalem* are thoroughly enmeshed in the expressive structures of Hollywood and pulp fiction, structures that the novel itself does not entirely escape.[9] Likewise, years after the release of his first feature film, Godard, one of the most vociferous champions of an independent *auteur* film practice, characterized *A bout de souffle* as "a picture that I've done for others. . . . [Y]ou don't make a movie, the movie makes you."[10] I want to suggest that the complications at play here (Faulkner claiming he was writing out of love when, of course, he also was writing for the market; Godard discovering that "self"-expression is always shaped by "outside" forces) reveal the difficulty Faulkner and Godard experienced in attempting to effect a clean separation between art and commerce that would allow them to safeguard the former even as they exploited the latter— a difficulty that made it impossible for them to pronounce the last word on the relationship between the two.

CUNNING

> I have lived for the last six months in such a peculiar state of family complications and back complications that I still am not able to tell if the novel is all right or absolute drivel. To me, it was written just as if I had sat on the one side of a wall and the paper was on the other and my hand and the pen thrust through the wall and writing not only on invisible paper but in pitch darkness too, so that I could not even know if the pen still wrote on paper or not.
>
> —WILLIAM FAULKNER, qtd. in Joseph Blotner, *Faulkner: A Biography*

The composition and publication history of the novel that would first appear under the title *The Wild Palms* is well known, but it is worth reviewing that history, as well as salient aspects of the novel's appearance and reception in France. As he would recollect during class conferences at the University of Virginia, Faulkner began work on the novel with "Wild Palms," the story of the extravagant, doomed love affair of Harry Wilbourne and Charlotte Rittenmeyer, but found "that it needed a contrapuntal quality like music. And so I wrote the other story ["Old Man"] simply to underline the story of Charlotte and Harry. I wrote the two stories by alternate chapters. I'd write the chapter of one and then I would write the chapter of the other just as the musician puts in—puts in counterpoint behind the theme that he is working with."[11] Faulkner's appeal to musical counterpoint to describe a novel that proceeds through two alternating and seemingly unrelated narratives is more metaphorical than exact, of course, but Thomas L. McHaney's study of the manuscript leads him to conclude that Faulkner did, indeed, write the novel as he claimed, and the musical analogy does convey not only the novel's effect on readers but also the critical interrelatedness of the two narratives, an interrelatedness expressed at levels both formal and thematic.[12] However, that interrelatedness was quite blithely ignored in the years following the novel's initial appearance, starting in 1946 when Malcolm Cowley scissored out "Old Man" for inclusion in his *Portable Faulkner*. Two years later New American Library, treating the Mississippi convict's narrative as a novel, issued a paperback entitled *The Old Man,* following up later in the year with a paperback of *The Wild Palms* that contained only Harry and Charlotte's story. In 1954, New American Library published yet another edition, this time including both stories, but printing them as individual wholes, ignoring Faulkner's initial conception of the novel's interleaved, "contrapuntal" form. Finally, two years later, "Old Man" appeared yet again by itself as one of the *Three Famous Short Novels* published by Modern Library. The effect of these various editions, McHaney notes, "was that most readers first came to only half of the novel in one of these divided texts, an experience that caused them to ignore altogether the question of Faulkner's meaning and the purpose of the intricately related plots" (xv).

Faulkner's novel received a similar, though not so long-lasting, disaggregation in France. *Les palmiers sauvages* was printed through the first four numbers of the 1951 volume of Sartre's *Les temps modernes,* a redaction that, among other things, did indeed make Harry Wilbourne's vow *la dernière phrase* of the work for its initial French readers. This was also the first new work of Faulkner's to appear in France after the Nobel Prize, which fact made the novella's publication in Sartre's journal something of an event. In 1952, the year Éditions Gallimard brought out the complete work, an essay on the novel by its translator, Maurice-Edgar Coindreau, appeared in the January issue of *Les temps modernes,* and it strongly urged readers to accept the challenge presented by such a seemingly disjointed text:

> The two sections of *The Wild Palms* . . . illuminate each other, and without their alternation the deepest meaning of each would remain concealed. But this meaning is the only one which matters. To say that "Old Man" gains by being printed and read independently of "Wild Palms" is to pretend that a fugue would be more beautiful if the answer and the counter-subject were detached from the subject. I realize that the separation of the two stories makes them easier to read. But if William Faulkner is occasionally obscure, he is not willfully so. His complexities, whether of content or form, are never gratuitous. Consequently, they ought to be respected.[13]

That this essay also appeared as the preface to the French edition of the novel perhaps accounts for the fact that, after its first, partial appearance in *Les temps modernes, Les palmiers sauvages* was subjected to none of the editorial indignities visited on its American counterpart: the French reading public apparently accepted Coindreau's assertion that the novel worked as an organic whole despite its segmented structure.

McHaney and Coindreau are both correct in asserting that Faulkner's original intentions for the novel are lost if its two narratives are separated from each other, but it is worth keeping in mind that these editorial shenanigans proceeded with Faulkner's approval, sometimes grudging but always given. It is not always easy, in fact, to divine Faulkner's feelings about proposals to "excerpt" his work: sometimes he objected strenuously; other times he acquiesced almost carelessly. A 1946 letter to Random House senior editor Robert N. Linscott, written to cover *The Sound and the Fury* "Appendix" Faulkner had just produced for Cowley's *Portable,* is exemplary in this regard. Faulkner objects strongly to treating the new piece as a kind of foreword to the novel (the idea "seems bad . . . a deliberate pandering to those who won't make the effort to understand the book"), yet he goes on to propose a new edition of *The Sound and the Fury* that would bind it together with the excerpted "Wild Palms" section of *The Wild Palms* (Blotner 228). Faulkner also gave his approval to what was one of the most flagrant examples of editorial meddling in his career, the aforementioned 1954 New American Library edition of *The Wild Palms* that printed the two stories back-to-back as self-contained units rather than as interlocked narratives. He admitted to his agent, Saxe Commins, that "dismembering *The Wild Palms* will in my opinion destroy the over-all impact which I intended," but, now post-Nobel, he seems to have concluded that his artistic reputation was finally such as to "not need petty defending" (Blotner 352). Faulkner appeared willing, in other words, to tolerate a fairly high level of potential misunderstanding of his work so long as the various publishing schemes inviting such misunderstanding kept his books selling. Here, the seductive allurements of the market appear to trump the rigorous demands of art.

Add to this publication history developments of the recent past—the appearance of the corrected text, which turned *The Wild Palms* into *If I Forget Thee, Jerusalem,* and the adoption of that text as the basis for a revised French translation, *Si je t'oublie Jérusalem* (which offers yet another candidate for the novel's last words: "'—Les femmes. Font chier!' fit le grand forçat"), and we find ourselves faced with a novel quite remarkably protean, even by the standards of an author who perpetually revisited and revised his material.[14] Partly because of this odd publication history, a body of scholarship on *If I Forget Thee, Jerusalem* has only begun to take shape in the last twenty or so years. McHaney's study was among the first to recognize the novel as the serious and complex work it is, pointing out the multiple connections between the narratives, drawing out its allusions to the work of Dante and Hemingway (not only *A Farewell to Arms* but also "Hills Like White Elephants"), finding parallels in the novel's "philosophy" (if it can be called that) to the work of Schopenhauer and of Nietzsche, and going so far as to offer an interpretation of Harry's masturbation as he chooses grief over nothingness (McHaney 172–74). As valuable as McHaney's study is, however, it is limited by its insistence on passing judgment on Harry and Charlotte, dressing out the text with a poorly fitting "sin and redemption" schematic that reads the novel as an instantiation of the "endure and prevail" ethos of the Nobel Prize speech, an interpretive gambit characteristic of much Cold War Faulkner scholarship. McHaney also gives "Old Man" a decidedly secondary status; though he adopts Faulkner's term, "counterpoint," to describe the relationship between the two stories, his reading treats "Old Man" more as an accompaniment to "Wild Palms" than an equal voice. Most discomfiting for contemporary scholars, however—and not unrelated to the study's moralistic, myth-critical framework—is McHaney's strong condemnation of Charlotte, a condemnation that at times seems nearly misogynist in its intensity. In McHaney's view, Charlotte is "a female love buccaneer whose high regard for what she calls 'bitching' approaches an implied nymphomania"; she is "false and commercial," producing a debased art that provides the model for Harry's later brief career as an author of "primer-bald . . . sexual gumdrop[s]" (*Jerusalem* 104); she is "deceived by notions of romantic love" (which McHaney assumes come from sentimental counterparts to the convict's detective fiction, though Charlotte's reading matter is never described), "and snar[es] the innocent Wilbourne into her scheme" (McHaney 11, 8, 31). McHaney's connecting of Charlotte's romanticism with the erotic titillations and deceptions of mass culture (Harry's onanism, by contrast, is read as "a symbolic elevation of the object of procreation . . . the will to live" [McHaney 173]), and his condemnation of this self-involved, sentimental womanhood as simultaneously cloying and vicious, can be seen as a manifestation of the sort of modernist anxiety diagnosed by Andreas Huyssen in *After the Great Divide,* and, unsurprisingly, much recent scholarship on the novel has drawn on the tools of feminist analysis to take issue with McHaney's view. Anne Goodwyn Jones has gone so far as to praise *If I Forget Thee, Jerusalem* as "one of the few places in Faulkner's fiction where one can find not only popular culture but also an adult woman who is both actively and happily sexual and also appears to have intelligence, imagination, and a certain independence of spirit," but other feminist analyses of the novel have been less optimistic, linking Charlotte's "painful, messy, sordid, and significantly 'female' death in a failed abortion" to the novel's last words in order to claim that, far from celebrating or even mourning Charlotte's desire, *If I Forget Thee, Jerusalem* means to punish her for it and to show that women are, indeed, shit.[15]

A middle space between these two extremes has been carved out by scholars attending to how the novel seems to interrogate the gender norms that nonetheless are so important to the narrative (Jones proposes a version of this view, as well). Thus John Duvall and Minrose Gwin, in formulations indebted to the theoretical positions developed by French feminism, see the novel as questioning "binary construction[s] of gender" and as revealing the "bisexual nature of Faulkner's art."[16] The weakness in these readings lies in the fact that, like McHaney's, they downplay the importance of "Old Man." Duvall and Jones write off the tall convict as the foil to Faulkner's cherished couple, an avatar of the patriarchal gender norms that Harry and Charlotte seek to evade and that, it is implied, ultimately defeat them; Gwin grounds her discussion of artistic bisexuality almost exclusively in "Wild Palms." In addition to paying so little attention to the issues highlighted in "Old Man," a narrative that blends Buster Keaton–style slapstick with highly wrought descriptions of a natural world gone haywire, these readings tend to render distinctly secondary the novel's concern with the entangled relationship between lowbrow mass culture and high art.

In recent years scholarship on the novel has redressed this lack of interest in "Old Man" by turning strongly toward this question, probing Faulkner's relationship to the culture industry (and the term coined by Theodor Adorno to describe the work of film, radio, publishing, and television manufactured under a capitalist regime of mass production is *apropos* here, since much of this scholarship reads Faulkner through Adorno). Though gender issues appear rarely in this criticism, it is the case that the central claim about the purpose of the novel's engagement with mass culture maps almost exactly (ideologically speaking) onto the gender readings of Gwin and Duvall (and other advocates of the novel's "androgynous" aesthetic). *If I Forget Thee, Jerusalem* seems to employ the tropes and techniques of culture industry in much the same fashion that it employs the tropes and techniques of misogyny: in order to hollow out an inhuman, despotic power and so make readers more aware of the social and political consequences of certain practices of cultural production and consumption. Thus over the course of several interrelated essays on the novel (the earliest cowritten with Pamela Rhodes), Richard Godden claims that Harry and the convict each appear as "prisoners" of "the same 'objective' reality, where reification touches every sphere of life," a reification exemplified through the novel's echoing of the discourses of hard-boiled fiction (particularly the work of James M. Cain and Horace McCoy) and Hollywood films in a tissue of intertextuality that points to the completely prefabricated nature of the protagonists' experiences.[17] In this reading, "intertextuality . . . is a contentless principle of structure that allows all literature, indeed all discourse, to intersect. Intertextuality could be read as literary criticism for advanced capitalism."[18] Thus "Old Man" produces scenes and language that force the text's "reified 'spectacle' . . . open, as Adorno said, 'irradiated by the light of its own self-determination'"; the convict's sojourn in the swamp, where he first appears to enjoy his unexpected freedom, "explodes with meanings, perceptual, judgmental, and economic, purging them of appropriation" (Rhodes and Godden, 104–5). Even though this liberatory moment is "as rare as it is brief," the convict's release from the reified terms of his existence serves to "nudge" readers along a "dialectical habit of mind" that cracks open both "Old Man" and "Wild Palms" along the seams of their narrative fashioning, making readers critically aware of the novel's reliance elsewhere on the modes and forms of the culture industry and so, presumably, critically aware of those modes and forms when they encounter them on the screen or between soft covers (Godden, *Fictions* 231).

Peter Lurie likewise traces the novel's engagement with the culture industry, but his reading departs from Godden's in a striking particular. Agreeing that "Old Man" clearly treats ironically the world of culture industry melodrama evoked by the narrative of "Wild Palms," Lurie privileges the narrative differently. In casting the flooded Mississippi as a two-dimensional mirror or movie screen that offers "no realist account of the landscape in which readers can place themselves," Faulkner "avoids the harbingers of novelistic 'verisimilitude and authenticity' such as realist description. . . . [T]he convict (despite his centrality in 'Old Man') possesses little interior life, depth, or psychology whereby readers are encouraged to (falsely) identify with him."[19] Thus for

Godden readers must identify with the convict in his brief idyll of "free labor" (in every sense: like the Polish miners of "Wild Palms," he's never paid) in order to win critical purchase on the rest of *If I Forget Thee, Jerusalem;* for Lurie, however, it is the novel's persistent denial of the comforts of identification that makes it a subversive text.

Like Gwin and Duvall, then, Lurie and Godden see *If I Forget Thee, Jerusalem* as working to reverse the terms of the discourse that bears it forward (in a sense, to make the narrative flow backward, much like the novel's flooded Mississippi). All four readings grant that *If I Forget Thee, Jerusalem* is deeply implicated in some rather distasteful, even disgusting, rhetorical modes, but each insists that the novel's posture toward this rebarbative material saves it from being completely engulfed by it, pointing to the text's implicit reliance on a classically modernist approach to the sentimental subject—irony—as the key attribute of this posture. The fact that they locate this irony in wildly differing aspects of the novel, however, indicates that further interpretive work needs to be done.

* * *

As is frequently noted, Faulkner's original title for the novel was drawn from Psalm 137. Following is the King James translation, the one Faulkner almost certainly knew best:

> By the rivers of Babylon, there we sat down, yea, we wept when we remembered Zion,
> We hanged our harps upon the willows in the midst thereof.
> For there they that carried us away captive required of us a song; and they that wasted us required of us mirth, saying, Sing us one of the songs of Zion!
> How shall we sing the Lord's song in a strange land?
> If I forget thee, O Jerusalem, let my right hand forget her cunning.
> If I do not remember thee, let my tongue cleave to the roof of my mouth; if I prefer not Jerusalem above my chief joy.
> Remember, O Lord, the children of Edom in the day of Jerusalem; who said, Rase it, rase it even to the foundations thereof.

> O daughter of Babylon, who art to be destroyed; happy shall he be, that rewardeth thee as thou hast served us.
> Happy shall he be, that taketh and dasheth thy little ones against the stones.

McHaney has connected the psalm to the novel's concern with issues of freedom and captivity, exemplified in the attempted escapes and fated imprisonments experienced by Harry and the tall convict; though he gestures toward a reading that would link the "cunning" hand of the psalm to Harry's hand as he masturbates in memory of Charlotte, he doesn't pursue the analogy. François Pitavy, in his foreword to the revised French translation of the corrected text, also notes the novel's concern with "cunning" hands, even though, as he points out, the French translation of the psalm does not speak of manual "cunning" (*"Si je t'oublie, Jerusalem, que ma droite m'oublie!"* [*Si je t'oublie* 16]), and even though the multiple English meanings of the homophone "palm" do not translate: French relies on two different words, *palmier* and *paume,* to indicate tree and hand (though Pitavy believes that French readers understand as well as their English counterparts the action accompanying Harry's last words).[20] For many Faulkner scholars, the invocation of the psalm, combined with the novel's engagement with the products of the culture industry, invites an analogy linking Faulkner's Hollywood screenwriting "exile" to the captivity of the Israelites; in this view, the cherished, never-to-be-forgotten "cunning" of the right hand is novel writing, even though the hand of the "cunning" writer also allows him to produce work that satisfies the demands of Babylon. Vincent King's reading of the novel draws out and develops precisely this point: Faulkner, like the psalmist of the Old Testament, employs a double strategy in order to sing the song demanded by Babylon while remaining true to his own artistic vision, and, as we have seen, much the same view subtends those analyses of the novel that see it as critical of its own discourse.[21]

If I Forget Thee, Jerusalem is indeed obsessed with what King calls the "use and abuse of fiction"—that is, the degree to which fictions of all brows and media, high, low, and middle, literary and cinematic, not only shape but confuse the conditions of freedom and imprisonment. In being arrested for attempting a crime modeled on his reading in the *Detectives' Gazette,* the tall convict is the novel's most frequently cited avatar of the cultural dupe, but, as the readings of Lurie and Godden make clear, no one in *If I Forget Three,*

Jerusalem works without a script, and especially not Faulkner. As compelling as this line of analysis is (and it is extraordinarily useful not only for interpreting *If I Forget Thee, Jerusalem* but also for understanding Godard's later discomfort with *A bout de souffle*), these readings of the novel's "cunning" falter in adopting a censorious view of Harry's final gesture. For Godden, Harry's "sealed onanistic chamber typifies the closed and rigid thought forms of commodity production, presenting themselves as immovable and eternal" (Rhodes and Godden 101); for Lurie, the scene "offers a model of the way commercial film, like all commodity culture, stimulates consumers' desire, only to frustrate (but then sustain) it by refusing satisfaction" (155). Thus the scene links Hollywood films to pornography, both "generic, commodified forms of pleasure . . . [that] are underpinned by a common motive: to manipulate audience's desires for the sake of profit. Faulkner's larger concern . . . is that generic forms such as melodrama, the historical film, pulp fiction, and pornography all rely on a pleasure that is produced by the culture industry and whose nature is, finally, the same: projective, solipsistic, and melancholy" (Lurie 155). Such interpretations of Harry's closing action are appealing not least because they set the novel down firmly on the side of the culturally righteous; however, the recent emergence of queer theory, which among other things has prompted reconsideration of representations of nonreproductive sex once deemed obviously morally suspect, should lead us to question what we might recognize, on further consideration, to be rather conventional (perhaps even vaguely Victorian) notions of sexual economy. It appears, in other words, that there remains an aspect of *If I Forget Thee, Jerusalem*'s engagement with the culture industry that even subversive readings of the novel find unredeemedly disgusting, and for reasons not so dissimilar, ultimately, from those McHaney gives for condemning Charlotte: the novel serves up as art material that, in the critics' view, is actually shit.

Harry's final words may well savor of the melodramatic, but they are also (as Patricia Franchini points out) quite beautiful, and in a way typically Faulknerian. It is possible, then, that Faulkner's aim in *If I Forget Thee, Jerusalem* was not simply diagnostic but also interrogatory, in the sense that its production of pleasure forces us to examine not only our blind acceptance of reified experience as "natural" but also our "natural" revulsions. This is not to claim that *If I Forget Thee, Jerusalem* exonerates or valorizes those modes of cultural expression so damaging as to be killing; it is, though, to take seriously the possibility that the novel is a kind of plea for the guilty:

> "This case is closed," the judge said. "The accused is waiting sentence. Make your statement from there." Rittenmeyer stopped. He was not looking at the judge, he was not looking at anything, his face calm, impeccable, outrageous.
>
> "I wish to make a plea," he said. For a moment the judge did not move, staring at Rittenmeyer, the gavel still clutched in his fist like a sabre, then he leaned slowly forward, staring at Rittenmeyer: and Wilbourne heard it begin, the long in-sucking, the gathering of amazement and incredulity.
>
> "You what?" the judge said. "A what? A plea? For this man? This man who willfully and deliberately performed an operation on your wife which he knew might cause her death and which did?" (*Jerusalem* 269)

Francis Rittenmeyer is not allowed to speak, so his plea is never heard; we must look elsewhere for our sense of what a plea for the guilty might sound like. Though, as I have noted, Psalm 137 is the most widely cited intertext of the novel, it is also true that its last three lines are generally not allowed to speak in the scholarship, even though the prediction that the Lord's revenge upon the daughter of Babylon will entail the destruction of her and her "little ones" bears a gruesome parallel to Charlotte's fate; indeed, it may be precisely because the hideous parallel can be drawn that scholars have been reluctant to engage it.[22] The daughter of Babylon is guilty insofar as she abets the captivity of the Israelites, and it could be said that Meta Carpenter abetted Faulkner's "captivity" in Hollywood. Indeed, the evidence suggests that she transformed it into an idyll of erotic pleasure whose contours bore a striking resemblance to that of Harry and Charlotte: the relationship was marked not only by intense sex but also by a "pattern of isolation and frugality" (Wilde and Borsten 60). To the extent that he surrendered to this captivity (and then sought to dash against stones the "little ones" it produced—perhaps the more sentimental, commercial aspects of his novel?), Faulkner was "guilty," too. Faulkner's own recollection of the link between the "ending" of the affair and the writing of the novel further complicates the relationship between psalm and text insofar as it admits to double casting: Carpenter, and by extension Hollywood (which Carpenter remembers Faulkner calling "this good ol' place" [Wilde and Borsten 277]), may be, no less than Yoknapatawpha and Oxford, the blissful, lost "Jerusalem" to be remembered. Finally, it is worth considering the possibility that it was in learning to appreciate the passions of his lover—Carpenter was an accomplished musician, and their two best friends in Hollywood were likewise musical—that Faulkner first got his idea for a "contrapuntal" novel. Thus the very structure of *If I Forget Thee, Jerusalem,* a crucial piece of evidence for those readings of the novel that see it as *only* critical of the culture industry (since the narrative alternation interrupts a potentially mesmerizing flow), may itself bear a guilty connection to Hollywood.

Taken together, Rittenmeyer's silent plea and the tangled web of correspondences indicated by the conclusion of the psalm point to the importance of what is probably the novel's least attractive rhetorical feature: its discourse of "meat," a trope registering simultaneous disgust and affection. Charlotte's sculpted Falstaff is "gross with meat" (*Jerusalem* 77); Charlotte and Harry's bourgeoisification in Chicago is "the mausoleum of love . . . the dead corpse borne between the olfactoryless walking shapes of the immortal unsentient demanding ancient meat" (*Jerusalem* 118); the convict resentfully describes the pregnant woman as "female meat" (*Jerusalem* 126, 144). The novel's obsession with "meat" reaches its apotheosis in Harry's musings on memory, musings that begin in a meditation on Charlotte's grave and end in his masturbation:

> he could imagine it, it would be a good deal like the park where he had waited, maybe even with children and nurses at times, the best, the very best; there would even be a headstone soon, at just exactly the right time, when restored earth and decorum stipulated, telling nothing; it would be clipped and green and quiet, the body, the shape of it under the drawn sheet, flat and small and moving in the hands of two men as if without weight though it did, nevertheless bearing and quiet beneath the iron weight of earth. *Only that cant be all of it* he thought. *It cant be. The waste. Not of meat, there is always plenty of meat. They found that out twenty years ago preserving nations and justifying mottoes—granted the nations the meat preserved are worth the preserving with the meat it took gone. But memory. Surely memory exists independent of the flesh.* But this was wrong too. *Because it wouldn't know it was memory* he thought. *It wouldn't know what it was it remembered. So there's got to be the old meat, the old frail*

eradicable meat for memory to titillate.... So it is the old meat after all, no matter how old. (*Jerusalem* 265, 272)

The "old meat" that memory titillates is Harry's penis (another, littler "old man"?), which, once taken in hand, "remembers" Charlotte in a way that makes Harry's body a kind of fleshly sonnet. As this passage implies, Harry concludes that total escape from the encumbrances of "meat" entails unacceptable "waste." One view of *If I Forget Thee, Jerusalem*, then, would take seriously the novel's economic refusal to let anything go to waste, no matter how repellent. This rejection of "waste," however, is undertaken in service to a most wasteful (indeed, some might even say self-abusive) economy of "high" literary art, and in fact the self-involved, densely allusive quality of much modernist literature can itself seem more than slightly onanistic. The gratifications of "high" modernist expression are, too, guilty pleasures, and not only for Marxist reasons (i.e., the guilt involved in creating "abstract," presumably politically disengaged, art). Indeed, Faulkner's description of the experience of producing the novel as a kind of alienated writing in the dark describes *both* Hollywood screenwriting *and* Oxford novel writing.

Thus one might say that *If I Forget Thee, Jerusalem* doesn't so much finally acquiesce to, or critique, a capitalist mode of mass production as weasel its way through it, and the work's sign for this cunning negotiation is the homophone (or pun), "palm," whose multiple meanings (as noun [a type of tree, the inside of the hand] and verb [to stroke with the inside of the hand, to trick, to defraud]) ramify through the text as a central revelation of the novel. On the one hand (so to speak), Faulkner produced a moving and dramatic narrative of boundless love despite moral censure and remarkable heroism in the face of natural disaster; on the other, he produced an extended, ruthless parody that ridiculed and pressed to the limits the pretensions not only of just such a narrative but also the equally highly stylized, putatively nonsentimental "art" literature of the prison world of "men without women" (among other things, Charlotte's fate reads beyond a prior fictional assurance that one particular matter of a woman's "meat" is "really not anything. It's just to let the air in").[23] The scandal at the heart of *If I Forget Thee, Jerusalem*, then, is that it fuses together high and low, art and commerce, in a common expressive project such that they illuminate each other, and transform each other, *equally,* in the manner of true counterpoint. Faulkner couldn't tell whether his novel was "all right or absolute drivel" because, like the pun, it signifies in two directions at once in a manner most unruly—a manner wild, even savage.

CON

> The cinema... can be everything at once, both judge and litigant.
> —JEAN-LUC GODARD, qtd. in Tom Milne, *Godard on Godard*

As we have seen, Bruce Kawin claims a central importance for *If I Forget Thee, Jerusalem* in Godard's *A bout de souffle*, but for Kawin Faulkner's centrality extends far beyond the moment of quotation in this single film and even beyond Godard: it encompasses the emergence of the New Wave itself. Kawin sees the 1952 publication of *Les palmiers sauvages* as a crucial moment for the development of New Wave cinema, insofar as its parallel but seemingly unrelated stories propose a model of narrative composition eschewing the long-dominant, Hollywood-based embrace of continuity editing in narrative film. Agnès Varda's 1956 *La pointe courte* "had placed together two separate plots . . . in an imitation of Faulkner's novel"; as Kawin notes, the film, which was edited by Alain Resnais, has been identified as "the first New Wave picture" (Kawin 147). Though *A bout de souffle* is concerned with only one narrative, its famous jump cuts and *faux raccords* can be seen as paralleling the discontinuity and "unresolution" of Faulkner's fiction (Kawin 150). Thus Kawin asserts a central place for Faulkner not only in literary history but in film history, a place that depends "not on Faulkner's films [that is, his screenplays] but on the influence of his fiction. . . . [H]e used such unusual tropes as montage, freeze-frames, superimposition, flashback, and perspective distortion, as well as sound-overlap and sound/image conflict" such that his work

> kept the traditions of radical subjectivity, of montage, and the "metaphysics of time" alive during the period when the coming of sound had rendered montage unfashionable and the economics of the film industry had militated against "visionary" experimentation. Although it remains to be established whether Faulkner hit on these techniques through the films he might have seen in Paris in 1925–26, or conceived them in strictly literary terms (finding most

of them in *Ulysses*), it is clear that he is one of the central figures in cinema's rediscovery of its own narrative—and *anti*-narrative—potential.... Godard has been putting Faulkner on film throughout his career. (Kawin 147–48, 153)

There is much merit in Kawin's analysis, but his desire to make a case for Faulkner's influence leads him to slight other developments within cinema itself that cannot be traced directly to Faulkner but that nonetheless had a strong effect on Godard's first picture (and on his subsequent cinematic practice). Not least of these is the unprecedentedly wide circulation of American films in France in the years immediately following World War II.

Before the war, France protected its domestic film industry with quotas restricting the importation of foreign films, especially American films. But in 1946, and almost certainly as a condition of access to Marshall Plan funds, France approved the Blum/Byrnes accord, an agreement that revoked the prewar quotas and established France as "a free market as far as the American [film] industry was concerned."[24] Rather than an import quota, the accord established a screen time quota, with just four weeks out of the year set aside for the screening of French films. The particulars of this treaty combined with what Motion Picture Association of America then-president Eric Johnston called a "tremendous backlog of pictures that had not been shown in most foreign countries" during the war to result in "these pictures flood[ing] in, even more than the countries could absorb" (Guback 16). Thus, within a year of the signing of the accord, French film production fell by 23 percent; by the end of 1947, "more than half of the French studios were said to have suspended operation, and unemployment reportedly rose to more than 75 percent in some branches of the industry" (Guback 22). According to Guback, the attendant outcry was such that in 1948 a new five-year agreement was signed that reinstated import quotas and raised the portion of screen time that exhibitors were required to devote to French films—though American films continued to enjoy preferential import treatment compared to that granted other countries (Guback 22).

It was against this volatile and hardly romantic *rapprochement franco-américain* that Godard and his cohorts at the *Cahiers du Cinéma* began their reassessment of the state of French cinema, and it was a reassessment that proceeded largely by comparing French and American films (with crucial detours into Italian neorealism). The hegemony of the American film industry, which enjoyed an economy of scale that the much smaller, war-damaged industries of Europe could not hope to match, was a sore point, and to some degree the championing in the pages of *Cahiers* of directors like Howard Hawks, Nicholas Ray, Alfred Hitchcock, Anthony Mann, Robert Aldrich, and Samuel Fuller (to offer a list indicating the catholic range of the *Cahiers* critics' enthusiasms) was deliberately provocative. Still, and as Jim Hillier points out, the upward revaluation of American film undertaken by the *Cahiers* crowd was not entirely unprecedented: André Bazin's work on Hollywood preceded his affiliation with the journal, and the critics at the more left-leaning *Positif* were embarked on a similarly revisionist project.[25] What distinguished the *Cahiers* view was the journal's willingness to take seriously films other critics wrote off as lightweight fluff or trash, and to see those films as having been *authored:*

> If the *politique des auteurs* caused ripples, and more, in French film culture and beyond, it was not because of the idea itself but because the idea was used in *Cahiers* with polemical brio to upset established values and reputations. There was nothing new or scandalous in . . . discussing, say, Murnau, Buñuel, Dreyer, Eisenstein, Renoir, Cocteau or Bresson or, from the USA, Stroheim or Welles or Chaplin, as the *auteurs* of their films. It was a slightly different matter—but only slightly—to propose, say, Howard Hawks as an *auteur,* mainly because, unlike Stroheim, Welles, or Chaplin, Hawks had not been noticeably in conflict with the production system. It was perhaps a significantly different matter when the cultural perspectives brought to bear on the proposal of Hawks as *auteur* of Westerns, gangster movies and comedies derived their terms from classical literature, philosophy or the history of art. It verged on positive outrage when, at the end of the 1950s and the beginning of the 1960s, such perspectives were brought to bear on, say, Vincente Minnelli or Samuel Fuller, not to mention Don Weis or Edward Ludwig. In other words, the closer *Cahiers* moved to what had been traditionally conceived as the "conveyor belt" end of the cinema spectrum, the more their "serious" discussion of film-makers seemed outrageously inappropriate. As it happens . . . the more they outraged in this way, the more acutely they raised crucial questions, however unsystematically, about the status and criticism appropriate to film as an art form in which unsystematic divisions were constantly being

made between art and commerce. If *Cahiers* came to be associated primarily with American cinema and a revaluation of its status, it was not because they talked about American cinema more than about other cinema—quite simply, they did not—but because American cinema as a whole, so generally ignored, misunderstood or undervalued, provided the most obvious site for engagement with these critical questions. (Hillier 7)

As an example of the dramatic, and swift, effect *Cahiers* criticism had on the European reception of Hollywood films, Hillier gives a striking "before and after" example in the *Guardian* reviews of Howard Hawks's *Rio Bravo*. At its first release in 1959, the film was described as "a typical Western of this age of the long-winded, large screen. . . . a soporific 'blockbuster.'" On its rerelease in 1963, however, it was hailed as a "gem": "*Rio Bravo* is . . . first and last a Howard Hawks film. For those who know Hawks this should be enough; for those who don't, it means that *Rio Bravo* is an example of the classical, pre-Welles school of American film-making at its most deceptively simple: broad lines, level glances, grand design, elementary emotions" (Hillier 11–12).

Certainly more than a portion of this revaluation was driven less by the quality of the films themselves than by an effort to find some way to live with the postwar "flooding" of American films into European theaters—to deliberately look away from the social, economic, and political issues in Gaullist France that the American invasion betokened. But Godard's film, produced in the moment of ascendancy of what some have termed *Cahiers*' "culturally conservative, politically reactionary attempt to remove film from the realm of social and political concern" (Hillier 6), shows that the implications of the *politique des auteurs* were at least as interrogative as they were recuperative. Tom Milne notes Annette Michelson's claim that, far from promoting a culturally conservative agenda, the *politique des auteurs* was "a concerted attempt to stem the advancing tide of American hegemony in the international market of the film industry, and in the domination of the studio system, whose model . . . had been the automotive industry's total rationalization and perfection of the principle of the division of labor."[26]

It is a commonplace in the criticism to note that *A bout de souffle* is stitched together out of quotations from American gangster pictures (what the French, in a renaming that has stuck, termed *film noir*), Westerns, and melodrama.

Like *If I Forget Thee, Jerusalem*, *A bout de souffle* is an intertextual text. The usual view of this use of allusion and quotation in Godard's film grants that it tends toward a cultural conservatism, but also praises its highly artistic (i.e., ironic) practice as a kind of cheeky *hommage* to genre pictures that has a certain philosophical point. As Dudley Andrew has observed: "The theme of the film, like the essence of its hero, is precisely the futile struggle to be original 'in the manner of' something or someone else. The notion of individuality and of forthrightness is as American as the movies, and as fully processed. Since there can be no escaping genre, since freedom is attainable only within or against genre, Godard the *cinéphile* embraces it. And he chooses the genre that most promoted and problematized freedom, the *film noir*" (Andrew 12). Though he is more interested in Godard's later meditations on the problem of freedom imagined through psychological coherence, and so less sanguine than Andrew, Kline too asserts that the film is imprisoned in its "free" expressive mode: "Michel, as character, enjoys a nonproblematical status guaranteed him by the warmed-over American essentialism of the film" (Kline 202); that is, Michel assumes a "liberty" that the canny critic recognizes as completely prefabricated (in Andrew's words, the "fully processed" American belief in "individuality" and "forthrightness"). This is not a surprising view given Kline's (rather odd) assertion that Faulkner, for Godard, presents an ultimately false model of American psychological "coherence" (Kline 220), but it is one deserving interrogation.

If I have suggested that Faulkner's novel is somewhat less than completely disdainful of the seductions of culture industry than has been claimed, I would like to propose also that Godard's film is less complacent in the face of those seductions than has been asserted. In the first spoken line of the film, Michel identifies himself as an idiot driven by compulsion ("All in all, I'm a dumb bastard. [*Après tout, j'suis con.*] All in all, if you've got to, you've got to!" [Andrew 33]), and through the course of the film he largely lives up to that self-description. Belmondo's undeniable charm, which Godard put to excellent use (the engaging way he addresses the camera while telling those who dislike France to go fuck themselves is a case in point), has worked to turn critics away from a too-careful exploration of the gap that opens up precisely between Michel's triumphalist American belief in absolute individual freedom and his deeply circumscribed postwar French reality, a disjunction that is crucial to the meaning of the film. Or rather, critics have preferred to trace that disjunction to Jean Seberg's Patricia, who is no less a dupe of US mass culture than Michel (he wants to be "Bogie," she wishes her name were Ingrid) but who, precisely by virtue of her Americanness, manages to escape the deadly consequences of this fantasy (*après tout,* her national fantasy, not Michel's) and so can be made out to be the target of all of the film's meditations on inauthenticity; many critics read Patricia in much the same way McHaney reads Charlotte (there is something of this in Kawin's interpretation, for example). But a *cherchez la femme* reading of cultural reification is no more satisfying for Godard's film than it is for Faulkner's novel, and for much the same reasons: *A bout de souffle*'s relationship to the culture industry is as disturbingly unsettled as that of *If I Forget Thee, Jerusalem,* with tropes both of complicity and of resistance attaching themselves to nearly every available surface.

As Pamela Falkenberg has pointed out, *A bout de souffle* "might be described as a simultaneous and double rewriting: the rewriting of the French commercial cinema (conceived of as a transformation) through the rewriting of the Hollywood commercial cinema (conceived of as a reproduction): the real art cinema as Hollywood."[27] I cannot do justice here to Falkenberg's suggestive essay, which adopts Jean Baudrillard's work on simulation in order to explore the relationship between Godard's "art" film and, on the one hand, the American crime melodramas that it cites and, on the other, Jim McBride's 1983 Hollywood remake, *Breathless.* However, Falkenberg's central claim—"The art cinema is both without and within the commercial cinema and exists on both sides of the difference that its vacillation secures" (Falkenberg 48)—captures exactly the point I mean to make here about the expressive complications Godard's film and Faulkner's novel face in attempting to produce a "successful" critique of culture industry (i.e., one that sells) by adopting expressive modes peculiar to it. Much as Faulkner's novel turns on the disquieting attributes of the homophone, Godard's film also is marked by a pun—*c'est pareil* (it's the same) and *séparé* (separated)—that literalizes the vacillation Falkenberg identifies. The pun unfolds over two widely separated (though parallel) scenes, the first in Patricia's room:

Michel: "Why did you slap me when I looked at your legs?"
Patricia: "It wasn't my legs."

Michel: "It's exactly the same." [*C'est exactement pareil.*]
Patricia: "The French always say things are the same [*sont pareil*] when they aren't at all."
Michel: "I've found something nice to say, Patricia."
Patricia: "What?"
Michel: "I want to sleep with you because you're beautiful."
Patricia: "No, I'm not."
Michel: "Then because you're ugly."
Patricia: "It's the same?" [*C'est pareil?*]
Michel: "Sure, my little girl, it's the same" [*c'est pareil*]. (Andrew 76)

And the second in the model's apartment:

Patricia: "It's sad to fall asleep. You have to ... sepa ..." [*sépa ...*]
Michel: "... ate" [... *ré*]
Patricia: "... to separate [*séparé*]. They say, 'sleep together,' but it's not true." (Andrew 134)

Along with *con* and *dégueulasse,* the words that open and close *A bout de souffle* and that are repeated throughout in varying contexts, this play of *c'est pareil/séparé* signals the central concern of the film: How are two ostensibly similar things nevertheless deemed separate? How do the separate become similar? What's truly idiotic, or disgusting? The pun in *A bout de souffle* works much as Faulkner's wild and cunning palm does in *If I Forget Thee, Jerusalem:* it opens up simultaneous and seemingly mutually contradictory possibilities of meaning precisely around the problem of determining "proper" (sexual, cultural, aesthetic) expression and gratification.

Thus the importance of Faulkner's novel to Godard's film lies less in the way the narrative of *If I Forget Thee, Jerusalem* aligns (whether sincerely or ironically) with that of *A bout de souffle* than in the fact that both author and *auteur* were embarked on similar projects of cultural interrogation. What Godard saw in Faulkner's novel, and what he put into his film, were not only its technical innovations in structure and expression, not only the "story line" of sex and death (separate, yet somehow the same), but also the work's problematic—indeed, tortured—effort to find a place to stand in a cultural landscape that had seen once-obvious distinctions between the high ground and the low flooded over and flattened out into a puzzling sameness. Godard's decision to combine high with low (Picasso, Renoir, Klee, Bach, Mozart—and Faulkner; Bogart, Aldrich, Fuller, Radio Luxembourg, *Paris Flirt* comics, and Preminger) illuminates that landscape in a manner he imagined to be both serious and substantive. Two years after the release of the film, though, Godard would describe *A bout de souffle* as "*Alice in Wonderland*" (Milne 175); later still, it would be "a film I've always been ashamed of . . . a film that came out of fascism" (Kline 185).

Michel may be a dumb bastard, but he is Godard's dumb bastard, and in one crucial respect he did in fact speak for his creator. In the wake of the movements of 1968, Godard embraced a Maoist politics and turned his back on commercial film production, choosing, over a career of compromising "grief," a life in cinema that for many years would be, at least commercially speaking, close to "nothing." As is well known, this is not the path that Faulkner chose. Though he complained about invasions of privacy in the post-Nobel period, Faulkner nevertheless enjoyed the acclaim and increasingly wrote, in the twilight of his career, works that were quite consonant with the demands of the market, both formally and ideologically (*The Town, The Reivers*). Both artists, in other words, turned away from an aesthetic practice that would persist in reading high art and mass culture in terms of each other so as to challenge the notion of a clearly legible cultural landscape. Deciding which turn is courageously liberatory, which delusionally complicit, is actually harder to do than may at first appear. Clearly, in the political realm, an unforgiving insistence on "all or nothing" can bend as easily toward terrorism as liberation, and, as Falkenberg makes clear, commerce and art are not so easily separated to begin with. Which is to say, finally, that though Faulkner and Godard moved on from (or rather, abandoned) the flooded fun-house cultural landscapes of *If I Forget Thee, Jerusalem* and *A bout de souffle*, they did so without having enjoyed the last word on the relationship between high and low. For those of us who persist in some final verdict, some summative judgment, both texts have the same nonanswer: Art, shit.

7

Making Camp

GO DOWN, MOSES

> In Camp there is often something *démesuré* in the quality of the ambition, not only in the style of the work itself. Gaudí's lurid and beautiful buildings in Barcelona are Camp not only because of their style but because they reveal—most notably in the Cathedral of Sagrada Família—the ambition on the part of one man to do what it takes a generation, a whole culture to accomplish.
> —SUSAN SONTAG, "Notes on Camp"

> I'm trying to say it all in one sentence, between one Cap and one period.
> —WILLIAM FAULKNER to Malcolm Cowley, November 1944

When Isaac McCaslin opens the plantation ledgers and begins his research into the entwined genealogies of the white McCaslin and Black Beauchamp families, his glance first falls not on an entry dealing with a member of those families—central though they are to *Go Down, Moses*—but on a citation registering his father's 1856 purchase of an "anomaly calling itself Percival Brownlee."[1] In the ensuing fourteen entries spread out over nine months, Ike reads how Brownlee proves himself so unsuited to slavery that Ike's father, Theophilus McCaslin (more usually identified in the text as Uncle Buck), and his father's twin brother, Amodeus (Uncle Buddy), decide to free him and then, when he refuses to leave the plantation, to rename him. The entries list a series of mishaps, any one of which could provide the pretext for a reason to "get shut of" Brownlee (meant to serve as a bookkeeper, Brownlee can't read; physically unsuited to any kind of fieldwork, he provokes an accident that ends in the death of a mule), but the ledgers posit his renomination as key to the "truth" of his "anomaly," and it is a truth deployed in the text as an open secret. Uncle Buddy gives Brownlee a Latin-ish name, Spintrius, that goes unglossed in the ledgers even as the novel elsewhere drops large hints of its meaning. Not simply an "anomaly," Brownlee is said to be "tragic and miscast." Leaving the plantation in 1856, he returns in 1862 and finds his "true niche . . . conducting impromptu revival meetings among the negroes, preaching and leading the singing also in his high sweet true soprano voice" (*GDM* 279); run off the plantation a second time, he reappears in the Jefferson town square four years later "in the entourage of a traveling Army paymaster," the two of them together creating the impression of "a man on an excursion during his wife's absence and with his wife's personal maid" (*GDM* 280). Catching sight of Uncle Buck, Brownlee gives his former owner "one defiant female glance" before leaving Yoknapatawpha forever. Twenty years later (that is, in 1888, the same year Ike McCaslin turns twenty-one and repudiates his heritage), McCaslin Edmonds, nephew of the McCaslin twins and now master of their plantation, hears that Brownlee has become "the well-to-do proprietor of a select New Orleans brothel" (*GDM* 280).

Long regarded as a kind of textual anomaly unassimilable to the tragic themes of racial injustice and environmental degradation central to *Go Down, Moses*, the Percival Brownlee episode has drawn attention in two recent analyses of William Faulkner's 1942 novel. In her exhaustive study of the work, Thadious Davis sees Brownlee's "feminization" and "homosexuality" as Faulkner's "attempt at humor" that "fails rather miserably . . . to satirize ownership and property rights."[2] While noting Brownlee's Bartleby-esque "passive resistance to being enslaved," she terms him a "cipher" too "sketchy" to be of serious interpretive interest (218). As a mirror of attributes "implicit in the story of Amodeus, Ike's Uncle Buddy"—who, the novel tells us, "should have been a woman to begin with" (*GDM* 260)—Brownlee "suggests a second story . . . that Ike cannot tell and that Faulkner does not explore. The silences" in Brownlee's narrative, Davis concludes, "are more pronounced than those in the narrative of Carothers's violation of his daughter" (the incest that, as the novel's most vile instantiation of the crime of slavery, generates much of the narrative of *Go Down, Moses*) and thus are indicative of Faulkner's unwillingness to interrogate the consequences of projecting "whiteness, race, and sexuality . . . onto a black male body" (219). Where Davis sees silences and lacunae indicative of Faulkner's inability or refusal to engage the full implications of his material, Richard Godden and Noel Polk draw out an entire parallel narrative that casts homosexual incest as the true crime of the McCaslin family history. For Godden and Polk, the "climax of the Brownlee episode comes in the revelation that Brownlee is homosexual and that his homosexuality is the single reason why Isaac's father bought him."[3] They posit a prior incest between Uncle Buck and Uncle Buddy ("Brownlee enters the ledgers as a thoroughly exogamous intruder over whom the brothers conduct, in the ledgers, an extended lovers' quarrel" [303]); and they conclude that Ike fabricates his grandfather's crime out of fragmentary and incomplete evidence almost entirely in order to block acknowledgment of his father's and uncle's (presumed greater) transgressions (358–59).[4]

I cite these readings because they represent the most recent efforts to make interpretive sense of Percival Brownlee; thus they introduce my own approach to this character's role in *Go Down, Moses* and limn the larger critical issues my analysis engages. For while I share key convictions driving both readings—that *Go Down, Moses* is a far more important text than generally acknowledged, and that Percival Brownlee is likewise underestimated—I question the theoretical assumptions underlying both interpretations, different though they may be, about how best to read Faulkner today. To a large degree, contemporary critical engagements in Faulkner's work are undertaken under something like an extended ironic quotation. To "read Faulkner" is actually not to read Faulkner but to read through Faulkner to some other, larger, narrative—history, usually, to put the broadest possible term into play, though sometimes also biography (or, best of all, biography as history).[5] It is entirely to be expected that drawing attention to silences and uncovering hidden narratives would emerge as important aspects of this critical project. Expanding the documentary record is the work of the historian *par excellence,* and it proceeds precisely through rigorous attention to what has gone unsaid, often drawing on previously disregarded evidence in order to piece together a more comprehensive narrative of the past. This is not, of course, an interpretive gambit peculiar to Faulkner scholarship, but it has become the dominant paradigm for study of the author, its ascendancy driven largely by the post–New Critical conclusion that Faulkner, by virtue of limitations deriving from his regional, racial, and (presumed) sexual identities, has largely failed in giving a true picture of his (again presumed) subject, the US South. As Eric J. Sundquist put it some years ago: "Although Faulkner's novels bring to a pitch the literary confrontation with race hatred in the early twentieth century, there are, by the same token, limitations to his vision. The fictional forms achieved by other authors, both black and white, in this way engage and complete those of Faulkner, reaching beyond the world of Yoknapatawpha and giving clearer voice to black lives and to the cultural traditions of race in America. The reconstruction of these traditions, their strands of signification and revising improvisations on the past, is today the main question for Faulkner's readers."[6]

I should make clear here the grounds for my engagements with this mode of analysis, since my questions are not at all hostile ones. I do not mean to imply that such scholarship is without merit; on the contrary, I admire it, and, as should be quite evident in the pages that follow, my own work attempts a similar interpretive project: history and biography have their roles to play in my reading of Brownlee as well. But it is no longer news that Faulkner fails (would fail, has failed, will always fail) in producing a "complete" picture of the ongoing US racial narrative; least of all would it be news to Faulkner, who repeatedly described himself and his work as failures (he was a failed poet, *The Sound and the Fury* was the "most splendid failure," etc.).[7] No doubt there is more than a small amount here of the *faux* humility that, post-Nobel, led Faulkner to describe himself at times as a farmer; no doubt there is even some defensiveness, some anxiety, at play as well. But it is also possible that Faulkner describes his work in terms of failure because, in some important way, he expected to fail. And while scholars have not ignored this aspect of his work, it is worth keeping in mind the possibility that readings driven by a desire to "complete" the Faulknerian project may themselves fail to take sufficient interpretive account of those "anomalous" aspects of his work that are fundamental to the text but that cannot be assimilated to an interpretive program driven by a desire to enlarge, or correct, the historical record.[8]

For as Percival Brownlee shows, reliance on the historical record (at least, the published record) as a tool of literary analysis is hardly foolproof. If one adopts the view that Brownlee is homosexual (an uncertain proposition, but one the text invites us to entertain), a turn to the historical record provides scant material with which to critique, let alone complete, Faulkner's representation of such a character. For now, at least, there is little scholarship on antebellum same-sex relations among African Americans, whether free or slave; what "knowledge" there is that circulates on homoeroticism and US slavery is highly speculative and largely shaped by the assumption that homosexuality was the "master's perversion," something forced on Black men by their owners.[9] Orlando Patterson's magisterial *Slavery and Social Death,* for example, pauses to discuss same-sex relations among the enslaved at precisely two points in history: in ancient Athens, where the "unusually high incidence of homosexuality among the slaveholding class" meant that male slaves were often purchased for sexual use and that concubinal manumission thus was a possibility for them as well as for women; and in medieval Persia, where strong discouragement of reproduction among the *ghilmān* meant that sexual expression among such slaves was either prevented (through castration) or channeled into homoeroticism.[10] The first instance flatly ascribes same-sex activity to masters; the second posits it as nothing more than a compensatory practice (i.e., "situational" homosexuality). My point here is not that Patterson's observations are *wrong;* it is, rather, that they are incomplete, and thus tending, insofar as they are seen *as* complete (and so as models for thinking about African American same-sex practices during slavery and after), to perpetuate invidious lines of analysis.[11] The thoughtful good sense of a study like James H. Sweet's—which raises the possibility that native same-sex practices were almost as surely lost to the enslaved as their native languages—is a helpful contribution to the scholarship.[12] Attempting to read Percival Brownlee primarily through what has so far emerged in historical scholarship, in other words, seems certain to render him even more anomalous than *Go Down, Moses* claims he is.

It is no easier to place Brownlee within the temporality of the author's consciousness—that is, Depression-era Jim Crow Mississippi. In many ways, knowing what lore Faulkner heard about Black same-sex practices in Mississippi in 1856, and how that lore squared with his own observations of the contemporary scene (if, indeed, he had any), would provide a more salient historical frame. Thanks partly to the importance of men like Bayard Rustin and James Baldwin, scholarship on twentieth-century African American homosexuality is more robust than its nineteenth-century counterpart. Work by Phillip Brian Harper, Roderick A. Ferguson, Kevin Mumford, and Robert Reid-Pharr is crucial to any effort to read Black queer life in twentieth-century

American history and culture, most especially to gaining an understanding of how Black queer authors themselves have talked back to political and cultural forces intent on silencing them.[13] However, these studies tend to emphasize the post–World War II period and the northern urban scene as frames for the Black writing and reading subject; thus they are of limited application in the effort to determine the function and effects of a character like Brownlee, deployed as he is in a pre–World War II text written by a white southerner and set in rural Mississippi.

Thus my approach to Percival Brownlee is not historically framed in the manner usually practiced today. That is, I do not read the episode against a background of recorded events and practices so that we can then judge the degree to which Faulkner fails or succeeds in supplying a "complete" picture of a man like Brownlee.[14] Rather, I read Brownlee through his names, both Percival and Spintrius, which the text signals as important and which themselves carry a historically inflected freight of meaning that, though not tied to the US South of 1856, 1866, 1888, or 1941 (the years of Brownlee's purchase and manumission; of his last appearance in Yoknapatawpha; of Ike's repudiation; and of Faulkner's writing, to name all the possible historical frames that could be brought to bear on the text), nonetheless has a certain analytic power.[15] In part I read his names as manifestations of what Lee Edelman has termed "homographesis"; to read in this way is to insist on Percival Brownlee as a textual effect, one whose "anomalous" status forces us to question long-standing assumptions about how to read Faulkner's novels and how to assess their cultural work. Thus this reading of Percival Brownlee not only affects our understanding of *Go Down, Moses* but also prompts reassessments in three broader interpretive realms. First, it demonstrates the fruitfulness of bringing the insights of queer theory to texts other than those produced by a "subject supposed to know"—a critical practice that sharpens our understanding not only of ostensibly "straight" texts but also of the full range of possibilities for queer theory itself in its concern with the sexually "anomalous." Second, it revives the discussion, faded but perhaps worth reengaging, of the political aesthetics of camp. And, finally, it provokes consideration of some renunciatory aspects of our own current critical practice that we might do well to reexamine.

Since my concern here is not only to show what a certain understanding of Brownlee does to our reading of *Go Down, Moses* but also to indicate what that understanding might do to our reading of Faulkner generally, I begin my discussion of Brownlee through a discussion of Faulkner—a discussion that makes clear my dependence on those biographical and historical modes of literary analysis about which I have already indicated my reservations. If this is to illustrate that I, too, must perforce "read Faulkner" before reading Faulkner, it is, I hope, also a way of making clear why I think it is useful to question an analytic posture even as one adopts it. Sometimes, what we call an end also works as a beginning.

BILLY THE QUEER

> He would dress carefully, knotting rich silk ties beneath high starched white collars. There was a kind of dandyism that came out now, and he had a graceful slim figure that the tight clothes flattered. His looks were changing too. Sometimes he would comb his hair in a high pompadourlike style without part above his generous forehead. [. . .] [A]s he moved into the higher grades, his alienation would prompt some of the students at the Oxford High School to tease him and call him "quair."
>
> —JOSEPH BLOTNER, *Faulkner: A Biography*

Queer theory has begun to make its presence known in Yoknapatawpha, though its progress has been wary and its appearance obscured in a thicket of disclaimers and caveats. In his 1994 exploration of homoeroticism in *Go Down, Moses* (one emphasizing the novel's oft-remarked marginalization of its woman characters but making no mention of Percival Brownlee), Neil Watson observes that even though "a case may be made for the subtext of homosexual desire" in the novel, "I certainly have no intention of making any claims about Faulkner, who as far as I know was as straight as they come."[16] This desire to defend Faulkner against the possible "taint" of homosexuality (to indulge what admittedly is the least generous reading of Watson's comment) diminishes somewhat in subsequent studies seeking to enlist queer theory in the study of Faulkner's work, but it never entirely disappears.[17] Minrose Gwin's reading of *Mosquitoes,* Faulkner's second, quite queer, novel, posits an author who "found the terrain, especially the male homoerotic terrain, of the queer abject treacherous footing for the successful male writer in the U.S." and who consequently abandoned that landscape for the presumably less perilous hill country of Yoknapatawpha.[18] Though Gwin takes pains to characterize Faulkner's abandonment as a consequence of "the regulatory powers of compulsory heterosexuality" (140), thus complicating a view of Faulkner as being "as straight as they come," her reading nevertheless casts the later, major novels as only tangentially addressing the issues raised in the work of his apprenticeship. In a paper presented at the same annual Faulkner conference in which Gwin offered her reading of *Mosquitoes,* John Duvall allows that "it would be possible to construct an argument that Faulkner's aesthetic is a gay aesthetic" but decides, finally, that litotes best captures the author's style: "the fiction of William Faulkner does not disavow male homosexuality."[19]

It is not hard to grasp the factors in Faulkner's life and work that have prompted these readings, however tentatively offered. Noted in the Faulkner biographies of both Frederick R. Karl and Joel Williamson, those factors have been well summarized by D. Matthew Ramsey in the course of his queer reading of the short story "Turnabout," a reading that pairs salient aspects of Faulkner's biography with attention to the story's unapologetic (and sympathetic) description of homoerotic attraction (to say that "Turnabout"—which dates not from Faulkner's apprenticeship but from the heart of the years that produced *The Sound and the Fury, As I Lay Dying, Sanctuary,* and *Light in August*—uses "gay codes" is to be too careful by half; very little of Bogard's attraction to Claude is coded).[20] The pertinent biographical details are well-known: the defiant adoption of a continental "dandy" persona in a prewar Mississippi small town deeply antipathetic to such display, a persona that included the serious pursuit of drawing and painting as well as writing poetry and dressing well and that earned Faulkner the soubriquet "Count No 'count"; the apartments shared with gay roommates in 1920s Greenwich Village and New Orleans; the lavish, unapologetic, and never-repudiated admiration for the work of Wilde, Swinburne, Housman, and Aiken.[21] There is, too, as Gwin notes, the evidence of the early work: not only *Mosquitoes* but also the short story "Divorce in Naples"; the sketch "Out of Nazareth," a description of a New Orleans encounter with a beautiful young hobo that references both the Old Testament love of Jonathan and David and Housman's *A Shropshire Lad;* and the intriguing, proto–*Midnight Cowboy* tale of two racetrack touts, "Damon and Pythias Unlimited."[22]

I frame my analysis of Percival Brownlee through this brief survey of efforts to read queerness in Faulkner's work so as to make two points. First, it is not clear to me what purpose is served by "defending" Faulkner from "charges" of homosexuality. The unmistakable sympathetic expressions of homoeroticism in Faulkner's texts, however partial or fraught, may be taken either as local illustrations of the author's own experience of sexual desire as fluid, unruly, and unsettling, or as signs of a strongly empathic creative imagination (and they may, of course, be both at once); neither requires apology. Second (and to return to the essays of Davis and Godden and Polk), given the evidence of the texts and the life, it seems to me a mistake to read Percival Brownlee under the assumption that, for Faulkner, homosexuality always and only signifies shame and abjection, a short-handed way of signaling a target for ridicule. To say that Faulkner is a gay-affirming author is clearly going too far; to assert that he was a homophobic one, however, is equally unreasonable. Ultimately, to the extent that Faulkner's fiction can be said to adopt a public posture toward homosexuality, that posture is probably best described as queerly *tortured*—which description, given all we have learned in two generations' worth of study of the man and the work, reveals Faulkner's approach to homosexuality to be hardly anomalous but, on the contrary, utterly typical.

SPINTRIUS

> To this very day, mankind has always dreamed of seizing and fixing that fleeting moment when it was permissible to believe that the law of exchange could be evaded, that one could gain without losing, enjoy without sharing . . . removing to an equally unattainable past or future the joys, eternally denied to social man, of a world in which one might *keep to oneself.*
>
> —CLAUDE LÉVI-STRAUSS, *The Elementary Structures of Kinship*

It is his renomination as "Spintrius" that seems to both identify and obscure Brownlee's putative status as "the homosexual" of *Go Down, Moses.* We are never told what the name means; but even before the novel goes on to ascribe to Brownlee behaviors "typical" of "homosexual" characters in twentieth-century fiction both homophobic and gay-friendly (i.e., his feminization, his insouciant refusal to accede to the demands of the dominant order, his irrepressibility), the fact that it is Uncle Buddy who proposes the new name invites readers, through the logic of "takes one to know one," to make the interpretive jump. Davis is right to see Uncle Buddy as a kind of pretext for Percival Brownlee; I would argue, however, that it is precisely the novel's refusal to stigmatize Uncle Buddy that is most salient. In many ways Uncle Buddy emerges as the more sympathetic of the twins, and precisely through those aspects of his personality that are most queer. His domestic care of his brother and apparently orphaned nephew McCaslin Edmonds is cast not only as feminized but praiseworthy; it is he who maintains, against his brother's blustering denial, that Eunice's death was no accident, but a suicide (and it is his laconic insistence in the ledgers on exactly this point that prompts Ike's insight into the nature of his grandfather's crime); his ledger entry recording the birth of James, Terrell and Tennie's first surviving infant ("both Well . . . both Well" [*GDM* 260–61]), hints at avuncular delight in the birth of a child as much his nephew as Cass and Ike. Buddy has to make explicit to his brother that his advice to "get shut of" Brownlee means freeing him, not selling him, but the attentive reader will have already made the connection between Buddy's locution and the twins' method of "shutting up" their slaves every evening in their father's unfinished mansion, a method that entails an elaborate display of nailing closed the front door of a building "which lacked half its windows and had no hinged back door at all" (*GDM* 251). If the "unspoken gentlemen's agreement" between the McCaslin twins and their slaves "that, after the white man had counted them and driven the home-made nail into the front door at sundown, neither of the white men would go around behind the house to look at the back door, provided that all the negroes were behind the front one when the brother who drove it drew out the nail again at daybreak" (*GDM* 251) strikes today's readers as perhaps savoring too much of a "don't ask don't tell" acquiescence to a repressive order better actively resisted, it nevertheless indicates a refusal to wholeheartedly endorse that order's dominant practice of domination, a practice that insists on difference—racial difference, gender difference, sexual difference—as natural and obvious even as it seeks to actively prohibit those "back door" freedoms that threaten to expose those differences as something less than natural and not all that obvious. To "get shut of" Percival Brownlee, then, entails recognizing the effectiveness of his mode of resisting enslavement.[23]

As Lee Edelman has noted, "though it can become . . . as dangerous to read as to fail to read homosexuality, homosexuality retains in either case its determining relationship to textuality and the legibility of signs."[24] Edelman describes the effort to write the homosexual as involving a "double operation" that simultaneously does and undoes notions of stable, or natural, sexual identity. On the one hand, there is a kind of writing involving "a category of homosexual person whose very condition of possibility is his relation to writing or textuality, his articulation, in particular, of a 'sexual' difference internal to male identity that generates the necessity of reading certain bodies as *visibly* homosexual" (*Homographesis* 9); such a writing can serve "the ideological purposes of a conservative social order intent on codifying identities in its labor of disciplinary inscription" (*Homographesis* 10). It seems to me that this first of the twin moves of homographesis does capture one aspect of Percival Brownlee that distinguishes him from Uncle Buddy: he is produced *as writing* (in the ledgers) and as *the* homosexual of *Go Down, Moses.* In being so produced within the domain of the ledgers, which are clearly linked to the artificial, "cultural" world of the McCaslin plantation, he serves to order our understanding of the wild, "natural" world of the hunt as distinctly *not*-homosexual. This making visible of homosexuality within *Go Down, Moses* can be seen as meant to guarantee that homosexuality is always visible; we are thus indirectly assured that, though only men hunt the Bottom, nothing but coffee or whiskey could have stained Ike McCaslin's mattress (*GDM* 333). In this way, homosexuality *means* only insofar as it props up the larger heterosexual order; the very terms of its existence derive from its marginal status, which Brownlee's own extremely brief appearance (his story takes up a total of five pages in a 365-page novel) would seem to confirm. In *Go Down, Moses*, this first gesture of homographesis appears quite readily on the surface of the text.

The diastole of Edelman's double operation of homographesis works to deconstruct the conditions of the first; it lets in everything that the first sought to exclude, involving a writing of homosexuality now "resistant to . . . categorization, intent on *de*-scribing the identities that order has so oppressively *in*scribed" (*Homographesis* 10). Or, as Edelman later puts it: "while homographesis refers to the act whereby homosexuality is put into writing under the aegis of writing itself, it also suggests the putting into writing—and therefore into the realm of *différance*—of the sameness, the similitude, or the essentializing metaphors of identity . . . that homographesis, in its first sense, is intended to secure" (*Homographesis* 12). Edelman draws on the example of the homograph—words that are identical in spelling but that mean different things—by way of demonstrating how this process works; as it happens, "bear," as both noun and verb, is the first example he offers (*Homographesis* 12–13).[25] And "by exposing the non-coincidence of what appears to be the same," Edelman writes, "the homograph, like writing, confounds the security of the distinction between sameness and difference" (*Homographesis* 13).[26]

Let me now turn to Percival Brownlee's "Latin" name by way of exploring how he fulfills the second of Edelman's homographic functions. As already noted, he is renamed Spintrius by Uncle Buddy on Christmas Day 1856, two months after he is freed as a result of the brothers' conclusion that he is "wrong . . . wrong . . . wrong" (*GDM* 253). Before this renomination, readers are given no clear sense of just what is "wrong" about Percival Brownlee; we are only given a litany of what he can't (or won't) do: "*No bookepper any way Cant read . . . Cant plough either Says he aims to be a Precher so may be he can lead live stock to Crick to Drink . . . Cant do that either Except one at a Time*" (*GDM* 252–53). The accident with the mule Josephine, about which we get no details, leads to Brownlee's manumission on the following day (*GDM* 253). Brownlee refuses to leave the plantation, however, and it is the effort to get him to leave—and to do this, as Buck puts it, as father would have done it—that results in the renomination. We are given to understand, then, that Lucius Quintus Carothers McCaslin would have handled the problem of Percival Brownlee mainly by relabeling him so as to make legible just exactly what was "wrong" about him.

Though Godden and Polk observe that "'*Spintrius*' derives from '*spintrae*,' Latin for 'perverts'" (309), the fact that the word exists only as a typically Faulknerian back-formed neologism indicates that the term deserves a closer look.[27] "Spintrius" is an attempted "masculinization" of a noun that, while denoting a class of men, exists only in a feminine-sounding form: a *sphintria* is a male prostitute. It derives from the same Greek root that gave rise to a second, etymologically related, Latin word, *sphinter.* This is the word from which we derive our own *sphincter;* the word had similar meaning in antiquity, but in Latin a *sphinter* is not only a muscle. It is also "a kind of bracelet or bangle," something that embraces or binds; it became a name for the muscle largely through metaphorical association.[28] And while a *sphinter* is something worn on the wrist (or carried deep inside oneself), something that may be said to bind an arm (or to embrace a lover), it is not a *manica*—a manacle. In naming Percival Brownlee "Spintrius," then, Uncle Buddy names his condition of "sameness," his "homo-ness," in a way that simultaneously does and undoes "What . . . father [would have] done" (*GDM* 254) by both affirming his difference and naming his freedom. The difference between Percival Brownlee and Spintrius is nothing more—and nothing less—than the difference between a manacle and a bracelet, a surface sameness that opens onto the difference between slavery and freedom.[29]

Thinking through this play of sameness and difference in the sexual and racial economies of *Go Down, Moses* as magnified and intensified by the appearance of Percival Brownlee makes clear how the text, however incompletely, entertains homosexuality as a realm free of the problems of incest and miscegenation that traumatize Ike McCaslin and lead to his repudiation of his heritage; indeed, homosexuality seems posited as the taboo whose breach carries the potential to heal the wounds created by the prior crimes, a return to "sameness" that yet forces liberation and social change. For homosexuality still entails exchange.

In the celebrated opening passages of *The Elementary Structures of Kinship*, Claude Lévi-Strauss posits the incest taboo as the structural "scandal" at the heart of the effort to discern the difference between nature and culture. The question he poses and his answer are well known, but worth briefly recapitulating in the context of reading Brownlee. If what is natural is what is universal in all human societies—leaving to the domain of culture all articulated "rules" of various social groups—what then to make of the proscription of incest, a "rule" that appears to be universal? For Lévi-Strauss, the existence of "a phenomenon which has the distinctive characteristics both of nature and its theoretical contradiction, culture" is "a formidable mystery to sociological thought."[30] The solution, he decides, lies in placing the incest prohibition "on the threshold of culture" (12). "The prohibition of incest is in origin neither purely cultural nor purely natural," he writes, "nor is it a composite mixture of elements from both nature and culture. It is the fundamental step because of which, but above all in which, the transition from nature to culture is accomplished. In one sense, it belongs to nature, for it is a general condition of culture. . . . The prohibition of incest is where nature transcends itself" (24–25). And for Lévi-Strauss, of course, culture emerged with the exchange of women, which the incest taboo works to ensure.

It is not difficult to see how Lévi-Strauss's formulation bears on the concerns of *Go Down, Moses*. If the incest taboo works to establish the world of culture—which exists somehow in opposition to nature—what to say of a domestic order, a culture—that is, the McCaslin family plantation—established in the breach of that taboo? Where, in other words, are we invited to find the locus of the "unnatural" in the world of *Go Down, Moses?* In the incestual insistence on the joys of keeping to oneself, or in an order of endogamous (so to speak), homosexual exchange? Ike's gesture of repudiation is a bid to free himself from his family's past, but it is also an effort to keep to himself, to evade the law of exchange; it thus bears an uncanny structural resemblance to Lucius Quintus Carothers McCaslin's founding crime (as Ike's later "advice" to Roth's rejected mistress makes clear).[31] Brother-sister incest traditionally has been read as the sign for those escapist utopias beyond the law of exchange that dot the Yoknapatawphan landscape (as imagined, for example, by Quentin Compson in *The Sound and the Fury*); in the wake of the irruption of father-daughter incest in *Go Down, Moses,* the homosexual in the person of Percival Brownlee emerges as a route to utopia that does not entail a rejection of exchange.[32]

The homographic function of Percival Brownlee thus puts to question not only an order that seeks to fix sexual identities in a regime of heterosexist, binary difference but also the taken-for-grantedness, the recognizability, of the "difference" between nature and culture itself—a questioning that ramifies through every register of the text. Readings accepting the notion that Ike is vouchsafed his vision of Old Ben only after he repudiates gun, compass, watch, and walking stick in order to shed the "taint" of culture and thus lose himself in an utterly natural and untamed wilderness miss crucial aspects of the scene. Ike does not encounter the bear as a consequence of surrendering himself to the wilderness; quite the contrary. It is only after he *returns* to the clearing where he'd left his watch and compass that "the wilderness coalesced. It rushed, soundless, and solidified—the tree, the bush, the compass and the watch glinting where a ray of sunlight touched them. *Then* he saw the bear" (*GDM* 200; emphasis added). Thus the central "truth" of Ike's encounter with Old Ben is not that "natural forces [are] bound to assert themselves" despite human intervention but, rather, that where Culture was, Nature shall be.[33]

PERCIVAL

"Dear Uncle, what ails you?"
—WOLFRAM VON ESCHENBACH, *Parzifal*

Like Mark Twain, Faulkner was given to public pronouncements deriding the pretensions of post-Reconstruction southern efforts to read the region's history as chivalric romance (whether out of Malory, Scott, or Tennyson), but, far more than Twain's, Faulkner's literary practice was deeply imbricated in what he ostensibly disavowed. Nowhere is this more evident than in *Go Down, Moses*, where Sophonsiba Beauchamp's ludicrous invocations of chivalry in "Was" give way, through Ike's dutiful assumption of the mortifications attendant on his quest to free a ravaged land languishing under a curse, to a full-bore redeployment of the Grail myth. The opening paragraph of "Was" frames both the story and the novel as haunted by narratives of "the old time, the old days," a phrase that punctuates Faulkner's text as a sign of both spurious nostalgia and genuine grief—but while this relentless verbal pressure is new in *Go Down, Moses*, the phrase itself appears, already fraught, in Faulkner's earliest work. "Thus it was in the old days" concludes *Mayday*, the handmade book Faulkner produced for Helen Baird in 1926 that, in its odd, brief tale of a medieval knight's successful quest for "little sister Death," blends the acerbity of Twain with the benignity of Tennyson and so anticipates the pied aesthetic that reaches its apotheosis in *Go Down, Moses*.[34]

If the parodic revision of the Grail itself that emerges through Hubert Beauchamp's slowly vanishing legacy of silver cup and gold coins were not sufficient to signal that Faulkner advances that hoariest avatar of modernist allusion, the tale of the Fisher King, as something other than a pious Eliotic mourning over the losses entailed in the turn to modernity, the appearance of *Percival* Brownlee makes it plain. Though Chrétien de Troyes's *Perceval*, Wolfram of Eschenbach's *Parzifal*, and Wagner's *Parsifal* differ significantly in their approaches to the tale of Percival, in all cases it is the appearance of this "fool" that signals the introduction of the Grail quest into the Arthurian romance and thus, to a significant degree, imposes a unifying interpretive structure on an otherwise highly paratactic narrative of knightly adventure.[35] Brownlee serves much the same function in *Go Down, Moses*. His appearance in the ledgers that inspire Ike's renunciation prompts the careful reader to consider the degree to which the text articulates the search for freedom as a quest upon which Ike McCaslin, in particular, imagines himself embarked.[36] Ike's repudiation is based on the belief that only by a revisionary repetition of his grandfather's gesture of repudiation can he redeem the land from its "curse," a naïve conviction that echoes the homeopathic logic of Wagner's *Parsifal* ("the wound is healed only by the spear that smote you"), but Ike seems unaware—indeed, almost completely unconscious—of the degree to which his repetition fails to reverse his grandfather's gesture: in his encounter with Roth's mistress, Ike's homeopathy indeed leads him to rearticulate his grandfather's command to Eunice ("Marry: a man in your own race" [*GDM* 346]). The competing and conflicting logics of Chrétien's, Wolfram's, and Wagner's treatments of the Grail legend thus constitute an important interpretive thread ushered into the text by Percival Brownlee.

In the fourth section of "The Bear," Ike attempts to explain to his cousin the reasons for his repudiation. Approaching this scene from the revelation of Lucius Quintus Carothers McCaslin's crimes might lead readers to assume that Ike's actions are driven by a kind of remorseful compassion, but careful attention to what he says reveals this is not the only, or even the chief, reason for his decision. Ike posits a neo-Calvinist eschatology of "blood" purification of the land, one in which succeeding generations of races have proven themselves unworthy of stewardship of the land entrusted to them: "Maybe He saw that only by voiding the land for a time of Ikkemotubbe's blood and substituting for it another blood, could He accomplish His purpose. Maybe He knew already what that other blood would be, maybe it was more than justice that only the white man's blood was available and capable to raise the white man's curse, more than vengeance when . . . He used the blood which had brought in the evil to destroy the evil as doctors use fever to burn up fever, poison to slay poison" (*GDM* 248). I have already described how this homeopathic therapeutics mimics the guiding redemptive principle of Wagner's *Parsifal;* the passage's recourse to a logic of blood makes clear that there is more than homeopathy binding Ike's vision to that subtending Wagner's opera. For in order for this scenario of "blood" redemption to work, the races must remain separate: to blend or combine "blood" would introduce such confusion into the heavenly "ledgers" as to compromise God's ability to keep track of each "blood's" successive attempt and failure to redeem the land. Ike's peculiar notion of what is meant by this "blood sacrifice" flows from his earlier vision of the Creation as a resembling nothing so much as a post-Reconstruction plantation novel: God "created the earth, made it and looked at it and said it was all right, and then He made man. He made the earth first and peopled it with dumb creatures, and then he Created man *to be His overseer on earth and to hold suzerainty over the earth and the animals on it in His name*" (*GDM* 246; emphasis added). Here, Heaven is the Big House, man the Master's overseer. This passage leads directly into the more famous (because more comforting) claim that man has failed to fulfill God's edict that the land be held "mutual and intact in the communal anonymity of brotherhood," but it is worth remembering the degree to which Ike affirms notions of hierarchy, and of blood, that his repudiation ostensibly critiques, not least because this then helps us make sense of his "advice" to Roth's rejected mistress: it is completely of a piece with his theory of racial redemption. We might consider, in other words, the degree to which Ike's withdrawal from his family's narrative of human and environmental exploitation—his effort to enact his own "blood sacrifice"—is driven less by compassionate grief for the sufferings of the descendants of Eunice and Tomasina than by an aesthetic desire that his gesture properly fit into a larger form, a "cold pastoral" of human history that, in the circular, symmetrical beauty of its narrative of successive attempts and successive failures, seems a kind of "eternal" truth.[37]

Seen through the multiply allusive, refractive lens of Percival, this facet of Ike's effort to free himself magnifies those aspects of the Grail myth that emphasize the cold forbearance of blood purification, rather than compassion, as key to the redemption of the land, aspects that are crucial to Wagner's *Parsifal*.[38] A streamlined version of the Grail myth meant to deliver a strongly racialized view of human error and salvation, Wagner's *Parsifal* offers a discomfiting gloss on Ike's repudiation that, among other things, renders more comprehensible the charge brought by Roth Edmonds's mistress: Ike indeed appears to have forgotten anything he "ever knew or felt or even heard about love" (*GDM* 346). Still, and as Faulkner's spelling of Brownlee's name indicates, *Parsifal* is not the only narrative of Percival; and though it is the one closest to Faulkner in chronological terms, it almost certainly was not, for him, the definitive version. Even a cursory reading of the romances would make clear to Faulkner that it is precisely the ambiguous and unsettled ("anomalous") nature of Percival (both the character and the tale) that is its most distinguishing feature.[39] So though Wagner's *Parsifal* prompts a critical appraisal of Ike's repudiation, other aspects of the legend invite a different view of his anguished gesture.

Wolfram's expansion and completion of Chrétien's unfinished narrative points the way toward a fuller consideration of what Faulkner ushers into his text in choosing to name Brownlee as he did. *Parzifal* is a romance of hidden, and so too long unacknowledged, family suffering (the ailing Grail king is Parzifal's uncle, a crucial detail scrubbed from Wagner's opera), a tale of sexual wounding that can only be assuaged by compassionate recognition and acceptance. Parzifal's sin lies in refusing to ask after the cause of his uncle's pain even after the instrument of that suffering is paraded before his eyes; he learns the cause of his uncle's grief elsewhere, in the course of his own lonely errantry, and it is only in returning to his uncle's side and asking the question to which he has learned the answer that Parzifal alleviates his uncle's pain, heals a suffering land, and accomplishes his own redemption. And while on the one hand aspects of this narrative might seem to strengthen the unflattering view of Ike ushered into the text by the allusion to Wagner's opera (insofar as they tend to confirm a lack of genuine compassion as central to Ike's failure), considering Uncle Ike *himself* as the grievously wounded guardian of a ravaged land points to a different interpretive strategy. What happens to *Go Down, Moses* if we take Parzifal's necessary question as our own: Dear Uncle, what ails you?[40]

In her essay "Melancholy Gender/Refused Identification," Judith Butler posits repudiation as the perhaps the single most potent gesture in the construction of a ostensibly whole and untroubled heterosexual subject, and it is a gesture that comes at formidable psychic cost: heterosexuality "is an identity based upon the refusal to avow [a homosexual] attachment and, hence, [a] refusal to grieve."[41] Butler is concerned to explain the phobic outbursts characteristic of a certain kind of hyperheterosexual identification as manifestations of this denied grief—but it is worth considering what a text (or a person) undertaking the task of finally grieving that repudiated attachment would look like. Until this moment, we have drawn on queer theory to read *Go Down, Moses;* here Faulkner's novel reads queer theory, for Butler leaves unexplored the possibility that any putatively heterosexual artist might choose to recollect, let alone represent, the grief of renouncing a beloved homosexual attachment. And if there is one aspect of *Go Down, Moses* that has received widespread agreement in the criticism, it is that the novel is saturated with a persistent, deeply felt, and unassuageable grief: Ike's grief for the loss of the wilderness, figured in the deaths of Old Ben and Sam Fathers; Rider's grief for Manny; Molly's grief for her lost grandson Samuel Worsham Beauchamp, her "Benjamin sold into Egypt"; Roth's grief for the loss of his Black family; Faulkner's grief for his nursemaid Caroline Barr, signaled in novel's dedication ("To Mammy"). A not-infrequent corollary of this grief is guilt: Ike's life as a hunter, in ways different from but parallel to his grandfather's life as a planter, clearly contributes to the death of what he claims to love; Roth's grief and shame over the loss of his Black foster-brother Henry does not change the fact that he himself repudiates the beloved connection; Faulkner's grief for the loss of a woman as much mother to him as his own does not erase or ameliorate the racist structures of southern domestic labor that brought him to her care in the first place.[42] In *Go Down, Moses* grief and guilt go together; and by this point it should be clear that I think the novel grieves another loss, and another guilt, beyond those already mentioned: the loss and guilt entailed in the refusal to embrace, or even clearly speak, the homosexual passions and possibilities gestured toward everywhere in the text. These possibilities include, but are not limited to, the loves of Zack and Lucas, of Roth and Henry, of Ike and Sam Fathers.[43] These grieved possibilities figure not only Ike's own losses but the history of similar losses that hail and so compel his own; they may figure Faulkner's losses, as well. Recognizing how the text signals its ongoing grief as a consequence not only of repudiation but also of the refusal to ask after the pain left in the wake of that repudiation brings readers to consider, to turn again to Butler, how the fleeting but nonetheless striking "mobility" of Brownlee functions as "a sign that a rigorously instituted logic of repudiation is not, after all, necessary" (*Power* 164). To read Percival and Spintrius together, in other words, is to see how *Go Down, Moses* gestures toward unrealized, scarcely articulated, but nonetheless deeply desired worlds of potential but denied action, affect, and freedom—unrealized worlds that haunt the novel.

ECCE HOMO

> Camp is a form of historicism viewed histrionically ... a disguise that fails.
> —PHILIP CORE, qtd. in *Camp: Queer Aesthetics and the Performing Subject*, ed. Fabio Cleto

To consider the various versions of the Percival romance that precede *Go Down, Moses* is not simply to recognize that there are different ways of shaping those aspects of the narrative that seem most indispensable to the story (the hero who begins his adventure knowing nothing of himself; the bleeding spear and glowing cup; the suffering knight; the failure to speak at the proper time that necessitates the return to articulate the unspoken question and so demonstrate compassionate concern): it is also to realize that there are different modes for expressing that material. The tale of Percival has aspects of the deepest tragedy and the highest comedy, and in fact Chrétien's and Wolfram's romances blend comedy and tragedy to often startling effect. However these mixtures may have struck the original audiences of these epics, for modern sensibilities such promiscuous blending is a hallmark of camp.

It is generally agreed that the humorous aspects of *Go Down, Moses* exist largely as residues of the flawed short stories Faulkner drew upon and revised in writing the novel. I want to suggest that the comic aspects of *Go Down, Moses* may also be understood as eruptions of camp, deliberate attempts to blend tragedy and comedy in a manner both artistically daring and politically provocative that model a kind of Nietzschean "gay scientific" approach to the grim truths of human bondage.[44] This is not to say that the text's use of humor is not often problematic; it is, rather, to offer a different, potentially more productive, explanation for this problem than heretofore proposed.

In an interview published ten years after the appearance of her groundbreaking and controversial essay "Notes on Camp," Susan Sontag admitted that the essay had its beginnings not in an abiding interest in camp itself but rather in "speculations of a rather general order" that coalesced into an ambition to "'name a sensibility,' to 'draw its contours, to recount its history.'"

> —that was the problem I started from, and then looked for an example, a model. And it seemed more interesting not to pick Sensibility X from among those heaped with ethical or aesthetic laurels, and to evoke instead a sensibil-

ity that was exotic and in obvious ways minor, even despised—as the rather quirky notion of a "sensibility" had itself been slighted, in favor of that tidier fiction, an "idea."

Morbidity was my first choice. I stayed with that for a while, attempting to systematize a long-term fascination with mortuary sculpture, architecture, inscriptions and other such wistful lore. . . . But the material was too detailed, and cumbersome to describe, so I switched to camp, which had the advantage of being familiar as well as marginal.[45]

Sontag describes her move from morbidity to camp largely as a consequence of formal—indeed, pragmatic and writerly—concerns: the detailed thickness of the morbid sensibility was simply *too much* to deal with, while camp's slender life on the margins of the familiar made it a far more flexible model. However, and as Caryl Flinn demonstrates, Sontag's shift from morbidity to camp is better understood not primarily as expedient but rather as a function of the relationship between morbidity and camp. For the two have more in common than simply a shared status as "despised," "minor," and "exotic" "sensibilities": the morbid and the camp both draw their affective power from their "wistful" relationship to the past, both the narratives of history and the figures of the dead. Camp articulates the longing (and grief) binding present to past, living to dead, but camp also puts that longing to the test by relentlessly exposing the hidden values and ideological assumptions that, as Susan Stewart has shown, are buried within the nostalgic impulse.

As Flinn points out, camp "might be said to function as a kind of *ironic* nostalgia," and though camp nostalgia thus always clearly separates itself from its ostensible love object and so always is expressed at a distance—as Sontag might say, expressed in quotation marks—it remains the case that camp nostalgia, like "straight" nostalgia, maintains a certain affection for its target.[46] Still, for camp, the narrative of history is useful not primarily as an explanation, a justification, or a rebuke, but as material for revisionary, potentially liberating, performance. Narrative becomes a stage; history becomes histrionic.

It is precisely this irreverent impulse that abets the persistent charge against camp that it lacks "depth" (which is to say, it lacks politics). Parallel to this charge, and indirectly buttressing it, is a secondary claim: that "even though homosexuals have been its vanguard, Camp taste is much more than homosexual taste. . . . [O]ne feels that if homosexuals hadn't more or less invented Camp, someone else would."[47] Critics of Sontag's essay long ago pointed out how these two claims—that camp has no politics and that camp is *not only* ("is much more than") a gay sensibility—operate together: Camp is denied a politics because it is denied its history as a response to an oppressive (and repressive) social regulation of sexual practices. Still, it's possible that the claim that camp taste "is much more than homosexual taste" arises from something other than homophobia. One could take Sontag's observation as an early manifestation of the epistemological shift that led to the revaluation and recruitment of the word "queer" as a means of indicating something deeply connected to, but "much more than," homosexuality.[48] Viewed through this lens, Sontag's observation can be seen as working less to minimize the "homosexual taste" of camp than to expand the field for camp action *and* homosexual taste, an expansion that, among other things, destabilizes our certainty about what is *not* camp (or homosexual).[49]

But granting this expanded camp ground does not solve the problem of determining the politics of camp: is it a resistant practice, a humorous, liberating "strategy for a situation"?[50] Or is it, to quote Andrew Britton, "little more than a kind of anaesthetic, allowing one to remain inside oppressive relations while enjoying the illusory confidence that one is flouting them"?[51] And what, exactly, does any of this have to do with reading Faulkner?

Undeniably, camp punctures any claim for the innocence of nostalgia by revealing its ideological moorings in the patriarchal family and in capitalist modes of production. It is hard to maintain certainty about the "naturalness" of the social order of "the old days, the old time" in the face of camp. However, camp operates not only against but *through* nostalgia, and so can be felt to maintain a sympathetic posture toward that which needs to be dismantled. It is in this apparent contradiction that the homographic double gesture emerges as crucial to understanding the blended discourse of camp. Camp's truth content rests precisely in its queer capacity to turn nostalgia against historicism, and this has been both its greatest strength and its greatest (perceived) weakness. Andrew Ross expressed this tension more than thirty years ago when he noted that camp "proposes working with and through existing definitions and representations, and in this respect it is opposed to the search for alternative, utopian, or essentialist identities which lay behind many of the countercultural and sexual liberation movements."[52] As a form, a practice, and a series of gestures, camp is *at once* critical and complicit, and it is precisely this queer doubleness that its detractors find most troubling. This doubleness, this excessive—truly, *démesuré*—insistence on "trying to say it all" is what many readers find most vexing about the Faulknerian text, as well, and particularly *Go Down, Moses*. How can a novel that begins with the farcical "Was" and that frames the grim tragedies revealed in the ledgers through the misadventures of a minor character like Percival Brownlee possibly articulate a sympathetic understanding of Black life under slavery and after?

To a significant degree, of course, *Go Down, Moses* admits its failure to enter into complete communion with the Black lives it purports to represent (an admission made most spectacularly in the postmortem narrative of the deputy sheriff in "Pantaloon in Black"), and making note of the novel's failure to accomplish what it seems to set out to do has become a commonplace in the criticism. To assume, though, that the only proper posture toward its material is one of uniform gravity is perhaps to assume too much; and while considering the humor in *Go Down, Moses* as a kind of camp efflorescence does not absolve the text from charges of failure, it does give us a different position from which to assess that failure. The text's unwillingness to take its tragedy completely straight, for instance, can be seen as an affirmative Nietzschean parody that insists on the liberating potential of the refusal to concede the sober terms of the historical narrative within which one finds oneself imprisoned. If it is true that, for Nietzsche as for Faulkner, "the role of art is to express the inner confusion of man confronted by humanity's drive for formal expression," a drive that speaks itself not only in art but also through and against those formal expressions of social "order" that posit clear racial, gender, and sex roles—if, to put it as Faulkner did, the central task of the artist is to express the human heart in conflict with itself—then the artist cannot help but function "parodically in relationship to all rigorous structuring."[53] And if it is additionally true, as Sander Gilman claims, that "Nietzsche views a successful parody as one which does not demean its prototype" (16), then Faulkner's deployment of humor in *Go Down, Moses* perhaps may be understood not only as indicating white contempt (the deputy sheriff) or obtuseness (Gavin Stevens) in the face of Black suffering. It may indicate, as well, an attempt to represent Black refusal to submit to white terms of existence—particularly if we understand the ghosted narrative of homosexuality in *Go Down, Moses* to be signaling something other than humiliation or abjection.

Finally: considering the role of Percival Brownlee in *Go Down, Moses* has led me to ponder how our current scholarly practice has been marked by the very same gesture of repudiation that marks *Go Down, Moses*. As I have already indicated, it is the gesture by which Lucius Quintus Carothers McCaslin is known—indeed, his crime consists chiefly in repudiating the kinship claims of daughter and son—and it is the gesture Ike repeats in rejecting his grandfather's plantation legacy. Ike's repudiation of his legacy arises not simply from the fact of his family's crime: as *Go Down, Moses* makes clear, it is also a consequence of his reading, in which he approaches the ledgers knowing "what he was going to find before he found it" and, having found what he expected, "never . . . look[ed] at [the ledgers] . . . again" (*GDM* 257, 259). I do not agree with those who claim that Ike fabricates a crime that may never have occurred (this is Godden and Polk's claim; Evans hints at this, as well)—he knew what he was going to find for good reason. But neither is Ike's reading practice any kind of model for scholarship, and it is worth pondering the degree to which we ourselves indulge in similarly hasty repudiations.[54] Rereading is necessary not because it changes the "facts" of a text but because our response to those facts will (need to) change.[55] Thus I have sought here to practice a particular kind of reading strategy in considering the meaning of Percival Brownlee: one based not on repudiation but on compassion; one that seeks not to prosecute the text for what it does not say but rather to attend to what it gestures toward. One that asks questions perhaps too long unspoken.

8

Unhistoricizing Faulkner

> All human beings are capable of making a homosexual object-choice and have in fact made one in their unconscious.
>
> —SIGMUND FREUD, *Three Essays on the Theory of Sexuality*

For more than twenty-five years, historicist modes of analysis have dominated literary study in the United States, and Faulkner studies have been no exception. Indeed, one could say that Faulkner scholars have been in the vanguard of the historicist movement, which is generally seen as having replaced excessively formalist New Criticism, hastily universalizing mythical readings, and rigidly allegorical "psychoanalytic" approaches with long-overdue attention to the economic, social, and political conditions under which authors and their texts come into being. Fredric Jameson's 1981 command to "always historicize!" was followed just two years later by Eric J. Sundquist's influential *Faulkner: The House Divided*, in which reconstructing "a context for Faulkner's fiction out of historical experience, contemporary literature, or political and sociological documents" is postulated as "the *only* way in which Faulkner's power and significance can be made to emerge."[1] As Sundquist predicted, Faulkner scholarship has come to grant privileged interpretive status to US southern history and its legacies of slavery, military conquest, and *de jure* racial segregation. Yet historicist modes of reading, like the allegorical ones they sometimes still resemble, are not limited to a single lens; and while the road to Yoknapatawpha, for good reason, lately has proceeded mostly through this landscape of racialized sectionalism, it has not been the only historical route through the novels. The nativist Faulkner, the New Deal Faulkner, the Cold War Faulkner, the postcolonial Faulkner, and, yes, the queer Faulkner: all are historically based interpretive constructs in one way or another.

Before going further I should make one thing clear. I am not at all opposed to historical literary and cultural analysis; in fact, I do it myself a lot of the time; in fact, one might say that there's nothing else I, or any one of us, can ever do, given our own temporality. But acknowledging one's own historically shaped epistemological limitations as a reader is rather a different thing from delimiting an artwork's historically determined zone of meaning. Certainly both gestures are foundational to any ethical or politically aware cultural analysis; but while the first is the cornerstone of humility, the second risks hubris, even cynicism. The emergence of the last of those contextual frames that I just listed—the sexual frame, which gives us the queer Faulkner—historically inflected as that emergence is, has highlighted the difference between these two ways of reading history in literary study, raising fundamental questions about the analytic categories informing most historicist modes of inquiry (for example, identity, teleology, and consciousness). We should not ignore these questions, if only because we would wish to be certain that, in our own interpretive work, we do not (to anticipate my discussion later in this chapter of an essay by Tim Dean) practice our politics at the expense of our ethics.[2]

It would be foolhardy, of course, to claim that reading Faulkner's sexualities through queer theory puts paid to a generation's worth of historically informed readings, many of them brilliant and illuminating both ethically and politically. Still, for a discussion of Faulkner's sexualities to be more than an occasion for one-liners ("Who knew that the Nobel Prize winner was ambidextrous?"),[3] we should acknowledge the questions queer theory poses for historicism. Toward that aim, I'll describe some recent developments in queer theory, a lively field of inquiry that has productively reopened questions long treated as closed. It will become clear how these developments press against many of the assumptions governing historicist literary analysis, but I want to emphasize certain of those pressure points so as to make plain the issues they raise. Since my research began with my own uncertainty over how to engage the many ways one could approach Faulkner's sexualities, I close with a discussion of the short story "The Leg"—an early story that I find helpful in illuminating how one angle on Faulkner's sexualities can lead to what we could call, following Jonathan Goldberg and Madhavi Menon, a more "unhistoricist" approach, one enabling "antihistoricist ways of formulating . . . historicity."[4]

Not unlike psychoanalysis, about which it has a good deal to say, queer theory is a *fin de siècle* development: two of its acknowledged foundational texts, Judith Butler's *Gender Trouble* and Eve Kosofsky Sedgwick's *Tendencies*, were published in 1990 and 1993, respectively.[5] If only because her prior work had been almost exclusively within the domain of gay literary and cultural analysis, Sedgwick's study more clearly marks the shift in thinking involved in moving from the post-Stonewall, strongly identitarian, antihomophobic mode of cultural inquiry to what Goldberg and Menon have called "the non- and even anti-identitarian" work of queer theory (1609), but Butler's rhetorical reading of sexuality and gender, which casts both as effects of "performative" language practices, was seen as the more radical and (as her title hopefully predicted) troubling of the two works. In postulating a hollowness at the core of any notion of sexual or gender identity, *Gender Trouble* offers one of the most strictly constructionist of the many social constructionist theses of human sexuality that arose in the wake of Michel Foucault's incomplete, multivolume *History of Sexuality,* a study often invoked as a prototype for the rigorously historicist work that has come to be associated with the constructionist thesis as such. The nature and consequences of Foucault's thought are contested to this day, but one does not have to read very far in the world of sexuality studies before bumping into the observation, widely attributed to the first of the three completed volumes of Foucault's *History,* that it was only in the mid-nineteenth century that a variety of sexual practices were named and configured as human "identities" in order to allow us to "not only seek the truth of sex, but demand from it our own truth." As Foucault sharply puts it, "We expect it [sex] to tell us who we are,"[6] and it would not be inaccurate to see much of his research as fundamentally engaged with demonstrating the unreasonableness of this expectation. In his analysis, homosexual and heterosexual identities emerge as effects of discourse, inventions of intellectual and emotional disciplines (in all senses of the word) that work both to incite and to police human sexual behavior. The merits of this thesis (and obviously I offer a potted summary here) lie in the degree to which it demonstrates how what we tend to assume as a transhistorical biological "truth" is in fact a Victorian-era construct stitched together out of tissue immanent to long-standing Western moral, racial, and religious beliefs—prejudices, really, that became objective and convincing largely through their rearticulation in the new discursive formations of anthropology, sociology, criminology, and psychology. This is a historicist reading insofar as a particular understanding of human sexuality is shown to have been a product of a particular moment in history, bearing the impressions of the social, educational, and economic conditions of its emergence. The truth of human sexuality is shown to be not timeless and fixed but rather contingent and malleable; a human creation, it is a truth open to revision.

A thesis meant to diminish delusion, enhance self-understanding, and enable liberation, this forcefully constructionist view of human sexuality, as rearticulated in Butler's *Gender Trouble* (a rearticulation that laid heavier emphasis than had Foucault's on deconstruction) initially faced some skepticism from feminists and advocates of lesbian and gay civil rights in the United States. Butler's strongest early criticism came from those who felt that she gave short shrift to "the body," a shorthand way of indicating all those physical attributes held to be unalterable through discourse or rhetoric and thus not amenable to subversive rearticulation in the manner of the drag queens Butler so admired. The ship of discourse (or rhetoricism, or constructionism—these are in some ways synonyms) can make no headway against the shoals of biology (or foundationalism, or essentialism, to again indicate like terms)—or so the criticism went, and thus in her follow-up study, *Bodies That Matter,* Butler worked harder to explain the enlightening and liberating properties of a rigorously rhetorical—which is to say, deconstructive—view of sexual identity.

Butler didn't convince all of her critics, and this standoff between biology and rhetoric (known in its largest contours as the essentialist-constructionist debate) might have continued indefinitely were it not for a series of articles in the late 1990s that broke the impasse by drawing on concepts developed in that branch of the "human sciences" that takes the relation between flesh and language as its chief concern: psychoanalysis. Perhaps no scholar has accomplished more in this area than Tim Dean, and in what follows I draw heavily on his work.[7] As he and others have pointed out, the problem with Butler's analysis lies less in her reliance on deconstruction than in her use of several key psychoanalytic concepts. In particular, Butler's uses of the theories of Jacques Lacan have drawn considerable commentary, but the question of

Butler's prowess as a reader of Lacan is less interesting for what it says about her theoretical acumen than for what it tells us about the ongoing seductive power of widely held assumptions regarding the "universalizing" "biologist" agenda said to drive psychoanalysis—an agenda whose totalizing pretensions are seen as best kept at arm's length via proper historicism.[8] It's worth recalling that a certain impatience with psychoanalysis informs Jameson's study, as well; in *The Political Unconscious,* "Freudian interpretation" is described as "a reduction and a rewriting of the whole rich and random multiple realities of concrete everyday experience into the contained, strategically prelimited terms of the family narrative . . . a system of allegorical interpretation in which the data of one narrative line are radically impoverished by their rewriting according to the paradigm of another narrative, which is taken as the former's master code or Ur-narrative and proposed as the ultimate hidden or unconscious *meaning* of the first one" (21–22). Here Jameson summarizes the argument of *Anti-Oedipus* by Gilles Deleuze and Félix Guattari,[9] which he characterizes as a "dramatic" (i.e., immoderate) attack on psychoanalysis even as he indicates some sympathy with its claims. Ultimately, Jameson judges psychoanalysis to be symptomatic of capitalism, and I will return to this issue of symptomatology later.[10] Here I want to stress that similarly narrow, if less theoretically developed, assumptions regarding what might be called the "evil genes" of psychoanalysis are held by Sedgwick as well, and while those assumptions can be traced to several sources (not least of them Freud himself), a good portion of the problem, according to Dean, lies in the unhappy transplantation of psychoanalysis to the United States, where the ideal of disinterested investigation into psychic operations was transformed into ego psychology, and where probing self-examination, whose aim was improved self-knowledge and an accompanying measure of self-acceptance, became reformist, adaptive therapy.

The psychic damage inflicted by US psychoanalysts seeking to enact a sexual "cure" in their lesbian and gay patients has been amply reported in both the popular and scholarly presses, and Butler and Sedgwick are right, given this, to question whether their purposes can be served by psychoanalysis. But in moving against psychoanalysis, Butler overlooks an important aspect of Foucault's thought. Foucault did indeed view with suspicion Freud's role in creating a world in which one's sexual practices are viewed as the "expression" of one's very being ("The West" 53). However, and as Arnold I. Davidson has noted, "the Freudian discovery of the unconscious represented for [Foucault] a decisive epistemological achievement" that "allowed one to question the old [Cartesian] theory of the subject.... However odd it may sound, the existence of the unconscious was a decisive component in Foucault's *antipsychologism*."[11] This is because the concept of the unconscious operates in much the same way as Foucault's institutional genealogies: to accept the existence of the unconscious is to accept the achievements of consciousness as precarious and contingent. Thus articulating Freud and Foucault together via the unconscious, in a manner more dialectical than oppositional, has drawn many theorists to explore how "psychoanalytic institutions have developed in directions antithetical to psychoanalytic concepts,"[12] leading to a revived interest in psychoanalysis as a philosophical and epistemological practice.

Though it was intended primarily to dispute the widely held view that Freud (like US-style psychoanalysis) was homophobic, and though it appeared before the emergence of queer theory, Henry Abelove's 1985 essay "Freud, Male Homosexuality, and the Americans" can be seen, in retrospect, to have begun this practice of rereading Freud with the aim of coming to a fuller appreciation of how his theories of human sexual desire cut across and complicate the notion of sexual "identity." Abelove's essay details Freud's lifelong refusal to posit homosexuality as an illness, opening with a discussion of Freud's 1935 letter to the mother of an American homosexual seeking treatment for her son; reminding us of Freud's 1903 assertion that "homosexuals must not be treated as sick people"; noting Freud's signing of a 1930 petition urging the Austrian decriminalization of homosexuality between consenting adults; and concluding with an illuminating reading of Freud's seven-year correspondence with James Jackson Putnam, an American psychoanalyst whose moralistic view of the talking cure plainly anticipates the turn to ego psychology and just as plainly repelled Freud.[13] In Putnam's view, patients needed "more than to simply learn to know themselves"; they needed to "try to improve their moral character and temperaments." Freud's response was unequivocally hostile: "Sexual morality as society—and at its most extreme, American society—defines it, seems very despicable to me. I stand for a much freer sexual life" (Abelove 386).

In describing Freud's refusal to judge homosexuality an illness, Abelove raised the question of just how Freud came to hold a position running so counter to that of most of his contemporaries. Careful readings of the 1915 footnote to the first of the 1905 *Three Essays on the Theory of Sexuality,* which provides the epigraph for this chapter, have gone some distance toward supplying an answer to that question, for this footnote reveals how, in Freud's view, a proper understanding of the unconscious—filled, as it is, with wishes and drives in which gender, sex, and temporal differences and distinctions are almost totally meaningless—militates against the notion that homosexual desire is "unnatural":

> Psycho-analytic research is most decidedly opposed to any attempt at separating off homosexuals from the rest of mankind as a group of special character. By studying sexual excitations other than those that are manifestly displayed, it has found that all human beings are capable of making a homosexual object-choice and have in fact made one in their unconscious. Indeed, libidinal attachments to persons of the same sex play no less a part as factors in normal mental life . . . than do similar attachments to the opposite sex. On the contrary, psycho-analysis considers that a choice of an object independently of its sex—freedom to range equally over male and female objects . . . is the original basis from which, as a result of restriction in one direction or the other, both the normal and the inverted types develop. Thus from the point of view of psychoanalysis the exclusive sexual interest felt by men for women is also a problem that needs elucidating and is not a self-evident fact. (*Three Essays* 145–46)

A politically progressive reading of this footnote in the mid-1980s like Abelove's entailed a normalizing view of homosexuality (despite Freud's use of the conventional opposition of his time between "normal" and "invert"); indeed, a view of homosexual desire as no less normal than heterosexual desire continues to inform today's lesbian and gay civil rights movement, and for good reason. Contemporary queer theory, however, takes a different interpretive approach. As Tim Dean and Christopher Lane explain, rather "than simply revealing homosexuality as a normal and natural expression of human erotic potential, Freud's connecting sexuality to the unconscious instead makes *all* sexuality perverse. . . . The idea of the unconscious dramatically changes how we can and should think about human sexuality" (Dean and Lane 4; emphasis added).[14]

How does it do this? By raising the possibility that the fundamental structuring differences of conscious life are meaningless to the unconscious. This observation has not gone unnoticed—Philip Weinstein reminds us how Freud's insight regarding the timelessness of unconscious mental processes made it possible for Faulkner, Kafka, and Proust to explore how "historical" events "remain unabsorbed, still registering their effects" in the present—but only recently have we begun to add to this awareness of the unconscious refusal to recognize temporal boundedness a full appreciation of its concomitant rejection of other constraints.[15] "To Freud's list of the characteristics of primary process thinking—the unconscious knows no negation, no contradiction, nothing of time—we now can add that the unconscious knows nothing of heterosexuality," Dean observes (*Beyond* 86). Realizing this, we can understand why Foucault valued Freud's discovery of the unconscious even as he viewed the institutionalization of psychoanalysis with suspicion: the unconscious works in much the same manner as Foucault's genealogies to puncture the notion of a human subject who, by dint of conscious effort conducted in keeping with immutable natural laws, will come to command its capacities. To uncover the ramshackle nature of so much of the "human sciences," to recognize how the existence of the unconscious means we will never be masters in our own house: these are rhyming insights, though arising from different opening assumptions.

Freud's theory of an ungovernably desiring unconscious has had historical consequences, though, as Dean and Lane observe: "Freud's originality stems not from his treating sexuality as historical, but paradoxically from his universalizing gestures" (11). This is to say, perhaps, that the unconscious is the place where biology and rhetoric—universalism and historicism, essentialism and constructionism—touch. Viewing the unconscious as both contingent and transcendent has two consequences for the argument I'm developing here. The first, and more indirect one, raises the possibility that historicist interpretations of sexuality in a text undertaken chiefly to abet judgment on an aspect of "sexual identity"—whether or not the author was "ambidextrous," whether characters are or are not recognizably lesbian or gay, whether or not a narrative is homophobic—no matter how well-meant politically, unhelpfully narrow our interpretive landscape. The second, and more direct, consequence lies in grasping how a certain rigidly historicist contextualism, even if intended to expand our political understanding of how texts arise and circulate in the world, can also limit literature's purchase on that world.

As I plan to explore the first point via my concluding discussion of "The Leg," I will take up the second one here. Queer theory's recognition of the unconscious as both universal and historical has consequences ranging beyond a concern with textual sexuality, and it is no surprise that two calls for change in literary critical business-as-usual have come from queer theory scholars. The first, Tim Dean's "Art as Symptom," shies away from a direct critique of Jamesonian Marxist historicism, but his shrewd reading of the liabilities of "the tendency to treat aesthetic artifacts as symptoms of the culture in which they were produced," centered though it is on the work of Slavoj Žižek, raises larger questions about the degree to which less avowedly psychoanalytic cultural analyses succeed in avoiding the seductions of a program of "demystification" that "elides the specificity of art" and transforms the critic into "a hermeneut with a particular relation to the world—a relation of suspicion and putative mastery" ("Art as Symptom" 29, 23). Dean's chief concern is the troubling ethical implications of an interpretive "conviction . . . that the work of art is duplicitous or ignorant of something, that it exhibits contradictions of which it is unaware and therefore needs the critic to help reveal. Neither artists nor their cultures are considered masters of the conflicts that produce their work; instead the role of mastery . . . falls to the demystifying critic" ("Art as Symptom" 30). This is not an entirely new complaint—cultural conservatives have long derided what they see as an insufficient contemporary reverence for artistic greatness in the work of canonical "masters."[16] What *is* new in Dean's account is his proposed intervention, an "associative" reading practice that addresses the problem of overweening critical mastery not by returning authority to the text via appeals to its formal autonomy (the cultural conservatives' approach) but rather by "enabling us to appreciate how enigmas aren't always puzzles to be decoded or obstacles to be overcome, but instead represent an ineliminable condition of existence" ("Art as Symptom" 39). As Dean's terminology indicates, he derives this "associative" reading practice from the psychoanalytic recognition that the workings of the unconscious present us with an "otherness [that] is a property of discourse" ("Art as Symptom" 38). In many ways psychoanalysis is committed to making sense of that otherness, to reducing its alien character, but, as Dean reminds us, psychoanalysis "thwarts interpretation even as it prompts it" ("Art as Symptom" 35).[17] Properly understood, this thwarting leads the "associative" critic to recognize how "the enigmas of otherness are exacerbated by art" ("Art as Symptom" 38). He continues:

> To the extent that art entails a practice or experience of defamiliarization in which otherness comes to the fore, it requires an ethical rather than an epistemological approach. From this perspective the ethics of psychoanalytic criticism would consist in refusing the imperative to overcome all enigmaticity through demystification. Such an ethics would encourage us to adopt a less knowingly superior attitude toward art.... The hermeneutics of suspicion that characterizes interpretive practices running the gamut from psychoanalysis to materialist to historicist criticism promotes a paranoid relation to cultural forms, fueling the impulse to critically master opacity or uncertainty through rigorous interpretation. But just as psychoanalysis indubitably contributes to this project by way of its theories of a cultural unconscious and attendant cultural symptoms, so too can psychoanalysis make us less paranoid, less insistent on uncovering meaning and significance everywhere we turn. ("Art as Symptom" 38–39)[18]

If Dean calls us to rethink Freud, Goldberg and Menon's "Queering History" comes at the problem via a reconsideration of Foucault. For Goldberg and Menon, the rigorously constructionist approach to sexuality has proven "inadequate to housing the project of queering" (1609). Taking queer theory's critique of identity to perhaps its limit, they argue against a view of history built on the belief that "the only modes of knowing the past are either those that regard the past as wholly other or those that can assimilate it to a present assumed identical to itself" (1616). Goldberg and Menon are troubled by what they see as a tendency to cast texts as entirely one or the other: either artifacts of a time utterly alien or evidence of how we have become what we are. In seeking a way around these unsatisfactory alternatives, Goldberg and Menon place Dipesh Chakrabarty's notion of the present as "not-one" next to Hayden White's call for a historical understanding of historiography in order to propose a mode of reading that would keep "alive the undecidable difference between difference and sameness [and thus] ... refuse what we might term the compulsory heterotemporality of historicism, whether it insists on difference or produces a version of the normative same" (1616).[19]

As Dean proposes an "associative" respect for textual enigma, so Goldberg and Menon call for a historical reading practice that would pay "attention to the question of sexuality *as a question*," one that insists neither on the past's radical alterity from, nor its teleological connection to, the present, but rather is sensitive to what they term its "idemtity": "a proportionality, likeness or similarity that is more an approximation than a substantialization" (1609–10). And as Dean's critique seeks to counter the aggression that can attend a reading practice grounded in suspicion and paranoia, so Goldberg and Menon press against the conviction "that history is the discourse of answers," since such a view produces "a discourse whose commitment to determinate signification . . . provides false closure, blocking access to the multiplicity of the past and to the possibilities of different futures" (1609).[20]

So what does all this have to do with reading Faulkner generally, or Faulkner's sexualities in particular? Let me approach that question via a return to Eric Sundquist's *House Divided,* and in particular its opening chapter, "The Myth of *The Sound and the Fury*." As this title implies, Sundquist aims to trouble the conventional view of Faulkner's fourth novel as an unquestioned masterpiece, and he goes at it hammer and tongs from almost the first page, asserting that "there is reason to believe that without Faulkner's work of the next ten years *The Sound and the Fury* would itself seem a literary curiosity" (3). In a chapter impressive not only for its interpretive rigor but also for the elegance of its prose, Sundquist argues that the importance of *The Sound and the Fury* emerges "only . . . in the larger context of novels to which it gives rise" (9). The ingeniousness of Sundquist's argument lies in his assertion that this indispensability of *The Sound and the Fury* cuts two ways: the novel prefigures both "the many problems in Faulkner's later fiction" (4) ("the dramatic parody and philosophical nonsense . . . the bulging prose and crude, idiosyncratic symbolism" of the work after 1942 [13, 14]) and the great novels that emerge once Faulkner takes on the "social and historical context" of his Jim Crow South: *Light in August, Absalom, Absalom!,* and *Go Down, Moses* (5).

Sundquist's charge that *The Sound and the Fury* is overrated has not gone undisputed; some of our finest Faulkner scholars have picked away at his claim that the novel is best viewed as a "preparation for things to follow, a search for a way to say things that had not been said" (6).²¹ For the most part, though, these critiques work by demonstrating the many ways in which the novel *does* engage with "the single most agonizing experience of [Faulkner's] region and nation: the crisis and long aftermath of American slavery" (6). I agree that Sundquist pays too little attention to the ways in which the novel dramatizes what it is "trying to say" about the southern racial *agon*—but the absolute merit of this corrective view is less interesting than the fact that it grants Sundquist his ground. That is, it concedes the truth of his larger claim: that only in writing explicitly about racial history did Faulkner become "great." This is a value judgment of a rather remarkable kind, postulating Faulkner's writing itself as a "house divided," torn between a virtuous engagement with historically derived literary material and an "eccentric" fascination with "experimental and 'modernist' ideas" (Sundquist 9). Sundquist's highest critical praise goes to the work he sees as most clearly expressive of those social and political "dis-eases" of which it is the speaking symptom. *The Sound and the Fury* is flawed because it mumbles its speech: its power is "determined by forces that exist even further beneath the nether reaches of consciousness . . . that only the historical depth of *Absalom, Absalom!* can reveal" (Sundquist 20). *The Sound and the Fury* is indeed opaque in many of its stylistic, formal, and structural aspects; but it seems rather a leap to claim that this opacity stems from a vaguely decadent or narcissistic "preoccupation with form rather than plot" (Sundquist 19). To claim that *The Sound and the Fury* is inferior work in this sense not only takes the notion of literary apprenticeship to a whole new level; it also betrays a certain moralizing impatience with "literariness" that, I submit, bears a family resemblance to the view that the only sex that should win our approval is heterosex, since only it has the potential to be meaningfully productive. Sundquist tips his hand in this moralizing direction when he characterizes "Faulkner's obsession with the unnamable [and] the inexpressible" as the author's "greatest hazard," adding that he finds it difficult "to tell why—or exactly at what point" the "poignant memories" of *The Sound and the Fury* "get transfigured into neurosis or bizarre, overbearing symbolism" and concluding that, finally, the novel's interests "remain largely unconscious" (19). This is not a good thing if one holds that the strength of art is to be found in its function as symptom, its ability to translate unconscious forces into articulations of contextual consciousness. Thus, brilliant as *House Divided* is, Sundquist's unwillingness to abide what Dean might term the enigmatic aspects of *The Sound and the Fury* reveals the limitations of a certain historicist criticism.

I want to caution that "unhistoricist" or "associative" reading practices are not rescue operations. Revealing the previously unrecognized ways in which a text can mean does not automatically make it a more beautiful or sophisticated work than it was before. Such textual revelations do, however, allow for recovery efforts that are genealogical in the best Foucauldian manner, bringing to light less-traveled paths through an imaginative landscape that, in their "idemtical" relationship to other textual routes, enrich our understanding. In this sense they are as useful for reading partially successful, even bad, work as they are for analyzing masterpieces. So let me now turn to some bad Faulkner to give you a sense of what this sort of queer reading of Faulkner's sexualities might entail.

Most readers know "The Leg" as one of the six stories comprising the closing "Beyond" section of Faulkner's 1950 *Collected Stories*. As Theresa M. Towner and James B. Carothers remind us, most of these stories were not on the list of titles first suggested by Robert Haas.[22] It is not hard to see why: all of the stories in "Beyond" are apprentice work, and it shows. However, they clearly had some meaning for Faulkner, who not only added them to the list Haas sent him but constructed the thematic "home" that would incorporate them into the larger geography of the *Collected Stories*. Faulkner posits the world of "Beyond" as nevertheless topologically connected to the world of Yoknapatawpha, in ways that other previously unpublished stories were not. And their placement flatly contradicts the temporal reality of their creation: written before Faulkner came into possession of his "cosmos," in *Collected Stories* they appear as way stations on the road out of Yoknapatawpha. This arrangement hints that though the stories of "Beyond" are immature work, it would be a mistake to take them as Sundquist takes *The Sound and the Fury:* of interest *only* because of what they later enable. Rather, we might consider the possibility that these tales are compelling precisely to the degree that they go nowhere: they are not studies for later novels (though it is striking that an Everbe Corinthia both opens and closes Faulkner's writing career), nor are they sketches of southern racial life. What these stories have in common with the others in the volume, then, is nothing so clear as theme or context but rather something both immanent to and beyond those historical concerns:

violence, mystery, and desire. We might approach the stories of "Beyond" as fantasies rather than representations—fantasies not only in the psychological sense but in the musical one. As Theodor Adorno put it in his introduction to *Quasi una Fantasia,* "In contrast to philosophy and the sciences, which impart knowledge, the elements of art which come together for the purpose of knowledge never culminate in a decision."[23] None of the stories of "Beyond" invite clear interpretive decisions, and this is particularly so of "The Leg."

Almost surrealistic in its wickedly apt linguistic slippages and canny deployment of psychoanalytic thinking, "The Leg" traces multiplying circuits of sexual fantasy and action, beginning with the implied couple of the American David and the English George, expanding to the (again implied) *ménage à trois* of David, George, and Everbe Corinthia (daughter of a lockkeeper who lives and works on a section of the Thames near Oxford), and proceeding—via the intervention of World War I, in which George is killed and David loses a leg—to the shattering concluding virtual *ménage à quatre* in which David's amputated "member," swollen into human form and imbued with a life that seems drawn in equal parts from David's flesh and George's spirit, seduces and destroys Corinthia.[24] Though lesser Faulkner, "The Leg" shows evidence of painstaking work on the part of the author, not only in its bold use of "Freudian" symbolism (obvious in the leg with a mind of its own) but also in its careful application of exactly the sort of elliptical narrative structure that so marks Faulkner's most famous sexual novel, *Sanctuary.*

My claim that George and David are the story's generative desiring couple is based on internal and external evidence. As other readers of the story have noted, characters named David appear in other early Faulkner writing in which the polymorphous aspects of sexual desire are often a subject. Faulkner's most homoerotic "David" passage, in the 1925 newspaper sketch "Out of Nazareth," describes an encounter he and his gay roommate, the artist William Spratling, have with a young hobo in New Orleans: "Spratling saw him first. 'My God,' he said, clutching me, 'look at that face.' And one could imagine young David looking like that. One could imagine Jonathan getting that look from David and, serving that highest function of which sorry man is capable, being the two of them beautiful in similar peace and simplicity—beautiful as gods, as no woman can ever be."[25] It seems clear the name carried a sexual freight for Faulkner in ways important to our reading of "The Leg," where (turning to the internal evidence) our narrator, David, seems as enamored of George as of his "mate's" (824) putative erotic interest, Everbe Corinthia. The story opens with George and David aboard a skiff in a lock on the Thames; David holds the boat in place as George flirtatiously "spouts" Milton at a "bridling" Corinthia, who, along with David, eyes with heightening anxiety a yawl awaiting its turn through the lock. The scene comes to its not-very-displaced climax when Corinthia opens her father's lock: David and the skiff are "shot through the gates" as George falls into the river (824). While George is sanguine about the mishap, David and Corinthia are deeply, and similarly, shaken: Corinthia sits on the ground, weeping, while David briefly loses consciousness (824–25). Corinthia and David take turns calling George a "damned fool" (825); for his part, George seems to enjoy the attentions of both.

A lyrical, retrospective interlude that heightens even further the romantic sense of David's attachment to George (829) links the episode on the Thames to the next scene in a World War I military hospital, where the wounded David, about to lose his leg, begs George to "be sure it's dead. They may cut it off in a hurry and forget about it. . . . That wouldn't do at all. They might bury it and it couldn't lie quiet. And then it would be lost and we couldn't find it to do anything" (830). Readers quickly realize that George is dead, though we are never given the means to decide whether we are to understand this and subsequent encounters David has with this friend as hallucinations or ghostly visitations. Certainly there is more than conversation happening in any case: lying "there surrounding, enclosing that gaping sensation below my thigh where the nerve- and muscle-ends twitched and jerked," David describes nights when "the gap . . . would become filled with the immensity of darkness and silence despite me" (833). On one of those nights David experiences "the gap" as "the dream . . . of the corridor and the invisible corner" permeated with "a rank, animal odor . . . [that] I had never smelled before . . . but . . . knew at once, blown suddenly down the corridor from the old fetid caves where experience began" (833). When David "awakens" from this dream to see George at his bedside, he blurts out, "It isn't anything. I won't again. I swear I shan't any more" (833). George responds cryptically, "I saw you on the river. You saw me and hid, Davy. Pulled up under the bank, in the shadow. There was a girl with you" (834). Fearful of future dreams, David stays awake for several nights; when sleep unavoidably comes, he discovers with relief that he had "eluded it" and "found a sort of peace" (834). He returns to service via training in the "Observer's School"—where he "had learned . . . to not observe what should not be observed"—his thigh "almost reconciled to the new [prosthetic] member" (834), when, without warning, he falls for a second time into the dream, experiencing "horror and dread and something unspeakable: delight" (834). The dream ends with George's silent re- and de-materialization at David's bedside, gazing down upon his friend with a look "implacable, sorrowful, but without reproach" as he slowly fades from view (835). David awakens to discover that "it" was gone, and, further, that "it took George with it" (835).

The final section of "The Leg" is framed in a conversation between David and a visiting priest who tells the story of the corruption of Everbe Corinthia by a man who comes to her in the evenings by punt. Home on army leave, Corinthia's brother Jotham witnesses her decline and eventual death but never sees her seducer: All he has to go on is the sound of a laugh, heard from the shadows near the shore. After searching the entire British Expeditionary Force "for a man whose laugh he had heard one time" (840), Jotham finds David and tries to stab him in his sleep. The story ends with Jotham's execution at dawn as David muses over a photograph found in Jotham's effects and given to him by the priest. Described by David as "a cheap thing such as itinerant photographers turn out at fairs," the photograph was "dated . . . in June of the summer just past," when David "was lying in the hospital talking to George" (841). David identifies the face in the photograph as his own, but yet not his: "it had a quality that was not mine: a quality vicious and outrageous and unappalled," the image bearing an inscription "written in a bold sprawling hand like that of a child: 'To Everbe Corinthia' followed by an unprintable phrase, yet it was my own face" (841–42). "The Leg" closes with David's repeated, despairing cry: "I told him to find it and kill it. . . . I told him to. I told him" (842).

Though I will not pursue the point in depth, I note that one psychoanalytic queer reading of "The Leg" would almost certainly linger over the title item and its resemblance to Lacan's *objet petit a,* the abjected thing that constitutes the foundation of desire "by standing in for loss" (Dean, *Beyond* 195). *Objet petit a* has come to bear considerable interpretive weight in recent queer theory, for "the logic of this concept . . . implies multiple, heterogeneous possibilities for desire" (Dean, *Beyond* 250). Here I stress that a queer reading of "The Leg" would focus not at all on finding "the homosexual" in the text (is it the feminized, "gapped" David who loves George, whose spirit then betrays David by possessing his leg in order to possess Corinthia? Or is it George who loves David, sacrificing his spiritual self to put an end to David's pursuit of the girl?) so as to invite judgment on the text's status as homophobic, homophilic, or closeted, but rather would openly acknowledge the enigmatic, multivalent nature of sexual desire. True, no one comes to a good end in "The Leg"—but how many sexual narratives in Faulkner do? It would be mistaken to take the story's grim conclusion as a moral about the hazards of non-normative sexuality; rather, "The Leg" is best understood as a fantasia on what we would all recognize as a constant theme in Faulkner: the self-shattering force of desire. This is "associative reading" insofar as it notes certain enigmatic aspects of the story as precisely that; it is "unhistoricist" in that it bypasses the temptation to cast the leg as "a symbol of the unleashed evil forces that have created the havoc and horror of the war."[26] It's worth noting that in refusing the consolations of historicism we bring our textual experience closer to that of Faulkner's earliest readers, who repeatedly remarked on the perverse violence and extremism of his texts. Thus the "unhistoricist" approach gives us another kind of entry into literary history, with the difference being that we now have revised critical tools for examining literary representations of the perverse or the extreme. Reading Faulkner's sexualities in this way gives us an "antihistoricist way of formulating . . . historicity" (Dean and Lane 30).

Further, approaching "The Leg" through queer theory allows us to see the text's merits and liabilities more clearly and dispassionately, without bending it to our will to make it do or be more (or less) than it is. This is a reading practice with obvious applications beyond the question of how to read sexuality, even as its genesis can be traced to the effort to respond to that question. To acknowledge the force of the unconscious in the author, in readers, and in the historical contexts within which works are both written and read is to acknowledge the ways in which a text eludes mastery. This necessarily is also to acknowledge that texts operate in ways both historical and unhistorical, and it obliges us to read so that we are always aware that efforts to represent the difficulties of "trying to say" or textual embodiments of the conviction that "words are no good" require more than a symptomatology that would push past the work in order to grasp what's "really" at stake.

Literature is not reducible to symptom—though we could say that Dean's call for associative reading as well as Goldberg and Menon's insistence on "idemtity" as a way of accounting for the past without being imprisoned in it are symptomatic insofar as both articulate a concern that our pursuit of the many benefits of historical literary analysis has led us to lose sight of the unhistorical aspects of literature. Those aspects lie in the "otherness" of art itself, which is always both anchored and transcendent—a truly ambidextrous enterprise, in which one hand describes our conscious world as the other points beyond.

POSTLUDE

Biographical criticism is one of the oldest forms of historicist literary analysis. This may seem a contrarian claim, given the seeming incompatibility of the hagiographic tendencies of traditional literary biography and the sharper critical sensibilities that are the hallmark of modern historicist scholarship. Yet the Faulkner biographies of the past twenty years or so—I'm thinking here of the work of Frederick R. Karl, Joel Williamson, and Judith Sensibar[1]—have largely eschewed the politesse and discretion so scrupulously observed by Joseph Blotner, Faulkner's first biographer, whose relationship with the author was, by his own admission, more filial than analytical. Admiration of the man, these newer biographies demonstrate, is not a necessary precondition for appreciating the work; knowledge of Faulkner's many personal and political failures contributes at least as much—in some cases, more—to the project of literary understanding as admiration for the sentiments expressed in his Nobel Prize speech. To be sure, psychoanalytic approaches to artists' biographies paved the way for these more gimlet-eyed studies—and psychoanalysis was for years seen as more athwart than aligned with historicism. But recent understandings of race, sex, class, and region as themselves historically produced phenomena with significant psychic effects have long since thoroughly complicated neat distinctions between inner and outer reality in shaping an author's life's work and its reception.

Seen through this lens, Phillip Gordon's *Gay Faulkner* emerges as a particularly interesting exercise in literary biography, yoking as it does a return to the romantic view of the author as troubled or wounded genius to a thoroughly contemporary queer reading of the fiction, an approach that appears to arise from the postulate that efforts to draw out the homosexual valences of

Faulkner's work will be convincing primarily insofar as they can be connected to identifiable corollaries in the life. To be sure, these valences are undeniably there, in the fiction and the life, as my preceding chapters and the analyses of the scholars whose work I've cited in those chapters make clear. What makes Gordon's approach to this interpretive work unusual is its project of crafting a novel sexual identity for the author—Gordon terms it an "apocryphal homosexuality"—that works both as way to think about Faulkner's own sexual sympathies and as a point of departure for certain themes in the fiction.[2] In doing so, he returns us to the landscape of author as hero, albeit a hero whose personal defiance of sexual norms was never fully on display.

There is no questioning the excellence of Gordon's intentions. Insofar as homosexuality remains demeaned and suspect in literary studies in manners paralleling those of the wider culture, interventions that successfully forestall or discredit dismissive or disdainful reactions to its complex, undeniable presence in Faulkner's life and work—and that do so in language both elevating and sympathetic—are wholly admirable. And reading the homosexual in Faulkner is, of course, a project with which I have enormous sympathy. How, then, to account for my sense that *Gay Faulkner* feels not only like a bold step forward but also a nostalgic glance backward?

The answer lies, I think, in Gordon's appeal to the suppositive, an interpretive tool that, while tempting, is best deployed judiciously. Once the study moves beyond the early years, the dominant mode of *Gay Faulkner* is speculative. More than once I was put in mind of John Irwin's classic text—less for any appeal to theory (there is little of that in *Gay Faulkner*) than for Gordon's high-wire speculations.[3] Indeed, "speculate" itself is a word that figures prominently in *Gay Faulkner*. Interestingly, the most striking speculations are not about Faulkner's sexual life: after all, the author's extensive youthful connections with the *gay milieux* of New York City and New Orleans are so well established as to render postulates about his own sexual behavior more reasoned inference than wide-eyed conjecture. No, the most remarkable speculations are literary: what Faulkner may (or may not) have read beyond Housman and Aiken, and what interpretations emerge when one decides that a character—Darl Bundren, V. K. Ratliff—not only is gay but that his gayness is the most important thing about him.

Like Irwin, then, Gordon offers an imaginative set of speculations that provide intriguing alternative avenues into the fiction. As is clear from the previous three chapters, I am not averse to interpretations employing associative and/or speculative reading practices. But there is a distinction between interpretations that seek to account for the range of associations a text might ignite in its readers and one that posits those associations as proof of aspects of the author's life.

And so, again like Irwin's work, *Gay Faulkner* strikes me as arising from energies more Faulknerian than Faulknerista, insofar as the author still emerges as the hero, canny and in command of his material and its implications. The increase in attention to expressions of queerness in Faulkner's work (and here I must mention not only Gordon's study but also important scholarship by Jaime Harker and Michael P. Bibler) is all to the good, and long overdue.[4] Still, while the deliberate engagement with themes and subjects long deemed *hors de combat* in Faulkner studies may be one important characteristic of the work of the Faulknerista, it does not, in and of itself, define the approach. I want to emphasize that this is not a criticism—Faulknerian readings remain important and useful, even necessary—so much as a distinction. It's also, perhaps, an observation that the differences within a difference are not only notable but also valuable, since it's in acknowledging and embracing those differences that we enlarge our capacity for insight and understanding.

9

What Television Is For; or, From "The Brooch" to *The Wire*

I take my text from the second book of Blotner, chapter 72, paragraph 5. It is mid-November 1958, and William Faulkner is at Princeton University, where, for a five-hundred-dollar fee (about $4,800 today), he is serving out the second half of a visiting writer's appointment. The arrangements at Princeton are rather different from those at Virginia, where Faulkner had been writer-in-residence for the entire 1957 and 1958 spring semesters. His agreement with Princeton had already seen him on campus for two weeks in March, and this weeklong November visit would close out the contract. Most of the heavy lifting had happened during the spring, when Faulkner conducted thirty-five "undergraduate interviews" and eight "group sessions," but the fall was hardly easier: six solid days of student meetings in an office in the library, with as many as thirteen individual appointments on a given day.[1] Then, too, there were the social obligations, often difficult for Faulkner but typical of this sort of thing. Saxe Commins, Faulkner's editor at Random House and a longtime Princeton resident, had died of a heart attack in July, but his widow, Dorothy Berliner Commins, nevertheless hosted two events at her home when Faulkner was in town, one of them a cocktail party whose invited guests were mostly members of the Institute for Advanced Study (IAS)—among them the Institute's director, the legendary physicist J. Robert Oppenheimer.

Blotner writes that Oppenheimer "had elicited Faulkner's sympathy in the loyalty controversy which had swirled up around him" in 1954, after the Atomic Energy Commission, acting in the McCarthyist spirit of day, revoked its top-secret security clearance from the man who had headed the Manhattan Project but whose wife and brother had belonged to the Communist Party in the 1930s. In July 1955 *Harper's* had published the essay "On Privacy," in which Faulkner deplored how a "pioneer in the simple science of saving the nation like Doctor Oppenheimer" had been "harassed and impugned ... until all privacy was stripped from him."² Faulkner mentions Oppenheimer twice in the essay, and this public expression of sympathy for one of Princeton's most celebrated residents may have been what prompted Dorothy Commins to plan the party. Faulkner, however, seems not to have been particularly keen to meet Oppenheimer, much less anyone from the IAS. "I don't understand their world," he complained to his hostess before the event, and indeed he spent most of the evening silently sitting "in a corner by himself, answering with yeses and noes when someone attempted a conversation with him" (Blotner 2:1704–5). Then Oppenheimer—"a shy man himself in some ways," Blotner writes—walked across the room and joined Faulkner. "I saw your story 'The Brooch' on television, Mr. Faulkner, and I enjoyed it," he said. "I wonder what you think of television as a medium for the artist." [Faulkner's answer] was a short one: "'Television is for niggers,' he said, and there was little more to the conversation" (Blotner 2:1705). And there you have it: Faulknerian bad behavior in the implosive, self-destructive mode, of a particularly distasteful sort. What could he have been thinking? Why would such a seemingly simple question draw such a vituperative response?

While I am not the first to try to answer these questions, it is a little surprising how few have preceded me in the effort, given that Faulkner's outburst lands feetfirst on two topics of long-standing interest in the scholarship (Faulkner and race, Faulkner and the culture industry)—topics that still generate good discussion today. Blotner, of course, does have something to say, and while his reading is not entirely satisfactory, it does cover a lot of bases. Dorothy Commins, he tells us, felt that Faulkner "meant that television was not a medium for the artist but rather one for entertaining a mass audience with a low level of appreciation," an excuse that mainly works to amplify the offensiveness of Faulkner's remark. Commins's pop psychology afterthought—"the answer [also] indicated a lack of breadth which [should be] blamed on the stultifying effect of [Faulkner's] native environment"—seems mostly an effort to contain the damage. Blotner himself decides that "the truth" of Faulkner's motivation in responding so nastily to Oppenheimer's friendly question lay in the intersection of the author's past failures as a writer ("like motion pictures, television was not his medium, and he was not particularly comfortable either writing for it or watching serious attempts at art on it") and present discomfort as a celebrity: "he was in a situation which . . . produced boredom and resentment, and he . . . struck out" (2:1705). Blotner thus ushers race into the discussion via Commins's remarks mostly to quietly escort it back out by effecting a clear separation between television and the N-word: the first word references something actual, a problem in Faulkner's past, whereas the second, however deplorable, should be understood as an unguarded expression of pique, a measure of the distress of the moment and little more. In his reading of Faulkner's teleplays of "The Brooch" and "Shall Not Perish" (Oppenheimer had seen the former on the *Lux Video Theatre*'s April 2, 1953, CBS broadcast), William Furry also briefly discusses the Oppenheimer exchange, adopting and slightly extending Blotner's first point: while "clearly dismissive of the medium," Faulkner's public display of contempt "may have masked a private frustration for his own failure with commercial television."[3] Furry is right to suspect Faulkner of protesting too much, even if he, no less than Blotner, wants to keep the focus on television and off race.

Frederick R. Karl and Richard Gray, the other two scholars who have written about Faulkner's outburst, take exactly the opposite tack. Much less interested in television than the N-word, they take an uncompromising approach to Faulkner's language. After rehearsing Commins's and Blotner's explanations, Karl concludes that "no explanation obtains except that [Faulkner] fell into the white man's most obvious retreat, using the Negro [sic] as someone so much lower in caste that the retort becomes unanswerable." Placing the comment in a wider context of Faulknerian speech habits, Richard Gray finds "Faulkner's frequent use of the word . . . disquieting." The epithet, he notes, "is used in an apparently uncritical way," and even though Faulkner sometimes seems simply "out to shock" a northern interlocutor with his diction, "more often than not the prejudice" expressed in the word "seems instinctive."[4] No less than Blotner's and Furry's, then, Karl's and Gray's interpretations of the retort are framed in contextual appeals to Faulkner's past experience, though here the salient history is not failed efforts to write for the movies or television but the failed intervention in the civil rights movement. For by November 1958 Faulkner's hard-earned reputation as a courageous white southern friend of desegregation and civil rights had taken quite a beating. Faulkner landed the first punch himself when, on March 5, 1956—three months into the Montgomery Bus Boycott—he published "A Letter to the North" in *Life* that offers the entirely unasked-for (and, for supporters of civil rights, thoroughly uncongenial) advice "to the NAACP and all the organizations who would compel immediate and unconditional integration: 'Go slow now'" (Faulkner, *Essays* 87). That same month saw the appearance in the biweekly magazine the *Reporter* of an interview conducted with London *Times* writer Russell Warren Howe, in which Faulkner expressed solidarity with white "Mississippi against the United States even if it meant going out into the street and shooting Negroes"; his insistence, later in the interview, that segregation was "wrong" and "untenable" did little to blunt the threat of violence detected by many readers in his confessed willingness "to make the same choice Robert E. Lee made" (Blotner 2:1591). Faulkner spent a good chunk of the rest of 1956 trying to clean up the ensuing mess, with little success. His letter to the *Reporter* characterizing his comments as "statements which no sober man would make, nor, it seems to me, any sane man believe" (*Essays* 225) was met by a respectful but firm reply from Howe that "all the statements attributed to Mr. Faulkner were transcribed by me from verbatim shorthand notes of the interview" (Blotner 2:1601). And to James Baldwin's excoriating "Faulkner and Desegregation," published in the fall 1956 issue of *Partisan Review,* Faulkner made no public reply whatsoever. One year later, his response to the crisis in Little Rock was only slightly less clumsy than the performances in *Life* and the *Reporter.* His four-paragraph letter to the editor of the *New York Times* opens on a daring note ("The tragedy of Little Rock is that it has at last brought out into the light . . . the fact that white people and Negroes do not like and trust each other, and perhaps never can" [*Essays* 230]) but quickly takes cover under the much-recycled, by then near-moribund prose of the Nobel Prize speech— prose that, in the letter's bombastic peroration, actually seems more a criticism than an endorsement of the federal government's decision to enforce *Brown*.[5]

These four readings of Faulkner's outburst, despite their different emphases, actually all derive from the same interpretive procedure: Blotner, Furry, Karl, and Gray split Faulkner's sentence down its spine, dividing it in half so as to argue for one of its two nouns as the governing interpretive term. What's not yet been attempted is a reading of Faulkner's retort taken intact, which is what I offer here. My approach involves focusing less on what television or the N-word might have meant for Faulkner than on what that small though quite complex word "for" is doing in the sentence. It doesn't take long for the realization to sink in: "television is for niggers" simultaneously articulates two distinct assertions about the relationship between television and Black America, one cultural—television is a denigrated art for a denigrated people—the other political: television is a champion of the disenfranchised and dispossessed. These claims have in turn a complex double relation to each other, and it is only in examining the terms of this double relation—this in many ways unreconciled two-ness—that we can begin to take the measure of Faulkner's outburst. Without doubt, television's uncanny capacity to embody and transmit the "warring ideals" of postwar life—those increasingly acute, and acutely felt, contradictions of modern American capitalism—was becoming quite clear by 1958.[6] Of course, television is not a folk; it possesses neither soul nor consciousness nor agency, even if its startlingly rapid colonization of key aspects of American life and culture quickly led to denunciations of it as a kind of living alien force, an invasive, electronic mind- and body-snatcher. Yet it is precisely television's capacity to make almost shockingly obvious how, in the words of Jacques Rancière, "a 'medium' is not a 'proper' means or material" but rather "a surface of conversion, a surface of equivalence," and to do so in ways that raise pointed questions about what connections might (or might not) obtain between equivalence and equality, that make it such an aesthetically troubling medium for the artist.[7]

Furry's 1996 discovery of the teleplays for "The Brooch" and "Shall Not Perish" (also written for *Lux Video Theatre,* and broadcast on February 11, 1954) in the archives of the J. Walter Thompson advertising agency at Duke University remains important; his careful reading of the many changes Faulkner made in adapting these stories for television is highly suggestive, though I do not address them in any detail here. While Furry notes that "no letters or office memos between Faulkner and the *Lux* producers detailing the terms of their relationship have turned up" (124), information pieced together from other sources seems to indicate that Faulkner's work for *Lux* was extremely lucrative (he received $2,500 for the two teleplays—about $24,000 today [125, 138]) and quickly dispatched: advance publicity for "The Brooch" claimed that the teleplay had been written by Faulkner in forty-eight hours.[8]

Already small beer as literature (in his 1948 story list for Robert K. Haas, his first editor at Random House, Faulkner himself called it "Topical, not too good"), the patriotic and sentimental "Shall Not Perish" makes for excruciating reading as a teleplay—the less said about it the better, frankly, and since it was not the broadcast seen by Oppenheimer, we can set it aside.[9] "The Brooch," first written in 1930 or 1931 and published in *Scribner's* in 1936 after several rejections and much revision, is obviously second-drawer Faulkner, though its grim, back-looping narrative of maternal malice, spousal betrayal, and suicide is not without interest. Yet the story bears little resemblance to the sappy, conventionally chronological teleplay, in which a good girl from the wrong side of the tracks prevails against her old meanie of a mother-in-law once her husband finally locates his spine. Jack Gould, the television critic for the *New York Times*, savaged "The Brooch," calling it a "synthetic" and "diluted" "soap opera," "a maudlin paean to young love." Acknowledging that Faulkner faced certain challenges in making a story with mature, disturbing content pass video code muster, Gould nevertheless asserts that "even under the television industry's purity code there was no reason for Mr. Faulkner to capitulate so completely to the video mores." Or rather, there was a reason, and it wasn't a good one: Gould insinuates that Faulkner "succumbed" "with eagerness" to "television's taboos" because the author himself, no less than the manufacturers of Lux Toilet Soap, was determined to cash in on his name. "Of all great American writers Mr. Faulkner undoubtedly is as entitled as any to enjoy a few of the materialistic pleasures which the fees paid by TV make possible," Gould observes:

> The small financial reward attendant to his literary efforts long has been a disheartening matter of record. If now he wants to whip out a few pot boilers for the video screen, his admirers may regret it but they will understand. At least no harm is done to his acknowledged artistic accomplishments of the past.
>
> But it is dismaying to find an author of Mr. Faulkner's stature and the producer of the Lux Video Theatre indulging in what amounts to literary sleight-of-hand. The advance fanfare over "The Brooch" obviously was an attempt to capitalize on Mr. Faulkner's justly earned fame: yet what the audience saw was substitute merchandise not of the quality advertised.[10]

Even more dismaying for Gould are the consequences of a sellout like Faulkner's for the future development of television as, precisely, a medium for the artist. "It is to the Faulkners that literally hosts of writers look for some inspiration and encouragement to do battle against puerile restrictions that so often in television gag the inquiring mind and the articulate voice," Gould writes. "If he intends to work further in TV, Mr. Faulkner must remember that his position carries with it certain inevitable responsibilities. He only betrays a new and promising medium if he accepts the theory that he will reserve his meaty stuff for other media and condone any literary hash for video."

In the final paragraph of "On Privacy"—the very essay in which he had expressed his solidarity with Oppenheimer in seeking "to preserve that privacy in which alone the artist and the scientist and humanitarian can function" (*Essays* 73)—Faulkner had scolded America for not yet having found any social role for the artist, "him who deals only in things of the human spirit, except to use his notoriety to sell soap or cigarettes or fountain pens or to advertise automobiles and cruises and resort hotels, or (if he can be taught to contort fast enough to meet the standards) in radio or moving pictures where he can produce enough income tax to be worth attention" (*Essays* 75). It's widely agreed that "On Privacy" was written primarily in response to Robert Coughlan's splashy, two-part, unauthorized profile of Faulkner, published in fall 1953 in *Life*. It seems to me more than a little likely that Gould's review of "The Brooch," published just five months before the *Life* profile, was another goad. It can hardly be a coincidence that soap appears among the items an artist's "notoriety" can sell: the broadcast of "The Brooch" concluded with a dressing-room "candid" with Sally Forrest (the actress cast in the role of Amy Boyd, the plucky wife), in which she describes herself as "one of the millions of people who admire William Faulkner and consider him to be one of the truly great writers of our time." She continues:

> I feel it a particular honor to have appeared in Mr. Faulkner's first television play, which he wrote especially for the Lux Video Theatre.
> I'm grateful to Lux for the opportunity and grateful to Lux for another reason, too.
> Having made as many pictures as I have, and lived in Hollywood as long as I have, I can heartily recommend Lux Toilet Soap. A beautiful complexion

is important to every woman—perhaps most of all to those of us who have to face cameras for a living—and that's why I depend on Lux for my complexion care. Why don't you? (Furry 178).

Adding Faulkner's experiences with the telecast of "The Brooch" to our contextual frame for reading "On Privacy" brings nearer to the surface of that essay a previously submerged defensiveness in Faulkner's tone. It also makes newly apparent the shock Faulkner must have felt to hear Oppenheimer himself (who, in truth, is really something of a sidelight in "On Privacy") bring up a major source of the bitterness and, I think, not inconsiderable shame that informed the writing of that essay—where, interestingly enough, it's radio and moving pictures, not television, that Faulkner fingers as the most lucrative media options for the artist eager to "produce income tax" but unwilling to sell only his notoriety. This was perhaps because television's connection to salesmanship already was so overdetermined by 1955 that it went without saying. After all, it was the wish to safeguard television's unprecedented reach as an advertising medium that accounted for the mostly self-imposed network censorship condemned by Gould as a block to significant artistic expression: no network wanted to risk losing viewers through challenging or possibly offensive programming. As Melvin Ely has shown, it was in part the threat of an organized, highly public boycott of Blatz Beer, corporate sponsors of the short-lived (but long syndicated) *Amos 'n' Andy* television show, that led officials at CBS to take seriously NAACP complaints about the show from the moment the civil rights organization contacted them.[11]

I mention *Amos 'n' Andy* not to open a discussion of the representation of Blacks in early television—that work has been done well by others, and I could do no more here than simply repeat it—but rather to develop my analysis by bringing further into the light a little-noted aspect of television programming's widely recognized contributions to the civil rights movement. Both J. Fred MacDonald and Sasha Torres have written persuasively about how television coverage of key developments in the civil rights movement—starting with Little Rock, which Taylor Branch has termed "the first on-site news extravaganza of the modern television era," and continuing through to the March 7, 1965, "Bloody Sunday" attack on Selma's Edmund Pettus Bridge—conveyed a sense of national urgency unachievable in any other medium.[12] What Torres describes as "the necessity of the imbrication of television with race trouble: on the one hand, race and racial conflict fed the medium's enormous appetite for visual spectacle; on the other, the mere fact of television's coverage served paradoxically to render racism visible in new ways, and to new audiences" is not likely to have escaped Faulkner's notice. Faulkner himself may not have been watching much television in 1957, but by then the TV was on for five hours a day in 85 percent of American households; market penetration in the South, long "retarded as a consumer of television," had finally been accomplished; and the coverage of Little Rock was "unrelenting: NBC led with John Chancellor's reports from Arkansas every night for a month" (MacDonald 66; Torres 20). Many white southerners—not all of them segregationists—blamed television itself for turning the civil rights movement from a local problem into a national crisis, "inflaming" "Negro unrest" by supplementing the live broadcasts of distressingly violent responses to peaceful protests with steady coverage of the issue in documentaries and talk shows like *Issues and Answers* and *Face the Nation*. Almost certainly, Faulkner heard some of this talk; his letters to *Life* and the *New York Times,* as well as the 1956 essay "If I Were a Negro," published in *Ebony* magazine, bespeak an effort to redirect the national discussion of civil rights away from television and back into literary channels where he felt more firmly in control. And in fact, there is considerable truth to the claim that television and the civil rights movement helped establish each other as legitimate forces in American life, though that truth goes well beyond television's reliance on conflict, "liveness," or spectacle to boost ratings.

For Samuel Ichiye Hayakawa, television's irreplaceable contribution to the civil rights movement lay in its power to directly address America's most oppressed citizens—the poor, the badly educated, the segregated—and not only with vivid visuals of protests aimed at securing voting rights and equal access to education. Called on to deliver the opening address of the August 1963 International Conference on General Semantics at New York University and taking television and race as his topic, Hayakawa (then an English professor at San Francisco State, later a US senator) observed that television had several "peculiar facts" as a medium that made it especially appealing to Blacks. Partly because "it by-passes literacy," television "spread with greater rapidity among the poor than the rich in the United States, among the uneducated than among the educated. . . . The poor and the uneducated being numerous in the Negro community, television spread with special rapidity among Negroes."[13] By providing entertainment in the home, television also allowed southern Blacks "to avoid the indignities of the ill-kept, humiliating, separate balconies of the segregated movie houses" (398). The final, crucial fact to be considered was television's high cost of production. As we have seen, it was this need to please advertising sponsors so as to make manageable television's steep economies of scale that led Gould to bemoan programming's aesthetic mediocrity, but Hayakawa read the situation otherwise. The fact that "all television programs are addressed pretty much to the whole community," he claimed, means that "whatever the television set says to white people, it also says to Negroes" (398). For Hayakawa, television was "profoundly democratizing" mostly because of its advertising:

> Here, for example, is a television commercial telling what fun and excitement children can have if they can persuade their parents to bring them to such-and-such an amusement park. The commercial does not bother to explain that they need not come if they are Negroes. Here is another commercial inviting the family to hop into the car and drive just twenty-five minutes from downtown to Woodland Acres, the beautiful new residential development, where three-bedroom ranch-type homes are now open for inspection. It does not tell you that if you are Negro, these homes are not for you. Here is an advertisement telling you to order this new, sparkling soft drink with the thrilling new flavor. It doesn't tell you that if you are Negro, you will have to drink it standing on the sidewalk outside the cafe.
>
> Now imagine that you are a Negro teen-ager, to whom the television set, with messages such as the foregoing, has been his constant baby-sitter and companion ever since he can remember. If you are this Negro teen-ager, you have spent more hours of your life in front of the television set than you have spent in school, according to the statistics given by audience research surveys. You do not know what your elders know, namely, which advertisements to heed and which to ignore as not being addressed to you. You only know that the friendly, friendly television set is always saying to you, "You are an American. You are entitled to eat and drink and wear what other Americans eat and drink and wear. You must think about the same political and world problems that other Americans think about. You are a member of this national community of Americans." (399–400)

In describing how political action arises as a consequence of this naïve response to televisual lures to consumption, Hayakawa proposes a view of the medium's contribution to the civil rights movement that accounts for both readings of Faulkner's outburst. It also steers fairly closely to Jacques Rancière's theory of the politics of aesthetics as being rooted less in an artwork's explicit (or implied) political "message" than in its formal capacity to alter the "distribution of the sensible" (*partage du sensible*) such that "new landscape[s] of the visible, the sayable, and the doable" come into imaginative being.[14] This is not to say that television advertising is art. It is, however, to begin to clear a space for considering television's potential as a medium for the artist by locating that potential *precisely* in all the ways that "television is for niggers" and, in turn, by highlighting how an understanding of medium as a means for expressing equivalence—advertising as politics, politics as spectacle, form as flow—has come to inform contemporary aesthetic practice.

Lest this discussion come to seem too theoretical or obscure, let me conclude with a brief reading of a scene from *The Wire,* the critically acclaimed television series that ran for five seasons (from June 2002 to March 2008) on the for-profit but subscriber-supported Home Box Office network. Much of the series's success grew from its ambitious and, in my view, successful effort to present what the show's creator and chief writer, David Simon, has called a "television novel" on contemporary themes: the costly failures of the war on drugs; the collapse of urban industry and the corresponding disappearance of the blue-collar middle class; the heartrending inadequacies of public city schools; the implosion of the daily newspaper business—all of them adjunctive to the series's single overriding theme, the fate of the city of Baltimore. The population of Baltimore is 63 percent Black, and a great deal has been written about the role of race in *The Wire,* where forty-two of the eighty-four featured actors are Blacks cast in roles ranging from police department chief to state senator and including teachers, drug lords, addicts, schoolroom strivers, street punks, detectives, and ministers. A proper discussion of this single issue in the show is beyond the scope of this chapter, but we can get a sense of how *The Wire* illuminates the linking of television and race through a quick look at what's come to be known as the "Chicken McNuggets" scene in the second episode of the first season. D'Angelo, Wallace, and Poot, all young men in the employ of drug kingpin Avon Barksdale, are seated on a castoff couch in the center courtyard of the McCulloh Homes housing project, which functions as an open-air drug market. D'Angelo keeps an eye on the surrounding transactions while the younger Wallace and Poot share a lunch of Chicken McNuggets.

Impressed by both the tastiness and convenience of the Chicken McNugget, Wallace expresses his admiration for the man he believes must have invented it: "Motherfucker got the bone all the way out the damn chicken. 'Til he came along nigger's just been chewing on drumsticks and shit, getting they fingers all greasy. He said, 'Later for the bone. Let's nugget that meat up and make some real money.'" When Poot wonders whether in fact the inventor of the Chicken McNugget was paid for his work, Wallace replies with certainty that he must be "richer than a motherfucker." This prompts a response from the older D'Angelo: "Nigger, please. The man who invented them things, he's just some sad-ass down at the basement of McDonald's, thinking up some shit to make some money for the real players." When Poot objects—"Naw, man, that ain't right."—D'Angelo goes off:

> Fuck right. It ain't about right, it's about money. Now you think Ronald McDonald gonna go down that basement and say, "Hey Mr. Nugget. You da bomb. We're selling chicken faster than you can tear the bone out. So I'm gonna write my clowny-ass name on this fat-ass check for you." Shit.
>
> And the nigger who invented them things is still working in the basement for regular wage thinking of some shit to make the fries taste better, some shit like that. Believe. (*The Wire,* season 1, episode 2)

Poot looks chastened, but Wallace does not back down. "Still had the idea though," he insists.

There are three aspects of this scene I want to emphasize. First, the use of the N-word to describe both the naively admiring Wallace and the apparently duped "Mr. Nugget." The word here continues to signify the downtrodden and despised, but it signifies something more: a talent to imagine, and to make, something new and different out of common, everyday material, and a grudging but real respect for that talent. The scene readily acknowledges that the respect may proceed from incorrect or insufficient information (as is the case for Wallace) and that the talent may wind up being exploited (as happens to D'Angelo's hypothetical Mr. Nugget), but that acknowledgment is not, it seems to me, intended as a dismissal of the talent itself. Second, the scene's bluesy, simultaneous sounding of two discordant notes: *both* a bitter emphasis on the bottom line as the ultimate determinate of worth—"it ain't about right, it's about the money"—*and* a dogged insistence on the intrinsic merit of creativity: "Still had the idea though." Third, the Chicken McNugget itself: trash tricked out as nutrition, pretty much the epitome of everything that's wrong with contemporary America, the Chicken McNugget nonetheless winds up being the vehicle for Wallace's reverie of imagination, invention, and grateful, lavish compensation. The entire scene—unfolding in an open-air drug market where the underlying background sound (the piping voices of playing children, the murmured exchanges of drug dealers and their clients, the muted but insistent rhythm track of a boom box) blends notes of domesticity and despair—is something of a crystallization of the aesthetic credo of *The Wire*, which is equal parts sociological and formal: to explore the equivalences between the drug trade and capitalism, between fighting crime and committing crime, between commerce and art, and to do all this by foregrounding television as a medium "for" the "nigger."

It seems to me that, in Faulkner's view, television was not just "*for* niggers": it *was itself* "nigger," the "sad ass" in the basement of the postwar American media ecology, ginning up money for the "real players"—not only the studio executives and producers but also writers like Faulkner himself, who, at least in the estimation of the *New York Times*'s Jack Gould, stood for media segregation by maintaining, either explicitly or implicitly, that between work produced for television and the modernist novel there could be no aesthetic equality. Certainly, that view seems to inform "On Privacy," where Faulkner strongly implies that "things of the human spirit" will never find expression in commercial media. Throughout the 1950s, Faulkner made a point of stressing his disdain for television, though never again (at least not publicly) in the violent terms he used with Oppenheimer. But as we all know, Faulkner had a lifelong tendency to misrepresent himself and his habits, so it should come as no surprise that this World War I flying ace spent more than a few hours of the last year of his life parked in front of the tube at the home of his Oxford neighbors Jim and Dutch Silver, watching his favorite television show, *Car 54, Where Are You?*, a comedy set in a Bronx police precinct that, at its premiere in 1961, was the only show of its type to employ Black actors in recurring roles (Blotner 2:1812; MacDonald 76). It's undoubtedly true that television's potential as a medium for the artist, and the crucial role Black America has played in making that potential a reality, was something Faulkner was unable to see. But it would be nice to imagine it's something he would have been willing to watch.

Postscript

This chapter initially was written in response to an invitation to contribute to a conference on Faulkner and modern media held in 2011 at the University of New South Wales's Centre for Modernism Studies. The ten years since that conference have seen growing scholarly interest in the topic within Faulkner studies—interest made possible in no small part by the papers presented at the conference itself, a predictable development.[15] A somewhat less predictable development in the intervening years has been growing discussion within academia around the circumstances under which one may print or say the epithet whose articulation sits at the heart of this chapter, a discussion that, so far, has produced few areas of agreement and shows no signs of abating. Here, I offer some observations on the current situation that I hope indicate how my analysis continues to offer useful food for thought in an increasingly charged atmosphere.

To be sure, observing that there are few areas of agreement today on when or how the N-word might appear in scholarship or class discussion is not to claim that widespread agreement existed in 2011—only that the issue was somewhat less publicly fraught. Pushing the historical horizon back even further, to 2002, brings us to an attempt to clarify why agreement seems so hard to come by: the publication of Randall Kennedy's lawyerly inquiry into "the strange career of a troublesome word," an inquiry that, in laying out the terms of the argument over the word's use, sought to interrogate what, back then, were seen as unusually intense efforts to establish, both in law and custom, an understanding of the N-word—"the paradigmatic slur" that "stands alone [in] its power to tear at one's insides"—as thoroughly unacceptable in any context.[16] In what he grants was a deliberately provocative gesture, Kennedy took the word as his study's primary title, not only to "inform (warn?) readers up front about the topic of the enterprise" but also, he admits, with "the hope of spurring publicity and snagging the attention of potential readers," even at the risk of giving offense (144). In this he was unquestionably successful: the study enjoyed solid sales and a great deal of attendant controversy.

Of course, Kennedy's goals extended beyond "snagging" readers. In an afterword to the paperback edition, he makes clear his position on the word itself ("I believe that it is a good thing that *nigger* is widely seen as a presumptively objectionable term. I think that people who use *nigger* in their speech should bear the risk that listeners overhearing them will misunderstand their intentions" [146]) on the way to identifying the interpretive "problem" he aims to highlight—the need "to make distinctions between [the word's] various usages" (146)—and his purpose in doing so. This purpose, he writes, is "to urge caution before attributing the worst meaning and motives to any word or symbol since all can be put to a variety of purposes, good as well as bad ... [and] to counsel likely targets of racist abuse to respond in ways that are self-empowering ... [rather than becoming] emotionally overwrought upon encountering racist taunts ... [and demanding that] authorities ... protect them ... by prohibiting *nigger* and other such words and punishing transgressions severely" (147). Writing at the turn of the twenty-first century, Kennedy believes he can offer this counsel thanks to changes within popular culture—he points to examples in hip-hop, athletics, cinema, and stand-up comedy—that he felt would, in time, lessen the word's bitter sting, complicating both its valence and its affective impact:

> The more aware ... [we] become of the ambiguity surrounding *nigger,* the less likely [we] will be to automatically condemn the actions taken by whites who voice the N-word. This tendency will doubtless, in certain instances, lead to unfortunate results, as decision makers show undue solicitude toward racists who use the rhetoric of complexity to cover their misconduct.
>
> Still, despite these costs, there is much to be gained by allowing people of all backgrounds to yank *nigger* away from white supremacists, to subvert its ugliest denotation, and to convert the N-word from a negative into a positive appellation. (138–39)

Kennedy envisioned a destiny for the N-word like that of "queer," a once primarily pejorative term that can now be used as a neutral, or even positive, signifier of identity. Twenty years on, the only thing we can confidently say about Kennedy's project of subversion and conversion is that it has not met with much success. Still, in 2011 (to return to the year of the conference), three years into Barack Obama's first term as the nation's first Black president, that project did not seem as far-fetched as it does today. Yes, the Tea Party movement and "birtherism" were slouching into the American political frame, but notions of an emerging "postracial" America sparked by Obama's election still had some currency. Back then, it was not entirely impossible to imagine that, to quote Kennedy again, "as a linguistic landmark, *nigger* is being renovated" (137) such that context—the when, where, why, and how of the word's articulation, in addition to the who—would become an important factor in judging whether, in fact, a slur had occurred.

The Australian conference was held in November. Three months later, George Zimmerman shot and killed Trayvon Martin. Zimmerman was acquitted in 2013; in response to the verdict, Patrisse Cullors, Alicia Garza, and Opal Tometi founded Black Lives Matter. In 2014, Michael Brown Jr., Tamir Rice, and Eric Garner died in the course of encounters with police in Ferguson, Missouri; Cleveland, Ohio; and New York City. In 2015, Freddie Gray Jr. and Sandra Bland died while in the custody of law enforcement in Baltimore and Waller County, Texas. On July 5, 2016, Alton Sterling was shot and killed by police in Baton Rouge, Louisiana; one day later, Philando Castile was shot and killed by an officer during a traffic stop in Falcon Heights, Minnesota. And three months after the death of Castile, Donald J. Trump—a man whose family real estate company's history of denying apartment rentals to Black applicants prompted a Department of Justice investigation; a man widely recognized as the most vocal proponent of the Obama "birther" falsehood—was elected president.[17]

It would take many months—more than a year, probably—to read all the newspaper columns, blog posts, and scholarly treatises written since that day aimed at explaining all the ways in which we should have seen Trump's election coming. At the time, though, much of the nation was in shock, profoundly unsettled in its sense of itself. Within the mini-nation that is the college campus, "unsettled" doesn't begin to describe the effects of Trump's election. Among faculty, staff, and students of color; among Deferred Action for Childhood Arrivals (DACA) students; and among international faculty and staff, feelings of betrayal, anxiety, and fear—never far from the surface to begin with for immigrant Americans and Americans of color, for good reason—became the dominant register of campus experience. And as colleges and universities became targets of white supremacist aggression—the August 2017 "Unite the Right" rally in Charlottesville being the most shocking example—campus experience itself increasingly emerged as a site for internal interventions aimed at reducing or eliminating racist harms. Desultory efforts at best at many colleges and universities, attempts to achieve diversity, equity, and inclusion experienced a profound sharpening and rapid acceleration—always rhetorically, and often in reality—following the May 2020 murder of George Floyd.

So it is not surprising, given the sincere and necessary work now underway at many colleges and universities to create a more supportive and inclusive learning environment, that any articulation of the N-word has emerged as an especially volatile flashpoint, with courses where textual or linguistic analyses play a key instructional role coming in for particular scrutiny. For the word is hardly avoidable: as Kennedy's analysis shows, it is deeply embedded in American culture, with complex, often contradictory uses and effects. In the study of American literature, for instance, diversifying the canon has not served to lower the word's profile: students will encounter it in the writings of Toni Morrison, James Baldwin, Richard Wright, Zora Neale Hurston, Frederick Douglass, Harriet Jacobs, Malcolm X, Audre Lorde, and Natasha Trethewey, to name only a few distinguished Black authors. And given the word's explosive power, chances are good that they will find it embedded in some of the most consequential passages of the work—passages that beg for classroom engagement and analysis.

In 2013, the *New York Times* published "In Defense of a Loaded Word," an editorial by Ta-Nehisi Coates that, nearly ten years on, remains deeply influential. Like Kennedy, Coates sees efforts to institute a wholesale ban on the use of the word as misguided. Coates, too, emphasizes context—though for Coates, the race of the speaker is contextually important to a greater degree than Kennedy allows. Articulated by Blacks, the N-word is "inappropriate" (here, Coates does not directly engage with the teasing or affectionate uses of the word that Kennedy explores); spoken by whites, it is "violent and offensive."[18] This is because, he explains, "within the boundaries of community relationships, words . . . are always spoken that take on other meanings when uttered by others." He continues:

A few summers ago, one of my best friends invited me up to what he affectionately called his "white-trash cabin" in the Adirondacks. This was not how I described the outing to my family. Two of my Jewish acquaintances once joked that I'd "make a good Jew." My retort was not, "Yeah, I certainly am good with money." Gay men sometimes laughingly refer to one another as "faggots." My wife and her friends sometimes, when having a good time, will refer to one another with the word "bitch." I am certain that should I decide to join in, I would invite . . . hard conversation.

Four years later, speaking at an event at Evanston Township High School in Illinois, Coates expanded on this point of linguistic ownership:

The question one must ask is why so many white people have difficulty extending . . . basic laws about how human beings interact to Black people. And I think I know why. When you're white in this country, you're taught that everything belongs to you. You think you have a right to everything . . . the laws and the culture tell you this. You have the right to go where you want to go, do what you want to do, be however, and people just have got to accommodate themselves to you. So here comes this word that, you know, you feel like you invented. And now somebody will tell you how to use the word that you invented. You know? "Why can't I use it? Everyone else gets to use it. That's racism, that I don't get to use it. That's racist against me. I have to inconvenience myself and hear this song and I can't sing along? How come I can't sing along?" You know what I mean? And I think, you know, for white people, I think the experience of being a hip-hop fan and not being able to use the word "nigger" is actually very, very insightful. It will give you just a little peek into the world of what it means to be Black. . . . So I think there's a lot to be learned from refraining.[19]

For Coates, the N-word is "the border, the signpost that reminds us that the old crimes don't disappear. It tells white people that, for all their guns and all their gold, there will always be places they can never go."[20]

Coates's view has taken hold within much of academe, where his sense of the educative value of white restraint has been enlarged by some into an assertion that there is ultimately no context—even the context of direct quotation—

in which white voicing of the N-word can escape its "violent and offensive" charge. Kennedy's admission that forbearance in the face of white use of the word risks producing "undue solicitude toward racists who use the rhetoric of complexity to cover their misconduct" is mostly seen today as a risk not worth taking. For beyond the issue of cultural ownership lies a suspicion felt by many students of color that any white use of the word, no matter the context, is an exercise in bad faith, an opportunity for the speaker to experience the thrill of racist transgression: a *sub-rosa,* passive-aggressive indulgence not dissimilar to gaslighting.

All this is to say, then, that context runs both ways: not only the context of articulation—we could call it the context of intent—but the larger cultural context that influences how the word is heard: the context of impact. For the past ten years, *that* context has been shaped by the ongoing Black death toll that, in the age of Trump and its rising tide of violent white supremacy and reaction ("Blue Lives Matter"), has created stratospheric levels of fear and anxiety among Black college students. Given this, efforts to defend speaking the word aloud in the pedagogical context of the classroom through appeals to academic freedom feel wholly inadequate to the moment. Even as he points out instances of damaging administrative overreaction in responses to student claims of racist classroom discourse, for example, Henry Reichman grants that "a more diverse student body and a more diverse faculty will inevitably pose questions for consideration in class that might not have been raised in more homogeneous settings."[21] The challenges are summed up neatly by Suzanne Nossel, the chief executive officer of PEN America: "Universities should never punish anyone for merely mentioning a word without any inflection of bigotry . . . , [yet] as stewards of learning professors should be conscious of where a rising generation draws its red lines. . . . [I]ndividual instructors need not turn their backs on academic freedom to reappraise the pedagogical value of speaking the word in full amid the risk that it will be heard as a slur" (Reichman 65–66).

That work of consciousness-raising and reappraisal is underway in Faulkner studies, proceeding along aural and textual tracks. For several years now, presenters at the annual Faulkner and Yoknapatawpha conference at the University of Mississippi have substituted "the N-word" for the epithet when it appears in direct quotation, alerting auditors in advance of this practice and, often, explaining their reasons for quoting the material in the first place. And in summer 2021, the *Faulkner Journal* editorial board (of which I am a member) approved the following statement of policy regarding appearance of the word in print:

> We encourage authors to avoid use of the term in question. If, however, one finds that a particular instance is important to an argument about that passage, character, or circumstance, it is in our readers' interests to encounter that usage in the form Faulkner wrote it. Avoiding all use of the word does not alter its appearance in Faulkner's texts or in the world about which he wrote. Not citing it, by contrast, prevents engaging with the historical situation that produced its use as a term of derision, subjugation, and hate. Our work as scholars is to understand and question that world.
>
> As Barbara Ladd of the journal's Advisory Board put it: "I would suggest that it's worth thinking through whether eliminating offensive language or substituting inoffensive words for the words an author wrote in a work of scholarship is truly an antiracist move, or whether antiracism comes in the act of facing the words we use and examining the worlds from which they arose." As an editorial colleague at another journal put it—Nathan Grant at *African American Review*—"[W]hat Faulkner, Morrison, Trethewey, and other writers are trying to achieve is the exposure of the many toxicities hurtful words ordinarily have to offer—less to normalize them than to show that racism, sexism, homophobia, etc., are the warp and weft of the country's fabric, each of which contributes to an ugly design and a poor fit for its wearers." This "poor fit," "ugly design," and the active examination of their role in the American social fabric is work to which *The Faulkner Journal* has been and remains committed.
>
> We think that there are differences in the ways the word in question appears in Faulkner's fiction. Therefore, we will not alter his language (using a substitute word or asterisks, for example). If the term appears in a manner that remains clear despite its omission or through contextualizing, and its appearance is not central to an interpretive or rhetorical emphasis, we ask that you not cite it directly. It is authors' individual decision about where that emphasis lies.[22]

Ten years ago, I wrote this chapter with the aim of directly facing the word Faulkner used in responding to Oppenheimer's innocent question and, in doing so, examining the world from which that use arose. Given that the word is central to the piece, I have retained it in quotation and identified it as "the N-word" elsewhere in the chapter.

Lurie's observation about what's lost in sanitizing Faulkner's language (such editorial interference "prevents engaging with the historical situation that produced" it) brings us back to my introduction and the discussion there of Joseph Blotner and Frederick Gwynn's decision to transcribe Faulkner's use of the epithet as "Negro" when it came time to translate the audio record of the class conferences into the print format of *Faulkner in the University*. Blotner's inclusion of the unexpurgated exchange with Oppenheimer contrasts interestingly with this earlier decision. Certainly, politics and the public relations realities of authorial representation played a hand here: *Faulkner in the University* was published in 1959, during Faulkner's lifetime, while the second volume of the biography appeared in 1974, twelve years after his death. Though we might wish for more truth in the earlier text, we should acknowledge and appreciate Blotner's decision to include the epithet in the later publication. As I have sought to show in this chapter, that instance of articulation, offensive as it is, has a great deal to tell us about Faulkner—and about television, too.

Notes

Preface and Acknowledgments

1. Stephen Railton, "Faulkner at Virginia: An Introduction," *Faulkner at Virginia: An Audio Archive:* http://faulkner.lib.virginia.edu/page?id=essays&section=intro.

Introduction: Musings of a Faulknerista

First epigraph: Railton and Plunkett identify this class meeting as "Frederick Gwynn's American Fiction Class." In the printed edition of the class conferences, Frederick L. Gwynn and Joseph L. Blotner identify this "Session One" as having been held during a "Graduate Course in American Fiction" (see Frederick L. Gwynn and Joseph L. Blotner, eds., *Faulkner in the University: Class Conferences at the University of Virginia, 1957–1958,* with an introduction by Douglas Day [1959; Charlottesville: University Press of Virginia, 1995], 1; hereafter cited as *FIU*). *Second epigraph:* William Faulkner, *The Sound and the Fury: The Corrected Text,* ed. Noel Polk (New York: Vintage International, 1990), 53.

1. Ann Thomas Moore (Grad English '58), "Learning Faulkner," in *Faulkner at Virginia: An Audio Archive,* http://faulkner.lib.virginia.edu/page?id=essays&section=intro.

2. Ibid.

3. Douglas Turner Day III, the biographer of Malcolm Lowry, is known to Faulkner scholars for his edition of the author's first novel, *Flags in the Dust;* he retired from the University of Virginia in 2000 and died in 2004. See his *New York Times* obituary: "Douglas Day, 72, Malcolm Lowry Biographer, Is Dead," https://www.nytimes.com/2004/10/19/books/douglas-day-72-malcolm-lowry-biographer-is-dead.html.

4. Gwynn asked about the relationship between the novel and the short story "That Evening Sun," following up with a question about whether Faulkner recalled "any kind of feeling of satisfaction when [he] finally finished *The Sound and the Fury*" ("February 15, 1957: Gywnn's Literature Class," in *Faulkner at Virginia: An Audio Archive,* http://faulkner.lib.virginia.edu/display/wfaudio01_1).

5. Stephen Railton, "Faulkner at Virginia: An Introduction," in *Faulkner at Virginia: An Audio Archive,* http://faulkner.lib.virginia.edu/page?id=essays&section=intro.

6. Ibid.

7. Stephen Railton, email message to author, January 16, 2012. In his introduction to the 1995 edition of *Faulkner in the University,* Day makes much the same observation: "Several days before Faulkner came to one of our classes, Gwynn would solicit potential questions from us. If he (or Blotner) were curious to hear a given question answered by Faulkner, one would be given a little slip of paper with the question on it, so that it might be posed to Faulkner during class discussion" (*FIU,* xii). In identifying all faculty interlocutors, the transcriptions included in *Faulkner at Virginia* reveal how frequently the faculty drove—in some cases dominated—classroom discussion.

8. William Faulkner, *The Portable Faulkner,* ed. Malcolm Cowley (New York: Viking, 1946).

9. Gwynn acknowledges these visitors in his opening remarks: "I'd like . . . to introduce this group to Mr. Faulkner. People generally in the back, as I see it, are dedicated souls who've given up a great deal, maybe even breakfast, to come in here and who are official auditors of this class today, and scattered toward the front are the real card-carrying, dues-paying members of a class in American fiction, who have a few questions and a few comments" (*Faulkner at Virginia: An Audio Archive,* http://faulkner.lib.virginia.edu/display/wfaudio01_1). These remarks do not appear in Gwynn and Blotner's volume.

The late Carol R. Rupprecht, for many years my colleague at Hamilton College, was one of those auditors, having accompanied her then-husband to UVA, where he was a graduate student. In her recollection, there were sometimes more auditors attending a Faulkner class than registered students, and there were always women among the auditors (personal conversation, spring 2000). Evidence of this last observation may be heard at the conclusion of the May 20, 1957, freshman English class. Faulkner says, "Thank you, ladies and gentleman," even though no women had spoken (and there would have been no female students in an undergraduate course at UVA in 1957): https://faulkner.lib.virginia.edu/display/wfaudio16_2.html.

Having noted this, I should acknowledge the possibility that the unidentified female interlocutor in the February 15, 1957, class conference might be an auditor rather than a student. I think this is unlikely, though, given the felt gravity of the encounter and given Gwynn's description of his students as "the real card-carrying, dues-paying" members of the audience "who have a few questions and a few comments," an introduction that would tend to discourage questions from auditors.

10. Considering that Mary Washington was a women's college, the editing of this session is remarkably sexist, even by Blotner and Gwynn's established standard. The audio record shows that Faulkner fielded a total of twenty-six questions, seventeen of them asked by women (the two links to this session can be found here: https://faulkner.lib.virginia.edu/browse.html). Gwynn and Blotner whittle this down to five questions—four of them posed by men (*FIU,* 89–91). They thus not only radically reduce the number of female speakers; they also reverse the original ratio of female to male interlocutors.

11. Railton told me that Douglas Day's voice isn't heard "on any of the tapes" of the class conferences (Railton, email message to author, January 16, 2012).

12. *Faulkner at Virginia: An Audio Archive,* http://faulkner.lib.virginia.edu/display/wfaudio01_1.

13. In introducing Faulkner to his class, Gwynn observes that "it might make this moment even more historical in our minds if I remind you that there is no writer in the world today whose

prestige is higher than this gentleman from Mississippi" (*Faulkner at Virginia, An Audio Archive*).

14. Founded in segregation, the University of Virginia had almost no Black students during Faulkner's residency. The slow process of desegregating UVA began in 1950, when Gregory Swanson sued to gain admission to the School of Law. Robert Bland, '59, an engineering major, was the first African American to graduate from the College of Arts & Sciences. He was one of just three undergraduate Black students admitted to the university in 1955 (see http://xroads.virginia.edu/~ug03/omara-alwala/harrison/Timeline.html).

15. Anna Creadick, "Reading Faulkner's Readers: Reputation and the Postwar Reading Revolution," in *Faulkner and History: Faulkner and Yoknapatawpha 2014,* ed. Jay Watson and James G. Thomas (Jackson: University Press of Mississippi, 2017), 166. While Creadick makes excellent use of the *Faulkner at Virginia* digital archive to demonstrate the important role "everyday" readers played in the creation of Faulkner's reputation, and while she rightly observes that "by excerpting Blotner and Gwynn's edited interviews in critical editions of Faulkner novels, scholars have continued to narrow what happened at Virginia into still smaller nuggets" (162), she does not pursue the explicitly gendered analysis of that narrowing that I offer here.

16. For Hellman's review and Scott's pamphlet, see John Bassett, ed., *William Faulkner: The Critical Heritage* (London: Routledge and Kegan Paul, 1975), 66–67 and 76–81.

17. This phenomenon—and women's efforts to combat it—received some national attention a few years ago thanks to a *Washington Post* story about the "amplification" strategy adopted by women White House advisors in the Obama administration, where two-thirds of the top aides were men. Already vexed by the extra effort entailed in making certain they were included in important meetings, the women found that their problems didn't end once they had gained access. For when they spoke up at these meetings that they had worked so hard to attend, their contributions often passed without acknowledgment, only to reappear minutes later in the comments of a male staffer, who was then credited with the idea. Determined to overcome this second barrier to full participation, the women chose to "amplify" each other. As the *Washington Post* reports: "When a woman made a key point, other women would repeat it, giving credit to its author. This forced the men in the room to recognize the contribution—and denied them the chance to claim the idea as their own" (Juliet Eilperin, "White House Women Want to Be in the Room Where It Happens," *Washington Post,* September 13, 2016: https://www.washingtonpost.com/news/powerpost/wp/2016/09/13/white-house-women-are-now-in-the-room-where-it-happens/). For a recent example of increased awareness of, and reaction to, this phenomenon as it plays out within higher education and the media, see Alexandra C. Kafka, "An NPR Show's Slight against a Tobacco Historian Lights up Twitter," *Chronicle of Higher Education,* July 15, 2019, https://www.chronicle.com/article/An-NPR-Show-s-Slight-Against/246688.

18. Olga Vickery, *The Novels of William Faulkner: A Critical Interpretation* (Baton Rouge: Louisiana State University Press, 1959); Myra Jehlen, *Class and Character in Faulkner's South* (New York: Columbia University Press, 1976); Thadious M. Davis, *Faulkner's "Negro": Art and the Southern Context* (Baton Rouge: Louisiana State University Press, 1982); Cleanth Brooks, *William Faulkner: The Yoknapatawpha Country* (New Haven, CT: Yale University Press, 1963); John T. Irwin, *Doubling and Incest, Repetition and Revenge: A Speculative Reading of Faulkner* (Baltimore: Johns Hopkins University Press, 1975); Eric J. Sundquist, *Faulkner: The House Divided* (Baltimore: Johns Hopkins University Press, 1983).

19. Minrose Gwin, "Feminism and Faulkner: Second Thoughts; or, What's a Radical Feminist Doing with a Canonical Male Text Anyway?," *Faulkner Journal* 4, no. 1–2 (Fall 1988/Spring 1989; published Fall 1991): 57; emphasis in original.

20. For a definition and exploration of the concept of cultural disidentification, see José Esteban Muñoz, *Disidentifications: Queers of Color and the Performance of Politics* (Minneapolis: University of Minnesota Press, 1999). As the subtitle indicates, Muñoz develops the notion of disidentification within the context of queer theory. Like all important theoretical concepts, though, the notion of disidentification has applications well beyond its locus of emergence.

1. Putting It All on One Pinhead

Epigraphs: William Faulkner, *The Sound and the Fury: The Corrected Text,* ed. Noel Polk (New York: Vintage International, 1990), 80. William Faulkner, qtd. in Malcolm Cowley, *The Faulkner-Cowley File: Letters and Memories, 1944–1962* (Harmondsworth, UK: Penguin, 1978).

1. Cowley, *The Faulkner-Cowley File: Letters and Memories, 1944–62,* 6.

2. Bernard De Voto "Witchcraft in Mississippi," *Saturday Review of Literature,* October 31, 1936, qtd. in Lawrence Schwartz, *Creating Faulkner's Reputation: The Politics of Modern Literary Criticism* (Knoxville: University of Tennessee Press, 1988), 13.

3. William Faulkner, "Address upon Receiving the Nobel Prize for Literature," in *William Faulkner: Essays, Speeches, and Public Letters,* ed. James B. Meriwether, updated ed. (1965; New York: Modern Library, 2004), 120.

4. Robert Penn Warren's *New Republic* review of *The Portable Faulkner,* cited in Malcolm Cowley, *The Faulkner-Cowley File: Letters and Memories, 1944–1962* (Harmondsworth, UK: Penguin, 1978), 94, 95. The Virginian Thomas Nelson Page, whose accomplishments include service as Woodrow Wilson's Italian ambassador, was a popular practitioner of the so-called "plantation genre" of fiction. His "Marse Chan" stories are sentimental apologias for slavery.

5. Joseph Blotner, *Faulkner: A Biography,* 2 vols. (New York: Random House, 1974), 2:1591.

6. William Faulkner, *The Sound and the Fury,* ed. David Minter (New York: Norton, 1987), 59.

7. For one example of this approach, see John Carlos Rowe, "The African-American Voice in Faulkner's *Go Down, Moses,*" in *Modern American Short Story Sequences: Composite Fictions and Fictive Communities,* ed. Gerald Kennedy, 76–97 (Cambridge: Cambridge University Press, 1995).

8. Lawrence Schwartz, *Creating Faulkner's Reputation: The Politics of Modern Literary Criticism* (Knoxville: University of Tennessee Press, 1988), 210.

9. William Faulkner, *Absalom, Absalom! The Corrected Text,* ed. Noel Polk (New York: Vintage International, 1990), 142.

10. For one discussion of the connection between Faulkner and Balzac, see Merrill Horton, "Faulkner, Balzac, and the Word," *Faulkner Journal* 19, no. 2 (2004): 91–106.

11. Faulkner added the "u" to the family name.

12. Joel Williamson, *William Faulkner and Southern History* (New York: Oxford University Press, 1993).

13. Faulkner's many lies about his service as a Canadian RAF pilot during World War I are another case in point. Though it appears that he did enlist, he never saw action.

14. William Faulkner, "An Introduction to *The Sound and the Fury*," *Mississippi Quarterly* 26 (1973), reprinted in William Faulkner, *The Sound and the Fury*, ed. David Minter (New York: Norton, 1994), 222.

15. Jean-Paul Sartre, "On *The Sound and the Fury:* Time in Faulkner," in *The Sound and the Fury*, ed. Minter, 259.

16. Eric J. Sundquist, *Faulkner: The House Divided* (Baltimore: Johns Hopkins University Press, 1983), 9.

17. John T. Matthews, *"The Sound and the Fury": Faulkner and the Lost Cause* (Boston: Twayne, 1991), 90.

18. Richard L. Godden, *Fictions of Labor: William Faulkner and the South's Long Revolution* (Cambridge: Cambridge University Press, 1997), 78.

19. Faulkner, "An Introduction to *The Sound and the Fury*," ed. Minter, 219.

20. William Faulkner, *Sanctuary: The Corrected Text*, ed. Noel Polk (New York: Vintage International, 1991), 321–22.

21. Pascale Casanova, *The World Republic of Letters*, trans. M. B. DeBevoise (Cambridge, MA: Harvard University Press, 2004), 336–37.

22. Ralph Ellison, *Shadow and Act* (New York: Vintage, 1972), 140.

23. Toni Morrison, "Faulkner and Women," in *Faulkner and Women: Faulkner and Yoknapatawpha 1985*, ed. Doreen Fowler and Ann J. Abadie, 296–97 (Jackson: University Press of Mississippi, 1986).

24. Jay Parini, *One Matchless Time: A Life of William Faulkner* (New York: HarperCollins, 2004); Judith L. Sensibar, *Faulkner and Love: The Women Who Shaped His Art* (New Haven, CT: Yale University Press, 2009); Michael Gorra, *The Saddest Words: William Faulkner's Civil War* (New York: Liveright, 2020).

2. Pulp Fictions

1. Philip Weinstein. *Faulkner's Subject: A Cosmos No One Owns* (Cambridge: Cambridge University Press, 1992), 146. Weinstein is referring to the hunting world of *Go Down, Moses*, but the phrase works metonymically to describe a certain view of Faulkner's literary corpus, as well.

2. These texts have a long history: Harry Runyan's *A Faulkner Glossary* (New York: Citadel, 1964) appeared just two years after Faulkner's death.

3. Toni Morrison, "Faulkner and Women," in *Faulkner and Women: Faulkner and Yoknapatawpha, 1985*, ed. Doreen Fowler and Ann J. Abadie (Jackson: University Press of Mississippi, 1986), 296.

4. Carol A. Kolmerten, Stephen M. Ross, and Judith Bryant Wittenberg, eds., *Unflinching Gaze: Morrison and Faulkner Re-Envisioned* (Jackson: University Press of Mississippi, 1997).

5. John T. Irwin's study is the *locus classicus* of any discussion of Faulknerian repetition. That the book was reissued in an expanded edition is one testimony to the importance of repetition (with and without difference) in the maintenance of cultural capital generally, and its importance in critical discourse on Faulkner in particular (*Doubling and Incest, Repetition and Revenge: A Speculative Reading of Faulkner*, expanded ed. [Baltimore: Johns Hopkins University Press, 1996]).

6. William Faulkner, *Absalom, Absalom! The Corrected Text,* ed. Noel Polk (1936; New York: Vintage International, 1990), 303; William Faulkner, *Light in August: The Corrected Text,* ed. Noel Polk (New York: Vintage International, 1990), 119; *The Sound and the Fury,* ed. David Minter, 2nd ed. (1929; New York: Norton, 1994), 3. Subsequent quotations from *The Sound and the Fury* are from this edition and are cited as *SF*.

7. William Faulkner, "An Introduction for *The Sound and the Fury*," ed. James B. Meriwether, *Southern Review* 8 (1972): 705–10; reprinted in *The Sound and the Fury,* ed. Minter, 226.

8. William Faulkner, "An Introduction to *The Sound and the Fury*," ed. James B. Meriwether, *Mississippi Quarterly* 26, no. 3 (Summer 1973): 410–15; reprinted in *The Sound and the Fury,* ed. Minter, 231.

9. I have in mind here Pierre Bourdieu's description of the homologous relationship between the investment of accumulated labor (i.e., time) in capital and the investment of time (i.e., mental labor) in culture (see "The Forms of Capital," in *Handbook of Theory and Research for the Sociology of Education,* ed. John G. Richardson, 241–58 [New York: Greenwood, 1986]). It is Bourdieu who first made significant use of the phrase "cultural capital," which has come to the fore in debates about canon formation (for example, in John Guillory's study *Cultural Capital: The Problem of Literary Canon Formation* [Chicago: University of Chicago Press, 1993]).

10. Pierre Bourdieu, *The Rules of Art: Genesis and Structure of the Literary Field,* trans. Susan Emmanuel (Stanford, CA: Stanford University Press, 1996), 325.

11. William Faulkner, "A Rose for Emily," in *Collected Stories* (1950; New York: Vintage, 1977), 129. Subsequent quotations are from this edition.

12. William Faulkner, *Selected Letters,* ed. Joseph Blotner (New York: Random House, 1977), 47.

13. "One day it suddenly seemed as if a door had clapped silently and forever to between me and all publishers' addresses and booklists and I said to myself, Now I can write. Now I can just write" (Faulkner, "An Introduction for *The Sound and the Fury*," reprinted in *The Sound and the Fury,* ed. Minter, 227).

14. Bruce Kawin, *Faulkner and Film* (New York: Frederick Ungar, 1977), 149.

15. Jeff Dawson, *Quentin Tarantino: The Cinema of Cool* (New York: Applause, 1995), 68.

16. Tarantino's mother, Connie Zastoupil, claims that during her pregnancy, "I was reading a Faulkner book, *The Sound and the Fury.* The heroine's name was Quentin, so I decided that my child was going to be named Quentin whether it was a male or a female" (Dawson 17). Ms. Zastoupil's unusual description of Caddy's daughter Quentin as "the heroine" of *The Sound and the Fury* raises the possibility that a more likely source for the name was the 1959 film adaptation of the novel, which featured only one Quentin, the "heroine," played by Joanne Woodward. Tarantino was born in 1963.

17. Quentin Tarantino and Roger Avery, *Pulp Fiction* (New York: Hyperion/Miramax Books, 1994), 85. Here I quote the published screenplay, which includes dialogue cut from the film; subsequent quotations are from this edition. Directed by Tarantino, *Pulp Fiction* was produced by A Band Apart, Jersey Films, and Miramax films, and released in the United States by Miramax in 1994.

18. Walter Benjamin, "The Work of Art in the Age of Mechanical Reproduction," in *Illuminations,* ed. Hannah Arendt; trans. Harry Zohn (New York: Schocken, 1969), 221. Benjamin's essay—

motivated by the emergence of cinema, "with its shock effect" (240), as fascism's favored artistic medium—describes how "that which withers in the age of mechanical reproduction is the aura of the work of art," going on to "generalize" this claim "by saying: the technique of reproduction detaches the reproduced object from the domain of tradition" (221). I will not attempt, in a single footnote, to address all the complications that follow on using Benjamin's essay to discuss Tarantino's film, but it is worth observing that *Pulp Fiction* toys with the notion of reproduction *itself* as the new location of the auratic and of "tradition."

19. Norman O. Brown, *Life Against Death* (Middletown, CT: Wesleyan University Press, 1959). In her essay on *Pulp Fiction,* Sharon Willis further links the constellation feces/gold/Oedipus to issues of cultural capital via Tarantino's nostalgia for 1970s pop culture: "To redeem a previous generation's trash may be, metaphorically, to turn its shit into gold, and to posit a certain reversibility of cultural authority in the process" (Willis, "The Fathers Watch the Boys' Room," *Camera obscura* 2, no. 32 [1993]: 48). Willis's reading of race in Tarantino's films strongly resembles the long-established critical tradition of psychoanalytically reading race in Faulkner.

20. Paul Woods, *King Pulp: The Wild World of Quentin Tarantino* (New York: Thunder's Mouth, 1996), 119.

21. It is worth pointing out, in the context of this remark, that the most often-heard criticism of Tarantino's films is that they amount to little more than tissues of cinematic quotation. The mini-controversy over Tarantino's appropriation (some would say plagiarism) of Ringo Lan's 1989 Hong Kong film *City on Fire* in *Reservoir Dogs* is a case in point (see Dawson 90–91).

22. Both Woods and Dawson mention Tarantino's fondness for this film; in Dawson's words, "one shouldn't underestimate the importance of Jim McBride's 1983 film *Breathless* in influencing Tarantino" (61).

23. Pamela Falkenberg's excellent analysis of the relationship between McBride's *Breathless* and Godard's *A bout de souffle* turns exactly on questions of repetition: "*Breathless* [is] the realistic representation of *A bout de souffle:* the simulation of a simulation that is itself a simulation of Hollywood" ("'Hollywood' and the 'Art Cinema' as a Bipolar Modeling System: *A bout de souffle* and *Breathless*," *Wide Angle* 7, no. 3 [1985]: 52). For another perspective on the importance of quotation in both the creation and circulation of cultural capital, see Guillory's discussion, in *Cultural Capital,* of Thomas Gray's commonplace books (87–89).

24. Irwin offers a comprehensive discussion of the relationship between incest and time in *The Sound and the Fury.*

25. Manohla Dargis, "A Bloody Pulp," *Vibe* 2, no. 8 (October 1994): 64–66.

26. Dawson and Wood both offer this explanation.

27. Todd Boyd, "Tarantino's Mantra? Pulp Director Has Wrongheaded Approach to the N-Word," *Chicago Tribune,* November 6, 1994, "Arts," 26.

28. William Faulkner, *Intruder in the Dust* (New York: Vintage International, 1991), 190.

29. Ken Burns, *The Civil War* (Florentine Films/PBS, 1989), episode 5, chap. 5.

30. Burns, *The Civil War,* episode 9, chap. 6.

31. Shelby Foote, *The Civil War, A Narrative: Red River to Appomattox* (New York: Random House, 1974), 1048. Burns uses Benson's words to construct a North-South reunion at the close of the television series, stressing the wish to "meet together . . . all sound and well." Foote's narra-

tive, however, emphasizes Benson's desire to fight the war again: "Reliving the war in words, he began to wish he could relive it in fact, and he came to believe that he and his fellow soldiers, gray and blue, might one day be able to do just that: if not here on earth, then afterwards in Valhalla" (Foote, 1048).

    32. bell hooks, *Reel to Real: Race, Sex, and Class at the Movies* (New York: Routledge, 1996), 48.

    33. For an excellent reading of the relationship between *Sanctuary* and *The Sound and the Fury*, see Kristin Fujie, "Trashing *Sanctuary*: The Material Origins of Faulkner's Art," in *Faulkner and Print Culture: Faulkner and Yoknapatawpha 2015*, ed. Jay Watson, Jaime Harker, and James G. Thomas Jr., 3–14 (Jackson: University Press of Mississippi, 2017).

    34. See Sarah Gleeson-White, "Faulkner Goes to Hollywood," in *William Faulkner in Context*, ed. John T. Matthews, 194–203 (Cambridge: Cambridge University Press, 2015); David M. Earle, "Faulkner and the Paperback Trade," in *William Faulkner in Context,* ed. John T. Matthews, 231–45 (Cambridge: Cambridge University Press, 2015); David M. Earle, "Yoknapatawpha Pulp, or What Faulkner *Really* Read at the P.O.," in *Fifty Years after Faulkner: Faulkner and Yoknapatawpha 2012,* ed. Jay Watson and Ann J. Abadie, 31–54 (Jackson: University Press of Mississippi, 2016); and Jaime Harker, "*The Wild Palms, The Mansion,* and William Faulkner's Middlebrow Domestic Fiction," in *Faulkner and Print Culture: Faulkner and Yoknapatawpha 2015,* ed. Jay Watson, Jaime Harker, and James G. Thomas Jr., 203–15 (Jackson: University Press of Mississippi, 2017).

3. Writing *A Fable* for America

Epigraph: "Gerechter Gott! Du hast gerichtet, / wie alles geschehen soll: / Gebührt dem Lohn, der gern anders möchte? / Oder dem, der nichts anders vermag?" (Arnold Schoenberg, *Moses und Aron,* trans. Allen Forte [Pacific Palisades, CA: Belmont Music Publishers, 1957], 2; translation slightly modified).

    1. Lawrence H. Schwartz, *Creating Faulkner's Reputation: The Politics of Modern Literary Criticism* (Knoxville: University of Tennessee Press, 1988), 1.

    2. Fredric Jameson's *The Political Unconscious: Narrative as a Socially Symbolic Act* (Ithaca, NY: Cornell University Press, 1981) is the *locus classicus* of this interpretive gesture, which brings to literary interpretation an attention to political-historical context understood to be greater than formalist readings allow.

    3. See especially chapters 5 and 6, "Forging a Postwar Aesthetic: The Rockefeller Foundation and the New Literary Consensus" and "The Triumph of the New Literary Consensus: Literary Elitism and Liberal Anti-Communism," 113–71. For two discussions of the emergence of the postwar liberal consensus that parallel Schwartz's analysis, see Andrew Ross, *No Respect: Intellectuals and Popular Culture* (New York: Routledge, 1989); and Thomas H. Schaub, *American Fiction in the Cold War* (Madison: University of Wisconsin Press, 1991).

    4. Important revisionary Faulkner scholarship of the period includes Myra Jehlen, *Class and Character in Faulkner's South* (1976; Secaucus, NJ: Citadel, 1978); John T. Matthews, *The Play of Faulkner's Language* (Ithaca, NY: Cornell University Press, 1982); Eric J. Sundquist, *Faulkner: The House Divided* (Baltimore: Johns Hopkins University Press, 1983); Thadious M. Davis, *Faulkner's "Negro": Art and the Southern Context* (Baton Rouge: Louisiana State University Press, 1983); James

Snead, *Figures of Division: William Faulkner's Major Novels* (New York: Methuen, 1986); and Michael Grimwood, *Heart in Conflict: Faulkner's Struggles with Vocation* (Athens: University of Georgia Press, 1987). These studies are not as skeptical of Faulkner's achievement as Schwartz's, but they cannot be described as continuations of the hagiographic mythic/formalist criticism of the early Cold War period.

It is worth noting that even "the establishment" within Faulkner scholarship found much to admire in Schwartz's study: in his omnibus review for *American Literary Scholarship,* M. Thomas Inge termed *Creating Faulkner's Reputation* "a carefully researched and impressively argued case study of the ways political trends, social forces, and aesthetic movements can be brought to bear on the creation of a writer's reputation" ("Faulkner, iii. Criticism: General," in *American Literary Scholarship: An Annual/1988,* ed. J. Albert Robbins, 141–42 [Durham, NC: Duke University Press, 1990]). See also Joseph R. Urgo, untitled review of *Creating Faulkner's Reputation, South Atlantic Review* 54, no. 4 [November 1989]: 104); and Myra Jehlen, untitled review of *Creating Faulkner's Reputation, Journal of American History* 76, no. 4 (March 1990): 1321.

5. Michael O'Brien, untitled review of *Creating Faulkner's Reputation, American Historical Review* 95, no. 3 (June 1990): 899.

6. Fred Pinnegar, untitled review of *Creating Faulkner's Reputation, Rocky Mountain Review of Language and Literature* 43, no. 4 (1989): 255.

7. Michel Gresset, "Postface," *Tandis que j'agonise* (*As I Lay Dying*), trans. Maurice Edgar Coindreau (1934; Paris: Éditions Gallimard, 1973), 247.

8. My thanks to Professor István Géher for this information.

9. Joseph Blotner indicates that Faulkner's earliest Swedish translations, by Thorsten Jonsson, a New York correspondent for Stockholm's *Dagens Nyheter,* were a postwar phenomenon (Blotner, *Faulkner: A Biography,* 2 vols. [New York: Random House, 1974], 2:1207). However, Hans H. Skei writes that Faulkner's works were available in Norwegian in the 1930s (*Soldiers' Pay* in 1932, *Light in August* in 1934) and implies that Danish and Swedish translations of Faulkner's novels were likewise available in the 1930s (see Skei, "Faulkner in Norway/Faulkner in Norwegian Literature," *Faulkner Journal of Japan* 1 [1999], http://www.faulknerjapan.com/journal/No1/SkeiRevd.htm).

10. Thus, for Pascale Casanova, Faulkner's importance lies precisely in how his fictions (as well as those of Joyce and Kafka), circulating in translation, "enable writers on the periphery who previously were denied access to literary modernity to take part . . . using instruments that they themselves have forged" (Casanova, *The World Republic of Letters,* trans. M. B. DeBevoise [Cambridge, MA: Harvard University Press, 2004], 328). Whether Casanova's analysis conduces toward a view of modern literary history as a series of artistic liberations or, conversely, as the tightening of a Western-internationalist stylistic straitjacket is a not a question I engage here (though for the purposes of my argument it's worth noting that, for Casanova, "Western" is not synonymous with "American"). For a sense of the issues at play, see the essays collected in the summer 2008 special issue of *New Literary History* (39, no. 3), "Literary History in the Global Age."

11. Three studies from the 1980s set the frame within which subsequent revisionary readings of Faulkner's late work would be set: Noel Polk, *Faulkner's "Requiem for a Nun": A Critical Study* (Bloomington: Indiana University Press, 1981); Matthews, *The Play of Faulkner's Language;* and Cheryl Lester, "To Market, to Market: *The Portable Faulkner,*" *Criticism: A Quarterly for Litera-*

ture and the Arts 29 (1987): 371–89. Polk's sympathetic attention to a novel long regarded as problematic, Matthews's demonstration of the uses of deconstruction in reading Faulkner's canonical novels, and Lester's recasting of the author's role in the creation of Cowley's *Portable Faulkner* as a kind of sabotage *sous rature* pointed the way for a view of the late work as self-questioning rather than bloviating. The strongest readings of this sort cast the later novels as critical reimaginings of earlier work (see Richard C. Moreland, *Faulkner and Modernism: Rereading and Rewriting* [Madison: University of Wisconsin Press, 1990]; and Joseph Urgo, *Faulkner's Apocrypha: "A Fable," "Snopes," and the Spirit of Human Rebellion* [Jackson: University Press of Mississippi, 1989]).

For a sampling of scholarship arguing for the merits of *A Fable*, see Noel Polk, "Woman and the Feminine in *A Fable*," in his study *Children of the Dark House: Text and Context in Faulkner* (Jackson: University Press of Mississippi, 1996), 196–218; "'Polysyllabic and Verbless Patriotic Nonsense': Faulkner at Midcentury—His and Ours," in *Faulkner and Ideology: Faulkner and Yoknapatawpha 1992*, ed. Donald M. Kartiganer and Ann J. Abadie, 297–328 (Jackson: University Press of Mississippi, 1995); "Roland Barthes Reads *A Fable*," in *Faulkner's Discourse: An International Symposium*, ed. Lothar Hönnighausen, 109–16 (Tübingen: Max Niemeyer, 1989); and "Enduring *A Fable* and Prevailing," in *Faulkner: After the Nobel Prize*, ed. Michel Gresset and Kanzaburo Ohashi, 110–26 (Kyoto: Yamaguchi, 1987). See also Warwick Wadlington, "Doing What Comes Culturally: Collective Action and the Discourse of Belief in Faulkner and Nathanael West," in *Faulkner, His Contemporaries, and His Posterity*, ed. Waldemar Zacharasiewicz, 245–52 (Tübingen: A. Francke, 1993), along with four essays in the collection *Faulkner: After the Nobel Prize*, ed. Gresset and Ohashi: "The Imagery in Faulkner's *A Fable*," by Lothar Hönnighausen (147–71); "The Indestructible Voice of the British Battalion Runner in *A Fable*," by Ikuko Fujihara (127–46); "The Critical Difference: Faulkner's Case in *A Fable*," by Fumiyo Hayashi (91–109); and "William Faulkner's Late Career: Repetition, Variation, Renewal," by Hans H. Skei (247–59).

12. Charles Rolo, writing in the *Atlantic*, called the book a failure; Brendan Gill, of the *New Yorker*, termed it a calamity. For the parody, see J. Maclaren-Ross, "A Cable, by W*ll**m F**lkn*r," *Punch*, October 5, 1955, 399–401.

13. John E. Basset, "*A Fable*: Faulkner's Revision of Filial Conflict," *Renascence* 40 (1987): 15; Richard H. King, "*A Fable*: Faulkner's Political Novel?," *Southern Literary Journal* 17, no. 2 (1985): 10; Harold Bloom, introduction to *Modern Critical Interpretations: William Faulkner's "Absalom, Absalom!*," ed. Bloom (New York: Chelsea House, 1987), 3; André Bleikasten, "A Private Man's Public Voice," in *Faulkner: After the Nobel Prize*, ed. Gresset and Ohashi, 59.

14. William Faulkner, *Selected Letters*, ed. Joseph Blotner (New York: Random House, 1977), 262. At the 2004 Modern Language Association annual convention, five scholars took the fiftieth anniversary of the work's appearance as an opportunity to press claims for the merits of *A Fable*. Members of the December 30, 2004, MLA panel ("Fifty Years after *A Fable*") included Keen Butterworth, David A. Davis, Caroline Miles, Noel Polk, Theresa M. Towner, and Joseph R. Urgo. More recently, John T. Matthews has described the novel's grasp of "how intersecting spheres of power—economic, military-industrial, political, cultural—were consolidating to form a global class of owners of means" as "a magnificent insight, one that is more timely today than ever." On the basis of this, he terms *A Fable* "the Faulkner novel of our times" (Matthews, *William Faulkner: Seeing through the South* [Oxford: Wiley-Blackwell, 2009], 271).

15. There is a long-established but underappreciated vein of scholarship on the conflicted nature of Faulkner's creative imagination. See Michael Millgate, "William Faulkner: The Two Voices," in *Southern Literature in Transition: Heritage and Promise,* ed. Philip Castille and William Osborne, 73–85 (Memphis, TN: Memphis State University Press, 1983); Grimwood, *Heart in Conflict;* and Doreen Fowler, "Introduction: Faulkner's 'Heart in Conflict,'" in *Faulkner: The Return of the Repressed* (Charlottesville: University Press of Virginia, 1997), 1–31. These studies mostly employ a psychological approach (Fowler's is a Lacanian psychoanalytic reading) to exploring Faulkner's "heart in conflict with itself"; Grimwood additionally sees Faulkner's simultaneous embrace and rejection of literature as a vocation as a function of "his attunement to the liabilities of pastoralism" (11).

16. Bleikasten, "A Private Man's Public Voice," 53. Faulkner's wholesale allegorization of the Passion Week in *A Fable* contrasts markedly with his selective, critically deconstructive, use of aspects of the Christ narrative in *The Sound and the Fury* (1929) and *Light in August* (1932).

17. A version of the Nobel Prize speech, studded as is the original with panegyrics on man's capacity to "prevail" and "endure," is given to the corrupt "old general" in the Thursday-night "temptation" scene. See *A Fable,* in *Faulkner: Novels, 1942–1954: "Go Down, Moses," "Intruder in the Dust," "Requiem for a Nun," "A Fable,"* ed. Joseph Blotner and Noel Polk (New York: Library of America, 1994), 994. Subsequent quotations from *A Fable* are from this edition.

18. Besides the New Testament and James Street's *Look Away!,* which Faulkner himself cites (incorrectly), the sources for *A Fable*'s borrowings include Humphrey Cobb's *Paths of Glory;* Erich Maria Remarque's *All Quiet on the Western Front* and *The Road Back* (the second reviewed by Faulkner in the *New Republic* in 1931); John Steinbeck's *Of Mice and Men* (rather shameless considering Faulkner's disdain for Steinbeck's work); and *War Birds: Diary of an Unknown Aviator.* Published in 1926, *War Birds* is a distillation by Eliot White Springs of the diaries of John McGavock Grider, a pilot killed during World War I. In 1932, while under contract with MGM, Faulkner did a treatment of *War Birds* for Howard Hawks.

19. Both Robert W. Hamblin and Joseph Urgo point out that the story of the condemned man and the bird appears nowhere in *Look Away!* (Hamblin, "James Street's *Look Away!* Source [and Non-Source] for William Faulkner," *American Notes & Queries* 21, no. 9–10 [May–June 1983]: 141–43; Urgo "Where Was That Bird? Thinking *America* through Faulkner," in *Faulkner in America: Faulkner and Yoknapatawpha, 1998,* ed. Joseph R. Urgo and Ann J. Abadie, 98–115 [Jackson: University Press of Mississippi, 2001]). The fact of Faulkner's mistake is less interesting to me than his belief that the story came from commercial media. Street worked as a reporter for a variety of newspapers in the South; *Look Away! A Dixie Notebook* (New York: Viking, 1936) gathers together some of his more memorable dispatches.

Faulkner had written other introductions to his fiction—for instance, the notorious preface to the 1932 Modern Library edition of *Sanctuary* and the two posthumously published 1933 prefaces to *The Sound and the Fury*—but never before had he felt compelled to acknowledge an imaginative debt.

20. "Interview with Jean Stein van den Heuvel," in *Lion in the Garden: Interviews with William Faulkner, 1926–1962,* ed. James B. Meriwether and Michael Millgate (New York: Random House, 1968), 239. Horkheimer and Adorno's discussion of mass media's dialectical reversal of the rebel-

lious detail into the "ready-made" "special effect" is an important but seldom-noted aspect of their critique of culture industry: "By emancipating itself, the detail had become refractory; from Romanticism to Expressionism it had rebelled as unbridled expression, as the agent of opposition, against organization.... Through totality, the culture industry is putting an end to all that. Although operating only with effects, it subdues their unruliness and subordinates them to the formula which supplants the work. It crushes equally the whole and the parts" (*Dialectic of Enlightenment: Philosophical Fragments,* ed. Gunzelin Schmid Noerr; trans. Edmund Jephcott [Stanford, CA: Stanford University Press, 2002], 99). Obviously, Adorno and Horkheimer's understanding of the "ready-made" in culture industry is something quite other than Marcel Duchamp's conceptualist exploration of the "readymade" in visual art: the first is not simply preformed, but predigested.

21. Philip M. Weinstein, ed., *The Cambridge Companion to William Faulkner* (Cambridge: Cambridge University Press, 1995), xix.

22. Both Polk, in "Roland Barthes reads *A Fable,*" and Nicholas Moseley, in "Faulkner's Fables" (*Review of Contemporary Fiction* 2, no. 2 [1982]: 79–86), claim, in different ways, that "*A Fable* is a fable about people's use of fables" (Moseley 80).

23. James B. Meriwether published the rejected preface as "A Note on *A Fable,*" *Mississippi Quarterly* 26 (1973): 416–17.

24. Faulkner promised Harold Ober that the finished story would "reveal its Christ-analogy through understatement," but on publication *A Fable* featured three crucifixes on its cover and a crucifix on the title page; throughout the text, the typographical device used to signal new chapters and breaks within chapters is the crucifix.

Faulkner's November 1943 letter to Ober is worth quoting at length, as it lays out quite clearly the importance *A Fable*'s commercial potential had for him:

> The idea belongs to a director in Hollywood. He told it in casual after-dinner talk to a producer for whom I had done a job which the producer liked. The producer... took fire, told the director I was the only man to write it, fired the director up. The three of us met, agreed that I should write the story, the other two put up the money, we would make the picture independently and own it between us, share and share alike. It was further agreed that I would write the story in any form I liked: picture script, play, or novel, any revenue from a play or novel to be mine exclusively. The picture rights of course are not for sale.
>
> I am still under contract with Warner, pending a readjustment of which, I cannot write moving picture script for anyone else. So, to kill two birds with one stone, I am writing this story in an elaborated, detailed, explicit synopsis form, from which I can write a script later when my status with Warner is cleared up, and which I can try to turn into a play now, or rewrite as a novelette-fable, either or both of which, under my leave of absence from Warner which reserved me the right to write anything but moving pictures while off salary, I can do.
>
> Is there enough of it here for you to show around for a sale or a reasonably definite commitment...? This is about half of it. It continues on, through the Three Temptations, the Crucifixion, the Resurrection. The Epilogue is an Armistice Day ceremony at the tomb of the Unknown Soldier.
>
> I would like to rewrite it as a magazine story... and as a play. As a magazine and book

piece, I will smooth it out, give the characters names, remove the primer-like biblical references and explanations, and let the story reveal its Christ-analogy through understatement. If anyone is interested, I can send the rest of this synopsis form on to you when I finish it, or you can send these fifty-one sheets back to me and I will rewrite and submit the finished product, whichever they like. . . . *no moving picture rights are for sale or included in any sale.* (Faulkner, *Selected Letters,* 178–79; emphasis in original)

Faulkner wrote Ober from Oxford, where he had returned from Hollywood on the strength of a thousand-dollar advance from Bacher for the fable treatment. He was able to write at home from mid-August 1943 to mid-February 1944, when financial pressures compelled his return to Hollywood (*Selected Letters,* 178, 180). Blotner's biography makes clear that money worries played a crucial role in Faulkner's decision to sign on to Bacher and Hathaway's scheme, which several other writers had already turned down (Blotner 2:1149–50).

25. Ephraim Katz, *The Film Encyclopedia,* 2nd ed. (New York: HarperCollins, 1994), 599.

26. Ronald Taylor, trans. and ed., *Aesthetics and Politics: Theodor Adorno, Walter Benjamin, Ernst Block, Bertolt Brecht, Georg Lukács* (New York: Verso, 1995), 123.

27. I here repeat and slightly modify a point made by Andreas Huyssen in *After the Great Divide: Modernism, Mass Culture, Postmodernism* (Bloomington: Indiana University Press, 1986), 34.

28. Walter L. Hixson's discussion of the USIA's "feature packets" describes the State Department's wide-bore consumption, reproduction, and dissemination of images of American virtue and prosperity during the "People's Capitalism" propaganda campaign of the mid-1950s. Feature packets with titles such as "The Hollywood Story" and "Hollywood and the Church" were circulated cheek-by-jowl with packets entitled "The Operas of Gian-Carlo Menotti" and "The Eisenhower Golf Stroke" (Hixson, *Parting the Curtain: Propaganda, Culture, and the Cold War, 1945–1961* [New York: St. Martin's, 1997], 134–37). I take the phrase "modernist conformism" from Peter Bürger's essay "The Decline of Modernism" (*The Decline of Modernism,* trans. Nicholas Walker [University Park: Pennsylvania State University Press, 1992], 38).

29. Susan Stewart, "Notes on Distressed Genres," in *Crimes of Writing: Problems in the Containment of Representation* (New York: Oxford University Press, 1991), 80.

30. See Richard Godden's two-part essay "*A Fable* . . . Whispering about the Wars," *Faulkner Journal* 17, no. 2 (Spring 2002): 25–84, which, by positing a series of semantic and thematic displacements, reads the novel's retelling of the Christ myth as Faulkner's engagement with the changing southern racial landscape via an "economically determined" allegory of "the black Jew" (78).

31. Shirley Samuels, introduction to *The Culture of Sentiment: Race, Gender, and Sentimentality in Nineteenth-Century America,* ed. Samuels (New York: Oxford University Press, 1992), 3.

32. Elizabeth Barnes, *States of Sympathy: Seduction and Democracy in the American Novel* (New York: Columbia University Press, 1997), 13.

33. Maureen Quilligan, *The Language of Allegory: Defining the Genre* (1979; Ithaca, NY: Cornell University Press, 1992), 22.

34. Janet Todd's study *Sensibility: An Introduction* (New York: Methuen, 1986) notes that "the sentimental impulse is recurrent in literature." Because "sentimental techniques and their appreciation" can be "associated with a variety of social and cultural phenomena" among which "there

is no hard association or simple cause and effect," the question of the virtues of sentimental literature "is, then, a matter of emphasis and number, not of complete identification and opposition" (10). Suzanne Clark's *Sentimental Modernism: Women Writers and the Revolution of the Word* (Bloomington: Indiana University Press, 1991) attends to the interdependencies of sentimental and modernist discourses. For various reasons, however, Clark is interested in continuing the discussion of sentimentality as a gendered phenomenon, and she does not connect sentimentalism with a commodified culture.

The bibliography on sentimentality in US culture has grown explosively. Besides the work of Barnes, Clark, Douglas, Samuels—and Jane P. Tompkins's well-known *Sensational Designs: The Cultural Work of American Fiction, 1790–1860* (New York: Oxford University Press, 1985)—see also Markman Ellis, *The Politics of Sensibility: Race, Gender, and Commerce in the Sentimental Novel* (New York: Cambridge University Press, 1996); Bruce Burgett, *Sentimental Bodies: Sex, Gender, and Citizenship in the Early Republic* (Princeton, NJ: Princeton University Press, 1998); Andrew Burstein, *Sentimental Democracy: The Evolution of America's Romantic Self-Image* (New York: Farrar, Straus and Giroux, 1999); Mary Chapman and Glenn Hendler, eds., *Sentimental Men: Masculinity and the Politics of Affect in American Culture* (Berkeley: University of California Press, 1999); John Phillips Resche, *Suffering Soldiers: Revolutionary War Veterans, Moral Sentiment, and Political Culture in the Early Republic* (Amherst: University of Massachusetts Press, 1999); Lori Merish, *Sentimental Materialism: Gender, Commodity Culture, and Nineteenth-Century American Literature* (Durham, NC: Duke University Press, 2000); Kristin Boudreau, *Sympathy in American Literature: American Sentiments from Jefferson to the Jameses* (Gainesville: University Press of Florida, 2002); Elizabeth White Nelson, *Market Sentiments: Middle-Class Market Culture in Nineteenth-Century America* (Washington, DC: Smithsonian Institution Press, 2004); and Lauren Berlant's summative *The Female Complaint: The Unfinished Business of Sentimentality in American Culture* (Durham, NC: Duke University Press, 2008).

35. Ann Douglas, *The Feminization of American Culture* (1977; New York: Doubleday, 1988), 189.

36. Steven C. Bullock, *Revolutionary Brotherhood: Freemasonry and the Transformation of the American Social Order, 1730–1840* (Chapel Hill: University of North Carolina Press, 1996), vii.

37. Lynn Dumenil, *Freemasonry and American Culture, 1880–1930* (Princeton, NJ: Princeton University Press, 1984), xii.

38. Mary Ann Clawson, *Constructing Brotherhood: Class, Gender, and Fraternalism* (Princeton, NJ: Princeton University Press, 1989), 39.

39. Arthur Koestler, "The Right to Say No: Four Contributions to the Congress for Cultural Freedom," in *The Trail of the Dinosaur and Other Essays* (London: Collins, 1955), 179.

40. The history of CIA funding of the Congress for Cultural Freedom is well known. See, for example, Christopher Lasch, *The Agony of the American Left* (New York: Knopf, 1969); and Frances Stonor Saunders, *The Cultural Cold War: The CIA and the World of Arts and Letters* (New York: New Press, 2000).

41. Andreas Huyssen, *After the Great Divide: Modernism, Mass Culture, Postmodernism* (Bloomington: Indiana University Press, 1986), 16–17.

42. See "Faulkner and the Culture Industry" in Weinstein, *Cambridge Companion*, 51–74.

43. I draw the phrase "driven into Paradise" from Arnold Schoenberg, "Two Speeches on the Jewish Situation," in *Style and Idea: Selected Writings of Arnold Schoenberg,* ed. Leonard Stein; trans. Leo Black (1975; Berkeley: University of California Press, 1984), 502. For a discussion of the modernist music scene that took root around Hollywood during the 1930s and afterward, see Dorothy L. Crawford, *A Windfall of Musicians: Hitler's Émigrés and Exiles in Southern California* (New Haven, CT: Yale University Press, 2009).

44. "So mache dich dem Volk verständlich; / auf ihm angemeßne Art" (Schoenberg, *Moses und Aron*).

45. Donald Jay Grout, *A History of Western Music,* rev. ed. (New York: Norton, 1973), 708. As Charles Rosen has observed:

In 1945, Arnold Schoenberg's application for a grant was turned down by the Guggenheim Foundation. The hostility of the music committee . . . was undisguised. The seventy-year-old composer had hoped for support in order to finish two of his largest music compositions, the opera *Moses und Aron* and the oratorio *Die Jakobsleiter* (*Jacob's Ladder*), as well as several theoretical works. Schoenberg had just retired from the University of California at Los Angeles; since he had been there only eight years, he had a pension of thirty-eight dollars a month with which to support a wife and three children aged thirteen, eight, and four. (*Arnold Schoenberg* [Chicago: University of Chicago Press, 1996], 1)

46. Bruce Kawin, "Sharecropping in the Golden Land," in *Faulkner and Popular Culture: Faulkner and Yoknapatawpha: 1988,* ed. Doreen Fowler and Ann J. Abadie, 196–206 (Jackson: University Press of Mississippi, 1990). In his letters, Schoenberg, like Faulkner, speaks frankly of his frustrations: "Now just think: I am surely the only composer of my standing there has been for at least a hundred years who could not live on what he made from his creative work without having to eke out his income by teaching" (*Arnold Schoenberg: Letters,* ed. Erwin Stein; trans. Eithne Wilkins and Ernst Kaiser [Berkeley: University of California Press, 1987], 163).

47. Alex Ross describes a 1934 meeting of Schoenberg and Irving Thalberg, head of production at Metro-Goldwyn-Mayer, to discuss the possibility of the composer scoring the studio's adaptation of Pearl Buck's *The Good Earth* (Ross attributes Thalberg's interest in Schoenberg to a radio encounter with "*Transfigured Night* or perhaps the Suite in G"—two of the composer's more accessible works). His outlandish request (by Hollywood standards) for "complete control over the sound" notwithstanding, Schoenberg was eager for the work and produced several sketches "leaning in a tonal direction." But he failed to land the commission, not, according to Ross, because of his compositional approach but because of money: Schoenberg set his fee at fifty thousand dollars, Thalberg quickly dropped the idea, and *The Good Earth* wound up being scored by MGM house composer Herbert Stothart (Alex Ross, *The Rest Is Noise: Listening to the Twentieth Century* [New York: Farrar, Straus and Giroux, 2007], 322–24). Though Schoenberg remained interested in writing for the movies, he apparently saw no reason to change his approach after this encounter with Thalberg: Roy M. Prendergast quotes a 1940 *New York Times* article by Bruno Ussher in which Schoenberg declared: "I would be willing to write music for a film. . . . I would want $100,000 for the score. They must give me a year to write it and let me compose what I want. And, of course, I would have to say something about the story" (Prendergast, *Film Music: A Neglected Art,* 2nd ed. [New York: Norton, 1992], 47).

For an example of Schoenberg's opinions about popular art, see his 1945 response to a Guggenheim committee query about the merit of an applicant's work: "I have no reason to change my opinion of Mr. Anis Fuleihan's talent.... It seems to me I can recommend the awarding of a Guggenheim Fellowship as warmly as I did the first time. And I am not surprised that he needs this support again. No serious composer in this country is capable of living from his *art*. Only popular composers earn enough to support oneself and one's family, and then it is *not art*" (*Schoenberg: Letters*, ed. Stein, 233; original emphases).

48. "'You want to go back to ranks,' the company commander said. 'You love man so well you must sleep in the same mud he sleeps in.'

"'That's it,' the other said. 'It's just backward. I hate man so.'" (*Fable* 721)

49. The story doesn't end there. The success of *The Robe* paved the way for Thomas Costain's *The Silver Chalice* (which tells the fate of the cup used by Christ at the Last Supper), a *Times* bestseller in 1952 and a Warner Brothers film in 1954. Lloyd Douglas repeated his winning formula with *The Big Fisherman*, his 1948 bestseller and a popular film in 1959.

50. The day before leaving for the hunting trip Faulkner mailed a one-page letter to the reporter, Sven Åhman of *Dagans Nyheter,* that, among other things, can be seen as a first draft of the Nobel Prize speech: "I hold that the award was made, not to me, but to my works, crown to thirty years of the agony and sweat of a human spirit, to make something which was not here before me, to lift up or maybe comfort or anyway at least entertain, in its turn, man's heart.... [I]t is my hope to find an aim for the money high enough to be commensurate with the purpose and significance of its origin" (Blotner 2:1345–46). It is hard not to see the irony in Faulkner's reference to the origin of the Nobel Prize endowment: Alfred Nobel (1833–96) obtained the first European patents on nitroglycerine and dynamite, and the fortune that endowed the Nobel Foundation was derived entirely from the manufacture of these and related explosive materials, which saw their first extensive military uses in World War I.

51. "It was [Faulkner's wife] Estelle ... who developed the argument that worked. She had no wish to go to Stockholm herself, she said, but Jill wanted to go, and when would she have another chance like this in her whole life? Actually, Jill was not anxious to go—she did not have all the clothes she would need, and she was more interested in a young man right there at home than in a trip to Europe on the verge of winter—but her father did not know this and finally capitulated." Around the same time Faulkner received a letter from Erik Boheman, Swedish ambassador to the United States, who wrote: "Being a farmer myself I understand only too well your reluctance to travel as far from your farm as across the ocean. I know, however, how immensely your presence in Stockholm on December 11 would be appreciated, not only by the institutions concerned but also by all your other Swedish admirers and I, therefore, venture to ask you whether it would be possible for you to make the trip" (Blotner 2:1349).

52. For the reluctance, see Blotner; for the resistance, see Urgo, *Faulkner's Apocrypha*. Though he proved a quick study, Faulkner entered into his Nobel laureateship with almost no understanding of cultural diplomacy. See, for example, a February 1946 letter to his agent regarding Italian translation and publication permissions (which the translator had initially pursued through United States Information Service): "You can write Sr. [Eugenio] Vaquer that I am happy to acquiesce, but ... what is U.S.I.S." (*Selected Letters* 227).

53. Faulkner traveled to Paris in April 1951 to be inducted into the Legion of Honor and to soak up French atmosphere for *A Fable*. He returned to the city a year later a year for the *Oeuvres du XXe Siècle* festival organized by the Congress for Cultural Freedom; while this was not a government-sponsored trip, his appearance had diplomatic overtones.

His work on Howard Hawks's 1955 film *Land of the Pharaohs* involved a December 1953–April 1954 trip through Switzerland and Italy to his final destination in Cairo.

54. For "coercive seductions," see Michael Zeitlin, "Marx and Freud in Recent Faulkner Criticism," in *A Companion to William Faulkner*, ed. Richard C. Moreland (Malden, MA: Blackwell, 2007), 97.

During Faulkner's trip to Japan, Leon Picon (the cultural aide in charge of the book program at the US embassy in Japan and the man responsible for the success of Faulkner's visit) "noticed something . . . which he used to sustain Faulkner's interest and keep the tone of the [literature seminar's] sessions from sagging. It seemed to him that Faulkner always did better when there was a pretty girl in the audience. Now he always saw to it that [embassy aide] Kyoko Sakairi was there, or a slim, boyish-looking little student named Midori Sasaki, a twenty-four-year-old teaching assistant at the Hiroshima Women's College" (Blotner 2:1555). The "intensely feminine" Sasaki made a particular impression on Faulkner, who covered some of her expenses when she later came to the United States to study at the University of North Carolina, Chapel Hill (Blotner 2:1558–59, 1627).

55. Letter from William Faulkner to "Mr. Howland," July 8, 1955, collection of the US State Department/United States Information Agency Bureau of Educational and Cultural Affairs (CU), Special Collections Division, University of Arkansas, box 144, file 17. Subsequent citations from this collection will be identified as CU, followed by box and file number. The letter is paraphrased in Blotner's biography (2:1541) and printed in full in *Selected Letters* (384–85).

56. Faulkner, "On Privacy (The American Dream: What Happened to It?)," in *William Faulkner: Essays, Speeches and Public Letters*, ed. James B. Meriwether (1965; London: Chatto and Windus, 1967), 70. Subsequent quotations are from this version of the essay and cited as *Essays*. For a detailed description of Robert Coughlan's efforts to get his story, and Faulkner's outrage over its publication, see Blotner 2:1390–93, 1466–69, and 1518–19; Robert Coughlan, "The Private World of William Faulkner," *Life*, September 29, 1953, 118–20, 122, 124, 127–28, 130, 133–34, 136; and "The Man behind the Faulkner Myth," *Life*, October 5, 1953, 55–58, 61–64, 66, 68.

57. "I'm trying to say it all in one sentence, between one Cap and one period. I'm still trying to put it all, if possible, on one pinhead" (Malcolm Cowley, *The Faulkner-Cowley File: Letters and Memories, 1944–1962* [1966; Harmondsworth, UK: Penguin, 1978], 14).

58. "Report of William Faulkner's visit to Greece, March 18 to March 31, 1957," May 13, 1957, Foreign Service Despatch 788 (from "Amembassy, Athens" to Department of State, Washington), signed by cultural affairs officer Duncan Emrich, 6, CU, box 144, file 14.

59. Deborah N. Cohn, "Faulkner, Latin America, and the Caribbean: Influence, Politics, and Academic Disciplines," in Moreland, *Companion*, 502. Given that the South American "boom" authors most vocal in their criticisms of US policy in Latin America (Carlos Fuentes, Gabriel García Márquez, Julio Cortázar, and Mario Vargas Llosa) have been among the region's greatest Faulkner admirers, it is puzzling to find Cohn later asserting that "Faulkner's [South American] visits

fulfilled the wildest dreams *and underlying political agenda* of the government that sponsored his travels by 'further[ing] understanding and good will' between the U.S. and Latin America" (511; emphasis added).

60. Richard Davenport-Hines, *Auden* (New York: Pantheon, 1995), 280. Blotner begins his narrative of Faulkner's misbehavior at the festival with the observation that the author arrived "prepared for a four-week holiday." He makes no mention of Faulkner's drunken use of racial epithets, though he does describe how the author snubbed Katherine Anne Porter and Glenway Wescott (Blotner 2:1421–22).

61. See the telegram dated August 13, 1954, in CU, box 144 file 13: "Faulkner ill requiring services doctor and male nurses. Total cost approximately $180. Please telegram authority pay." The reply, also in CU, box 144, file 13, notes that "Department has no funds available to cover medical services for United States Specialists. However, Department has authorized salary at $23.07 per day for William Faulkner to off-set this emergency."

62. CU, box 144, file 18. At the time Frederick A. Colwell was director of the American Specialists program within State's International Educational Exchange Services program.

63. William Faulkner to Frederick A. Colwell, letter dated May 31, 1958, CU, box 144, file 18. See also *Selected Letters*, 412–13.

64. See Adorno's 1938 essay "On the Fetish Character in Music and the Regression of Listening," in *The Culture Industry*, ed. J. M. Bernstein, 26–52 (New York: Routledge, 1991). See also Adorno and Horkheimer's discussion of the role of repetition in culture industry in *Dialectic of Enlightenment*, 119, 122.

65. A version of this point informs Hixson's observation on the effects of the fall of the Iron Curtain: "The revolutionary events of 1989–91 found Soviets and East Europeans embracing Western models such as market economics, parliamentary democracy, and political pluralism. But the peoples of these states were in pursuit of something deeper (or perhaps shallower). They sought to become part of the modern, consumer-driven, mass-mediated society associated with the West" (Hixson, *Parting the Curtain*, 230–31).

66. See Carol Polsgrove, *Divided Minds: Intellectuals and the Civil Rights Movement* (New York: Norton, 2001), 5–6.

67. Polsgrove cites the typescript "Faulkner and Civil Rights," in the James W. Silver papers at the University of Mississippi.

68. See Mary L. Dudziak, *Cold War Civil Rights: Race and the Image of American Democracy* (Princeton, NJ: Princeton University Press, 2002).

69. A 1952 graduate of Miles College, Lucy had been accepted into the graduate program at Alabama that year, but the university rescinded its offer of admission when it learned she was Black. Lucy approached the NAACP very soon after; her attorneys in the case—Thurgood Marshall, Constance Baker Motley, and Arthur D. Shores—began court action in July 1953. The NAACP won its court order forbidding Alabama from using Lucy's race as a reason to deny admission in June 1955.

70. The NAACP charged the university with acting in support of the mob and sued; it later withdrew its case, but university officials used the lawsuit as a rationale for expelling Lucy. In 1992, forty years after she was admitted, Autherine Lucy graduated from the University of Alabama with

a master's degree in elementary education (see "Campus Life: Alabama: 36 Years after the Hate, Black Student Triumphs," *New York Times,* April 26, 1992, sec. 1, p. 43, col. 1).

71. Russell Warren Howe, "A Talk with William Faulkner," *Reporter,* March 22, 1956, 19; the interview was first published in the March 4, 1956, London Sunday *Times.*

72. "A Letter to the North" appeared in *Life,* March 5, 1956; it is reprinted in Meriwether's *Essays* as "Letter to a Northern Editor," 86–91. "If I Were a Negro," published in the September 1956 issue of *Ebony,* appears in the Meriwether volume under the title "A Letter to the Leaders of the Negro Race," 107–12. Subsequent quotations are from Meriwether's edition.

73. "I have at hand an editorial from the *New York Times* of February 10th [1956] on the rioting at the University of Alabama because of the admission as a student of Miss Lucy, a Negro. The editorial said: 'This is the first time that force and violence have become a part of the question.' That is not correct. To all Southerners, no matter which side of the question of racial equality they supported, the first implication, and—to the Southerner—even promise, of force and violence was the Supreme Court decision itself" (*Essays* 88).

74. See Grace Elizabeth Hale and Robert Jackson, "'We're Trying Hard as Hell to Free Ourselves': Southern History and Race in the Making of William Faulkner's Literary Terrain," in Moreland, *Companion,* 33, 31.

75. First published in the June 1956 issue of *Harper's,* "On Fear: The South in Labor" is reprinted under the title "On Fear: Deep South in Labor: Mississippi," in *Essays* 92–106.

76. Roy Bongartz, "Give Them Time . . . Reflections on Faulkner," *Nation,* March 31, 1956, 239.

77. Albert Murray and John F. Callahan, eds., *Trading Twelves: The Selected Letters of Ralph Ellison and Albert Murray* (2000; New York: Vintage, 2001), 117. Ellison and Murray's strongest comments are prompted not by the Howe interview but by Faulkner's *Life* essay "A Letter to the North." Ellison's comments on the Howe piece are brief but categorical: "Faulkner wrote a letter . . . denying that crap he dropped on the world, but the reporter stuck to his guns and insisted that he reported true. Which I believe he did" (*Trading Twelves* 127).

78. "Faulkner and Desegregation" was republished in Baldwin's 1961 collection, *Nobody Knows My Name: More Notes of a Native Son,* where it achieved wide circulation. The essay also appears in *James Baldwin: Collected Essays,* ed. Toni Morrison (New York: Library of America, 1998), 209–14.

79. James Baldwin, "Faulkner and Desegregation," *Partisan Review,* Fall 1956, 568.

80. Albert Murray, "Me and Old Uncle Billy and the American Mythosphere," in *Faulkner at 100: Retrospect and Prospect: Faulkner and Yoknapatawpha, 1997,* ed. Donald M. Kartiganer and Ann J. Abadie (Jackson: University Press of Virginia, 2000), 249.

81. Arnold Rampersad, *Ralph Ellison: A Biography* (New York: Knopf, 2007), 324. For the comment about Faulkner as a literary ancestor, see Ralph Ellison, "A Rejoinder," *New Leader,* February 3, 1964, 22. This essay and its precursor (a response to Irving Howe's 1963 essay "Black Boys and Native Sons," published in the autumn 1963 issue of *Dissent*) have been published together as "The World and the Jug," in *Shadow and Act* (New York: Vintage, 1972), 107–43.

82. "I was working at Bill's house when he was doing Nat Turner, and we used to talk about it—or around it—from time to time. Bill comes from Virginia where the insurrection occurred. So it seemed to me that it was part of my inheritance and was also part of his. I didn't read the book so much as a confession of Nat Turner but as a confession of Bill Styron, and I don't mean that as

a 'put-down.' He had taken an historical event which belongs to everybody and especially to the man it torments the most, and he tried to make some kind of peace with it, to tell the truth—very much like Faulkner, although I didn't always agree with Faulkner, especially as he got older" (David C. Estes, "An Interview with James Baldwin," in *Conversations with James Baldwin,* ed. Fred L. Standley and Louis H. Pratt [Jackson: University Press of Mississippi, 1989], 279). Estes's interview with Baldwin originally appeared in the fall 1986 edition of the *New Orleans Review.*

83. Toni Morrison, "Faulkner and Women," in *Faulkner and Women: Faulkner and Yoknapatawpha, 1985,* ed. Doreen Fowler and Ann J. Abadie, 296–97 (Jackson: University Press of Mississippi, 1986). Morrison's engagements with Faulkner's *oeuvre* have been the subject of much scholarly attention. See, for example, Philip M. Weinstein, *What Else but Love? The Ordeal of Race in Faulkner and Morrison* (New York: Columbia University Press, 1996); the essays collected in Carol A. Kolmerten, Stephen M. Ross, and Judith Bryant Wittenberg, eds., *Unflinching Gaze: Morrison and Faulkner Re-Envisioned* (Jackson: University Press of Mississippi, 1997); and Evelyn Jaffe Schreiber, *Subversive Voices: Eroticizing the Other in William Faulkner and Toni Morrison* (Knoxville: University of Tennessee Press, 2002).

84. Schwartz, *Creating Faulkner's Reputation,* 5, 202.

85. Catherine Gunther Kodat, "Writing *A Fable* for America," in *Faulkner in America: Faulkner and Yoknapatawpha 1998,* ed. Joseph R. Urgo and Ann J. Abadie, 82–97 (Jackson: University Press of Mississippi 2001).

86. Catherine Gunther Kodat, *Don't Act, Just Dance: The Metapolitics of Cold War Culture* (New Brunswick, NJ: Rutgers University Press, 2015). Schwartz's work was deeply influenced by Serge Guilbaut's *How New York Stole the Idea of Modern Art: Abstract Expressionism, Freedom, and the Cold War,* trans. Arthur Goldhammer (Chicago: University of Chicago Press, 1983).

87. Catherine Gunther Kodat, "Unsteady State: Faulkner and the Cold War," in *William Faulkner in Context,* ed. John T. Matthews, 156–65 (New York: Cambridge University Press, 2015).

88. See Greg Barnhisel, "Packaging Faulkner as a Cold War Modernist," in *Faulkner and Print Culture: Faulkner and Yoknapatawpha 2015,* ed. Jay Watson, Jaime Harker, and James G. Thomas Jr., 158–74 (Jackson: University Press of Mississippi 2017); Deborah Cohn, "William Faulkner's Ibero-American Novel Project: The Politics of Translation and the Cold War," *Southern Quarterly* 42, no. 1 (Winter 2004): 5–18; "Combating Anti-Americanism during the Cold War: Faulkner, the State Department, and Latin America," *Mississippi Quarterly* 59, no. 3–4 (Summer–Fall 2006): 396–413; and "Faulkner, Latin America, and the Caribbean: Influence, Politics, and Academic Disciplines," in *A Companion to William Faulkner,* ed. Richard C. Moreland, 499–518 (Malden, MA: Blackwell 2007); Alan Nadel, "'We—He and Us—Should Confederate': Stylistic Inversion in *Intruder in the Dust* and Faulkner's Cold War Agenda," in *Fifty Years after Faulkner: Faulkner and Yoknapatawpha 2012,* ed. Jay Watson and Ann J. Abadie (Jackson: University Press of Mississippi, 2016); Helen Oakley, "William Faulkner and the Cold War: The Politics of Cultural Marketing," in *Look Away! The U.S. South in New World Studies,* ed. Jon Smith and Deborah Cohn (Durham, NC: Duke University Press, 2004); and Harilaos Stecopoulos, "William Faulkner and the Problem of Cold War Modernism," in *Faulkner's Geographies: Faulkner and Yoknapatawpha 2011,* ed. Jay Watson and Ann J. Abadie, 143–62 (Jackson: University Press of Mississippi, 2015).

4. A Postmodern *Absalom, Absalom!*, a Modern *Beloved:*
The Dialectic of Form

Epigraphs: William Faulkner, *Selected Letters,* ed. Joseph Blotner (New York: Random House, 1977), 84; Toni Morrison qtd. in Mervyn Rothstein, "Toni Morrison, in Her New Novel, Defends Women," *New York Times,* August 26, 1987, C17

1. The values the oral tradition of signifying offers to literary analysis have been outlined in Henry Louis Gates Jr., *The Signifying Monkey: A Theory of African-American Literary Criticism* (New York: Oxford University Press, 1988).

2. Charles Lewis's rewarding comparative reading of *Beloved* and *The Scarlet Letter* argues that Morrison's novel in fact "reads" New Historicist criticism in ways that reveal exactly that critical school's inabilities to read *Beloved.* Yet, like so many critics of *Beloved,* Lewis doesn't explore the work's relationship to literary modernism, though he does say that his article is concerned with "the irony of romance in unexpected places" (Lewis, "The Ironic Romance of New Historicism: *The Scarlet Letter* and *Beloved,*" *Arizona Quarterly* 51, no. 1 [Spring 1995]: 33).

3. Alan Benson, prod. and dir., "Toni Morrison," interview by Melvyn Bragg, *The South Bank Show* (BBC, 1987). In this particular interview, Morrison insists that she was not planning to write about slavery *at all* when she began *Beloved:* "It would never occur to me to go into that area—I didn't think I had the emotional resources." It is possible, of course, that Morrison decided to cast the initiating impulse for the novel in "universal" terms for the benefit of her (mostly white) interviewers (similarly, the theme of self-sabotage appears more or less anchored in feminist concerns according to the interests of the interviewer). However, the conversation with Gloria Naylor in *Southern Review* indicates otherwise, as I later discuss.

4. In almost every interview given at *Beloved*'s publication, Morrison describes her discovery of Margaret Garner's story while editing *The Black Book* (the news clipping about the case appears at the top of page 10 of that anthology): see Middleton Harris, *The Black Book,* with the assistance of Morris Levitt, Roger Furman, and Ernest Smith (New York: Random House, 1974); for two representative examples, see the *New York Times* interview with Rothstein and the interview with Marsha Jean Darling in the *Women's Review of Books* ("In the Realm of Responsibility: A Conversation with Toni Morrison," *Women's Review of Books* 5, no. 6 [March 1988]: 5–6).

The inspiration for *Jazz* came from a photograph in *The Harlem Book of the Dead,* which featured photographs by James Van Der Zee, poems by Owen Dodson, and an interview of Van Der Zee by Camille Billops. Morrison edited this project, writing the book's foreword, in 1978; the photograph of the woman who was the model for Dorcas appears on page 53 (James Van Der Zee, Owen Dodson, and Camille Billops, *The Harlem Book of the Dead* [Dobbs Ferry, NY: Morgan and Morgan, 1978]).

5. Gloria Naylor and Toni Morrison, "A Conversation," *Southern Review* 21, no. 3 (Summer 1985): 584.

6. Morrison has said that her characters usually start as ideas rather than as personalities (Nellie McKay, "An Interview with Toni Morrison." *Contemporary Literature* 24, no. 4 [Winter 1983]: 418).

7. Joseph Blotner, *Faulkner: A Biography*, 2 vols. (New York: Random House, 1974), 1:890. See 888–909 for a chronology of the novel's creation.

8. Theodor Adorno, *Negative Dialectics*, trans. E. B. Ashton (New York: Continuum, 1973), 5. For Adorno, modernist formalism is intimately bound up with this notion of the nonidentical: "Form is constituted only through dissimilarity, only in that it is different from the nonidentical; in form's own meaning, the dualism persists that form effaces" (Adorno, *Aesthetic Theory*, trans. and ed. Robert Hullot-Kentor [Minneapolis: University of Minnesota Press, 1997], 162). Modernism thus "comes into its own" precisely to the extent that we are able to recognize, in its formal properties, its struggle with its "own" meaning.

9. Faulkner's anachronism has drawn considerable critical attention. For two representative examples, see Richard Godden, "*Absalom, Absalom!*, Haiti and Labor History: Reading Unreadable Revolutions," *ELH* 61, no. 3 (Fall 1994): 685–720; and John T. Matthews, "Recalling the West Indies: From Yoknapatawpha to Haiti and Back," *American Literary History* 16, no. 2 (Summer 2004): 238–62.

10. William Faulkner, *Absalom, Absalom! The Corrected Text*, ed. Noel Polk (1936; New York: Vintage International, 1990), 109. Subsequent quotations from *Absalom, Absalom!* are from this edition and cited as *AA*.

11. Fredric Jameson, *Postmodernism; or, The Cultural Logic of Late Capitalism* (Durham, NC: Duke University Press, 1991), ix.

12. "Forms" here has a double charge, indicating both those African American aesthetic practices that have influenced American modernism and the bodies of African Americans themselves, so often deployed as symbolic characters in modernist works.

13. Joseph Frank, "Spatial Form in Modern Literature," in *The Widening Gyre: Crisis and Mastery in Modern Literature* (Bloomington: Indiana University Press, 1968), 60.

14. Allen Tate, foreword to *The Widening Gyre: Crisis and Mastery in Modern Literature* (Bloomington: Indiana University Press, 1968), ix.

15. "I would suggest that judgments on Afro-American 'modernity' and the 'Harlem Renaissance' that begin with notions of British, Anglo-American, and Irish 'modernism' as 'successful' objects, projects, and processes to be emulated by Afro-Americans are misguided. It seems to me that Africans and Afro-Americans—through conscious and unconscious designs of various Western 'modernism'—have little in common with Joycean or Eliotic projects. Further, it seems to me that the very *histories* that are assumed in the chronologies of British, Anglo-American, and Irish modernisms are radically opposed to any adequate and accurate account of the history of Afro-American modernism" (Houston A. Baker Jr., *Modernism and the Harlem Renaissance* [Chicago: University of Chicago Press, 1987], xv–xvi).

16. Linda Krumholz describes Morrison's technique in this section as modernist ("The Ghosts of Slavery: Historical Recovery in Toni Morrison's *Beloved*," *African American Review* 26, no. 3 [Fall 1992], 396), but she does not explore why Morrison would decide that a modernist method was particularly suitable there. Jean Wyatt argues that Morrison is seeking to represent "a maternal symbolic" in this section. This seems to me generally true; but, given the imaginative and historic continuity between psychoanalysis and modernism, it seems a partial answer (Wyatt, "Giving

Body to the Word: The Maternal Symbolic in Toni Morrison's *Beloved*," *Publications of the Modern Language Association* 108, no. 3 [May 1993]: 474–88).

17. See, for instance, the interviews with Nellie McKay, Claudia Tate, Charles Ruas, Christina Davis, Thomas LeClair, Jane Bakerman, and Paul Gilroy, as well as Morrison's own essays on her aesthetic (particularly "Unspeakable Things, Unspoken," "Memory, Creation, and Fiction," and "The Site of Memory") in Toni Morrison, *The Source of Self-Regard: Selected Essays, Speeches, and Meditations* (New York: Knopf, 2019).

18. Chloe Ardellia Wofford, "Virginia Woolf's and William Faulkner's Treatment of the Alienated," A Thesis Presented to the Faculty of the Graduate School of Cornell University for the Degree of Master of Arts, September 1955, 1. As is now well-known, Toni Morrison is the *nom de plume* of Chloe Wofford; Morrison was the last name of the author's ex-husband.

19. See Jean-Paul Sartre, "Time in Faulkner: *The Sound and the Fury*," in *William Faulkner: Two Decades of Criticism*, ed. Frederick J. Hoffman and Olga W. Vickery (East Lansing: Michigan State College Press, 1951).

20. Interestingly, Morrison's thesis makes no mention of Clytie; she mentions Faulkner's Black characters only once, as "those capable of restoring the order needed . . . [those] who 'endured'" (35).

21. Toni Morrison, "Faulkner and Women," in *Faulkner and Women: Faulkner and Yoknapatawpha, 1985*, ed. Doreen Fowler and Ann J. Abadie, 295–96 (Jackson: University Press of Mississippi, 1986).

22. Emily Miller Budick, "Absence, Loss, and the Space of History in Toni Morrison's *Beloved*," *Arizona Quarterly* 48, no. 2 (Summer 1992): 135; Caroline M. Woidat, "Talking Back to Schoolteacher: Morrison's Confrontation with Hawthorne in *Beloved*," *Modern Fiction Studies* 39, no. 3–4 (Fall/Winter 1993): 527–46; Jan Stryz, "The Other Ghost in *Beloved*: The Spectre of *The Scarlet Letter*," *Genre* 24, no. 4 (Winter 1991): 417–34. Two exceptions to this trend toward reading *Beloved* with or against *The Scarlet Letter* are John N. Duvall, "Authentic Ghost Stories: *Uncle Tom's Cabin, Absalom, Absalom!,* and *Beloved*," *Faulkner Journal* 4, no. 1–2 (Fall 1988/Spring 1989): 83–97; and Richard C. Moreland, "'He Wants to Put His Story Next to Hers': Putting Twain's Story Next to Hers in Morrison's *Beloved*," *Modern Fiction Studies* 39, no. 3–4 (Fall/Winter 1993): 501–25.

23. Indeed, Pèrez-Torres's essay (inadvertently, I believe) casts modernism as exactly a huge nothing out of which *Beloved* arises: "The narrative emerges, then, at the point at which premodern and postmodern forms of literary expression cross" (Rafael Pèrez-Torres, "Knitting and Knotting the Narrative Thread—*Beloved* as Postmodern Novel," *Modern Fiction Studies* 39, no. 3–4 [Fall/Winter 1993]: 690). Modernism thus becomes a gigantic hole, a ghost, as it were, haunting the scene of its emergence.

24. Toni Morrison, "Unspeakable Things Unspoken: The Afro-American Presence in American Literature," *Michigan Quarterly* 28, no. 1 (Winter 1989): 11; *Playing in the Dark* (Cambridge, MA: Harvard University Press, 1992), 5.

25. An important companion to Gates's work for any consideration of the conjunctions of African American expressivity and Western modernism is Paul Gilroy's *The Black Atlantic* (Cambridge, MA: Harvard University Press, 1993). Eric Lott's work on the minstrel tradition in America

is also useful in its careful tracing of white habits of "borrowing" Black cultural traditions (Lott, *Love and Theft: Blackface Minstrelsy and the American Working Class* [New York: Oxford University Press, 1993]).

26. *Absalom, Absalom!* also toys with this notion of "restriction"; however, the incomplete scope of its succeeding narratives invites creative "play" rather than paranoid exclusion.

27. Darling, "In the Realm of Responsibility," 6.

28. For a thorough examination of Margaret Garner's story that Morrison might have read, see Julius Yanuck, "The Garner Fugitive Slave Case," *Mississippi Valley Historical Review* 40, no. 1 (June 1953): 47–66. Another likely source for Morrison would have been *Reminiscences of Levi Coffin* (1898; New York: Arno, 1968). Yanuck's essay cites scores of articles from various newspapers that covered the Garner case, any one of which Morrison could have perused.

29. Some newspaper accounts describing the murder say the child died a gruesome, lingering death, in which the mother "hacked" repeatedly at the girl's throat with a butcher knife (Yanuck, "The Garner Fugitive Slave Case," 52). Levi Coffin claimed that the child was killed mercifully, "with one stroke" (Coffin, *Reminiscences,* 560).

30. All the accounts, for instance, agree that the murdered girl was three years old, not almost two (and so in the preoedipal phase of development), as she is in Morrison's novel. Rendering Beloved as a preoedipal infant is certainly crucial to Morrison's artistic project and has been remarked on by many critics of the novel. See, for instance, Wyatt, "Giving Body to the Word"; Moreland, "He Wants to Put His Story"; and Deborah Horvitz. "Nameless Ghosts: Possession and Dispossession in *Beloved*," *Studies in American Fiction* 17, no. 2 (autumn 1989): 157–67.

31. It is not hard to imagine why Morrison would have decided against depicting a mother's desperate dash for freedom across the frozen Ohio River.

32. Yanuck, "The Garner Fugitive Slave Case," 52; Harris, *The Black Book,* 10.

33. Coffin, *Reminiscences of Levi Coffin,* 563.

34. Christina Davis, "Interview with Toni Morrison," *Présence Africaine* 145 (1988): 142.

35. I am partly drawing here on Richard C. Moreland's reading of the novel in his study *Faulkner and Modernism* (Madison: University of Wisconsin Press, 1990), in which Rosa and Mr. Compson are seen as Faulkner's efforts to work through and critique the two dominant methods available to his effort to "tell about the South": a backward-looking nostalgia and an ironic detachment.

36. Shreve's claim that "in a few thousand years, I who regard you will also have sprung from the loins of African kings" (*AA* 302) carries a postmodern ironic charge for contemporary readers, knowing, as we do, that twentieth-century archaeological work has conclusively determined that we all are in truth sprung from the loins of Africa.

37. For a discussion of the European and Euro-American trope of African blackness as blankness, see Henry Louis Gates Jr., *Figures in Black: Words, Signs, and the Racial Self* (New York: Oxford University Press, 1987), 21–24.

38. Budick argues that "the novel's endorsement of and almost hypnotic descent into oblivion in its final pages . . . can hardly represent simple encapsulation of the novel's wisdom" (Budick, "Absence, Loss, and the Space of History in Toni Morrison's *Beloved*," 117). Margaret Homans comments that the conclusion of *Beloved* is "curious" and "paradoxical, because, of course, the novel *is there*" ("Feminist Fictions and Feminist Theories of Narrative," *Narrative* 2, no. 1 [1994]: 11).

39. James Phelan, "Toward a Rhetorical Reader-Response Criticism: The Difficult, the Stubborn, and the Ending of *Beloved*," *Modern Fiction Studies* 39, no. 3–4 (Fall/Winter 1993): 721.

40. Benson, "Toni Morrison."

41. Paul Gilroy, "Living Memory: A Meeting with Toni Morrison," in *Small Acts: Thoughts on the Politics of Black Cultures* (London: Serpent's Tail, 1993), 179.

42. William Troy, "The Poetry of Doom," *Nation* 143, no. 18 (October 31, 1936): 524; Harold Strauss. "Mr. Faulkner Is Ambushed in Words," *New York Times,* November 1, 1936, 7; Clifton Fadiman, "Faulkner, Extra-Special, Double-Distilled," *New Yorker,* October 31, 1936, 62.

43. For an influential discussion of Faulkner's Cold War reputation, see Lawrence H. Schwartz, *Creating Faulkner's Reputation: The Politics of Modern Literary Criticism* (Knoxville: University of Tennessee Press, 1988). I engaged with Schwartz's analysis more deeply in the preceding chapter.

44. For one example of how Faulkner's psychology might be mined for its history, see John T. Matthews, "The Rhetoric of Containment in Faulkner," in *Faulkner's Discourse: An International Symposium,* ed. Lothar Hönnighausen, 55–67 (Tübingen: Max Niemeyer, 1989); Godden's essay also combines psychoanalytic and Marxist insights in its reading of *Absalom, Absalom!*

45. Thomas R. Edwards, "Ghost Story," *New York Review of Books,* November 5, 1987, 19.

46. Margaret Atwood, "Haunted by Their Nightmares," *New York Times Book Review,* September 13, 1987, 49; Stanley Crouch, "Aunt Medea," *New Republic,* October 19, 1987, 40.

47. Judith Thurman, "A House Divided," *New Yorker,* November 2, 1987, 175.

48. Carol A. Kolmerten, Stephen M. Ross, and Judith Bryant Wittenberg, eds., *Unflinching Gaze: Morrison and Faulkner Re-envisioned* (Jackson: University Press of Mississippi, 1997).

49. Hermione Hoby, "Toni Morrison: 'I'm Writing for Black People... I Don't Have to Apologize,'" *The Guardian,* April 25, 2015, https://www.theguardian.com/books/2015/apr/25/toni-morrison-books-interview-god-help-the-child.

50. While I was fortunate to be able to secure a copy of the thesis in the mid-1990s, I understand that Cornell University denies duplication requests today. It's not clear if that prohibition was established at Morrison's request. While she never made a secret of her thesis, she was scrupulous in denying Faulkner any direct influence on her own writing.

51. George Hutchinson, "Tracking Faulkner in the Paths of Black Modernism," 59; and Jay Watson, introduction, xi, in *Faulkner and the Black Literatures of the Americas: Faulkner and Yoknapatawpha 2013,* ed. Jay Watson and James G. Thomas Jr. (Jackson: University Press of Mississippi, 2016).

5. Posting Yoknapatawpha

Epigraph: Roland Barthes, *Empire of Signs,* trans. Richard Howard (New York: Hill and Wang, Noonday Press, 1982), 4.

1. Meg Wolitzer and Christopher Niemann, "Two Things That Depress Me When I Open a Novel," *New York Times Book Review,* February 6, 2000, 31.

2. The quote is drawn from an introduction to *The Sound and the Fury* Faulkner wrote in 1933 for a proposed but never published new edition by Random House. After his death two different

versions of this preface were found among his papers and published within a year of each other, one in the *Southern Review* and the other in the *Mississippi Quarterly*; both were edited by James B. Meriwether. Here I quote the version published in 1972 in the *Southern Review* and republished in *The Sound and the Fury*, ed. David Minter (1929; New York: Norton, 1994), 227.

3. William Faulkner, *Requiem for a Nun*, in *Novels, 1942–1954: "Go Down, Moses," "Intruder in the Dust," "Requiem for a Nun," "A Fable"* (New York: Library of America, 1994), 611. "Again. Sadder than was. Again. Saddest of all. Again" (Faulkner, *The Sound and the Fury*, ed. Minter, 61). That Temple, in *Requiem*, sentences after her "Again," cries out, "Tomorrow and tomorrow and tomorrow . . . ," citing the passage in *Macbeth* that gave Faulkner the title of his earlier novel, deepens the sense of compulsion underlying the repetition.

4. William Faulkner, *The Town*, in *Novels, 1957–1962: "The Town," "The Mansion," "The Reivers"* (New York: Library of America, 1999), 267. Attention to the discrepancies among the Snopes volumes has had a small but persistent place within the criticism, beginning with Cowley's discussions with Faulkner preserved in *The Faulkner-Cowley File*. Just one example of what's involved here: In *The Hamlet* Mink's murder victim is named Jack Houston. His wife, Lucy Pate, is killed by his own horse, which he executes in its stall moments after the accident (William Faulkner, *The Hamlet: The Corrected Text*, ed. Noel Polk [New York: Vintage International, 1991]; see 231 for the name of Houston's wife, 239 for her death and the subsequent shooting of the horse). In *The Town* he is called Zack Houston; his wife is Letty Bookright; and Ratliff asserts that Houston was riding "that same blood stallion [that] killed her" when he was shot by Mink, an assertion nowhere gainsaid in the novel (*The Town* 69).

5. John T. Irwin, *Doubling and Incest, Repetition and Revenge: A Speculative Reading of Faulkner*, expanded ed. (1975; Baltimore: Johns Hopkins University Press, 1996). Irwin is absolutely correct to see repetition as central to Faulkner's aesthetic. My concerns are different from his in two ways: I am interested in how Faulkner's habit of repeating himself undermines as well as forwards his aesthetic vision, and I am not convinced that the most important aspect of Faulknerian repetition is its oedipal dimension.

6. Along these lines, see Saul Rosenberg's "Delta Faulkner," the first-place winner in the first year of the "Faux Faulkner" contest, which presents Faulkner's *oeuvre* as real estate subject to endless speculation and development:

Each year there would be a little less of the rich unbroken alluvial virgin ground: the new critics and there was plenty of room because it was just a trickle and the structuralists and there was still plenty left and the poststructuralists and it was a stream but that was all right because streams until at last it was a flood and all right still because when the new historicists (and who to know till then that the old historicists were old) came the deconstructionists had gone ahead clearing the ground before them. . . . ("Delta Faulkner," in *The Best of Bad Faulkner: Choice Entries from the Faux Faulkner Contest*, ed. Dean Faulkner Wells [New York: Harcourt Brace Jovanovich, 1991], 22).

7. Michael Grimwood, *Heart in Conflict: Faulkner's Struggles with Vocation* (Athens: University of Georgia Press, 1987); Richard C. Moreland, *Faulkner and Modernism: Rereading and Rewriting* (Madison: University of Wisconsin Press, 1990). Grimwood's study is exemplary in that his analysis of Faulkner's aesthetic vision reveals it to be at once both productive and destructive.

8. Joseph Urgo, *Faulkner's Apocrypha: "A Fable," "Snopes," and the Spirit of Human Rebellion* (Jackson: University Press of Mississippi, 1989).

9. Cheryl Lester, "To Market, to Market: *The Portable Faulkner,*" *Critique* 29, no. 3 (Summer 1987): 371–89; Malcolm Cowley, introduction to *The Portable Faulkner,* rev. and expanded ed. (1946; New York: Penguin, 1977), viii.

10. William Faulkner. "Interview with Jean Stein Vanden Heuvel," in *Lion in the Garden: Interviews with William Faulkner, 1926–1962,* ed. James B. Meriwether and Michael Millgate (New York: Random House, 1968), 225. The interview first appeared in the *Paris Review* in 1956.

11. Though to be fair to Cowley (and to anticipate my later point about the similarity of his and Urgo's analyses), he frankly admits to being awed by Faulkner's capacity for ceaseless invention: the author's "creative power was so unflagging that he could not tell a story twice without transforming one detail after another" (Malcolm Cowley, *The Faulkner-Cowley File: Letters and Memories, 1944–1962* [New York: Penguin, 1978], 45–46).

12. In its own way, Urgo's study practices a kind of metaphysics, working as it does to establish a correlation between Faulkner's novels and the apocrypha of sacred Judeo-Christian narrative. It's worth recalling that Faulkner, in describing the emergence of Yoknapatawpha, uses not a noun but an adjective (he does *not* say, "by sublimating the actual into an apocrypha"). And according to the *OED,* "apocryphal" has had secular applications since at least the seventeenth century ("of doubtful authenticity; spurious, fictitious, false; fabulous") that, among other things, are synonymous with "mythical," Cowley's preferred term for Yoknapatawpha.

13. Jacques Lacan, *The Four Fundamental Concepts of Psychoanalysis,* ed. Jacques-Alain Miller; trans. Alan Sheridan (New York: Norton, 1978), 165–66. In less provocative language, Jean Laplanche and Jean-Baptiste Pontalis explain sublimation as the "process postulated by Freud to account for human activities which have no apparent connection with sexuality but which are assumed to be motivated by the force of the sexual instinct. The main types of activity described by Freud as sublimated are artistic creation and intellectual inquiry" (Jean Laplanche and Jean-Baptiste Pontalis, *The Language of Psycho-Analysis,* trans. Donald Nicholson-Smith [New York: Norton, 1973], 431).

14. See especially the introduction, "Masks and Mirrors," to *The Ink of Melancholy: Faulkner's Novels from "The Sound and the Fury" to "Light in August"* (Bloomington: Indiana University Press, 1990).

15. Carvel Collins, ed., *William Faulkner: Early Prose and Poetry* (Boston: Little, Brown, 1962), 115–16. The essay was originally published in April 1925 in the New Orleans literary journal the *Double Dealer.*

16. The second phrase appears almost word-for-word in the *Mississippi Quarterly* version of the preface as well. John T. Irwin correctly points to the importance of the "feminine" position in this view of the artistic process, though Irwin's commitment to an oedipal paradigm entails a view of the feminine that emphasizes lack: Faulkner "understood that a writer's relation to his material and to the work of art is always a loss, a separation, a cutting off, a self-castration that transforms the masculine artist into the feminine-masculine vase of the work" (Irwin, *Doubling and Incest/Repetition and Revenge,* 171). I am more drawn to a reading of Faulkner's introduction that is grounded in a consideration of the multiple aspects of "release" (to lose, but also to liberate, and to recirculate).

17. For readings of sex and narrative, see, for example, Peter Brooks, *Reading for the Plot: Desire and Intention in Narrative* (New York: Knopf, 1984); and Judith Roof, *Come as You Are: Sexuality and Narrative* (New York: Columbia University Press, 1996).

18. *Flags in the Dust*, Faulkner's third novel and the first set in Yoknapatawpha, was completed in 1927 and rejected by the publisher Horace Liveright in early 1928. A shorter, much-cut version was finally published by Harcourt Brace in January 1929 as *Sartoris*. Between rejection and publication of this novel Faulkner wrote *The Sound and the Fury*; his friend Ben Wasson did most of the editing required to turn *Flags in the Dust* into *Sartoris*.

In his two-volume biography of Faulkner, Joseph Blotner reports that an early version of what would become "There Was a Queen," entitled "Through the Window," was first rejected by *Scribner's* in July 1929; it would take four years and several revisions before the magazine finally published the piece (Blotner, *Faulkner: A Biography*, 2 vols. [New York: Random House, 1974], 1:664, 791).

19. Frederick L. Gwynn and Joseph L. Blotner, eds., *Faulkner in the University: Class Conferences at the University of Virginia, 1957–1958* (Charlottesville: University Press of Virginia, 1959), 285. In the *Mississippi Quarterly* version of the 1933 preface to *The Sound and the Fury*, Faulkner describes the effect of this rejection as if "a door had clapped silently and forever to between me and all publishers' addresses and booklists and I said to myself, Now I can write. Now I can just write" ("An Introduction," *Mississippi Quarterly*, as reprinted in *The Sound and the Fury*, ed. Minter 230). In the *Southern Review* version of the preface, Faulkner asserts that this profoundly private, ecstatic writing produced "something to which the shabby term Art not only can, but must, be applied" (Minter 226).

20. William Faulkner, *Flags in the Dust*, ed. Douglas Day (New York: Vintage, 1974), 110. Subsequent quotations from *Flags in the Dust* are from this edition and cited as *Flags*.

21. See, for example, John T. Matthews's discussion of Byron's letters, in which he points out that "Byron's writing obsesses him precisely because representation cannot make absence a presence" (*The Play of Faulkner's Language* [Ithaca, NY: Cornell University Press, 1982], 54). In a formulation that draws very close to the focus of my analysis, Bleikasten notes that "in Byron's raw fantasies and ungrammatical language Horace's 'unravish'd bride' [i.e., Narcissa herself] becomes an available whore" and concludes that "Byron's sordid story provides the novel with a kind of parodic subplot, a grimacing replica in low life of what goes on in the upper spheres" (Bleikasten, *Ink of Melancholy*, 34). Bleikasten does not postulate this echoing series of gestures—revisiting, rewriting, re- and disfiguring—as having application beyond the world of *Flags in the Dust*, however.

22. Details on Faulkner's career as postmaster at the University of Mississippi are drawn from Blotner 1:325–66.

23. Blotner later notes that Faulkner thought highly enough of this remark to repeat it in a letter to Ben Wasson (1:366).

24. The building housing the University of Mississippi post office included "a book store in the back, and a general, typical eating place with a soda fountain in front. Then, there was the post office in the other side of the front with the boxes making one side of the hall which led back to the book store and to a barber shop immediately behind the post office.... Above the boxes a sort of heavy cage material furnished the wall on to the ceiling. This gave the postal workers inside seats

to all of the outside gossip, which might have been passed in the belief that it was confidential" (Blotner 1:328).

25. Faulkner's spelling of "desperate" as "desprate" fuses two verbs that perfectly describe Byron's condition: despairing and prating.

Flags in the Dust postulates several avatars of the "failed poet" (as Faulkner called himself on occasion), all named for celebrated writers—Horace, Virgil, Byron—and all unwilling (or unable) to sublimate desire into art. As Bleikasten has noticed, in a formulation that points up the similarities between Byron's career as a writer and that of the early Faulkner, "writing, for Faulkner, was at first little more than the literary encoding of a series of private moves: a way of playing hide-and-seek with his theatrical selves, a way of parading and a way of wooing" (*Ink of Melancholy* 9). Indeed, for Bleikasten, Byron's letters constitute a kind of sardonic revision of Faulkner's own apprentice work:

> The addressees of the neatly hand-lettered, hand-illustrated, and hand-bound *art nouveau* booklets which Faulkner produced between 1921 and 1926 [i.e., mostly while postmaster] were nearly all women: *Vision in Spring,* an early sequence of love poems, was written for Estelle Oldham Franklin, his boyhood sweetheart and future wife; one copy of *The Marionettes* was dedicated to her daughter; *Mayday* and *Helen: A Courtship* were gifts for Helen Baird, another woman he loved; *The Marble Faun,* his first published book, was dedicated to his mother, the first object of his affections. These booklets were not only texts *about* desire and love; they were their messengers and would probably not have been manufactured with such excruciating care had they not been intended as signed offerings, graceful propitiatory gestures in a coy game of seduction. (*Ink of Melancholy* 9)

26. Arthur C. Danto, *Playing with the Edge: The Photographic Achievement of Robert Mapplethorpe* (Berkeley: University of California Press, 1996), 31. Danto's distinction in many ways is an elaboration on the Kantian notion of the aesthetic as disinterested regard. (Using this definition, Danto finds Mapplethorpe's work definitely *not* pornographic.)

27. However, it is worth remembering that all of Byron's letters reproduced in the novel are those written in Virgil's hand. "As Snopes read, [Virgil] transcribed in his neat, copybook hand, pausing only occasionally to inquire as to the spelling of a word"—and perhaps pausing not at all to inquire after punctuation (*Flags* 117). The novel never reproduces Byron's final letter, the one he leaves behind in place of the others and the only one offered to Narcissa in his own hand.

28. For a reading of Byron's obsession that emphasizes its class aspects, see Pamela Rhodes, "'I Remember Them Letters': Byron Snopes and Interference," in *Faulkner's Discourse: An International Symposium,* ed. Lothar Hönnighausen (Tübingen: Max Niemeyer, 1989), 77–89. For discussion of "There Was a Queen" that reads the story as an investigation of the combined erotic and economic demands of the commercial short story market Faulkner both resented and hoped to exploit, see Matthews, "Shortened Stories: Faulkner and the Market," in *Faulkner and the Short Story: Faulkner and Yoknapatawpha, 1990,* ed. Evans Harrington and Ann J. Abadie, 3–37 (Jackson: University Press of Mississippi, 1992). "The binding together of the erotic and the economic" (Matthews, "Shortened," 12) is as good a definition as any of the pornographic.

29. Along the same lines, see the *Mississippi Quarterly* version of the 1933 preface to *The Sound*

and the Fury: "Because it is himself that the Southerner is writing about, not about his environment; who has, figuratively speaking, taken the artist in him in one hand and his milieu in the other and thrust the one into the other like a clawing and spitting cat into a croker sack.... [It is] a matter of violent partizanship, in which the writer unconsciously writes into every line and phrase his violent despairs and rages and frustrations or his violent prophesies of still more violent hopes" (229).

30. William Faulkner, *Selected Letters*, ed. Joseph Blotner (New York: Random House, 1977), 235. Blotner's note indicates that Linscott returned the version of the introduction that was later published in the *Southern Review*.

31. Yi-Fu Tuan, *Space and Place: The Perspective of Experience* (Minneapolis: University of Minnesota Press, 1977), 3.

32. All definitions but the last come from the *OED*. The meaning of post as "an act of coition" (and, relatedly, "to ride a post: as 'to copulate'") comes from J. S. Farmer and W. E. Henley, eds., *Slang and Its Analogues* (1890–1904; New York: Arno, 1970), 261, 263. My thanks to John O'Neill, professor of English emeritus at Hamilton College, for this last definition.

33. Critical examinations of Yoknapatawpha have always been a mainstay of the criticism, and recent scholarship has expanded that work to include investigations into allied questions of place, space, and race, through readings of its connections to the Caribbean, Mexico, the Black US South, and the Global South. For a sample of this work, see the essays collected in Jay Watson and Ann J. Abadie, eds., *Faulkner's Geographies: Faulkner and Yoknapatawpha 2011* (Jackson: University Press of Mississippi 2015).

Similarly, explorations of Faulkner's treatment of sex and sexuality have recently expanded to include non-normative sexuality. For one example of this work, see Jaime Harker, "Queer Faulkner: Whores, Queers, and the Transgressive South," in *The New Cambridge Companion to William Faulkner*, ed. John T. Matthews, 107–18 (New York: Cambridge University Press, 2015). Faulkner's forays into writing sex are the subject of my next three chapters.

Interlude

1. See, for example, the essays collected in *William Faulkner in the Media Ecology*, ed. Julian Murphet and Stefan Solomon (Baton Rouge: Louisiana State University Press, 2015); and *Faulkner and Print Culture: Faulkner and Yoknapatawpha 2015*, ed. Jay Watson, Jaime Harker, and James G. Thomas Jr. (Jackson: University Press of Mississippi, 2015).

2. See, for example, Michael Gorra, *The Saddest Words: William Faulkner's Civil War* (New York: Liveright, 2020).

6. "C'est vraiment dégueulasse":
Last Words in *A bout de souffle* and *If I Forget Thee, Jerusalem*

Epigraph: Éric Rohmer qtd. in *Cahiers du Cinéma: The 1950s: Neo-Realism, Hollywood, New Wave*, ed. Jim Hillier (Cambridge, MA: Harvard University Press, 1985), 91.

1. Dudley Andrew, *Breathless: Jean-Luc Godard, Director* (New Brunswick, NJ: Rutgers Uni-

versity Press, 1988), 88. English translations of the film's dialogue are drawn from Andrew. French dialogue is taken from the Winstar DVD.

2. Bruce Kawin, *Faulkner and Film* (New York: Ungar, 1977), 151.

3. William Faulkner, *If I Forget Thee, Jerusalem,* ed. Noel Polk (New York: Vintage International, 1990), 20. Subsequent quotations from the novel are from this edition and cited as *Jerusalem.* T. Jefferson Kline, *Screening the Text: Intertextuality in New Wave French Cinema* (Baltimore: Johns Hopkins University Press, 1992), 199.

4. William Faulkner, *The Wild Palms* (New York: Random House, 1939), 339; William Faulkner, *Les palmiers sauvages,* trans. Maurice-Edgar Coindreau (Paris: Éditions Gallimard, 1952), 348.

5. Jean-Luc Godard, *A bout de souffle* (Impéria Films, Société de Vouvelle de Cinéma, 1960; Winstar Video DVD, 2001); all French dialogue is drawn from this DVD.

6. Tom Milne suggests that Inspector Vital was named for Jean-Jacques Vital, a French film producer whose projects Godard strongly disdained (see *Godard on Godard* [1972; Cambridge, MA: Da Capo, 1986], 99).

7. Meta C. Wilde and Oren W. Borsten, *A Loving Gentleman: The Love Story of William Faulkner and Meta Carpenter* (New York: Simon and Schuster, 1976), 166.

8. William Faulkner, *Selected Letters of William Faulkner,* ed. Joseph Blotner (New York: Random House, 1977), 338.

9. Richard Gray, *The Life of William Faulkner: A Critical Biography* (Oxford: Blackwell, 1994), 247.

10. Colin McCabe, *Godard: Images, Sound, Politics* (London: Macmillan, 1980), 45.

11. Frederick L. Gwynn and Joseph L. Blotner, eds., *Faulkner in the University: Class Conferences at the University of Virginia, 1957–1958* (Charlottesville: University Press of Virginia, 1959), 171.

12. Thomas McHaney, *William Faulkner's "The Wild Palms": A Study* (Jackson: University Press of Mississippi, 1975), xiv–xv, 37.

13. Maurice Edgar Coindreau, *The Time of William Faulkner: A French View of Modern American Fiction,* trans. George McMillan Reeves (Columbia: University of South Carolina Press, 1971), 62.

14. William Faulkner, *Si je t'oublie, Jérusalem,* trans. Maurice-Edgar Coindreau and François Pitavy (Paris: Éditions Gallimard, 2001), 351.

15. Anne Goodwyn Jones, "'The Kotex Age': Women, Popular Culture, and *The Wild Palms,*" in *Faulkner and Popular Culture: Faulkner and Yoknapatawpha, 1988,* ed. Doreen Fowler and Ann J. Abadie (Jackson: University Press of Mississippi, 1990), 145; Diane Roberts, *Faulkner and Southern Womanhood* (Athens: University of Georgia Press, 1994), 207.

16. Minrose C. Gwin, *The Feminine and Faulkner: Reading (Beyond) Sexual Difference* (Knoxville: University of Tennessee Press, 1990), 126; John N. Duvall, *Faulkner's Marginal Couple: Invincible, Outlaw, and Unspeakable Communities* (Austin: University of Texas Press, 1990), 37.

17. Richard Godden, *Fictions of Labor: William Faulkner and the South's Long Revolution* (Cambridge: Cambridge University Press, 1997), 221.

18. Pamela Rhodes and Richard Godden, "*The Wild Palms:* Degraded Culture, Devalued Texts," in *Intertextuality in Faulkner,* ed. Michel Gresset and Noel Polk (Jackson: University Press of Mississippi, 1985), 97.

19. Peter Lurie, *Vision's Immanence: Faulkner, Film, and the Popular Imagination* (Baltimore: Johns Hopkins University Press, 2004), 133, 134.

20. François Pitavy, email message to author, November 2, 2004.

21. Vincent Allan King, "The Wages of Pulp: The Use and Abuse of Fiction in William Faulkner's *The Wild Palms*," *Mississippi Quarterly* 51, no. 3 (Summer 1998): 503–25.

22. Michael Grimwood's work is the exception here (see *Heart in Conflict: Faulkner's Struggles with Vocation* [Athens: University of Georgia Press, 1987], 89–90).

23. Ernest Hemingway, *Men Without Women: Stories* (1928; London: Jonathan Cape, 1931), 75.

24. Thomas H. Guback, *The International Film Industry: Western Europe and America since 1945* (Bloomington: Indiana University Press, 1969), 21.

25. Hillier, *Cahiers du Cinéma*, 1–2.

26. Tom Milne, *Godard on Godard* (1972; Cambridge, MA: Da Capo, 1986), vi.

27. Pamela Falkenberg, "'Hollywood' and the 'Art Cinema' as a Bipolar Modeling System: *A bout de souffle* and *Breathless*," *Wide Angle* 7, no. 3 (1985): 44.

7. Making Camp: *Go Down, Moses*

Epigraphs: Susan Sontag, "Notes on Camp," in *Camp: Queer Aesthetics and the Performing Subject*, ed. Fabio Cleto (Ann Arbor: University of Michigan Press, 1999), 59; Malcolm Cowley, *The Faulkner-Cowley File: Letters and Memories, 1944–1962* (Harmondsworth, UK: Penguin, 1978), 14.

1. William Faulkner, *Go Down, Moses* (1942; New York: Vintage International, 1990), 252. Subsequent quotations of *Go Down, Moses* are from this edition and are cited as *GDM*.

2. Thadious M. Davis, *Games of Property: Law, Race, Gender, and Faulkner's "Go Down, Moses"* (Durham, NC: Duke University Press, 2003), 218, 219.

3. Richard Godden and Noel Polk, "Reading the Ledgers," *Mississippi Quarterly* 55, no. 3 (2002): 302.

4. Godden and Polk's reading is provocative on several fronts. Beginning with the not unreasonable assertion that Brownlee's "anomaly" is sexual, they proceed to make a series of ever more extreme claims about how that "anomaly" matters. These include not only the claim that Buck and Buddy engaged in an "incestuous liaison" that is interrupted "by Buck's homosexual miscegeny with a slave" (302) but the further assertion that Brownlee is a "stock-diddler" and that the mule Josephine breaks her leg as a consequence of being sexually assaulted by him (307). This conclusion is reached by reading the single line "*Wrong stall wrong niger wrong everything*" (*GDM* 253) in the context of an earlier complaint ("*may be he can lead live stock to Crick to Drink . . . Cant do that either Except one at a Time*" [*GDM* 252–53]) and then treating the sexual inference as the sole logical explanation. That Brownlee can't drive livestock because he lacks skill or experience and that "wrong stall" could mean that the wrong mule was fetched for a job are interpretive possibilities equally alive in these passages, of course. In their effort to make Brownlee's "perversion" serve, in Paul Morrison's phrase, as "the explanation for everything," Godden and Polk illustrate how Brownlee works his strongest effects not on the other characters but rather on his readers: trying to figure out Brownlee's place in the novel reveals how we expect homosexuality to be deployed in a text (as opposed to how it actually is deployed, or whether it is clearly deployed at all) and how we believe it should matter. In this sense, then, Brownlee may indeed be seen to be a queering force in *Go Down, Moses* (see Paul Morrison. *The Explanation for Everything: Essays on Sexual Subjectivity* [New York: New York University Press, 2001]).

As my later discussion of Lee Edelman's *No Future* makes clear, Davis's almost offhand linking of Bartleby and Brownlee dovetails with his call in *No Future* for a radical queer refusal of the status quo. However, Davis downplays Brownlee's resistance, preferring instead to assert that his "feminization" and "homosexuality" serve only to abject him.

5. See, for example, Joel Williamson, *William Faulkner and Southern History* (New York: Oxford University Press, 1993).

6. Eric Sundquist, "Faulkner, Race, and the Forms of American Fiction," in *Faulkner and Race: Faulkner and Yoknapatawpha, 1986,* ed. Doreen Fowler and Ann J. Abadie (Jackson: University Press of Mississippi, 1987), 2. To read Faulkner's constitutively limited yet moving engagement with southern racial history, and to read Black and white literary traditions with and against each other, are of course the guiding principles behind Sundquist's own *Faulkner: The House Divided* and *To Wake the Nations.*

7. Instances of this kind of talk are almost too numerous to mention, but a good flavor of Faulkner's rhetoric can be gotten in the inaugural class conference during his residency at the University of Virginia, where some form of "to fail" appears nine times in the first five pages: *The Sound and the Fury,* Quentin Compson, Quentin Compson's father, and the Nobel Prize speech are all described as failures (Frederick L. Gwynn and Joseph L. Blotner, eds., *Faulkner in the University: Class Conferences at the University of Virginia, 1957–1958* [Charlottesville: University Press of Virginia, 1959], 1–5).

8. For scholarship that engages Faulknerian failure, see, for example, André Bleikasten, *The Most Splendid Failure: Faulkner's "The Sound and the Fury"* (Bloomington: Indiana University Press, 1976); and *The Ink of Melancholy: Faulkner's Novels from "The Sound and the Fury" to "Light in August"* (Bloomington: Indiana University Press, 1990); as well as Michael Grimwood, *Heart in Conflict: Faulkner's Struggles with Vocation* (Athens: University of Georgia Press, 1987).

9. The *locus classicus* here is Harriet Jacobs's description, in her 1861 narrative, of a master's use of his male slave in "a nature too filthy to be repeated" (Harriet Jacobs, *Incidents in the Life of a Slave Girl,* ed. Jean Fagan Yellin [1861; Cambridge, MA: Harvard University Press, 1987], 192). That Jacobs's narrative, which is concerned in no small degree to explain her own sexual behavior, was produced for a Christian abolitionist audience would seem useful to keep in mind. For a discussion of the contemporary effects of this sort of denunciatory narrative of cross-racial same-sex expression, see Lee Edelman's essay "The Part for the (W)Hole: Baldwin, Homophobia, and the Fantasmatics of 'Race,'" in *Homographesis: Essays in Gay Literary and Cultural Theory* (New York: Routledge, 1994).

Obviously I cannot offer here a survey of the rapidly growing body of scholarship on same-sex relations in human history, but I would like to indicate my debts. The work of Judith Butler, Lee Edelman, David Halperin, D. A. Miller, Paul Morrison, and Eve Kosofsky Sedgwick has guided my thinking, even when (or especially when) they disagree with each other. I understand the dangers and complications of positing a modern-style "homosexual identity" within antebellum and Reconstruction Black communities and, wherever possible, try to indicate my awareness of these issues through my diction; thus, "same-sex," "homoerotic," and "homosexual" do *not* all mean the same thing but are employed (necessarily as a kind of shorthand) precisely in order to indicate different, historically inflected, aspects of sexual expression. My use of the term "queer" is meant to indicate precisely the kind of sexual "anomaly" a character like Brownlee presents, insofar as reading him as "homosexual" solves at the risk of oversimplifying our understanding of his textual function and effects. The word thus has a slightly closer connection to homosexuality than is usually the case in queer theory—a connection emphasized in Edelman's *No Future*.

As to the immediate issue: while the published record of antebellum African American same-sex relations is thin, it is not nonexistent. See, for instance, Jonathan Ned Katz's *Gay American History: Lesbians and Gay Men in the U.S.A.* (New York: Crowell, 1976), which describes evidence of same-sex practices among African Americans in documents from the seventeenth and nineteenth centuries, and the entry "African Americans" in the *Encyclopedia of Lesbian, Gay, Bisexual, and Transgender History in America*, 3 vols. (New York: Scribners, 2004), 1:10–16; though the entry is uncredited, it was written by Marc Stein, and I am grateful to him for sharing it with me. B. R. Burg's study of the diaries of mid-nineteenth-century US seaman Philip C. Van Buskirk seems to indicate that African American sailors participated in same-sex relations with the same frequency as their Anglo-American counterparts, and it includes at least one example of a cross-racial same-sex encounter that likely was reciprocal (B. R. Burg, *An American Seafarer in the Age of Sail: The Erotic Diaries of Philip C. Van Buskirk, 1851–1870* [New Haven, CT: Yale University Press, 1994], 74; my thanks to Lynn Adrian for drawing my attention to this work). See also Karen V. Hansen, "'No Kisses Like Youres': An Erotic Friendship between Two African-American Women during the Mid-Nineteenth Century," *Gender and History* 7, no. 2 (1995): 153–82. While it does not offer a discussion of nineteenth-century African American same-sex practice, Robert Aldrich's recent study on homosexuality and colonialism, *Colonialism and Homosexuality* (New York: Routledge, 2003), seems to me a model of what is needed; thanks to John Stauffer for mentioning it to me. Thanks also to Ian Lekus and Rob Corber for their helpful emails on this issue.

10. Orlando Patterson, *Slavery and Social Death: A Comparative Study* (Cambridge, MA: Harvard University Press, 1982), 231, 312.

11. As with Molefi Kete Asante, who flatly claims that "homosexuality is a deviation from Afrocentric thought . . . fed by the prison breeding system" and existing solely as an effect of slavery and racism. Asante adds that Black "homosexuality cannot be condoned or accepted" and concludes, "we can no longer allow our social lives to be controlled by European decadence" (*Afrocentricity* [Trenton, NJ: Africa World Press, 1988], 57).

Though their volume is concerned almost entirely with twentieth-century sexual practices, Stephen O. Murray and Will Roscoe offer an intriguing speculation about one possible source of the view that same-sex activity among Blacks is either an unwelcome infliction or a compensatory exigence when they note that

> among the many myths Europeans have created about Africa, the myth that homosexuality is absent or incidental in African societies is one of the oldest and most enduring. For Europeans, black Africans—of all the native peoples of the world—most epitomized "primitive man." Since primitive man was supposed to be close to nature, ruled by instinct, and culturally unsophisticated, he had to be heterosexual, his sexual energies and outlets devoted exclusively to their "natural" purposes: biological reproduction. If black Africans were the most primitive people in all humanity—if they were, indeed, human, which some debated—then they had to be the most heterosexual. (*Boy-Wives and Female-Husbands: Studies in African Homosexualities* [New York: St. Martin's, 1998], xi)

See also their collection's concluding essay, "Diversity and Identity: The Challenge of African Homosexualities," in which they remind us that "absence of evidence can never be assumed to be evidence of an absence" (267).

12. Sweet's discussion of the same-sex practices of the Central African *jinbandaas* is laudable not least because he seems, elsewhere in his study, more comfortable with the notion that same-sex practices among New World slaves were primarily manifestations of "situational" homosexuality. His observations on the fate of the *jinbandaa* in the diaspora are worth quoting:

> The spiritual capacity of the transvested homosexual was so universally known [in Central Africa] that they were referred to not by their patterns of dress or by their sexual behavior, but by their roles as religious leaders. Only when these Africans encounter the Western world do we begin to see the breakdown of the gender-defined organization of this kinlike, transvestite, religious society.
>
> This disjuncture between the gendered, religious space in Central Africa and the lack of such a space in the diaspora indicates several sobering things. First, those transvested homosexuals who were brought to Europe and its colonies as slaves were isolated not only according to race, but also according to their gender and their sexuality. Given the evidently small number of *jinbandaas* in the diaspora, there was no way for them to replicate their gender-defined communities in their new surroundings. Second, Western/Christian prejudice and repression against the feminine and against the passive homosexual contributed to the attrition of a seemingly well-defined African gender category that defied Western norms. And finally, the institutional foundation that gave this collection of transvested homosexuals religious power all but disappeared. Because they could no longer meet collectively to share knowledge and affirm their religious power, these powers were effectively diluted. Indeed, in Brazil, the very meaning of the term *jinbandaa* was transformed, at least within the white community. Rather than referring to an individual with religious power, the term *jinbandaa* became synonymous with the passive "sodomite." (*Recreating Africa: Culture, Kinship, and Religion in the African-Portuguese World, 1441–1770* [Chapel Hill: University of North Carolina Press, 2003], 56–57)

Thank you to Stephanie Y. Evans for bringing Sweet's work to my attention.

13. See Robert Reid-Pharr, *Black Gay Man: Essays* (New York: New York University Press, 2001) and *Conjugal Union: The Body, the House, and the Black American* (New York: Oxford University Press, 1999); Kevin Mumford, *Interzones: Black/White Sex Districts in Chicago and New York in the Early 20th Century* (New York: Columbia University Press, 1997); Roderick A. Ferguson, *Aberrations in Black: Toward a Queer of Color Critique* (Minneapolis: University of Minnesota Press, 2004); and Phillip Brian Harper, *Are We Not Men? Masculine Anxiety and the Problem of African-American Identity* (Oxford: Oxford University Press, 1996).

It is worth observing that the current thinness of the scholarship on nineteenth-century Black nonnormative sexuality vis-à-vis its twentieth-century counterpart has the paradoxical effect of making Baldwin and Rustin seem more anomalous than they likely were. It has also led to an effort to make a special claim for the effects of Black urban migration and corresponding proletarianization on the proliferation of so-called "perverse" forms of Black sexuality (Ferguson and Mumford suggest this). While urban overcrowding clearly made Black queer life more visible, and thus more available to policing and sociological surveillance, it is doubtful whether it can be said to have caused it. John Howard's study *Men Like That: A Southern Queer History* (Chicago: University of Chicago Press, 1999) makes clear that southern rural life had (and has) its queer aspects.

14. Insofar as I mean to question prevailing assumptions about southern history, sexuality, and the figuring of these two in Faulkner's texts, my discussion of Percival Brownlee can be seen as an example of the "unhistoricist" approach recently described by Jonathan Goldberg and Madhavi Menon ("Queering History," *Publications of the Modern Language Association* 120, no. 5 [October 2005]: 1608–17). I engage their approach directly in the next chapter.

15. The production of *Go Down, Moses* presents a complicated case, in terms of establishing a time frame for analysis. Faulkner pieced the novel together through extensive revision of a group of preexisting stories (originally not far removed, tonally, from the "darky tales" of post-Reconstruction plantation fiction) and new composition. For analyses that interpret the novel through this composition history, see Joanne V. Creighton, *William Faulkner's Craft of Revision: The Snopes Trilogy, "The Unvanquished," and "Go Down, Moses"* (Detroit: Wayne State University Press, 1977); James Early, *The Making of "Go Down, Moses"* (Dallas, TX: Southern Methodist University Press, 1972); and Grimwood, *Heart in Conflict*.

16. Neil Watson, "The 'Incredibly Loud . . . Miss-fire': A Sexual Reading of *Go Down, Moses*," in *William Faulkner: Six Decades of Criticism*, ed. Linda Wagner-Martin (East Lansing: Michigan State University Press, 2002), 208.

17. Though I am sympathetic to aspects of Watson's reading, his interest in the homoerotic subtext of *Go Down, Moses* is anchored almost entirely in a view of the novel's "pervasiveness of despair" over heterosexual relations and procreation, a reading that casts "homoerotic tension" largely as a symptom of heterosexual failure (210, 207). While I agree that grief is the founding emotion of *Go Down, Moses*, I do not share his diagnosis of the source of that grief.

18. Minrose Gwin, "Did Ernest Like Gordon? Faulkner's *Mosquitoes* and the Bite of 'Gender Trouble,'" in *Faulkner and Gender: Faulkner and Yoknapatawpha 1994*, ed. Donald M. Kartiganer and Ann J. Abadie (Jackson: University Press of Mississippi, 1996), 139.

19. John Duvall, "Faulkner's Crying Game: Male Homosexual Panic," in *Faulkner and Gender: Faulkner and Yoknapatawpha 1994*, ed. Donald M. Kartiganer and Ann J. Abadie (Jackson: University Press of Mississippi, 1996), 50, 53.

20. D. Matthew Ramsey, "'Turnabout' Is Fair(y) Play: Faulkner's Queer War Story," *Faulkner Journal* 15, no. 1–2 (Fall 1999/Spring 2000): 61–81. "Turnabout" was revised into the screenplay for the 1933 Howard Hawks film *Today We Live*, one of Faulkner's earliest Hollywood assignments. Told he needed to create a leading role in the film for Joan Crawford, Faulkner is reported to have replied, "I don't seem to remember a girl in the story" (Joseph Blotner, *Faulkner: A Biography*, 2 vols. [New York: Random House, 1974], 1:307).

21. The roommates were the writer Stark Young in Manhattan and the artist William Spratling in New Orleans. Also worth noting is Faulkner's long friendship with the gay editor Ben Wasson, who described himself as "dazzled" when Faulkner recited poetry to him during their first meeting at the University of Mississippi (Blotner 1:49).

22. "Out of Nazareth" and "Damon and Pythias Unlimited" are reprinted in William Faulkner, *William Faulkner: New Orleans Sketches*, ed. Carvel Collins (London: Chatto and Windus, 1958).

23. It should be clear, then, that I disagree with Godden and Polk's claim that Buck purchased Brownlee for his sexual services and is therefore unable to resell him. Were that the case, Buddy's claim that Buck "put [himself] out of Market" (*GDM* 253) in buying Brownlee makes no sense: presumably there would be other buyers with similar sexual tastes who would be willing to purchase Brownlee. Rather, Buck can only be described as being "out of Market" if, in fact, he has purchased a man who simply refuses to be a slave. As should be clear from my reading, I think that is the case with Brownlee and, further, that the novel casts his "anomalous" sexuality as the sign of his resistance.

24. Lee Edelman, *Homographesis: Essays in Gay Literary and Cultural Theory* (New York: Routledge, 1994), 7.

25. Faulkner absolutely was aware of the productively unsettling work of the homograph "Caddy."

26. Though Edelman calls this process "*homo*graphesis," and though elsewhere he articulates his theoretical interests in what seems to be an exclusively homosexual frame, I take the central critical action of homographesis—its drive to deconstruct "essentializing metaphors of identity"—to be one that opens a text to its fullest queer possibilities, and not only to its exclusively "homosexual" meaning. As I note later in this essay, Edelman makes precisely this argument ten years after the publication of *Homographesis*.

27. Godden and Polk here build on the discussion of the word in Nancy Dew Taylor, *Annotations to William Faulkner's "Go Down, Moses"* (New York: Garland, 1994), 151–52, by further connecting the definition spintrius = pervert to a 1931 Modern Library edition of Suetonius's *The Lives of the Twelve Caesars* that was in Faulkner's library (309). In the passage they cite, the word used is *spintrae* (not spintrius). While Godden and Polk move directly from "pervert" to "homosexual," I think it useful to keep in mind that the word "pervert" contains any number of possibilities (indeed, the Suetonius passage they quote describes "monstrous feats of lubricity" by "girls and perverts" [309])—a semantic unsettledness that emphasizes Brownlee's *queer* status in the novel.

28. P. G. Glare, ed., *Oxford Latin Dictionary* (New York: Oxford University Press, 1983), 1805. Thanks to Barbara Gold and Carl Rubino for their patient and generous help with the Latin and Greek etymologies.

29. This play of sameness and difference appears more explicitly in the novel at the moment when Ike, setting out on the woodland foray that culminates in his vision of Old Ben, recalls Sam's advice about how to comport himself in the wilderness: "Be scared. You cant help that. But dont be afraid. Aint nothing in the woods going to hurt you if you dont corner it or it dont smell that you are afraid. A bear or a deer has got to be scared of a coward the same as a brave man has got to be" (*GDM* 198–99). Here, the similarity between being afraid and being scared is articulated as a difference.

30. Claude Lévi-Strauss, *The Elementary Structures of Kinship*, trans. James Harle Bell and ed. John Richard Von Sturmer and Rodney Needham (1949; rev. ed., Boston: Beacon Press, 1969), 10. Subsequent quotations will be cited parenthetically within the text. My summary of Lévi-Strauss's thesis is descriptive, not normative. I do not have space here to more than indicate my appreciation for the critiques of his work offered by Jacques Derrida ("Structure, Sign, and Play in the Discourse of the Human Sciences," in *Writing and Difference,* trans. Alan Bass [Chicago: University

of Chicago Press, 1978], 278–93) and Gayle Rubin ("The Traffic in Women: Notes on the Political Economy of Sex," in *Toward an Anthropology of Women,* ed. Rayna R. Reiter [New York: Monthly Review Press, 1975], 157–210), who each point out how *The Elementary Structures of Kinship* assumes as givens precisely what should be questioned (the premise of an originary gesture; the notion of women as property). I draw on the theories of Lévi-Strauss here mainly in order to open an interrogation of the development of "natural" human attachment that is more fully engaged in my later discussion of Judith Butler's work.

31. On this point, see the chapter on *Go Down, Moses* in James A. Snead, *Figures of Division: William Faulkner's Major Novels* (New York: Methuen, 1986).

32. Along these lines, Werner Sollors, in his reading of *Absalom, Absalom!,* wonders "whether it is not male homosexual attraction that has been a hidden player on the stage of incest and miscegenation":

> The homoerotic axis of the novel extends from Sutpen's naked fights with his "wild negroes," witnessed by his white daughter Judith as if it were a primal scene, to Charles's "seduction" of Henry and the double entendre of Charles's taunt "unless you stop me." The axis reaches its culminating point, however, in the encounter between Quentin and Shreve, out of whose obvious attraction for each other the reconstruction of incest and miscegenation in the house of Sutpen is made possible and fleshed out, so that even their joint depiction of Judith's supposed surprise that Bon kissed her "like your brother would—provided of course your brother ever thought of, could be brought to, kissing you on the mouth" seems to resonate with their own late-night, demiclad, college-roommate interaction. The ideal of *fraternité* is thereby taken to a point that may have been implied but has rarely been explicit in Faulkner's precursors. His recognition of how the "abstraction" of "the Negro" and the fantasies of "race" have served as the screen for all sorts of repressed desires has been rendered in a form in which themes, especially deep and politically volatile themes, become understandable not as natural givens but as the consequence of narrative structures and the partial points of view that may underlie these structures. (*Neither Black nor White Yet Both: Thematic Explorations of Interracial Literature* [Cambridge, MA: Harvard University Press, 1997], 331–32)

In this view of *Absalom, Absalom!,* narratives of incest and miscegenation emerge in one register of the text in order to drain away, or manage, homoerotic attractions existing in another. In their reading of *Go Down, Moses,* Godden and Polk literalize this approach through their claim that Ike manufactures Lucius Quintus Carothers McCaslin's crime in order to block recognition of his father's homosexual incest and miscegeny. My own view is that Sollors's observations are more suited to *Absalom, Absalom!* than to the later novel. It is of course true that homosexual yearning plays an important role in *Go Down, Moses;* there, however, incest and miscegenation are much less potentially fictive: characters (and readers) are granted evidence that does not exist in *Absalom, Absalom!* (not the least being Lucas Beauchamp's physical resemblance to his white grandfather). Finally, though, my chief objection to Sollors's and Godden and Polk's readings lies with how they equate incest, miscegenation, and homosexuality: the first two terms read the third as similarly abominable. That Ike's reading of Percival Brownlee does not arouse anything approaching the level of revulsion called up by his recognition of the relationship among his grandfather, Eunice, and Tomasina is one indication, I think, of the flaw in this assumption.

For another, important reading of the incest motif in Faulkner, see Karl Zender, "Faulkner and the Politics of Incest," *American Literature* 70, no. 4 (December 1998): 739–65.

33. Lawrence Buell, "Faulkner and the Claims of the Natural World," in *Faulkner and the Natural World: Faulkner and Yoknapatawpha, 1996,* ed. Donald M. Kartiganer and Ann J. Abadie (Jackson: University Press of Mississippi, 1999), 5. My counter to Buell's claim is indebted to John T. Matthews's reading of this moment: Old Ben "coalesces out of the wilderness [as] . . . actually a derived presence. . . . [I]t is not until Ike rediscovers the watch and compass that Ben appears" (*The Play of Faulkner's Language* [Ithaca, NY: Cornell University Press, 1982], 254–55). Relatedly, see also David H. Evans's discussion of the thoroughly hierarchical world of the hunt; as he points out, Ike's experience of "the natural world is organized throughout by social orders" (Evans, "Taking the Place of Nature: 'The Bear' and the Incarnation of America," in *Faulkner and the Natural World: Faulkner and Yoknapatawpha, 1996,* ed. Donald M. Kartiganer and Ann J. Abadie [Jackson: University Press of Mississippi, 1999], 188).

34. As Carvel Collins observes in his introductory notes to *Mayday,* in ending his tale this way Faulkner gestures directly toward James Branch Cabell's *Jurgen* (1919), a parodic treatment of medieval themes that, thanks to its "leering pornographic elements," enjoyed something of a *succès de scandale* (William Faulkner, *Mayday,* introd. Carvel Collins [Notre Dame, IN: University of Notre Dame Press, 1978], 22). Possibly important for our consideration of *Go Down, Moses* is not only *Jurgen*'s engagement with medieval romance but also the novel's subtitle: "A Comedy of Justice."

35. Faulkner had a copy of Thomas Bulfinch's redaction of Malory's *Mort d'Arthur* in his library, but of course the sources for his knowledge of Arthurian romance in general, and the Fisher King Grail legends in particular, would have been multiple, not least among them T. S. Eliot's footnotes to "The Waste Land" and Tennyson's *Idylls of the King.* In *Mayday,* for instance, Faulkner draws on the legend of Tristram and Isoude (I follow here Malory's spellings as adopted in Bulfinch); that he spells the princess's name "Yseult" indicates a familiarity with sources other than Bulfinch.

I realize that in moving from Wolfram to Wagner I am passing over many versions of the legend, not the least among them Malory's and Tennyson's, that are of interest both formally and thematically (certainly it is worth noting, for example, that Tennyson's Percivale, like Faulkner's Ike, fails in his quest, withdraws from the world, and adopts an elegiacal mode of expression). However, my concern here is not to provide a detailed discussion of textual antecedents but rather to point out those links between *Go Down, Moses* and the Grail legend most pertinent to my overall analysis. Finally, it's worth remembering that *Go Down, Moses* is also a paratactic narrative. The text's principles of unity so escaped Faulkner's publishers that the first edition appeared under the title *"Go Down, Moses" and Other Stories,* to Faulkner's dismay.

36. Faulkner's use of the Grail legend in *Go Down, Moses* is complex and cross-cutting in a contradictory manner that is typically Faulknerian: Ike McCaslin resembles both Parzifal and Anfortas; Percival Brownlee incorporates attributes of Parzifal, Kundry, and Galahad. That other characters in *Go Down, Moses*—not only Percival and Ike but also Sam Fathers, Fonsiba Beauchamp, Molly Beauchamp, and Samuel Worsham Beauchamp—likewise seek freedom echoes those aspects of the Arthurian romance that posit the Grail quest as a project at once individual and communal. To put it another way: the allusion works kaleidoscopically and fractally, not allegorically.

37. Like "Ode on a Grecian Urn," the poem that is its totem, "The Bear" is divided into five

sections. Section four of the story corresponds to the fourth stanza of the poem, which describes the vase's tableau of animal sacrifice. For a complementary reading of Ike's interview with Roth's mistress, see Glenn Cannon Arbery, "Victims of Likeness: Quadroons and Octoroons in Southern Fiction," in *Interracialism: Black-White Intermarriage in American History, Literature, and Law*, ed. Werner Sollors (New York: Oxford University Press, 2000), 393–407.

38. Wagner's extremely complex opera has been read, variously, as the apotheosis of his racialized, anti-Semitic aesthetic (see, for example, Theodor Adorno, *In Search of Wagner*, trans. Rodney Livingstone [1952; London: Verso, 1991]; Paul Lawrence Rose, *Wagner: Race and Revolution* [London: Faber and Faber, 1992]; and Marc A. Weiner, *Richard Wagner and the Anti-Semitic Imagination* [1995; Lincoln: University of Nebraska Press, 1997]); as a representation of the medical, social, and moral aspects of syphilis (Linda Hutcheon and Michael Hutcheon, *Opera: Desire, Disease, Death* [Lincoln: University of Nebraska Press, 1996]); as a parable anticipating Lacanian theories of subject formation (Slavoj Žižek, "'The Wound Is Healed Only by the Spear That Smote You': The Operatic Subject and its Vicissitudes," in *Opera through Other Eyes*, ed. David J. Levin [Stanford, CA: Stanford University Press, 1994], 177–214); and as crucial step in the transition from musical romanticism to modernism (see Carl Dahlhaus, *Between Romanticism and Modernism*, trans. Mary Whittall [1974; Berkeley: University of California Press, 1980]; and Lucy Beckett, *Richard Wagner: "Parsifal"* [Cambridge: Cambridge University Press, 1981]). Every one of these readings has some bearing on Faulkner's use of the Grail myth to address sex and race in *Go Down, Moses;* space limitations simply make it impossible for me to pursue these connections.

39. Arthur Groos and Norris J. Lacy note that Parsifal's mutability is the "basic element of his individual history . . . and a crucial factor in his longevity as an Arthurian hero" (Groos and Lacy, eds., *Perceval/Parzifal: A Casebook* [New York: Routledge, 2002], 2).

40. Here I can only gesture toward Eve Kosofsky Sedgwick's important discussion of the role aunts and uncles have played in "representing nonconforming or nonreproductive sexualities," those "alternative life trajectories" so often occluded in both literature and life (Sedgwick, *Tendencies* [London: Routledge, 1993], 63). See her chapter "Tales of the Avunculate: Queer Tutelage in *The Importance of Being Earnest*," in *Tendencies*. It seems to me that the many aunts and uncles of *Go Down, Moses* signal, in registers both racial and sexual, these occluded, lost, and grieved "alternative life trajectories."

41. Judith Butler, *The Psychic Life of Power: Theories in Subjection* (Stanford, CA: Stanford University Press, 1997), 140.

42. For one discussion of Caroline Barr's relationship to the Falkner family as well as to William Faulkner, see Judith Sensibar, "Who Wears the Mask? Memory, Desire, and Race in *Go Down, Moses*," in *New Essays on "Go Down, Moses*," ed. Linda Wagner-Martin (Cambridge: Cambridge University Press, 1996), 101–27.

43. That this yearning is repeatedly linked to precisely the kind of cross-racial communion that Ike cannot bring himself to accept points, again, to the text's persistent linking of homosexuality and freedom.

44. As the opening epigraphs of this essay indicate, I think an argument could be made for much of Faulkner's work as participating in a camp aesthetic; *Go Down, Moses* here has the status of a local example.

There is ample evidence that Faulkner was familiar with the work of Friedrich Nietzsche (as he was familiar with the writings of Henri Bergson and Arthur Schopenhauer). For studies that discuss the author's engagement with Nietzsche, see John T. Irwin, *Doubling and Incest/Repetition and Revenge: A Speculative Reading of Faulkner* (1975; Baltimore: Johns Hopkins University Press, 1996); and Thomas L. McHaney, *William Faulkner's "The Wild Palms": A Study* (Jackson: University Press of Mississippi, 1975). Recent scholarship investigates the connections between Nietzsche's homosexuality and his philosophy; while such scholarship has an obvious bearing on my analysis, this is not the place for an in-depth examination. See, for example, Joachim Köhler, *Zarathustra's Secret: The Interior Life of Friedrich Nietzsche,* trans. Ronald Taylor (1989; New Haven, CT: Yale University Press, 2002); and Rüdiger Safranski, *Nietzsche: A Philosophical Biography,* trans. Shelley Frisch (2000; London: Granta, 2002).

45. Maxine Bernstein and Robert Boyers, "Women, the Arts, and the Politics of Culture: An Interview with Susan Sontag," in *Conversations with Susan Sontag, ed.* Leland Poague (Jackson: University Press of Mississippi, 1995), 69. In saying that her first ambition in writing "Notes on Camp" was to "name a sensibility, draw its contours, to recount its history," Sontag quotes the second paragraph of the essay itself.

46. Caryl Flinn, "The Deaths of Camp," in *Camp: Queer Aesthetics and the Performing Subject,* ed. Fabio Cleto (Ann Arbor: University of Michigan Press, 1999), 436.

47. Susan Sontag, "Notes on Camp," in *Camp: Queer Aesthetics and the Performing Subject,* ed. Fabio Cleto (Ann Arbor: University of Michigan Press, 1999), 64.

48. One manifestation of this shift appears in Edelman's *No Future:* "In the preface to *Homographesis* I wrote that the signifier 'gay,' understood 'as a figure for the textuality, the rhetoricity, of the sexual . . . designates the gap or incoherence that every discourse of "sexuality" or "sexual identity" would master.' Extending that claim, I now suggest that queer sexualities" operate in much the same manner (see Lee Edelman, *No Future: Queer Theory and the Death Drive* [Durham, NC: Duke University Press, 2004], 26; ellipses in original).

49. Certainly homosexual panic is the most well-known response to the recognition of expanded possibilities for (emotional, sexual) expression; but, as the example of *Go Down, Moses* shows, it is not the only one.

I cannot begin to summarize the scholarship on camp, not all of it written in response to Sontag's essay. Cleto's is the most comprehensive of the several camp anthologies published in the 1990s.

50. Esther Newton, *Mother Camp: Female Impersonators in America* (Chicago: University of Chicago Press, 1979), 105.

51. Andrew Britton, "For Interpretation: Notes Against Camp," in *Camp: Queer Aesthetics and the Performing Subject,* ed. Fabio Cleto (Ann Arbor: University of Michigan Press, 1999), 138.

52. Andrew Ross, *No Respect: Intellectuals and Popular Culture* (New York: Routledge, 1989), 161.

53. Sander Gilman, *Nietzschean Parody* (1976; Aurora, CO: Davies Group, 2001), 21.

54. Among other things, I am expanding here on Evans's observation that "in passing judgment on Ike, readers replicate his own gesture, to the extent that they also imagine themselves to have the moral 'high ground,' from which to discover the inherent value of Ike's decision and to fit it into a moral historical pattern" (Evans, "Taking the Place of Nature," 194).

55. At the risk of stating the obvious, I should make clear that I am not advocating some sort of *faux*-dialectical "repudiation of repudiation," nor am I claiming that repudiation is in and of itself somehow "wrong." Sometimes repudiation is the right and necessary thing, and sometimes it works. That much seems plain. Rather, I am calling for closer attention to *the conditions under which* the repudiating gesture is performed, keeping in mind that repudiation may not simply fail to achieve its ends. It may actually work to perpetuate the conditions it aims to abolish—as *Go Down, Moses* teaches us.

8. Unhistoricizing Faulkner

Epigraph: Sigmund Freud, *Three Essays on the Theory of Sexuality*, in *The Standard Edition of the Complete Psychological Works of Sigmund Freud*, ed. and trans. James Strachey et al. (London: Hogarth, 1953), 145.

1. Fredric Jameson, *The Political Unconscious: Narrative as a Socially Symbolic Act* (Ithaca, NY: Cornell University Press, 1981), 9; Eric J. Sundquist, *Faulkner: The House Divided* (Baltimore: Johns Hopkins University Press, 1983), x; emphasis added.

2. Tim Dean, "Art as Symptom: Žižek and the Ethics of Psychoanalytic Criticism," *diacritics* 32, no. 2 (Summer 2002): 22.

3. Frederic Koeppel, "Book Folks: 'Faulkner's Sexualities,' Anyone?," *Memphis Commercial Appeal*, July 1, 2007.

4. Jonathan Goldberg and Madhavi Menon, "Queering History," *Publications of the Modern Language Association* 120, no. 5 (October 2005): 1609.

5. Eve Kosofsky Sedgwick, *Tendencies* (London: Routledge, 1993); Judith Butler, *Gender Trouble* (1990; New York: Routledge 1999).

6. Michel Foucault, "The West and the Truth of Sex," trans. Daniel W. Smith, in *Homosexuality and Psychoanalysis*, ed. Tim Dean and Christopher Lane (Chicago: University of Chicago Press, 2001), 53.

7. See especially Tim Dean, *Beyond Sexuality* (Chicago: University of Chicago Press, 2000) and "Art as Symptom."

8. See, for example, James Penney, "(Queer) Theory and the Universal Alternative," *diacritics* 32, no. 2 (Summer 2002): 3–19. Dean's chapter "Bodies That Mutter," in *Beyond Sexuality* (174–214), offers a thorough analysis of Butler's use of Lacan.

9. Gilles Deleuze and Félix Guattari, *Anti-Oedipus: Capitalism and Schizophrenia*, trans. Robert Hurley, Mark Seem, and Helen R. Lane (New York: Viking, 1977).

10. Jameson sees Freud's theory of unconscious wish-fulfillment mechanisms as "abstractions" derived from the capitalist abstraction of labor (*Political Unconscious* 66). But to claim that "we can think abstractly about the world only to the degree to which the world has itself has already become abstract" (66), and to imply that this capacity emerges first (or only) with the rise of capitalism, is to ignore realms of abstract thinking about the world (Euclidean geometry, for instance) whose appearance well predates capitalism. Though I do not have the space here to develop this point, it seems to me that what Jameson calls the "political *un*conscious" of cultural artifacts is better understood as *conscious* knowledge, repressed. My thanks to Michael Zeitlin for

pointing me toward passages in *The Political Unconscious* that helped focus my thinking about Jameson's argument.

11. Arnold I. Davidson, *The Emergence of Sexuality: Historical Epistemology and the Formation of Concepts* (Cambridge, MA: Harvard University Press, 2001), 209–10.

12. Tim Dean and Christopher Lane, *Homosexuality and Psychoanalysis* (Chicago: University of Chicago Press, 2001), 5.

13. Henry Abelove, "Freud, Male Homosexuality, and the Americans," in *The Lesbian and Gay Studies Reader,* ed. Abelove, Michèle Aina Barale, and David M. Halperin (New York: Routledge, 1993), 382. Subsequent quotations are from this edition. Abelove's essay was first published in the winter 1985–86 issue of *Dissent.*

14. Arnold I. Davidson first noted that careful reading of the *Three Essays* leads to the conclusion that, from 1915 onward, "perversion is no longer a legitimate concept" within psychoanalytic thought ("How to Do the History of Psychoanalysis: A Reading of Freud's *Three Essays on the Theory of Sexuality,*" *Critical Inquiry* 13, no. 2 [Winter 1987]: 275). While Abelove emphasizes Freud's progressiveness in refusing to see homosexuality as pathological, Davidson takes a more critical view of Freud's less than eager willingness to admit the most radical consequences of his theory.

15. Philip Weinstein, *Unknowing: The Work of Modernist Fiction* (Ithaca, NY: Cornell University Press, 2005), 87.

16. And in 1964, long before the onset of the "culture wars," Susan Sontag articulated a similar complaint in "Against Interpretation."

17. Dean turns to Jean Laplanche's elaboration of Lacan's "enigmatic signifier" in order to demonstrate the ways in which psychoanalytic interpretation can work "against rather than toward the consolations of sense" (Dean, "Art as Symptom," 35).

18. For a similar view, see Leo Bersani, "Psychoanalysis and the Aesthetic Subject," *Critical Inquiry* 32, no. 2 (Winter 2006): 161–74.

19. Dipesh Chakrabarty, *Provincializing Europe: Postcolonial Thought and Historical Difference* (Princeton, NJ: Princeton University Press, 2000), 249, qtd. in Goldberg and Menon 1610; Hayden White, *Tropics of Discourse: Essays in Cultural Criticism* (Baltimore: Johns Hopkins University Press, 1978), 29, qtd. in Goldberg and Menon 1615–16.

20. Though aspects of their critique resemble those of the self-described "New Formalists," Dean, Goldberg, and Menon are not mentioned in Marjorie Levinson's omnibus review of New Formalist scholarship. This is perhaps because their work remains closely tied to queer theory: for Levinson, the "mixed bag" of New Formalism lacks a theoretical anchor (see Levinson, "The Changing Profession: What Is New Formalism?," *Publications of the Modern Language Association* 122, no. 2 [March 2007]: 558–69). My thanks to Peter Lurie for suggesting I consider queer theory's relationship to New Formalism through this essay.

21. See John T. Matthews, "The Rhetoric of Containment in Faulkner," in *Faulkner's Discourse: An International Symposium,* ed. Lothar Hönnighausen, 55–67 (Tübingen: Max Niemeyer, 1989); and Richard Godden, "Quentin Compson: Tyrrhenian Vase or Crucible of Race?," in *New Essays on "The Sound and the Fury,"* ed. Noel Polk, 99–137 (Cambridge: Cambridge University Press, 1993).

22. Theresa M. Towner and James B. Carothers, *Reading Faulkner: Collected Stories* (Jackson: University Press of Mississippi, 2006), 415, 423, 431, 448.

23. Theodor Adorno, "Music and Language: A Fragment," in *Quasi una Fantasia: Essays on Modern Music,* trans. Rodney Livingstone (New York: Verso, 1998), 4.

24. William Faulkner, "The Leg," in *Collected Stories* (1950; New York: Vintage, 1977), 834. Subsequent quotations are from this edition.

25. William Faulkner, *William Faulkner: New Orleans Sketches,* ed. Carvel Collins (London: Chatto and Windus, 1958), 47. Widely interpreted as homosexual, the passion of Jonathan and David is described in 1 Samuel 18.

26. Edmund L. Volpe, *A Reader's Guide to William Faulkner: The Short Stories* (Syracuse, NY: Syracuse University Press, 2004), 57, qtd. in Towner and Carothers 430.

Postlude

1. Frederick R. Karl, *William Faulkner: American Writer* (New York: Weidenfeld and Nicolson, 1989); Joel Williamson, *William Faulkner and Southern History* (New York: Oxford University Press, 1993); Judith L. Sensibar, *Faulkner and Love: The Women Who Shaped His Art* (New Haven, CT: Yale University Press, 2009).

2. Phillip Gordon, *Gay Faulkner: Uncovering a Homosexual Presence in Yoknapatawpha and Beyond* (Jackson: University Press of Mississippi, 2020), 3.

3. John T. Irwin, *Doubling and Incest, Repetition and Revenge: A Speculative Reading of Faulkner,* expanded ed. (Baltimore: Johns Hopkins University Press, 1996).

4. Jaime Harker, "Queer Faulkner: Whores. Queers, and the Transgressive South," in *The New Cambridge Companion to William Faulkner,* ed. John T. Matthews (New York: Cambridge University Press, 2015), 107–18; Michael P. Bibler, *Cotton's Queer Relations: Same-Sex Intimacy and the Literature of the Southern Plantation, 1936–1968* (Charlottesville: University of Virginia Press, 2009).

9. What Television Is For; or, From "The Brooch" to *The Wire*

1. Joseph Blotner, *Faulkner: A Biography,* 2 vols. (New York: Random House, 1974), 2:1609, 1704.

2. William Faulkner, "On Privacy (The American Dream: What Happened to It?)," in *William Faulkner: Essays, Speeches, and Public Letters,* ed. James B. Meriwether, updated (1965; New York: Modern Library, 2004), 70–71.

3. William Furry, "Faulkner in a Haystack: The Search for William Faulkner's Television Adaptations of 'The Brooch' and 'Shall Not Perish,'" *Faulkner Journal* 16, no. 1–2 (Fall 2000/Spring 2001): 136.

4. Frederick R. Karl, *William Faulkner: American Writer* (New York: Weidenfeld and Nicolson, 1989), 988–89; Richard Gray, *The Life of William Faulkner* (1994; Oxford: Blackwell, 1996), 38. Most of the recent scholarly biographies of Faulkner that adopt an explicitly sociopolitical, historicist approach to the fiction or that offer revaluations of the author's post-Nobel career as a public intellectual do not discuss the Oppenheimer incident.

5. "Against that principle which by physical force compels man to relinquish his individuality into the monolithic mass of a state dedicated to the premise that the state alone shall prevail, we . . . may have to represent that last community of unified people dedicated to that opposed

premise that man can be free by the very act of voluntarily merging and relinquishing his liberty into the liberty of all individual men who want to be free" (Faulkner, *Essays,* 231).

6. W. E. B. Du Bois, *The Souls of Black Folk,* ed. Henry Louis Gates Jr. and Terri Hume Oliver (New York: Norton), 11.

7. Jacques Rancière, *The Future of the Image,* trans. Gregory Elliott (2003; New York: Verso, 2007), 75.

8. Michael Millgate, *The Achievement of William Faulkner* (1966; Athens: University of Georgia Press, 1989), 50. Furry claims that Faulkner "dashed off" the teleplays of both "The Brooch" and "Shall Not Perish" during a trip to New York City early in 1953, citing as evidence a March 31 letter to Else Jonsson (125, 138). However, Blotner's footnote to a February 22 letter to Jonsson, in which Faulkner writes that he "will make a television play of one of my stories this week" (346), indicates that Faulkner was working not on "The Brooch" or "Shall Not Perish" but on the adaptation of the "Old Man" section of *The Wild Palms.* Though the phrasing is ambiguous, Millgate seems to believe that the adaptation of "Shall Not Perish" was written in 1954, again on a tight schedule before the February 11 broadcast. For the letters to Jonsson, see William Faulkner, *Selected Letters,* ed. Joseph Blotner (New York: Random House, 1977), 346–47.

9. Faulkner, *Selected Letters,* ed. Blotner, 274. Given the hiding he got in the *New York Times* for his teleplay of the "The Brooch," it seems odd that Faulkner, offered a second chance to prove himself, would produce such a poor script—an improbability that indirectly lends credence to Furry's theory that the adaptations of "The Brooch" and "Shall Not Perish" were written at the same time.

10. Jack Gould, "'The Brooch' on TV / William Faulkner Runs Afoul of Video's / 'Code' and Comes Off Second Best," *New York Times,* April 12, 1953, xii.

11. See Melvin Patrick Ely, *The Adventures of "Amos 'n' Andy": A Social History of an American Phenomenon* (1991; Charlottesville: University of Virginia Press, 2001), esp. chap. 10.

12. Taylor Branch, *Parting the Waters: America in the King Years, 1954–63* (New York: Simon and Schuster, 1988), 223; J. Fred MacDonald, *Blacks and White TV: Afro-Americans in Television since 1948* (Chicago: Nelson-Hall, 1983); Sasha Torres, *Black, White, and in Color: Television and Black Civil Rights* (Princeton, NJ: Princeton University Press, 2003).

13. S. I. Hayakawa, "Communication: Interracial and International," *ETC: A Review of General Semantics* 20, no. 4 (December 1963): 397.

14. Jacques Rancière, *Dissensus: On Politics and Aesthetics,* ed. and trans. Steven Corcoran (New York: Continuum International, 2010), 149.

15. The essays presented at the University of New South Wales conference were collected and published in 2015 as *William Faulkner in the Media Ecology,* ed. Julian Murphet and Stefan Solomon (Baton Rouge: Louisiana State University Press, 2015).

16. Randall Kennedy, *Nigger: The Strange Career of a Troublesome Word* (2002; New York: Vintage, 2003), 22.

17. "'No Vacancies' for Blacks: How Donald Trump Got His Start, and Was First Accused of Bias," *New York Times,* August 28, 2016, 1, www.nytimes.com/2016/08/28/us/politics/donald-trump-housing-race.html.

18. Ta-Nehisi Coates, "In Defense of a Loaded Word," *New York Times,* November 23, 2013, 1, www.nytimes.com/2013/11/24/opinion/sunday/coates-in-defense-of-a-loaded-word.html.

19. German Lopez, "Ta-Nehisi Coates Has an Incredibly Clear Explanation for Why White People Shouldn't Use the N-Word," *Vox,* November 9, 2017, www.vox.com/identities/2017/11/9/16627900/ta-nehisi-coates-n-word.

20. Coates, "In Defense."

21. Henry Reichman, *Understanding Academic Freedom* (Baltimore: Johns Hopkins University Press, 2021), 64–65. Examples Reichman cites of administrative overreaction to student complaints include the widely reported 2020 firing of an adjunct faculty member at the University of Southern California Marshall School of Business for saying a Chinese word "that could sound similar to the English N-word, but means something entirely different" (68) and an effort by administrators at the University of Waterloo in Canada to issue an outright ban on the word, drawing objections from Black faculty (65).

For an overview and analysis of recent misguided and damaging administrative actions on this issue, see Kimberly A. Yuracko, "When Administrators Make Mistakes," *Chronicle of Higher Education,* December 29, 2021, www.chronicle.com/article/when-administrators-make-mistakes.

22. Peter Lurie, "Editorial Statement—Racial Quoting," *Faulkner Journal* 32, no. 2 (Fall 2018): 193.

Bibliography

Abadie, Ann, and Annette Trefzer, eds. *Faulkner's Sexualities: Faulkner and Yoknapatawpha 2007.* Jackson: University Press of Mississippi, 2010.
Abelove, Henry, Michèle Aina Barale, and David M. Halperin, eds. *The Lesbian and Gay Studies Reader.* New York: Routledge, 1993.
Adorno, Theodor. *Aesthetic Theory.* Translated and edited by Robert Hullot-Kentor. Minneapolis: University of Minnesota Press, 1997.
———. *Negative Dialectics.* Translated by E. B. Ashton. New York: Continuum, 1973.
———. "On the Fetish Character in Music and the Regression of Listening." In *The Culture Industry,* edited by J. M. Bernstein, 26–52. New York: Routledge, 1991.
———. *Quasi una Fantasia: Essays on Modern Music.* Translated by Rodney Livingstone. New York: Verso, 1998.
Adorno, Theodor, and Max Horkheimer. *Dialectic of Enlightenment: Philosophical Fragments.* Edited by Gunzelin Schmid Noerr; translated by Edmund Jephcott. Stanford, CA: Stanford University Press, 2002.
Aldrich, Robert. *Colonialism and Homosexuality.* New York: Routledge, 2003.
Andrew, Dudley. *Breathless: Jean-Luc Godard, Director.* New Brunswick, NJ: Rutgers University Press, 1988.
Arbery, Glenn Cannon. "Victims of Likeness: Quadroons and Octoroons in Southern Fiction." In *Interracialism: Black-White Intermarriage in American History, Literature, and Law,* edited by Werner Sollors, 393–407. New York: Oxford University Press, 2000.
Baker, Houston A., Jr. *Modernism and the Harlem Renaissance.* Chicago: University of Chicago Press, 1987.
Baldwin, James. *James Baldwin: Collected Essays.* Edited by Toni Morrison. New York: Library of America, 1998.
Barnes, Elizabeth. *States of Sympathy: Seduction and Democracy in the American Novel.* New York: Columbia University Press, 1997.
Barnhisel, Greg. "Packaging Faulkner as a Cold War Modernist." In *Faulkner and Print*

Culture: Faulkner and Yoknapatawpha 2015, edited by Jay Watson, Jaime Harker, and James G. Thomas, Jr., 158–74. Jackson: University Press of Mississippi, 2017.

Barthes, Roland. *Empire of Signs.* Translated by Richard Howard. New York: Hill and Wang, Noonday Press, 1982.

Bassett, John, ed. *William Faulkner: The Critical Heritage.* London: Routledge and Kegan Paul, 1975.

Benjamin, Walter. *Illuminations.* Edited by Hannah Arendt; translated by Harry Zohn. New York: Schocken, 1969.

Berlant, Lauren. *The Female Complaint: The Unfinished Business of Sentimentality in American Culture.* Durham, NC: Duke University Press, 2008.

Bibler, Michael P. *Cotton's Queer Relations: Same-Sex Intimacy and the Literature of the Southern Plantation, 1936–1968.* Charlottesville: University of Virginia Press, 2009.

Bleikasten, André. *The Ink of Melancholy: Faulkner's Novels from "The Sound and the Fury" to "Light in August."* Bloomington: Indiana University Press, 1990.

———. *The Most Splendid Failure: Faulkner's "The Sound and the Fury."* Bloomington: Indiana University Press, 1976.

Blotner, Joseph. *Faulkner: A Biography.* 2 vols. New York: Random House, 1974.

Boudreau, Kristin. *Sympathy in American Literature: American Sentiments from Jefferson to the Jameses.* Gainesville: University Press of Florida, 2002.

Bourdieu, Pierre. *The Rules of Art: Genesis and Structure of the Literary Field.* Translated by Susan Emmanuel. Stanford, CA: Stanford University Press, 1996.

Branch, Taylor. *Parting the Waters: America in the King Years, 1954–63.* New York: Simon and Schuster, 1988.

Brooks, Cleanth. *William Faulkner: The Yoknapatawpha Country.* New Haven, CT: Yale University Press, 1963.

Brown, Norman O. *Life Against Death.* Middletown, CT: Wesleyan University Press, 1959.

Bullock, Steven C. *Revolutionary Brotherhood: Freemasonry and the Transformation of the American Social Order, 1730–1840.* Chapel Hill: University of North Carolina Press, 1996.

Burgett, Bruce. *Sentimental Bodies: Sex, Gender, and Citizenship in the Early Republic.* Princeton, NJ: Princeton University Press, 1998.

Burstein, Andrew. *Sentimental Democracy: The Evolution of America's Romantic Self-Image.* New York: Farrar, Straus and Giroux, 1999.

Butler, Judith. *Gender Trouble.* 1990. New York: Routledge 1999.

———. *The Psychic Life of Power: Theories in Subjection.* Stanford, CA: Stanford University Press, 1997.

Casanova, Pascale. *The World Republic of Letters.* Translated by M. B. DeBevoise. Cambridge, MA: Harvard University Press, 2004.

Chapman, Mary, and Glenn Hendler, eds. *Sentimental Men: Masculinity and the Politics of Affect in American Culture.* Berkeley: University of California Press, 1999.

Clark, Suzanne. *Sentimental Modernism: Women Writers and the Revolution of the Word.* Bloomington: Indiana University Press, 1991.
Clawson, Mary Ann. *Constructing Brotherhood: Class, Gender, and Fraternalism.* Princeton, NJ: Princeton University Press, 1989.
Cleto, Fabio, ed. *Camp: Queer Aesthetics and the Performing Subject.* Ann Arbor: University of Michigan Press, 1999.
Coffin, Levi. *Reminiscences of Levi Coffin. 1898.* New York: Arno, 1968.
Cohn, Deborah N. "Combating Anti-Americanism during the Cold War: Faulkner, the State Department, and Latin America." *Mississippi Quarterly* 59, no. 3-4 (Summer/Fall 2006): 396-413.
———. "Faulkner, Latin America, and the Caribbean: Influence, Politics, and Academic Disciplines." In *A Companion to William Faulkner,* edited by Richard C. Moreland, 499-518. Malden, MA: Blackwell, 2007.
———. "William Faulkner's Ibero-American Novel Project: The Politics of Translation and the Cold War." *Southern Quarterly* 42, no. 1 (Winter 2004): 5-18.
Coindreau, Maurice Edgar. *The Time of William Faulkner: A French View of Modern American Fiction.* Translated by George McMillan Reeves. Columbia: University of South Carolina Press, 1971.
Cowley, Malcolm. *The Faulkner-Cowley File: Letters and Memories, 1944-1962.* Harmondsworth, UK: Penguin, 1978.
Crawford, Dorothy L. *A Windfall of Musicians: Hitler's Émigrés and Exiles in Southern California.* New Haven, CT: Yale University Press, 2009.
Creadick, Anna. "Reading Faulkner's Readers: Reputation and the Postwar Reading Revolution." In *Faulkner and History: Faulkner and Yoknapatawpha 2014,* edited by Jay Watson and James G. Thomas Jr., 158-76. Jackson: University Press of Mississippi, 2017.
Creighton, Joanne V. *William Faulkner's Craft of Revision: The Snopes Trilogy, "The Unvanquished," and "Go Down, Moses."* Detroit: Wayne State University Press, 1977.
Darling, Marsha Jean. "In the Realm of Responsibility: A Conversation with Toni Morrison." *Women's Review of Books* 5, no. 6 (March 1988): 5-6.
Davenport-Hines, Richard. *Auden.* New York: Pantheon, 1995.
Davidson, Arnold I. *The Emergence of Sexuality: Historical Epistemology and the Formation of Concepts.* Cambridge, MA: Harvard University Press, 2001.
Davis, Thadious M. *Faulkner's "Negro": Art and the Southern Context.* Baton Rouge: Louisiana State University Press, 1982.
———. *Games of Property: Law, Race, Gender, and Faulkner's "Go Down, Moses."* Durham, NC: Duke University Press, 2003.
Dawson, Jeff. *Quentin Tarantino: The Cinema of Cool.* New York: Applause, 1995.
Dean, Tim. "Art as Symptom: Žižek and the Ethics of Psychoanalytic Criticism." *diacritics* 32, no. 2 (Summer 2002): 22.
———. *Beyond Sexuality.* Chicago: University of Chicago Press, 2000.

Dean, Tim, and Christopher Lane, eds. *Homosexuality and Psychoanalysis.* Chicago: University of Chicago Press, 2001.

Deleuze, Gilles, and Félix Guattari. *Anti-Oedipus: Capitalism and Schizophrenia.* Translated by Robert Hurley, Mark Seem, and Helen R. Lane. New York: Viking, 1977.

Derrida, Jacques. *Writing and Difference.* Translated by Alan Bass. Chicago: University of Chicago Press, 1978.

Douglas, Ann. *The Feminization of American Culture.* 1977. New York: Doubleday, 1988.

Dudziak, Mary L. *Cold War Civil Rights: Race and the Image of American Democracy* Princeton, NJ: Princeton University Press, 2002.

Dumenil, Lynn. *Freemasonry and American Culture, 1880–1930.* Princeton, NJ: Princeton University Press, 1984.

Duvall, John N. "Authentic Ghost Stories: *Uncle Tom's Cabin, Absalom, Absalom!,* and *Beloved.*" *Faulkner Journal* 4, no. 1–2 (Fall 1988–Spring 1989): 83–97.

———. *Faulkner's Marginal Couple: Invincible, Outlaw, and Unspeakable Communities.* Austin: University of Texas Press, 1990.

Earle, David M. "Faulkner and the Paperback Trade." In *William Faulkner in Context,* edited by John T. Matthews, 231–45. New York: Cambridge University Press, 2015.

———. "Yoknapatawphan Pulp, or What Faulkner *Really* Read at the P.O." In *Fifty Years after Faulkner: Faulkner and Yoknapatawpha 2012,* edited by Jay Watson and Ann J. Abadie, 31–45. Jackson: University Press of Mississippi, 2016.

Early, James. *The Making of "Go Down, Moses."* Dallas, TX: Southern Methodist University Press, 1972.

Edelman, Lee. *Homographesis: Essays in Gay Literary and Cultural Theory.* New York: Routledge, 1994.

———. *No Future: Queer Theory and the Death Drive.* Durham, NC: Duke University Press, 2004.

Ellis, Markman. *The Politics of Sensibility: Race, Gender, and Commerce in the Sentimental Novel.* New York: Cambridge University Press, 1996.

Eschenbach, Wolfram von. *Parzifal.* Translated by T. Hatto. Harmondsworth, UK: Penguin, 1980.

Faulkner, William. *Absalom, Absalom! The Corrected Text.* Edited by Noel Polk. New York: Vintage International, 1990.

———. *Collected Stories.* New York: Vintage, 1977.

———. *Flags in the Dust.* Edited by Douglas Day. New York: Vintage, 1974.

———. *Go Down, Moses.* 1942. New York: Vintage International, 1990.

———. *The Hamlet: The Corrected Text.* Edited by Noel Polk. New York: Vintage International, 1991.

———. *If I Forget Thee, Jerusalem.* New York: Vintage International, 1990.

———. "An Introduction for *The Sound and the Fury.*" Edited by James B. Meriwether.

Southern Review 8 (1972): 705–10. Reprinted in *The Sound and the Fury,* ed. Minter, 225–28.

———. "An Introduction to *The Sound and the Fury.*" Edited by James B. Meriwether. *Mississippi Quarterly* 26, no. 3 (Summer 1973): 410–15. Reprinted in *The Sound and the Fury,* ed. Minter, 228–32.

———. *Les palmiers sauvages.* Translated by Maurice-Edgar Coindreau. Paris: Éditions Gallimard, 1952.

———. *Light in August: The Corrected Text.* Edited by Noel Polk. New York: Vintage International, 1990.

———. *The Portable Faulkner.* Edited by Malcolm Cowley. New York: Viking, 1946.

———. *Selected Letters.* Edited by Joseph Blotner. New York: Random House, 1977.

———. *Si je t'oublie, Jérusalem.* Translated by Maurice-Edgar Coindreau and François Pitavy. Paris: Éditions Gallimard, 2001.

———. *The Sound and the Fury: The Corrected Text.* Edited by Noel Polk. New York: Vintage International, 1990.

———. *The Sound and the Fury: An Authoritative Text, Backgrounds and Contexts, Criticism.* 2nd ed. Edited by David Minter. New York: Norton, 1994.

———. *The Sound and the Fury: An Authoritative Text, Backgrounds and Contexts, Criticism.* 3rd ed. Edited by Michael Gorra. New York: Norton, 2014.

———. *The Wild Palms.* New York: Random House, 1939.

———. *William Faulkner: Early Prose and Poetry.* Edited by Carvel Collins. Boston: Little, Brown, 1962.

———. *William Faulkner: Essays, Speeches, and Public Letters.* Edited by James B. Meriwether. 1965. Updated. New York: Modern Library, 2004.

———. *William Faulkner: New Orleans Sketches.* Edited by Carvel Collins. London: Chatto and Windus, 1958.

Ferguson, Roderick A. *Aberrations in Black: Toward a Queer of Color Critique.* Minneapolis: University of Minnesota Press, 2004.

Foucault, Michel. "The West and the Truth of Sex." Translated by Daniel W. Smith. In *Homosexuality and Psychoanalysis,* edited by Tim Dean and Christopher Lane. Chicago: University of Chicago Press, 2001.

Fowler, Doreen. *Faulkner: The Return of the Repressed.* Charlottesville: University Press of Virginia, 1997.

Fowler, Doreen, and Ann J. Abadie, eds. *Faulkner and Popular Culture: Faulkner and Yoknapatawpha: 1988.* Jackson: University Press of Mississippi, 1990.

———. *Faulkner and Race: Faulkner and Yoknapatawpha, 1986.* Jackson: University Press of Mississippi, 1987.

———. *Faulkner and Women: Faulkner and Yoknapatawpha 1985.* Jackson: University Press of Mississippi, 1986.

Frank, Joseph. *The Widening Gyre: Crisis and Mastery in Modern Literature.* Bloomington: Indiana University Press, 1968.

Freud, Sigmund. *Three Essays on the Theory of Sexuality.* In *The Standard Edition of the Complete Psychological Works of Sigmund Freud,* edited and translated by James Strachey et al. London: Hogarth, 1953.

Furry, William. "Faulkner in a Haystack: The Search for William Faulkner's Television Adaptations of 'The Brooch' and 'Shall Not Perish.'" *Faulkner Journal* 16, no. 1-2 (Fall 2000/Spring 2001): 119-48.

Gates, Henry Louis, Jr. *Figures in Black: Words, Signs, and the Racial Self.* New York: Oxford University Press, 1987.

———. *The Signifying Monkey: A Theory of African-American Literary Criticism.* New York: Oxford University Press, 1988.

Gilroy, Paul. *The Black Atlantic.* Cambridge, MA: Harvard University Press, 1993.

Gleeson-White, Sarah. "Faulkner Goes to Hollywood." In *William Faulkner in Context,* edited by John T. Matthews, 194-203. New York: Cambridge University Press, 2015.

Godden, Richard. "*Absalom, Absalom!,* Haiti and Labor History: Reading Unreadable Revolutions." *ELH* 61, no. 3 (Fall 1994): 685-720.

———. *Fictions of Labor: William Faulkner and the South's Long Revolution.* Cambridge: Cambridge University Press, 1997.

Godden, Richard, and Noel Polk. "Reading the Ledgers." *Mississippi Quarterly* 55, no. 3 (2002): 301-59.

Gorra, Michael. *The Saddest Words: William Faulkner's Civil War.* New York: Liveright 2020.

Goldberg, Jonathan, and Madhavi Menon, "Queering History." *Publications of the Modern Language Association* 120, no. 5 (October 2005): 1608-17.

Gordon, Phillip. *Gay Faulkner: Uncovering a Homosexual Presence in Yoknapatawpha and Beyond.* Jackson: University Press of Mississippi, 2020.

Gray, Richard. *The Life of William Faulkner: A Critical Biography.* Oxford: Blackwell, 1994.

Grimwood, Michael. *Heart in Conflict: Faulkner's Struggles with Vocation.* Athens: University of Georgia Press, 1987.

Grout, Donald Jay. *A History of Western Music.* Rev. ed. New York: Norton, 1973.

Guback, Thomas H. *The International Film Industry: Western Europe and America since 1945.* Bloomington: Indiana University Press, 1969.

Guillory, John. *Cultural Capital: The Problem of Literary Canon Formation.* Chicago: University of Chicago Press, 1993.

Gwin, Minrose C. *The Feminine and Faulkner: Reading (Beyond) Sexual Difference.* Knoxville: University of Tennessee Press, 1990.

———. "Feminism and Faulkner: Second Thoughts; or, What's a Radical Feminist Doing with a Canonical Male Text Anyway?" *Faulkner Journal* 4, no. 1–2 (Fall 1988/Spring 1989; published Fall 1991): 55–65.

Gwynn, Frederick L., and Joseph L. Blotner, eds. *Faulkner in the University: Class Conferences at the University of Virginia, 1957–1958.* With an introduction by Douglas Day. 1959. Charlottesville: University Press of Virginia, 1995.

Hale, Grace Elizabeth, and Robert Jackson, "'We're Trying Hard as Hell to Free Ourselves': Southern History and Race in the Making of William Faulkner's Literary Terrain." In *A Companion to William Faulkner,* edited by Richard E. Moreland. Malden, MA: Blackwell, 2007.

Harker, Jaime. "Queer Faulkner: Whores, Queers, and the Transgressive South." In *The New Cambridge Companion to William Faulkner,* edited by John T. Matthews, 107–18. New York: Cambridge University Press, 2015.

———. "*The Wild Palms, The Mansion,* and Faulkner's Middlebrow Domestic Fiction." In *Faulkner and Print Culture: Faulkner and Yoknapatawpha 2015,* edited by Jay Watson, Jaime Harker, and James G. Thomas Jr., 203–15. Jackson: University Press of Mississippi, 2017.

Harper, Phillip Brian. *Are We Not Men? Masculine Anxiety and the Problem of African-American Identity.* Oxford: Oxford University Press, 1996.

Harris, Middleton. *The Black Book.* With the assistance of Morris Levitt, Roger Furman, and Ernest Smith. New York: Random House, 1974.

Hillier, Jim, ed. *Cahiers du Cinéma: The 1950s: Neo-Realism, Hollywood, New Wave.* Cambridge, MA: Harvard University Press, 1985.

Hixson, Walter L. *Parting the Curtain: Propaganda, Culture, and the Cold War, 1945–1961.* New York: St. Martin's, 1997.

Hoffman, Frederick J., and Olga W. Vickery, eds. *William Faulkner: Two Decades of Criticism.* East Lansing: Michigan State College Press, 1951.

hooks, bell. *Reel to Real: Race, Sex, and Class at the Movies.* New York: Routledge, 1996.

Horvitz, Deborah. "Nameless Ghosts: Possession and Dispossession in *Beloved.*" *Studies in American Fiction* 17, no. 2 (autumn 1989): 157–67.

Howard, John. *Men Like That: A Southern Queer History.* Chicago: University of Chicago Press, 1999.

Hutchinson, George. "Tracking Faulkner in the Paths of Black Modernism." In *Faulkner and the Black Literatures of the Americas: Faulkner and Yoknapatawpha 2016,* edited by Jay Watson and James G. Thomas Jr., 59–73. Jackson: University Press of Mississippi, 2016.

Huyssen, Andreas. *After the Great Divide: Modernism, Mass Culture, Postmodernism.* Bloomington: Indiana University Press, 1986.

Irwin, John T. *Doubling and Incest, Repetition and Revenge: A Speculative Reading of Faulkner.* 1975. Expanded ed. Baltimore: Johns Hopkins University Press, 1996.

Jacobs, Harriet. *Incidents in the Life of a Slave Girl*. 1861. Edited by Jean Fagan Yellin. Cambridge, MA: Harvard University Press, 1987.

Jameson, Fredric. *The Political Unconscious: Narrative as a Socially Symbolic Act*. Ithaca, NY: Cornell University Press, 1981.

———. *Postmodernism; or, The Cultural Logic of Late Capitalism*. Durham, NC: Duke University Press, 1991.

Jehlen, Myra. *Class and Character in Faulkner's South*. New York: Columbia University Press, 1976.

Karl, Frederick R. *William Faulkner: American Writer*. New York: Weidenfeld and Nicolson, 1989.

Kartiganer, Donald M., and Ann J. Abadie, eds. *Faulkner and Gender: Faulkner and Yoknapatawpha 1994*. Jackson: University Press of Mississippi, 1996.

———. *Faulkner and the Natural World: Faulkner and Yoknapatawpha, 1996*. Jackson: University Press of Mississippi, 1999.

———. *Faulkner at 100: Retrospect and Prospect: Faulkner and Yoknapatawpha, 1997*. Jackson: University Press of Virginia, 2000.

Kawin, Bruce. *Faulkner and Film*. New York: Frederick Ungar, 1977.

Kennedy, Randall. *Nigger: The Strange Career of a Troublesome Word*. 2002. New York: Vintage, 2003.

Kline, T. Jefferson. *Screening the Text: Intertextuality in New Wave French Cinema*. Baltimore: Johns Hopkins University Press, 1992.

Kodat, Catherine Gunther. *Don't Act, Just Dance: The Metapolitics of Cold War Culture*. New Brunswick, NJ: Rutgers University Press, 2015.

Koestler, Arthur. *The Trail of the Dinosaur and Other Essays*. London: Collins, 1955.

Kolmerten, Carol A., Stephen M. Ross, and Judith Bryant Wittenberg, eds. *Unflinching Gaze: Morrison and Faulkner Re-Envisioned*. Jackson: University Press of Mississippi, 1997.

Lacan, Jacques. *The Four Fundamental Concepts of Psychoanalysis*. Edited by Jacques-Alain Miller; translated by Alan Sheridan. New York: Norton, 1978.

Laplanche, Jean, and Jean-Baptiste Pontalis. *The Language of Psycho-Analysis*. Translated by Donald Nicholson-Smith. New York: Norton, 1973

Lasch, Christopher. *The Agony of the American Left*. New York: Knopf, 1969.

Lester, Cheryl. "To Market, to Market: *The Portable Faulkner*." *Criticism: A Quarterly for Literature and the Arts* 29 (1987): 371–89.

Levinson, Marjorie. "The Changing Profession: What Is New Formalism?" *Publications of the Modern Language Association* 122, no. 2 (March 2007): 558–69.

Lévi-Strauss, Claude. *The Elementary Structures of Kinship*. 1949. Rev. ed. Translated by James Harle Bell; edited by John Richard Von Sturmer and Rodney Needham. Boston: Beacon, 1969.

Lewis, Charles. "The Ironic Romance of New Historicism: *The Scarlet Letter* and *Beloved.*" *Arizona Quarterly* 51, no. 1 (Spring 1995): 33

Lott, Eric. *Love and Theft: Blackface Minstrelsy and the American Working Class.* New York: Oxford University Press, 1993.

Lurie, Peter. *Vision's Immanence: Faulkner, Film, and the Popular Imagination.* Baltimore: Johns Hopkins University Press, 2004.

MacDonald, J. Fred. *Blacks and White TV: Afro-Americans in Television since 1948.* Chicago: Nelson-Hall, 1983.

Matthews, John T, ed. *The New Cambridge Companion to William Faulkner.* New York: Cambridge University Press, 2015.

———. *The Play of Faulkner's Language.* Ithaca, NY: Cornell University Press, 1982.

———. "Recalling the West Indies: From Yoknapatawpha to Haiti and Back." *American Literary History* 16, no. 2 (Summer 2004): 238–62.

———. *The Sound and the Fury: Faulkner and the Lost Cause.* Boston: Twayne, 1991.

———. *William Faulkner: Seeing through the South.* Oxford: Wiley-Blackwell, 2009.

McHaney, Thomas. *William Faulkner's "The Wild Palms": A Study.* Jackson: University Press of Mississippi, 1975.

Merish, Lori. *Sentimental Materialism: Gender, Commodity Culture, and Nineteenth-Century American Literature.* Durham, NC: Duke University Press, 2000.

Meriwether, James B., and Michael Millgate, eds. *Lion in the Garden: Interviews with William Faulkner, 1926–1962.* New York: Random House, 1968.

Millgate, Michael. *The Achievement of William Faulkner.* 1966. Athens: University of Georgia Press, 1989.

Milne, Tom. *Godard on Godard.* 1972. Cambridge, MA: Da Capo, 1986.

Moreland, Richard C., ed. *A Companion to William Faulkner.* Malden, MA: Blackwell, 2007.

———. *Faulkner and Modernism: Rereading and Rewriting.* Madison: University of Wisconsin Press, 1990.

———. "'He Wants to Put His Story Next to Hers': Putting Twain's Story Next to Hers in Morrison's *Beloved.*" *Modern Fiction Studies* 39, no. 3–4 (Fall/Winter 1993): 501–25.

Morrison, Paul. *The Explanation for Everything: Essays on Sexual Subjectivity.* New York: New York University Press, 2001.

Morrison, Toni. *Beloved.* New York: Knopf, 1987.

———. "Faulkner and Women." In *Faulkner and Women: Faulkner and Yoknapatawpha 1985*, edited by Doreen Fowler and Ann J. Abadie, 296–97. Jackson: University Press of Mississippi, 1986.

———. *Playing in the Dark.* Cambridge, MA: Harvard University Press, 1992.

———. *The Source of Self-Regard: Selected Essays, Speeches, and Meditations.* New York: Knopf, 2019.

Mumford, Kevin. *Interzones: Black/White Sex Districts in Chicago and New York in the Early 20th Century.* New York: Columbia University Press, 1997.

Muñoz, José Esteban. *Disidentifications: Queers of Color and the Performance of Politics.* Minneapolis: University of Minnesota Press, 1999.

Murphet, Julian, and Stefan Solomon, eds. *William Faulkner in the Media Ecology.* Baton Rouge: Louisiana State University Press, 2015.

Murray, Albert, and John F. Callahan, eds. *Trading Twelves: The Selected Letters of Ralph Ellison and Albert Murray.* 2000. New York: Vintage, 2001.

Nadel, Alan. "'We—He and Us—Should Confederate': Stylistic Inversion in *Intruder in the Dust* and Faulkner's Cold War Agenda." In *Fifty Years after Faulkner: Faulkner and Yoknapatawpha 2012,* edited by Jay Watson and Ann J. Abadie. Jackson: University Press of Mississippi, 2016.

Nelson, Elizabeth White. *Market Sentiments: Middle-Class Market Culture in Nineteenth-Century America.* Washington, DC: Smithsonian Institution Press, 2004.

Newton, Esther. *Mother Camp: Female Impersonators in America.* Chicago: University of Chicago Press, 1979.

Oakley, Helen. "William Faulkner and the Cold War: The Politics of Cultural Marketing." In *Look Away! The U.S. South in New World Studies,* edited by Jon Smith and Deborah Cohn. Durham, NC: Duke University Press, 2004.

Patterson, Orlando. *Slavery and Social Death: A Comparative Study.* Cambridge, MA: Harvard University Press, 1982.

Pèrez-Torres, Rafael. "Knitting and Knotting the Narrative Thread—*Beloved* as Postmodern Novel." *Modern Fiction Studies* 39, no. 3-4 (Fall/Winter 1993): 689-707.

Phelan, James. "Toward a Rhetorical Reader-Response Criticism: The Difficult, the Stubborn, and the Ending of *Beloved.*" *Modern Fiction Studies* 39, no. 3-4 (Fall/Winter 1993): 709-28.

Polsgrove, Carol. *Divided Minds: Intellectuals and the Civil Rights Movement.* New York: Norton, 2001.

Prendergast, Roy M. *Film Music: A Neglected Art.* 2nd ed. New York: Norton, 1992.

Quilligan, Maureen. *The Language of Allegory: Defining the Genre.* 1979. Ithaca, NY: Cornell University Press, 1992.

Railton, Stephen, and Michael Plunkett, eds. *Faulkner at Virginia: An Audio Archive.* http://faulkner.lib.virginia.edu.

Rampersad, Arnold. *Ralph Ellison: A Biography.* New York: Knopf, 2007.

Ramsay, D. Matthew. "'Turnabout' Is Fair(y) Play: Faulkner's Queer War Story." *Faulkner Journal* 15, no. 1-2 (Fall 1999/Spring 2000): 61-81.

Rancière, Jacques. *Dissensus: On Politics and Aesthetics.* Edited and translated by Steven Corcoran. New York: Continuum International, 2010.

———. *The Future of the Image.* Translated by Gregory Elliott. 2003. New York: Verso, 2007.

Reichman, Henry. *Understanding Academic Freedom.* Baltimore: Johns Hopkins University Press, 2021.

Reid-Pharr, Robert. *Black Gay Man: Essays.* New York: New York University Press, 2001.

——. *Conjugal Union: The Body, the House, and the Black American.* New York: Oxford University Press, 1999.

Resche, John Phillips. *Suffering Soldiers: Revolutionary War Veterans, Moral Sentiment, and Political Culture in the Early Republic.* Amherst: University of Massachusetts Press, 1999.

Rhodes, Pamela. "'I Remember Them Letters': Byron Snopes and Interference." In *Faulkner's Discourse: An International Symposium,* edited by Lothar Hönnighausen, 77–89. Tübingen: Max Neimeyer, 1989.

Rhodes, Pamela E., and Richard Godden. "*The Wild Palms:* Degraded Culture, Devalued Texts." In *Intertextuality in Faulkner,* edited by Michel Gresset and Noel Polk. Jackson: University Press of Mississippi, 1985.

Roberts, Diane. *Faulkner and Southern Womanhood.* Athens: University of Georgia Press, 1994.

Rosen, Charles. *Arnold Schoenberg.* Chicago: University of Chicago Press, 1996.

Ross, Alex. *The Rest Is Noise: Listening to the Twentieth Century.* New York: Farrar, Straus and Giroux, 2007.

Runyan, Harry. *A Faulkner Glossary.* New York: Citadel, 1964.

Samuels, Shirley, ed. *The Culture of Sentiment: Race, Gender, and Sentimentality in Nineteenth-Century America.* New York: Oxford University Press, 1992.

Saunders, Frances Stoner. *The Cultural Cold War: The CIA and the World of Arts and Letters.* New York: New Press, 2000.

Schoenberg, Arnold. *Arnold Schoenberg: Letters.* Edited by Erwin Stein. Translated by Eithne Wilkins and Ernst Kaiser. Berkeley: University of California Press, 1987.

——. *Style and Idea: Selected Writings of Arnold Schoenberg. 1975.* Berkeley: University of California Press, 1984.

Schwartz, Lawrence. *Creating Faulkner's Reputation: The Politics of Modern Literary Criticism.* Knoxville: University of Tennessee Press, 1988.

Sedgwick, Eve Kosofsky. *Tendencies.* London: Routledge, 1993.

Sensibar, Judith L. *Faulkner and Love: The Women Who Shaped His Art.* New Haven, CT: Yale University Press, 2009.

Snead, James. *Figures of Division: William Faulkner's Major Novels.* New York: Methuen, 1986.

Sollors, Werner, ed. *Interracialism: Black-White Intermarriage in American History, Literature, and Law.* New York: Oxford University Press, 2000.

Sontag, Susan. *Against Interpretation and Other Essays.* 1966. New York: Macmillan/Picador, 2001.

———. "Notes on Camp." In *Camp: Queer Aesthetics and the Performing Subject*, edited by Fabio Cleto, 53–65. Ann Arbor: University of Michigan Press, 1999.

Stecopoulos, Harilaos. "William Faulkner and the Problem of Cold War Modernism." In *Faulkner's Geographies: Faulkner and Yoknapatawph 2011*, edited by Jay Watson and Ann J. Abadie, 143–62. Jackson: University Press of Mississippi, 2015.

Stewart, Susan. *Crimes of Writing: Problems in the Containment of Representation*. New York: Oxford University Press, 1991.

Stryz, Jan. "The Other Ghost in *Beloved*: The Spectre of *The Scarlet Letter*." *Genre* 24, no. 4 (Winter 1991): 417–34.

Sundquist, Eric J. *Faulkner: The House Divided*. Baltimore: Johns Hopkins University Press, 1983.

———. *To Wake the Nations: Race in the Making of American Literature*. Cambridge, MA: Belknap Press of Harvard University Press, 1998.

Taylor, Nancy Dew. *Annotations to William Faulkner's "Go Down, Moses."* New York: Garland, 1994.

Taylor, Ronald, trans. and ed. *Aesthetics and Politics: Theodor Adorno, Walter Benjamin, Ernst Block, Bertolt Brecht, Georg Lukács*. New York: Verso, 1995.

Todd, Janet. *Sensibility: An Introduction*. New York: Methuen, 1986.

Tompkins, Jane P. *Sensational Designs: The Cultural Work of American Fiction, 1790–1860*. New York: Oxford University Press, 1985.

Torres, Sasha. *Black, White, and in Color: Television and Black Civil Rights*. Princeton, NJ: Princeton University Press, 2003.

Towner, Theresa M., and James B. Carothers. *Reading Faulkner: Collected Stories*. Jackson: University Press of Mississippi, 2006.

Urgo, Joseph. *Faulkner's Apocrypha: "A Fable," "Snopes," and the Spirit of Human Rebellion*. Jackson: University Press of Mississippi, 1989.

Urgo, Joseph R., and Ann J. Abadie, eds. *Faulkner in America: Faulkner and Yoknapatawpha, 1998*. Jackson: University Press of Mississippi, 2001.

Van Der Zee, James, Owen Dodson, and Camille Billops. *The Harlem Book of the Dead*. Dobbs Ferry, NY: Morgan and Morgan, 1978.

Vickery, Olga. *The Novels of William Faulkner: A Critical Interpretation*. Baton Rouge: Louisiana State University Press, 1959.

Watson, Jay. Introduction to *Faulkner and the Black Literatures of the Americas: Faulkner and Yoknapatawpha 2013*, vii–xxiv. Jackson: University Press of Mississippi, 2016.

Watson, Jay, and Ann J. Abadie, eds. *Faulkner's Geographies: Faulkner and Yoknapatawpha 2011*. Jackson: University Press of Mississippi, 2015.

———. *Fifty Years after Faulkner: Faulkner and Yoknapatawpha 2012*. Jackson: University Press of Mississippi 2016.

Watson, Jay, Jaime Harker, and James G. Thomas Jr., eds. *Faulkner and Print Culture: Faulkner and Yoknapatawpha 2015*. Jackson: University Press of Mississippi, 2015.

Watson, Jay, and James G. Thomas Jr., eds. *Faulkner and the Black Literatures of the Americas: Faulkner and Yoknapatawpha 2013.* Jackson: University Press of Mississippi 2016.

———. *Faulkner and History: Faulkner and Yoknapatawpha 2014.* Jackson: University Press of Mississippi, 2017.

Weinstein, Philip, ed. *The Cambridge Companion to William Faulkner.* Cambridge: Cambridge University Press, 1995.

———. *Faulkner's Subject: A Cosmos No One Owns.* Cambridge: Cambridge University Press, 1992.

———. *Unknowing: The Work of Modernist Fiction.* Ithaca, NY: Cornell University Press, 2005.

———. *What Else but Love? The Ordeal of Race in Faulkner and Morrison.* New York: Columbia University Press, 1996.

Wilde, Meta C., and Oren W. Borsten. *A Loving Gentleman: The Love Story of William Faulkner and Meta Carpenter.* New York: Simon and Schuster, 1976.

Williamson, Joel. *William Faulkner and Southern History.* New York: Oxford University Press, 1993.

Willis, Sharon. "The Fathers Watch the Boys' Room." *Camera obscura* 2, no. 32 (1993): 41–74.

Wofford, Chloe Ardellia [Toni Morrison]. "Virginia Woolf's and William Faulkner's Treatment of the Alienated." A Thesis Presented to the Faculty of the Graduate School of Cornell University for the Degree of Master of Arts, September 1955.

Wolitzer, Meg, and Christopher Niemann. "Two Things That Depress Me When I Open a Novel." *New York Times Book Review,* February 6, 2000.

Woidat, Caroline M. "Talking Back to Schoolteacher: Morrison's Confrontation with Hawthorne in *Beloved.*" *Modern Fiction Studies* 39, no. 3–4 (Fall/Winter 1993): 527–46.

Woods, Paul. *King Pulp: The Wild World of Quentin Tarantino.* New York: Thunder's Mouth, 1996.

Yanuck, Julius. "The Garner Fugitive Slave Case." *Mississippi Valley Historical Review* 40, no. 1 (June 1953): 47–66.

Žižek, Slavoj. "'The Wound Is Healed Only by the Spear That Smote You': The Operatic Subject and Its Vicissitudes." In *Opera through Other Eyes,* edited by David. J. Levin, 177–214. Stanford: Stanford University Press, 1994.

Index

Abelove, Henry, 185–86
abolitionists, 96–97, 255n9
A bout de souffle (film), 44, 131–35, 148, 151–55, 229n23
Absalom, Absalom! (Faulkner), 22–25, 85–106, 108, 246n26, 247n44, 260n32
actual and apocryphal, 108, 111–14, 123–24, 249n12. *See also* sublimation
Adorno, Theodor, 54, 75–76, 87, 140–41, 193, 233–34n20, 244n8
advertising, 208–11
aestheticism, 47–48, 88, 102–3, 109, 133, 155, 161, 163, 211, 244n12, 248n5, 248n7, 251n26
African Americans: Black characters in Faulkner, 40–42, 245n20; and the canon, 217; and desegregation, 77–79; and failure of *Go Down, Moses*, 178; and Faulkner studies, 105–6; Faulkner studies and Black authors, 26–27, 81–82; and history and high modernist techniques, 87–88; and homosexuality, 160–61; and masculinity, 41; and reclamation of history, 98–99; signifying tradition, 85, 94, 105, 243n1; and television, 205, 213–14
Africanist aesthetics and modernism, 88, 93–95, 101
After the Great Divide (Huyssen), 139, 235n27
alienation, 90–91
allegoresis, 55

allegory, 21, 52, 55–59, 61
allusion, 52–53. *See also* Grail myth
"American Literature through French Eyes" (Peyre), 50
Amos 'n' Andy (television show), 208
ancient tragedy, 10
Andrew, Dudley, 152
anecdote, as inspiration for *The Sound and the Fury*, 7–10
Anglo-American modernism, 94
anticommunism, 47–48, 55, 73
Anti-Oedipus (Deleuze and Guattari), 184
antipsychologism, 185
apocrypha, 111–13, 123, 249n12
"apocryphal homosexuality," 199
"Appendix: Compson" (Faulkner), 111, 138
apprenticeship. *See* literary apprenticeship
art. *See* commerce and art
"Art as Symptom" (Dean), 188–89
Asante, Molefi Kete, 256n11
As I Lay Dying (Faulkner), 18, 24–25, 26, 114, 163
associative reading, 188–89, 192, 196–97
Athens, ancient, 160
Atwood, Margaret, 103
Auden, W. H., 71–72
aunts and uncles, 262n40
auteurs, 42, 135, 150–51, 154. *See* also *politique des auteurs*
authority. *See* cultural authority

Bacher, William, 52, 54, 65–66, 235n24
Baker, Houston A., Jr., 89
Balch Writer-in-Residence, 3–7
Baldwin, James, 80–82, 204, 257n13
Balzac, Honoré de, 20
Barnes, Elizabeth, 56–58
Baudrillard, Jean, 153
Bazin, André, 150
Bellow, Saul, 74
Beloved (Morrison), 85–106, 243nn2–4, 245n23, 246n30, 246n38
Bibler, Michael P., 200
bilateral exchange agreement, 73
biographical criticism, 21–22, 34, 158–59, 163, 198–200
biographical studies, 28. *See also* Blotner, Joseph
biology, and rhetoric, 183
Bleikasten, André, 51–52, 114, 120–21, 250n21, 251n25
Blotner, Joseph: account of cultural diplomacy, 72–74; admiration of Faulkner, 198; and everyday readers, 225n15; and *Faulkner in the University,* 3–10, 13; and Faulkner on desegregation, 77–78; and Hollywood, 54, 235n24; and Linscott, 252n30; and literary rejections of Faulkner, 250n18; narrative of Faulkner's misbehavior, 240n60; and Nobel Prize trip, 66–67; and Oppenheimer exchange, 201–5; sanitizing Faulkner's language, 221; and Swedish translations, 231n9; and teleplays, 267n8
Blum/Byrnes accord, 149
Bodies That Matter (Butler), 183
Borges, Jorge Luis, 50
Bourdieu, Pierre, 32–34, 228n9
Boyd, Todd, 42
Branch, Taylor, 208
Breathless (film), 38–39, 132, 153, 229nn22–23
Breit, Harvey, 73–74
Britton, Andrew, 177
"The Brooch" (Faulkner), 202–8
Brooks, Cleanth, 10

brotherhood, 55, 57, 59–62, 90, 172
brother-sister incest, 169
Brown, Norman O., 37
Brown decision, 76, 79
Bullock, Steven C., 59
Burns, Ken, 43–44, 229n31
Butler, Judith, 173–74, 182–84, 255n9

Cabell, James Branch, 261n34
Cahiers du Cinéma, 135, 149–51
The Cambridge Companion to William Faulkner, 53
camp, 161, 175–79, 263n49
capitalism, 23, 54–55, 57–58, 60–62, 83–84, 140–41, 205, 264n10
captivity, 143–45
Car 54, Where Are You? (television show), 213–14
careful reading, 32, 82, 265n14
Carothers, James B., 192
Carpenter, Meta, 135, 145–46
Casanova, Pascale, 26, 231n10
CCF. *See* Congress for Cultural Freedom (CCF)
censorship, 133, 208
centenary, at the University of Mississippi, 81
Chakrabarty, Dipesh, 189
chivalry, 170. *See also* Grail myth
Chrétien de Troye, 170–73, 175
Christianity and sentimentalism, 55, 58–59. *See also* *A Fable* (Faulkner)
"Chronology of William Faulkner's Life and Works" (Weinstein), 53
cinema. *See* film
civil rights movement, 16–17, 77, 81, 203–4, 208–11
The Civil War (Burns), 43–44, 229n31
class conferences, 1–10, 13, 221, 224n7, 224n9, 255n7. *See also* *Faulkner in the University*
Clawson, Mary Ann, 60
Clutch Cargo (cartoon), 35
Coates, Ta-Nehisi, 217–19
coeducation at UVA, 9

Cohn, Deborah N., 23n59, 71
Coindreau, Maurice-Edgar, 26, 50, 137–38
Cold War: and American cultural imaginary, 49, 55, 83–84; and cultural diplomacy, 66–72; and formalist criticism, 85–86; and modernism and the culture industry, 53–54, 62–64; reputation of Faulkner, 17, 25–26, 46–49, 50–51, 71, 76–77, 80–83, 103; and Schwartz, 17, 25–26, 46–49. See also *A Fable* (Faulkner); "On Privacy" (Faulkner)
Collected Stories (Faulkner), 192–96
colleges and universities, 217–19. *See also* class conferences
commerce and art, 45, 63–64, 134–35, 155
Commins, Dorothy Berliner, 201–3
Commins, Saxe, 53, 79, 138, 201–3
communism. *See* anticommunism
Congress for Cultural Freedom (CCF), 61–62, 236n40, 239n53
constructionist approach to sexuality, 182–83, 189
consumerist mass culture, 53–55
context of impact, 219
continuity editing, in narrative film, 148
contrapuntal form, in *If I Forget Thee, Jerusalem,* 136–37, 146–48
Cornell University, 82, 89–90, 247n50
corporatism, 58–62
Coughlan, Robert, 69, 207, 239n56
counterpoint, 136, 139, 148
Cowley, Malcolm, 5, 15–16, 21, 46, 110–13, 121, 123, 136–38, 232n11
Creadick, Anna, 9–10, 225n15
Creating Faulkner's Reputation (Schwartz), 17, 46–49, 76, 231n4
creative imagination, 112, 164, 233n15
critical mastery, 93, 101–2, 129, 188, 196
Crouch, Stanley, 103
cultural authority, 32, 34–35, 38–40, 93, 229n19
cultural capital, 32–35, 39, 42–44, 227n5, 228n9, 229n19, 229n23. *See also* quotation
cultural diplomacy, 67–76, 80, 83–84, 238n52
cultural disidentification, 226n20

cultural hegemony, 53–55
cultural ownership, 218–19
cultural supremacy, 50
culture and nature, 168–69
culture industry, 34, 62–64, 69, 83, 140–44, 146, 152–53, 234n20

"Damon and Pythias Unlimited" (Faulkner), 163
Darling, Marsha Jean, 96–97
Davidson, Arnold I., 185, 265n14
Davis, Christina, 98
Davis, Thadious, 10, 18, 157–58, 164–65
Day, Douglas, 8–9, 223n3, 224n11
Dean, Tim, 183–84, 186–90, 192, 197, 265n17
Declaration of Independence, 56
deconstructive analytical tools, 49, 117
Deleuze, Gilles, 184
democratic capitalism, 60–62
Denver, CO, 75
desegregation, 76–77, 79, 203–4, 225n14
dialectic between form and content. *See* form and content (formalist criticism)
divided reading, 33–34
"Divorce in Naples" (Faulkner), 163
domination, 165
double consciousness, 94
Douglas, Ann, 57–58
Douglas, Lloyd C., 66, 238n49
"Dry September" (Faulkner), 50
Duke University, 205
Duvall, John, 140–42, 163

Earle, David M., 45
Ebony (magazine), 17, 78, 209
Edelman, Lee, 161, 165–67, 255n4, 256n9, 259n26, 263n48
Éditions Gallimard, 137
Edwards, Thomas R., 103
Eisenhower, Dwight D., 73–74
The Elementary Structures of Kinship (Lévi-Strauss), 168, 260n30
Ellison, Ralph, 26–27, 79–81, 241n77
Ely, Melvin, 208

Eschenbach, Wolfram von, 170–73, 175
European reputation of Faulkner, 49–50
Evans, David H., 179, 261n33, 263n54
Evanston Township High School, 218
everyday readers, 9–10, 225n15

A Fable (Faulkner), 51–84; brotherhood in, 59–62; as Christian allegory, 55–59, 233n16; and cultural diplomacy of Faulkner, 67–76, 239n53; and literary sentimentalism, 56–59; and mass cultural entertainment, 53–55, 63–64; multiple borrowings in, 52, 233n18; reception of, 48–49, 51–53, 65–66; and reputation of Faulkner, 82–83; and Schoenberg's *Moses und Aron,* 64–65; and Schwartz, 48–49; self-referentiality in, 52; struggle to finish, 66–68; and *Uncle Tom's Cabin,* 56–58
Fadiman, Clifton, 102
failure, 13–14, 22, 158–59, 178, 198, 202–3, 251n25, 255nn7–8
Falkenberg, Pamela, 153, 155, 229n23
Falkner, John Wesley Thompson, 21
Falkner, William Clark, 21
familial structures, 57–59
father-daughter incest, 157, 169
Faulkner: The House Divided (Sundquist), 180, 190–92
Faulkner, William: alcoholism, 28, 63, 67, 72, 78; apprenticeship work, 21–22, 115–16, 163, 191–92, 251n25; approach to homosexuality, 162–64; as Balch Writer-in-Residence, 3–7; and Baldwin, 80–82, 204; and Balzac, 20; biographic sketch sent to *Forum* magazine, 34; Bourdieu on, 32–34; and camp, 161, 175–79, 263n49; and civil rights movement, 16–17, 77, 203–4; in *The Civil War* miniseries, 43; and class conferences, 1–10, 13, 221, 224n7, 224n9, 255n7; and Cold War critical revaluation, 50; creative imagination of, 112, 164, 233n15; and cultural capital, 32–35, 42–44; and cultural diplomacy, 67–76, 80, 83–84, 238n52; and culture industry, 34, 62–64, 69, 83, 140–44, 146, 152–53, 234n20;

and Eisenhower, 73–74; and failure, 13–14, 158–59, 198, 251n25, 255nn7–8; feminist readings of, 10, 16–17, 49, 139–40; and fiction and history, 20–25; and fiction's resemblance to Greek tragedy, 10; and film, 35–39, 44, 66, 126–27, 131–35, 144, 148–55, 229; "Freedom American Style" speech, 68–69; and Godard, 35, 44, 131–35, 148–49, 151–55, 229n23; historicist and queer readings of, 130; and Hollywood, 25, 54, 62–66, 127, 135, 143–47, 234–35n24, 258n20; identity critique of, 18; on issues of race, 16–17; Kawin on, 35, 132–33, 148–49; keys to, 30; late work, 110, 231–32n11; legacy of, 25–27; life and work of, 20–25; literary recognition of, 46–47; and mass culture, 53–55; and Nobel Prize, 16, 48–52, 66–67, 75–76, 91, 139, 198, 204, 233n17, 238n50, 255n7; N-word use, 4–5, 202–3; and *Oeuvres du XXe Siècle* festival, 71–72, 239n53; and People-to-People program, 73–75; political statements of, 76–77; as postmaster, 118–19; and *Pulp Fiction* (film), 35–44, 228–29n17–19; queer theory in study of, 162–64; rebarbative in, 109, 125, 142; representations of race, 49, 208–9; reputation of, 16–20, 25–26, 46–51, 71, 76–77, 80–83, 103, 138, 203–4; role of, in contemporary culture, 35; and Schoenberg, 54, 64–65, 237–38nn45–47; and Schwartz, 17, 25–26, 46–50, 67, 76, 80, 231n4; screenwriting of, 135, 143, 147; and sexualities, 181–82, 190–92, 196; sexual life, 199; speech habits, 4–6, 203; and State Department, 67–76; and structure of tension and antagonism, 44; and sublimation, 113–22, 123–24, 249n13; and Tarantino, 35–42, 44, 228nn16–17, 229n19, 229n21; and teaching, 29–32; and time, 29–32; translations of, 26, 50, 231n9; and women, 6–11, 17. *See also* historicism; literary modernism; repetition; Yoknapatawpha County; *and individual works by*
"Faulkner and Desegregation" (Baldwin), 80–82, 204, 241n78

Faulkner and Yoknapatawpha conference, 84, 91–92, 105–6, 219–20
Faulkner at Virginia (website), 3–7, 225n15
Faulknerians, 10–13
Faulkner in the University, 3–9, 221, 224n7
Faulknerista model, 11–14, 106, 130, 200
Faulkner Journal, 220
Faulkner's Apocrypha (Urgo), 110–12
fellow feeling, 59–60
feminist analyses, 10, 16–17, 49, 139–40. *See also* women
Ferguson, Roderick A., 160–61
feuilleton, 107
fiction and history, 20, 20–25. *See also* historicism
Fields, Barbara J., 43
film(s), 35–39, 44, 66, 126–27, 131–35, 144, 148–55, 229; American, 149–51; European reception of Hollywood films, 150–51; *film noir,* 151–52; French, 149–51. *See also A bout de souffle* (film); Hollywood; screenwriting; Tarantino, Quentin; television
Finnegans Wake (Joyce), 63
Flags in the Dust (Faulkner), 21, 115–20, 250n18, 251n25
Flinn, Caryl, 176
Foote, Shelby, 43, 229–30n31
forbidding style, 102–3
formal properties, of literary modernism, 18–19, 94–95, 244n8
form and content (formalist criticism), 18, 25, 87–88. *See also* New Criticism
Forrest, Sally, 207–8
Forum magazine, 32–34
Foucault, Michel, 182–85, 187, 189
fragmented narrative method, 89–90, 94–95, 100
France, 26, 49–50, 71–72, 136–37, 149–51, 239n53
Frank, Joseph, 89, 95
fraternalism, 59–60
freedom: academic, 219; capitalistic, 83–84; and domination, 165; Godard on, 152; and Grail myth, 171, 261n36; and homosexuality, 262n43; and imprisonment, 143; intellectual, 61–62; rhetoric of, via ideologies of brotherhood, 55; right to say no, 61–62; and Spintrius, 168
"Freedom American Style" (speech), 68–69
Freemasonry, 59–62
French New Wave, 38, 132–34
French translations: of Faulkner, 26, 50, 137–38; of Psalm 137, 143
Freud, Sigmund, 113–15, 184–89, 249n13, 265n14
"Freud, Male Homosexuality, and the Americans" (Abelove), 185
Fugitive Slave Law, 96–97
Furry, William, 203–5, 267n8

Garner, Margaret, 95–100, 243n4, 246n28
Gates, Henry Louis, Jr., 94, 243n1, 245n25
Gay Faulkner (Gordon), 130, 198–200
gender-defined communities in Central Africa, 257n12
gendered representation, 6–9
gender norms, 140–41
gender representation. *See* women
Gender Trouble (Butler), 182–83
genealogies, of Foucault, 185, 187, 192
genealogy, 107–9
Germano, William, 12
Gilman, Sander, 178
Gilroy, Paul, 102
Gleeson-White, Sarah, 45
Godard, Jean-Luc, 35, 44, 131–35, 148–49, 151–55, 229n23
Godden, Richard L., 23–24, 141–44, 158, 167, 179, 254n4, 259n23, 259n27, 260n32
Go Down, Moses (Faulkner), 156–79; and aunts and uncles, 262n40; and Cabell's *Jurgen,* 261n34; and camp aesthetic, 175–79, 262n44; and dialectic between form and content, 25; and failure, 178; and fiction and history, 21; and Grail myth, 170–74, 261nn35–36, 262n38; homoerotic subtext,

Go Down, Moses (continued)
 162–64, 258n17; homosexuality in, 164–68, 260n32, 263n49; humorous aspects of, 175–79; and Lévi-Strauss, 168–69; and queer theory, 161, 173–74; and repudiation, 173–74, 179, 264n55; southern racial theme, 22–23; time frame for analysis, 258n14; and Weinstein, 227n1. *See also* Percival Brownlee
Goldberg, Jonathan, 181–82, 189–90, 197, 258n14
"The Gold Watch" (Tarantino), 35–44
Göncz, Árpád, 50, 71
Gordon, Phillip, 130, 198–200
Gorra, Michael, 28
Gould, Jack, 206–8, 210, 213
Grail myth, 170–73, 261nn35–36, 262n38
Gray, Richard, 135, 203–4
Greece, 70
grief, 131, 134, 139, 170–74, 258n17. *See also* loss
Grimwood, Michael, 110, 233n15, 248n7
Guardian, 151
Guattari, Félix, 184
Guback, Thomas H., 149
guilt and grief, 174
Gwin, Minrose, 11, 140, 162–63
Gwynn, Frederick L., 2–10, 13, 221, 223n4, 224n7, 224nn9–10, 225n15

Haas, Robert K., 192, 206
Haiti, 24
Hale, Grace Elizabeth, 79
Hamblin, Robert W., 18, 233n19
The Hamlet (Faulkner), 25, 110, 248n4
Harker, Jaime, 45, 200
Harper, Phillip Brian, 160–61
Harper's, 68–69, 81, 202
Hathaway, Henry, 52, 54, 66, 235n24
Hawks, Howard, 150–51, 233n18, 239n53, 258n20
Hawthorne, Nathaniel, 93
Hayakawa, Samuel Ichiye, 209–11
Hellman, Lillian, 10
Hemingway, Ernest, 51

heterosexuality, 173–74, 182–83
high art, 140, 155
high modernism, 62–63, 83, 85, 87–88, 94, 147
Hillier, Jim, 150–51
historical literary analysis, 181, 197
historical record, 97–99, 159–60. *See also* revision
historicism, 23, 30, 103–4, 129–30, 176–77, 180–84, 187–90, 192, 196, 198
History of Sexuality (Foucault), 182
Hixson, Walter L., 235n28, 240n65
Hollywood, 25, 54, 62–66, 127, 135, 143–47, 150–51, 153–54, 234–35n24, 258n20. *See also Cahiers du Cinéma;* film(s)
homoeroticism, 160, 162–64, 193, 255n9, 258n17, 260n32
homographesis, 161, 166–67, 169, 259n26
homosexuality: Asante on, 256n11; and camp, 176–77; and exchange, 168–69; Faulkner's approach to, 162–64; and Foucault, 182; and freedom, 262n43; and Freud, 185–86, 265n14; Godden and Polk's reading, 254n4; homographesis, 161, 259n26; homographic function of Percival Brownlee, 164–66; homosexual panic, 263n49; homosexual yearning, 260n32; and incest and miscegenation, 260n32; *jinbandaas,* 257n12; and New World slaves, 257n12; Percival Brownlee, 157–60, 169; reading of, in Faulkner, 198–99; scholarship on, 255–56n9. *See also* queer theory
hooks, bell, 44
Horkheimer, Max, 75, 233–34n20
Howe, Irving, 81, 241n81
Howe, Russell Warren, 17, 77–79, 204, 241n77
Howland, Harold E., 68–70
hubristic faith, 70, 82–83
Hungary, 50, 71
Huyssen, Andreas, 62–63, 139, 235n27

IAS. *See* Institute for Advanced Study (IAS), 201–2

identities: homographesis, 166, 259n26; identity critique of Faulkner, 18; and queer theory, 185, 189; and sentimental Christianity, 55; sexual identities, 158–59, 166, 169, 182–83, 187, 199, 263n48

If I Forget Thee, Jerusalem (Faulkner), 138–55; and *A bout de souffle* (film), 132–35, 148–55; and censorship, 133–34; as contrapuntal, 146–48; and culture industry, 140–44, 152–53; feminist analysis, 139–40; French translation of, 138–39; and intertextuality, 132–33, 152–55; meat trope, 146–47; and Psalm 137, 142–43; publication history, 138–39; and pulp fiction, 135

"If I Were a Negro" (Faulkner), 78–79, 209, 241n72

imaginary, Cold War American cultural, 49, 55, 83–84

incest, 21, 39, 157–58, 168–69, 229n24, 260n32

"In Defense of a Loaded Word" (Coates), 217–19

indirection, strategies of, 88–89

Institute for Advanced Study (IAS), 201–2

integration, 78–79

intellectual freedom, 61–62

International Conference on General Semantics, 209–10

interrogation, of southern racial history, 76–77

intertextuality, 132–34, 141–42, 145, 152–55

irony, 85, 100–101, 142

Irwin, John T., 10, 110, 199–200, 227n5, 229n24, 248n5, 249n16

isolation, 90–91

-ista suffix, 12–13

J. Walter Thompson advertising agency, 205

Jackson, Robert, 79

Jacobs, Harriet, 255n9

Jameson, Fredric, 88, 103, 180, 184, 230n2, 264–65n10

Jazz (Morrison), 86–87, 243n4

Jehlen, Myra, 10

jinbandaas, 257n12

Johnston, Eric, 149

Jones, Anne Goodwyn, 139–40

Joyce, James, 20, 63

Jurgen (Cabell), 261n34

Karl, Frederick R., 163, 198

Kawin, Bruce, 35, 44, 132–33, 148–49

Kennedy, Randall, 214–19

King, Vincent, 143

Kline, T. Jefferson, 132–33, 152

Koestler, Arthur, 61–62

Kosztolányi, Dezső, 50

Lacan, Jacques, 113–14, 183–84, 195, 265n17

Lane, Christopher, 186–87, 196

language, 94–95, 114–15, 220–21. *See also* N-word

La pointe courte (Varda), 148

latitude/longitude paradigm, 113. *See also* sublimation

"Law School Wives," 7

Lee, Muna, 67, 75

"The Leg" (Faulkner), 181, 188, 192–96

Les palmiers sauvages. See *The Wild Palms* (Faulkner)

Les temps modernes (Sartre), 137

Lester, Cheryl, 110–12, 232n11

"A Letter to the North" (Faulkner), 78, 204, 241n72, 241n77

Levinson, Marjorie, 265n20

Lévi-Strauss, Claude, 168–69, 259–60n30

Lewis, Charles, 243n2

liberation, 26, 155, 168, 183

Life magazine, 69, 78, 204, 207–9, 241n72, 241n77

Light in August (Faulkner), 18, 21–25, 76, 190

linguistic ownership, 217–18

Linscott, Robert N., 123, 138, 252n30

literary apprenticeship, 21–22, 115–16, 163, 191–92, 251n25

literary classics and film, 38–39

literary Left, 89

literary mastery. *See* critical mastery
literary modernism: Baker on, 244n15; and capitalistic freedom, 83; and culture industry, 62–64; and Faulkner's Cold War critical revaluation, 50; feminist analysis, 139; formal properties of, 18–19, 94–95, 244n8; ideological reading of, 88–89; influenced by African American aesthetic practices, 244n12; and irony, 142; and media segregation, 213; and Morrison, 89–95, 99–102, 243n2, 244n16, 245n23; and postmodernism, 104; Schwartz on, 47. See also *Absalom, Absalom!* (Faulkner); *A Fable* (Faulkner); *The Sound and the Fury* (Faulkner)
literary stock, 18, 46–47. *See also* reputation
literary technique, 86
Look Away! (Street), 52, 233nn18–19
loss, 31–32, 122–23, 174. *See also* grief
Lucy, Autherine, 17, 77, 240nn69–70, 241n73
Lukács, Georg, 20, 89
Lurie, Peter, 141–44, 221
Lux Video Theatre, 203, 205, 207–8

MacDonald, J. Fred, 208–9
manipulation of time, in narrative structures, 32–34
map as spatialization of time, 108–9
Marshall Plan funds, 149
Mary Washington College, 7, 224n10
masculinization, 114–15, 167–68
Masonic movement, 59–62
mass culture, 53–55, 62, 65, 139–40, 155
Masses & Mainstream, 76
Matthews, John T., 23, 62–63, 261n33
Mayday (Faulkner), 170, 261nn34–35
McBride, Jim, 38–39, 153, 229nn22–23
McHaney, Thomas L., 136–40, 143–44, 153
meat discourse, 146–48
media segregation, 213
medieval Persia, 160
"Melancholy Gender/Refused Identification" (Butler), 173
memoranda, State Department, 70–71

Memphis Commercial Appeal, 76
Menon, Madhavi, 181–82, 189–90, 197, 258n14
Metropolitan Club, 74
Michelson, Annette, 151
military victory, 55
Milne, Tom, 151, 253n6
Minell, Abram, 75
misogyny, 140–41
Monogram Pictures, 132
Montgomery Bus Boycott, 204
Moore, Ann Thomas, 2–3, 9, 10
morbidity, 176
Moreland, Richard C., 110, 246n35
Morrison, Toni: *Beloved* and *Absalom, Absalom!*, 86–104; characters of, 243n6; effect of Faulkner on, 27, 92–93; and Faulkner and Yoknapatawpha Conference, 91–93; Garner's story, 243n4, 246n28; Lewis on, 243n2; linking of past and future, 31; maternal symbolic in, 244n16; and Oprah, 18; pre-oedipal infant in, 246n30; scholarly attention to, 242n83; and slavery, 243n3; thesis of, 82, 89–91, 245n20, 247n50
Moses und Aron (Schoenberg), 54, 64–65
Mosquitoes (Faulkner), 10, 162–63
Mumford, Kevin, 160–61
Muñoz, José Esteban, 226n20
Murray, Albert, 79–81, 241n77
musical counterpoint, 136–37, 146

NAACP, 77–79, 204, 208, 240nn69–70
Nagano, Japan, 68–69, 75
narrative transcendence, 99–100
The Nation, 79
National Conference of the US National Commission for UNESCO, 75
nature and culture, 168–69
Naylor, Gloria, 86–87
negative dialectics, 87
neologism. *See* Spintrius
New American Library, 136–38
New Criticism, 47, 86, 180
New Formalist scholarship, 265n20

New Leader, 76
New Wave cinema, 38–39, 132–35, 148–49
New York Herald Tribune, 10
New York intellectuals, 47
New York Times, 209, 217
New York Times Book Review, 107–8
Niemann, Christopher, 107–9
Nietzsche, Friedrich, 178–79, 263n44
nineteenth-century romance, 93
Nobel Prize, 16, 48–52, 66–67, 75–76, 91, 139, 198, 204, 233n17, 238n50, 255n7
No Future (Edelman), 255n4, 256n9, 263n48
non-normative sexuality, 196, 252n33
North American Association, 72
Nossel, Suzanne, 219
nostalgia, 100, 176–77, 246n35
"Notes on a Horsethief" (Faulkner), 59–62, 80
"Notes on Camp" (Sontag), 175–77, 263n45
Nouvelle revue française, 26, 50
Novás Calvo, Lino, 50
N-word, 4–5, 41–42, 203, 205, 212, 214–21, 268n21

Obama, Barack, 216, 225n17
Ober, Harold, 234–35n24
objet petit a, 195–96
O'Brien, Michael, 49
Oeuvres du XXe Siècle festival, 71–72, 239n53
The Old Man (Faulkner), 136–37
"Old Man" section, 132–33, 136–37, 139–41, 267n8. *See also* "Wild Palms" section
"On Privacy" (Faulkner), 68–70, 202, 207–8, 213
Oppenheimer, J. Robert, 201–3, 207–8, 213, 221, 266n4
Oprah Winfrey book club, 18
otherness, 188–89, 197. *See also* psychoanalysis
"Out of Nazareth" (Faulkner), 163, 193
Oxford, MS, 20

Page, Thomas Nelson, 226n4
paradox, 99–102
Parini, Jay, 28

Paris, France, 71–72, 239n53
Parsifal (Wagner), 170–73, 262n38
Partisan Review, 47, 59, 63–64, 80, 204
Patterson, Orlando, 160
People-to-People program, 73–75
Percival Brownlee, 156–79; Davis on, 157–58, 255n4; Godden and Polk's reading, 254n4, 259n23, 259n27; and Grail myth, 170–73, 261n36; and historical record, 159–61; and homoeroticism, 163–64; and incest and miscegenation, 260n32; and repudiation, 174, 179; and resistance, 255n4, 259n23; Spintrius renomination, 164–69; and unhistoricist approach, 258n14
Pèrez-Torres, Rafael, 93, 245n23
Peyre, Henri, 50
Phelan, James, 101
Picon, Leon, 72, 239n54
Pinnegar, Fred, 49–50
Pitavy, François, 143
pleasure, 31–32, 144–45
The Political Unconscious (Jameson), 184, 230n2
politico-cultural imaginary, 55
politics, sentimental, 56–57
politics and ethics, 181
politics of aesthetics, 211
politics of camp, 161, 177
politique des auteurs, 135, 150–51
Polk, Noel, 158, 167, 179, 232n11, 254n4, 259n23, 259n27, 260n32
Polsgrove, Carol, 76–77
pornographic modes of writing sex, 116–22, 124
pornography, 144
The Portable Faulkner (Cowley), 5, 16, 34, 46, 111–13, 121, 123, 136–38, 232n11
Positif (magazine), 150
postage stamp image, 110–12, 115, 119, 124
postmodernism, 88, 93–94, 102–4
post-Reconstruction efforts, 170–72
Pound, Ezra, 74
primary process thinking, 187
Princeton University, 201–2

privacy, 68–70, 155, 202, 207–8. *See also* "On Privacy" (Faulkner)
Psalm 137, 142–46
psychoanalysis, 183–89, 198, 244n16, 265n14, 265n17
public diplomacy. *See* cultural diplomacy
pulp fiction, 135
Pulp Fiction (film), 35–44, 228–29nn17–19
Punch, 51
purposeful restrictions, 94–98
Putnam, James Jackson, 185

Quasi una Fantasia (Adorno), 193
"Queering History" (Goldberg and Menon), 189–90
queer theory, 162–64; and camp, 177–78; and cultural disidentification, 226n20; and Edelman, 161, 259n26, 263n48; and *Go Down, Moses,* 161, 173–74; and Gordon, 198–200; and historicist approach to sexuality, 181–82, 188–89; and homosexuality, 185–86, 255–56n9; *If I Forget Thee, Jerusalem*'s engagement with the culture industry, 144; "The Leg" reading, 192–96; and New Formalist scholarship, 265n20
Quilligan, Maureen, 57
quotation, 37–44, 132–33, 151–52, 229n21, 229n23

race: and cultural ownership, 218–19; failure to produce a complete US racial narrative, 159; Faulkner on issues of, 16–17; and historical context in Faulkner, 76–77, 190–91; racialized sectionalism, 180–81; racial redemption, 79, 171–72; representations of, 49, 208–9; in *The Sound and the Fury,* 40; southern racial theme, 22, 24–25, 76, 235n30, 255n6; and television, 208–9. *See also* civil rights movement; N-word
Railton, Stephen, 3–5
Raimbault, René-Noël, 50
Ramsey, D. Matthew, 163

Rancière, Jacques, 205, 211
realist narrative discourse, 99–100
reception, modernism and postmodernism as phenomena of, 88
redefinition, 112
redemption, 50, 79, 139, 171–73
rediscovery of self in writing, 120, 122. *See also* sublimation
Reichman, Henry, 219, 268n21
Reid-Pharr, Robert, 160–61
The Reivers (Faulkner), 110–11, 123, 155
religion and commerce, 58
repetition, 31–32; in *Absalom, Absalom!,* 100–101; and aesthetic vision of Faulkner, 109, 248n5; and cultural capital, 44; in film, 36–41, 229n23; and Irwin, 227n5; problem of, 121–23; and repudiation, 171; revisionary repetition, 52–53, 109–10; and sublimation, 115–16; and Tarantino, 36–41
Reporter, 78, 204
representations of race, 49, 208–9
representations of women, 17
repudiation, 173–74, 179
reputation, 16–20, 25–26, 46–51, 71, 76–77, 80–83, 103, 138, 203–4
Reservoir Dogs (film), 44, 229n21
Resnais, Alain, 148
revision: and Morrison, 93, 95, 99–100; and readings of Faulkner's late work, 231–32n11; and reframing, 110–11; revisionary repetition, 52–53, 109–10; revisionary scholarship, 230–31n4
right to say no, 61–62
Rio Bravo (film), 151
The Robe (Douglas), 66, 238n49
Rockefeller Foundation grants, 47
"A Rose for Emily" (Faulkner), 32–34, 50
Ross, Alex, 237n47
Ross, Andrew, 177–78
Rowan Oak, 20
The Rules of Art (Bourdieu), 32–34
Rupprecht, Carol R., 224n9

sameness and difference, 57, 166–68, 189–90, 259n29
Samuels, Shirley, 56
Sanctuary (Faulkner), 17, 24–25, 50, 63, 121–22, 193
sanitizing Faulkner's language, 4–5, 220–21
Sartre, Jean-Paul, 22, 137
The Scarlet Letter (Hawthorne), 93, 243n2
Schoenberg, Arnold, 54, 64–65, 237–38nn45–47
Schwartz, Lawrence H., 17, 25–26, 46–50, 67, 76, 80, 231n4
Scott, Evelyn, 10
screen time quota, 149
screenwriting, 135, 143, 147
Scribner's, 115, 206, 250n18
Seberg, Jean, 153
Sedgwick, Eve Kosofsky, 182–85, 255n9, 262n40
self-sabotage, 86–87, 243n3
Sensibar, Judith, 28, 198
sentimentalism, literary, 54–61, 235–36n34. *See also* irony
Sewanee Review, 47
sex, writing of, 114–22, 252n33
sexual economy, 144
sexual identity, 158–59, 166, 169, 182–83, 187, 199, 263n48
sexuality, historicist approach to, 181–82, 188–89
"Shall Not Perish" (Faulkner), 203, 205–6, 267n8
signifying style, 85, 94, 105, 243n1
Si je t'oublie Jérusalem (French translation), 138
Silver, James W., 77
Simon, David, 211–12
"situational" homosexuality, 160, 257n12
slavery, 86–89, 95–98, 101–3, 156–60, 165, 243n3, 255n9, 257n12
Slavery and Social Death (Patterson), 160
social injustice, 95, 99

Sollors, Werner, 260n32
The Song of Bernadette (Werfel), 66
Sontag, Susan, 175–77, 265n16
The Sound and the Fury (Faulkner): anecdote as inspiration for, 7–10; appendix, 138; Black characters in, 40–42; Caddy's silence, 7–10, 13; Christ narrative in, 233n16; and "The Gold Watch," 39–41; Hungarian translation of, 50, 71; incest and time in, 39, 229n24; and literary apprenticeship, 21–22; and literary modernism, 24; Matthews on, 23; Morrison's reading of, 90–91; obsession with loss, 123; and Oprah Winfrey's book club, 18; pinhead imagery, 19–20; posthumously published introduction, 31; prefaces, 114–15, 121–23, 233n19, 247–48n2; Quentin Compson section of, 19–20; Sartre's review of, 22, 26; Scott's pamphlet blurbing, 10; southern racial theme, 22–23; and sublimation, 114–15, 120–21; Sundquist on, 22–23, 190–92; and Tarantino, 228n16
southern racial theme, 22, 24–25, 76, 235n30, 255n6
Soviet Union, 73–74, 240n65
Spanish translations, 50
Spintrius, 164–69, 174, 259n27
State Department, US, 67–76
Steinbeck, John, 74, 233n18
Stevenson, Adlai, 73
Stewart, Susan, 55, 176
Stone, Phil, 118
Stowe, Harriet Beecher, 56, 58
Strauss, Harold, 102
Street, James, 52, 233nn18–19
sublimation, 113–22, 123–24, 249n13
Sundquist, Eric J., 10, 22–23, 159, 180, 190–92
Sweet, James H., 160, 257n12

Tabori, George, 74
Tarantino, Quentin, 35–42, 44, 228nn16–17, 229n19, 229n21
Tate, Allen, 89, 95

television, 35, 43, 202–14
temporal manipulations, 32–35, 37–39, 44
Tendencies (Sedgwick), 182
textuality, 130, 165–66, 263n48
"That Evening Sun" (Faulkner), 50
Thayer, Thatcher, 58
"There Was a Queen" (Faulkner), 115–20, 250n18, 251n28
Three Essays on the Theory of Sexuality (Freud), 186, 265n14
Three Famous Short Novels (Faulkner), 137
Thurman, Judith, 103–4
Till, Emmett, 76
Today We Live (film), 258n20
Todd, Janet, 235n34
Torres, Sasha, 208–9
The Town (Faulkner), 109–10, 155, 248n4
Towner, Theresa M., 192
translations, 26, 50, 231n9
Troy, William, 102
Trump, Donald J., 216
Tuan, Yi-Fu, 124
"Turnabout" (Faulkner), 163, 258n20
"Two Things That Depress Me When I Open a Novel" (Wolitzer), 107–9

Uncle Tom's Cabin (Stowe), 56, 58
unconscious, 184–89, 196, 264n10
Unflinching Gaze (Kolmerten, Ross, and Wittenberg), 31
unhistoricist approach, 180–97, 258n14
United Press International, 76
universalism, 86–87
University of Alabama, 17, 77–78, 240n69, 241n73
University of Mississippi, 81, 91–92, 118, 219–20, 250n24
University of New South Wales's Centre for Modernism Studies, 214–16
University of Virginia, 2–9, 224n9, 225n14
Urgo, Joseph, 110–13, 233n19, 249n12

Van Der Zee, James, 243n4
Varda, Agnès, 148
Venezuela, 72
The Vicarious Element in Nature and Its Relation to Christ (Thayer), 58
vicarious relations, 57–60
Vickery, Olga, 10
"Virginia Woolf's and William Faulkner's Treatment of the Alienated" (Wofford), 82, 89–90

Wagner, Richard, 170–73, 262n38
Walken, Christopher, 36
waste, 147
Watson, Neil, 162, 258n17
Weber, Mark, 118–19
Weinstein, Arnold, 18
Weinstein, Philip M., 53, 187, 227n1
Werfel, Franz, 66
Western modernity, 93–94
White, Hayden, 189
white America: and cultural authority, 42–44; and cultural ownership, 218–19; and literary modernism, 93–95; and racial redemption, 79; and the South, 78; white supremacy, 24, 217–19
The Wild Palms (Faulkner), 25, 131–34, 136–38, 148
"Wild Palms" section, 132–33, 136–42. *See also* "Old Man" section
William Faulkner and Southern History (Williamson), 21
Williams, William Carlos, 74
Williamson, Joel, 21, 163, 198, 203–5
Willis, Sharon, 41–42, 229n19
The Wire (television series), 211–13
Wofford, Chloe A. *See* Morrison, Toni
Wolitzer, Meg, 107–10
women, 6–11, 17, 56, 224nn9–10, 225n17. *See also* feminist analyses
Women's Review of Books, 96–97, 243n4
Woolf, Virginia, 89–91

"The World and the Jug" (Ellison), 26
writing sex, 114–22, 252n33. *See also* "The Leg" (Faulkner)

Yoknapatawpha County, 107–25; and apocrypha, 249n12; "Beyond" section, 192; and Cowley, 16; critical examinations of, 252n33; fiction and history, 20–21; and *Flags in the Dust,* 250n18; and sublimation, 113–22

Žižek, Slavoj, 188

CPSIA information can be obtained
at www.ICGtesting.com
Printed in the USA
LVHW042215060123
736550LV00003B/262